The Tonkin Gulf
YACHT CLUB

THOMAS
McKELVEY CLEAVER

The
Tonkin
Gulf
YACHT CLUB

NAVAL AVIATION IN THE VIETNAM WAR

OSPREY PUBLISHING
Bloomsbury Publishing Plc
Kemp House, Chawley Park, Cumnor Hill, Oxford OX2 9PH, UK
29 Earlsfort Terrace, Dublin 2, Ireland
1385 Broadway, 5th Floor, New York, NY 10018, USA
E-mail: info@ospreypublishing.com
www.ospreypublishing.com

OSPREY is a trademark of Osprey Publishing Ltd

First published in Great Britain in 2021

ISBN: HB 9781472845955; PB 9781472845948; eBook 9781472845924;
ePDF 9781472845917; XML 9781472845931

23 24 25 26 27   10 9 8 7 6 5 4 3 2 1

Maps by www.bounford.com
Index by Zoe Ross

Originated by PDQ Digital Media Solutions, Bungay, UK
Printed and bound in Great Britain by CPI (Group) UK Ltd, Croydon CR0 4YY

Osprey Publishing supports the Woodland Trust, the UK's leading woodland
conservation charity.

To find out more about our authors and books visit www.ospreypublishing.com.
Here you will find extracts, author interviews, details of forthcoming events
and the option to sign up for our newsletter.

CONTENTS

LIST OF MAPS AND ILLUSTRATIONS

MAPS

PLATES

VPAF pilots, 923rd Fighter Regiment, with MiG-17s. (VPAF Official)
MiG-21MFs of 921st Fighter Regiment, 1972. (VPAF Official)
USS *Maddox* in the Tonkin Gulf. (USN Official)
An E-1B Tracer, known as "Willy Fudd," 1965. (USN Official)
An F-8C Crusader lands on *Coral Sea*, 1965. (USN Official)
A Kaman SH-2 Seasprite. (USN Official)
An A-1H Skyraider launches from *Coral Sea*, 1966. (USN Official)
Coral Sea takes on fuel at Yankee Station, 1966. (USN Official)
A-4C Skyhawks, RA-5C Vigilantes, and an E-1B Tracer aboard
    Enterprise, 1966. (USN Official)
F-4Gs of VF-113 with experimental camouflage. (USN Official)
F-4B Phantoms VF-112 "Aardvarks"/F-4Gs aboard *Kitty Hawk*, 1966.
    (USN Official)
Oriskany on fire in the Tonkin Gulf, 1966. (USN Official)
A KA-3B Skywarrior catapults from *Coral Sea*, 1967. (USN Official)
Forrestal on fire, July 29, 1967. (USN Official)
An RF-8G Crusader prepares to launch from *Coral Sea*, 1967. (USN
    Official)
An F-5 "Aggressor" used by Top Gun. (USN Official via Fred Johnsen)
Captain Dan Pedersen. (USN Official)
A-6A Intruders bomb North Vietnam, 1968. (USN Official)

FOREWORD

Tom Cleaver has captured the dramatic history – action, triumphs, successes, and failures – of Naval Aviation's combat record in Vietnam in a manner worthy of the classic historical novel. From the first shot fired in the Tonkin Gulf in August 1964 – heard, if not around the world, certainly within the contending political and military circles – through the early engagements in April/June 1965, to the final salvo in April and May 1975, Tom weaves an accurate tale, sculpted as if by an artist, full of the color and fury of battle, courage, suspense, and thrill of victory – as experienced and portrayed on both sides of the conflict.

It's almost as if Tom had been there at the beginning, observing and recording the formation of the VPAF defense: the use of North Korean "experts," the establishment of the ground support defenses of AAA and SAM sites, the development of the VPAF inventory of MiG-17/19/21 aircraft and the manpower to ensure readiness, repair, and re-equipment of resources; i.e., bridges, POL, AAA and missile sites, etc. – not to mention the anti-US propaganda that became so effective throughout the world during the fray. Too bad Tom couldn't have gotten into McNamara's mind and inserted reality and military logic in the determination and selection of a winning strategy.

But even with the forces arrayed against the US effort, including the highly effective unconventional methods employed by the Viet Cong and North Vietnam and the Johnson Administration's imposition of draconian rules of engagement that served to literally hamstring and frustrate the objectives and actions of our air combat forces, Tom weaves the air-to-air and air-to-ground successes and failures – and aircrew losses – into a mosaic that reflects the reality that commands and aircrews experienced while struggling to maintain overall morale and motivation sufficient to ensure effective mission accomplishment.

Take position on his right wing as Tom sets the stage and defines the struggles of initial air-to-air employment, engagements, action, and results – mostly mixed, often tragic. Naval Aviation fighter escorts, Combat Air Patrols and strike/fighter sections and divisions endeavor to hold their own, contesting the decidedly inferior assets arrayed against them. Tom weaves and jinks his way through Operation *Pierce Arrow* (bet you never heard of that one) and breaks hard into *Rolling Thunder* as Crusaders lead the tally of victories with their gun and AIM-9; the F-4 finds little success with its Fleet Air Defense radar system/AIM-7 package and discovers – almost too late – that aircraft and system design and philosophy have high and, possibly, unacceptable risks and costs in mission accomplishment. Missed opportunities, missile failures, aircrew mistakes and miscues even result in friendly fire incidents and tragic loss of aircrews in the early air-to-air encounters.

From initial engagements in the mid-sixties through the end of the decade, Naval Aviation's successes (kills) barely exceeded its losses. The attitudes and enthusiasm of Navy aircrews were waning – if not shredded – by the inability of the state-of-the-art technology to best what most observers considered the outmoded – even primitive – first-generation jet fighters like the MiG-17/MiG-19. The match between Naval Aviation and North Vietnam through the period 1967–71 ended in what can only be called "a draw," with both sides panting for breath and frustrated with lack of purpose. Naval Aviation scored successes during 1966–68; however, there were no kills in 1969, one in 1970, and none in 1971.

Enter Captain Frank Ault and the Ault Report. The lull in action between the end of *Rolling Thunder* and *Linebacker* gave rise to the resurgence of US air superiority; the venue: Top Gun. The changes in aircrew training, tactics, and weapons system employment proved to be the remedy so badly needed in reasserting mastery over an intensely dedicated and determined enemy. The Top Gun lessons learned began to take effect in early 1972, and May 1972 became the "icing on the cake" that heralded a taste of victory for Naval Aviation and surely left a bitter taste in the minds and hearts of the North Vietnamese fighter community.

But the "Thrill of Victory" that marked the war's longest day, and most productive year in confirmed "kills" by Navy fighter aircrews would also be marked by the ever-increasing feeling – and knowledge – that ultimate victory was not to be. The military exigencies would be preempted by political posturing and restrictions having the effect of neutering the US forces' action needed for ultimate success and victory over the dedicated and unrelenting forces being fed and fortified by the communist ideology in Hanoi and beyond.

Finally, Naval Aviation earned its wings in the final years of the Vietnam War and acquitted itself superbly with valuable lessons learned in attitude, tactics, and system design and employment. These elements and the formation of Top Gun are the legacy – and constitute the DNA of each and every participant – and student – of the actions depicted. Read it, dream it, and relive the memories of "The Tonkin Gulf Yacht Club – Naval Aviation in Vietnam!"

Captain Roy Cash, Jr., USN (Ret)
Former CO, Top Gun

INTRODUCTION

As for many of my generation, the war in Vietnam and my participation in it changed my life completely. Forever. Looking back, I divide my life in two parts: Before Tonkin Gulf, and After Tonkin Gulf. I will never, ever forget the moment in late September 1964, when I decided to stop in a bar on the main street of Olongapo, the "service town" outside the Subic Bay Naval Base, that I was passing to get out of the tropical sun. USS *Pine Island*, an ungainly seaplane tender that was flagship for the admiral's command, of whose staff I was an enlisted member, had docked that morning for a break after our first deployment to Da Nang, following what we all knew was the first step to a war in Vietnam that involved us – the "Maddox Incident" as we in the Navy called it.

Inside, sitting at the bar, was my best friend from Navy boot camp, who I hadn't seen since we had both gone through firefighting training at the San Diego Naval Station the year before while awaiting transport to our separate destinations in WestPac. His ship's patch was on his shoulder: "*USS Maddox*." I'd forgotten that was his destination.

Taking the seat to his left, I took note of the outline of the missing petty officer's "crow" on his sleeve. The outline of holes where the crow had been sewn told its own story – he'd been busted. Recently. I bought us each a San Miguel, and answered his questions about what I'd been doing: I worked in the operations office on the staff of Commander Patrol Forces Seventh Fleet, which I noted had been *Maddox*'s operational commander at that event. He frowned at that. Another round of San Miguel was ordered, and it was my turn to question him. As delicately as I could, I asked "How'd that happen?" pointing at his sleeve.

"Got busted."

I expected him to tell me he'd gotten a "captain's mast" for coming back late from liberty, something that could happen to any of us and nothing to make a big deal of. No. He'd been court-martialed. Hmmm – a summary court was a little more serious, so I asked "what for?"

"Failure to obey a direct order." Now *that* was serious indeed.

"What order?"

"'Open fire.' Said 'no' three times." *Yikes!*

And then, while he told me there had been no enemy torpedo boats attacking *Maddox* or *Turner Joy* that night I'd been awakened at 0200 hours as the duty yeoman in the operations office to take the FLASH message of the attack to the Chief of Staff, how he had been the senior fire control technician in the ship's gunnery control tower and had three times refused to open fire with the six 5-inch guns he controlled, telling his captain each time that the only target out there in the darkness was the other American destroyer, my life changed forever.

Never again, after those minutes in that Olongapo bar, would I ever believe without proof anything said by any official of the government of my country, a country whose constitutional government I had sworn to protect against all enemies, foreign or domestic. Little did I know then that, after I got home the following year and returned to civilian life, I would spend the next seven years consumed by my opposition to the war I had learned that day was a lie.

I came to learn during those years that there is a profound difference between loving one's country and supporting its government.

I have studied the Vietnam War in detail in the years since I returned home and told my father that first night back that "You know absolutely nothing about what's really going on in that war." That was the beginning of the Seven Years' War of the Cleavers – with my father finally saying in 1987 that I had been right, during what turned out to be our last face-to-face conversation. It's why I spent a considerable bit of time in the late sixties involved with the late Dr. Peter Dale Scott, who was dedicated to tracking down the witnesses to the lie that began what had come to be known as the "War of Lies" and discovering that what I had discovered that afternoon in an Olongapo bar was almost only the least of it. It's why I ended up with a degree in History. It's why I was overjoyed the day I laid hands on a copy of the "Pentagon Papers," where for the first time I read an account of the event that changed my life that comported with the reality I had discovered.

It turns out that even now, 50 years later, there are secrets from that night still to be examined. Others have studied the Tonkin Gulf Incident, and it is now known that those "lights in the water" mistakenly identified as enemy torpedo boats were in fact the reflections of the moon and lightning flashes on the enormous school of flying fish that transits the Tonkin Gulf at that time of year. Lyndon Johnson was more right than he knew when he exclaimed, on being first informed of the event, that "those dumb, stupid sailors were just shooting at flying fish." In that moment, he knew more about the war than all his advisors ever did.

One can nowadays ask Google the right questions, input an old code name, and be rewarded with a PDF of a document previously classified Top Secret, now declassified through the Fifty Year Rule, and find that they knew! They knew all the mistakes, all the missed opportunities, everything! They knew them and either let them continue or took actions that exacerbated them.

Perhaps the best news to come from that war is that the men who were in the cockpits of the MiGs, and their opponents in the cockpits of the Phantoms and Crusaders, have come to know each other personally, have visited each other in their homes, have become friends. They recognize and respect each other. Peace has been declared.

This book could not have been written without the active help of those who were there: Rear Admiral H. Denny Wisely from Fighter Squadron 114 (VF-114) and the war's first years, Captain Roy Cash, Jr., who served in VF-33 in the middle years, and Commander Curt "Dozo" Dosé of VF-92 and Lieutenant Michael M. "Matt" Connelly of VF-96, who flew in 1972's "new war." Their willingness to go over their experiences in detail and to review the manuscript for accuracy was critical to completing this project. The late Don Davis, the Associated Press war correspondent who originally reported the "Higbee Incident," provided essential information on the event that the Navy's History and Heritage Command now claims never happened. Rear Admiral James A. Lair of Attack Squadron 22 (VA-22) as well as Captain Ken Burgess, Captain Timothy Prendergast, and Captain Richard Heinrich of VF-51, Lieutenant Commander William Crumpler of HC-1, and Admiral James W. Alderink, then commander of Air Group 21 aboard

USS *Hancock*, recalled their experiences during Operation *Frequent Wind*, the evacuation of Saigon in 1975, and the Mayaguez Incident.

Importantly, through Roy Cash and Curt Dosé, I was also put in contact with retired Lieutenant General Pham Phu Thai, who ended a 30-year career as deputy commander of the Vietnam People's Air Force (VPAF), and retired VPAF Colonel Tu De, the last living participant in the Higbee Incident, who shared their experiences as young pilots of "the other side." Dr. Nguyen Sy Hung, Historian of the VPAF and author of *Aerial Engagements in the Skies of Vietnam Viewed From Both Sides*, considered by American participants who have read it to be a far more accurate and honest account of events they were party to than official US sources, provided an English translation of this important book, without which it would not have been possible to write a history that puts both sides in the air together. After 50 years, it's time to try to tell the whole story.

Examining any facet of the Vietnam War inevitably leads to the question, "Were there any lessons learned?" Sadly, a five-minute examination of the daily paper can quickly lead to the answer: no, no lessons were learned.

If there is a lesson, it is this by foreign policy analyst Adam Garfinkle, analyzing Vietnam and our wars since:

Finally but most important, U.S. expeditionary forces operating in any non-Western cultural zone are very unlikely to win a war at reasonable cost and timetable, employing levels of violence acceptable to the American people, unless the U.S. effort includes a serious effort to understand the country, and unless it has a local ally that is competent and legitimate in the eyes of the population it would rule. In none of these cases did those conditions apply.

This book is for those who cannot forget this history.

Thomas McKelvey Cleaver
Los Angeles, California, 2021

I

SHOOTING AT FLYING FISH

On July 18, 1964, USS *Maddox* (DD-731) departed Kiaosiung Harbor on Formosa, and took up a southerly heading through the Formosa Straits (today known as the Taiwan Straits), headed for the Tonkin Gulf. *Maddox* was no stranger to the waters of Southeast Asia over the previous 20 years. She was an Allen M. Sumner-class destroyer – perhaps the most pugnacious American destroyers ever built – named after Captain William A.T. Maddox, a Marine who made a name for himself at the Battle of Santa Clara during the American conquest of California in the Mexican–American War. She was the third destroyer to bear this name, given her when she was laid down at the Bath Iron Works Corporation on October 28, 1943, in memory of the second *Maddox* (DD-622), a Gleaves-class destroyer sunk by a Luftwaffe Ju-88 in the Battle of Gela on July 19, 1943, during the invasion of Sicily.

Launched on March 19, 1944 and commissioned on June 2 of that year, *Maddox* arrived at Ulithi Anchorage in the Western Pacific on October 21, just too late to participate in the Battle of Leyte Gulf, which saw the end of the Imperial Japanese Navy as a significant fighting force. She was assigned as an escort in Task Group 38.4 commanded by Rear Admiral Ralph Davison aboard the fabled USS *Enterprise* (CV-6), part of Admiral John S. McCain's Task Force 38. *Maddox* first traversed the waters of the Tonkin Gulf in January 1945 when the aviators of Admiral William F. Halsey Jr.'s Third Fleet became the first Americans to enter combat over Vietnam – then known as French Indochina – with a series of air strikes from Hanoi in the north to Saigon in the south.

In June 1950, *Maddox*, then newly arrived back in the Western Pacific, formed part of Task Force 77, which struck the North Korean capital of Pyongyang on July 4. The strikes both saved naval aviation by demonstrating that the Navy could take on a mission no other force could have accomplished, and saved the American position in South Korea by convincing Soviet dictator Josef Stalin to renege on his promise to North Korean leader Kim il-Sung to provide direct Soviet air cover for the invading North Korean army. Six months later, the destroyer became the first ship to sail the Formosa Strait as part of the Formosa Strait Patrol Force.

Maddox's current assignment was an outgrowth of that old assignment in 1950. The Formosa Strait Patrol Force had become the Seventh Fleet Patrol Force (PatFor7thFlt), with destroyers assigned by mission, and patrol bomber squadrons assigned long term to cover the communist-controlled coastline of East Asia from the Sea of Japan in the north to the Tonkin Gulf in the south. The command flag was at the time aboard the newly arrived seaplane tender USS *Pine Island* (AV-12), which was then conducting independent seaplane operations involving patrols along the Chinese coast through the Formosa Straits with the SP-5B Marlin flying boats of Philippines-based Patrol Squadron 40 (VP-40) in Buckner Bay, Okinawa.

The ships and planes followed specific search patterns, each code-named with the name of a make of wristwatch, while specific search tasks were code-named for American cars. *Maddox* was sailing on the Bulova track, and squadron commodore Captain John Herrick was to conduct a Desoto patrol along the coast of the Democratic Republic of Vietnam. "Desoto" was the code name for a signals intelligence collection program begun in 1962 in which naval SIGINT (signals intelligence) direct support units (DSUs) were placed on board destroyers patrolling the Asian coastline. The objective of the Desoto patrols was to collect signals intelligence by activating communist radar and radio systems as they cruised off the coast in international waters just beyond the claimed territorial limit, while officially asserting the right of freedom of navigation in international waters. Occasionally, a communist patrol ship might come out and shadow the US ship, but normally little else happened.

As *Maddox* headed across the South China Sea, no one aboard could imagine that this patrol, so indistinguishable from so many others the ship had undertaken during her career, would change history.

In the summer of 1964, Southeast Asia was balanced on a knife edge, as the possibility of direct American military involvement in the ongoing Vietnamese civil war became more and more likely.

The Central Intelligence Agency (CIA) had organized secret operations to destabilize the North Vietnamese and strengthen the South Vietnamese position in the years since 1957, when the North decided to renew the war of independence in South Vietnam after it became clear that the elections called for in the 1954 Geneva Convention, which had seen the French depart their Indochina colonies, would not be held in 1955 as agreed. The elections had been aborted by the South Vietnamese government with the active support of the United States, since everyone involved on all sides had expected that the communist leader Ho Chi Minh, the leader of the successful war of independence, would win.

Shortly before the overthrow of South Vietnamese President Ngo Dinh Diem in early November 1963, the US government had contemplated an unannounced withdrawal of US forces from South Vietnam, following a confidential report to the Pentagon submitted in the summer of 1963 by US Army military advisor Lieutenant Colonel John Paul Vann in which he expressed his belief that the Army of the Republic of Viet Nam (ARVN), as then organized and led, would never be the equal of the communist National Liberation Front (NLF or "Viet Cong," VC) due to the massive corruption in the upper ranks and the low morale of the combat troops. President Kennedy had reluctantly read the *New York Times'* Vietnam War correspondent David Halberstam's book *The Making of a Quagmire*, which had been published in August 1963, and marked the first public questioning of American policy in South Vietnam. With Halberstam's public account of the mistakes and misjudgments made in South Vietnam since the president had announced he was sending American military advisors in 1961, and Vann's private assessment, the president had privately concluded that the United States needed to separate itself from the government of South Vietnam since the necessary reform was not happening. Given the nature of his political relationship with his vice-president, he said nothing about this decision to Lyndon Baines Johnson. Kennedy's assassination in Dallas, a mere three weeks after the assassination of Diem in Saigon, changed everything.

Lyndon Johnson, along with every other senior leader in the Kennedy Administration, had lived through the days of McCarthyism in the early 1950s, during which the right wing of the Republican Party, then known as "the China Lobby," had mounted a political campaign against the Democrats over the political question "Who lost China?" accompanied by Senator Joseph McCarthy's wild charges of massive communist infiltration of the Truman Administration. A charge of being "soft on communism" was one no Democratic politician wanted made against him by these people. Fear of the far right's demagoguery had led in the fall of 1950 to the disastrous decision to cross the 38th parallel after the successful expulsion of the invading North Koreans from South Korea in order to "roll back communism," which had led directly to intervention by the People's Republic of China and what then-Secretary of State Dean Acheson had called "the greatest defeat of American arms since the Second Battle of Bull Run" that winter. No one mentioned now that the most ardent proponent of "crossing the parallel" had been Dean Rusk, then Undersecretary of State for Far Eastern Affairs and now Secretary of State, and again one of the strongest proponents of US involvement in the developing world to oppose "communism." No one in the new Johnson Administration ever wanted to be asked "Who lost South Vietnam?" With the Republican Party almost certain to nominate far right candidate Senator Barry Goldwater for president in the coming presidential campaign – a man who already advocated stronger US action to "win" in Vietnam – none wished to appear "soft on communism." The fire ten years earlier had burned hot and deep. Thus, in January 1964, American involvement in the continuing civil war for Vietnamese independence was close to becoming a formal military commitment. Once again, American domestic political considerations dominated and controlled actions with regard to foreign policy.

Following President Kennedy's assassination on November 22, 1963, new President Lyndon B. Johnson had taken the advice of his more aggressive hold-overs from the Kennedy Administration, and increased the US commitment to South Vietnam. Whereas President Kennedy had authorized an increase in American advisors to the South Vietnamese armed forces to 12,000 in June 1962, Johnson authorized a further increase to 15,000 in December 1963.

In January 1964, as a result of these changes, the Department of Defense assumed control of the covert missions from the CIA and organized new missions through the military-developed Operations Plan (OPLAN) 34A-64, which were under the active control of the Military Assistance Command – Vietnam (MACV). Originally, these OPLAN 34A operations would be a program of selective intrusions and attacks against the North Vietnamese using graduated intensity, which would last 12 months. Their purpose was to "convince the Democratic Republic of Vietnam (DRV) leadership that their continued direction and support of insurgent activities in the Republic of Vietnam (RVN) and Laos should cease."

This plan reflected the then-current US strategy for escalating the war through "graduated response." Under this strategy, four action levels were established, in which each proceeding action was a qualitative and quantitative increase over what had gone before regarding the sensitivity of target selection and the intensity with which force would be applied in the event that the lesser option was unsuccessful. Level One involved harassment attacks whose cumulative effect, though labeled "unspectacular," would make the DRV leadership aware of the attacks to the extent that they would allocate forces to counter them. In the event that this approach failed, Level Two, termed "attritional," would involve attacks against important military and civil installations in which the loss of such facilities could cause "temporary immobilization of important resources" which, in turn, might create or increase opposition by the population of North Vietnam against the government. Level Three was termed "punitive," and was intended to cause damage, displacement, or destruction of facilities and installations that were critical to the North Vietnamese economy, industry, or military security. At this level of escalation, the North Vietnamese government would have to redeploy resources used to support the war in the South to the needs of internal security. While the planners admitted that operations at this level would necessarily involve large enough forces that they would be overt, they believed these attacks could be attributed to the South Vietnamese armed forces.

Step Four of the OPLAN was the commencement of an American-led aerial bombing campaign that would damage North Vietnam's capacity to support the actions of the NLF in the South, or cripple the North Vietnamese economy sufficiently to make the North Vietnamese leadership decide that the extent of the losses was not worth continued support of the war in the South. At this point, the planners in

Washington expected that the North Vietnamese reaction to the attacks would be based on two factors: willingness to accept critical damage to the North Vietnamese economy by continuing their support of the war in the South, and the possibility of military-economic support by the People's Republic of China.

While several senior military commanders, most pointedly Pacific Fleet commander Admiral Ulysses S. Sharp, expressed reservations about the potential negative effects of these plans and activities, no one in Washington responsible for producing these plans took any time to look back at the ineffectiveness of the aerial bombing campaign against North Korea ten years earlier, which had aimed to end the Korean War, and in which the United States had dropped more bombs on that country than it had dropped on Germany in World War II, to no positive military outcome. There were certainly no experts in Washington who knew that, while China and Korea had a long history of cooperation and support, China and Vietnam had an even longer history of mutual dislike going back to the expulsion of what became the Vietnamese people from their ancestral homeland in what was now southern China by the Han Empire some 2,000 years earlier; several wars had been fought between the two in the years following as the Vietnamese fought for their national independence from imperial China. There was also no real American understanding of the self-inflicted destruction of the Chinese economy in the so-called "Great Leap Forward" that had begun in 1958 and actually set things back to a level below what had existed at the time the communists had taken power in 1949, with several million deaths from famine as peasants were directed to abandon their fields in favor of creating backyard steel mills. Certainly, there was no knowledge outside of the communist faction closest to Chairman Mao Tse-Tung that his response to the disruption of the Great Leap and the resulting instability would be a "Cultural Revolution" that would leave the country unable to intervene anywhere outside its borders for the next generation.

So far as Washington was concerned, the Vietnamese were part and parcel of the International Communist Conspiracy bent on world domination, working with their Chinese and Soviet overlords to destabilize the "free" nations of Southeast Asia, in order to lead to the loss of the region to the communists as each national "domino" fell to their control. The only thing the United States needed to do was tailor whatever military action it planned so as not to provoke the Chinese to intervene as they had done so powerfully in Korea.

The initial results of these operations were disappointing, since the North Vietnamese quickly became very competent in opposing them. Rather than the failure leading to any reconsideration of the basic usefulness of the strategy, the Johnson Administration became more deeply involved as it sought a stronger approach. OPLAN 37-64, which had been developed jointly by the National Security Council, the Joint Chiefs of Staff (JCS) and MACV, was presented in June 1964. The new plan outlined a three-pronged approach to "eliminate to negligible proportions DRV support of VC insurgency in the Republic of Vietnam." These options included ground action by the ARVN in Cambodia and Laos to eliminate sanctuaries and supply points; increased-intensity 34A attacks on North Vietnamese coastal military installations; and bombing 98 pre-selected targets in North Vietnam by the Republic of Vietnam Air Force (VNAF) and USAF and US naval air units.

By this time, American air units were already directly involved in at least some of the fighting in Southeast Asia. In May, Air Force and Navy reconnaissance planes were authorized to gather information on what would come to be known as "the Ho Chi Minh Trail," with the information passed on to the South Vietnamese who were conducting raids against the trail where it passed out of North Vietnam into Laos before turning back into northern South Vietnam. By June 9, 130 photo reconnaissance missions had been flown and the extent of the North Vietnamese transport system became known. Three days earlier, Lieutenant Charles Klusmann of Light Photographic Squadron 63 (VFP-63) ejected from his RF-8A Crusader when he was hit by Pathet Lao gunfire over Laos. Captured by the Pathet Lao, he managed to escape on September 4. The day following Klusmann's loss, the Navy started providing fighter escort for the photo missions, with the escort authorized to retaliate against antiaircraft artillery (AAA) fire. VF-111's commanding officer, Commander Doyle W. Lynn, was shot down over central Laos on one of the first escort missions, but was rescued by the Air Force the next day. The loss of Klusmann and Lynn resulted in the Navy ceasing to fly low-level missions over the trail, restricting them to a minimum altitude of 10,000 feet and routing them away from known hot spots. Such missions would continue through the rest of the year, as part of what was called in Washington the "war short of a war" that was played out over Southeast Asia.

OPLAN 34A's major operational components included airborne operations (AIROPS) to insert intelligence and commando teams into North Vietnam, and maritime operations (MAROPS) involving hit-and-run commando raids on coastal installations. These missions operated under the code name "Timberwork."

OPLAN 34A was almost revealed in a story that appeared in the *New York Times* on July 22, reporting a public statement by South Vietnamese Air Marshal Nguyen Cao Ky, commander of the VNAF, to the effect that his aircraft were dropping commando teams into North Vietnam to engage in sabotage. Such reports were quickly followed by statements from leading members of the Johnson Administration that only "limited steps" were being taken that in no way would lead to a wider war.

In fact, the operations described by Air Marshal Ky were not solely Vietnamese. American military pilots were involved. One such was Navy Lieutenant Daniel Robert White. White had become a naval aviator in 1957, assigned to fly the Douglas AD-6 Skyraider attack aircraft with VA-25. Following an assignment to teach USAF pilots to fly Skyraiders that were being supplied to the VNAF to replace their aging ex-French Grumman F8F-1 Bearcats in 1962, White had volunteered for "special operations" and arrived in South Vietnam wearing civilian clothes in May 1964, with a cover story that he was a Douglas tech rep whose job was to oversee maintenance training for the VNAF Skyraiders. In actuality, he was assigned to the Special Operations Group (SOG) of MACV. He was a pilot in the OPLAN 34A operations, flying un-marked Fairchild C-123 Provider cargo planes that dropped South Vietnamese commandos and other nationalities hired as mercenaries from their base at Nha Trang in northern South Vietnam. White had never flown a C-123 before he arrived at the base, but after three flights in the right seat as co-pilot and three in the left as pilot in command, he was designated an aircraft commander. The black airplanes were ostensibly the property of China Airlines, a CIA front that operated as an actual airline in Southeast Asia, based in Taipei, Taiwan. White was generally the only American on any flight, with a Nationalist Chinese co-pilot and flight engineer. White and a Marine captain who was a fellow member of the team were in charge of the air operation.

Of the eight air drops that had taken place by mid-July, none had been more than "moderately successful" and casualty rates among the teams were so high due to the North Vietnamese having become proficient at intercepting them that the ARVN paratroops assigned considered them suicide missions; paratroopers now failed to report for duty and officers showed up drunk in hopes of being declared unfit to proceed on the missions.

Around the time that Lieutenant White arrived in South Vietnam, US Pacific Fleet commander Admiral Ulysses S. Sharp sent a memorandum to Secretary McNamara in which he noted that nearly all his early reservations about implementing the covert program had "become reality," warning that North Vietnamese defenses "may be more extensive and effective than originally assessed." The maritime commando teams were composed of South Vietnamese Special Forces, known as *Luc Long Dac Biet* or *Biet Kich*, with Chinese and Korean foreign mercenaries crewing the attack craft. American involvement, which was extensive in planning, training, and logistics, was otherwise minimized in order to allow US officials to deny involvement in case the raids were publicized by the North Vietnamese.

Regardless of the planning effort, senior American intelligence and military officials continued to express little confidence in the effectiveness of the OPLAN 34A missions. CIA Director John McCone stated "they will not seriously affect the DRV or cause them to change their policies." Following his return from an inspection trip to South Vietnam in March 1964, Defense Secretary Robert S. McNamara described OPLAN 34A as "a program so limited that it is unlikely to have any significant effect," though his response after so saying was to press for greater program development in order to make it become the successful operation he wanted. Other officials used terms like "pinpricks" and "pretty small potatoes."

The last Desoto patrol in the Tonkin Gulf had been undertaken by USS *John R. Craig* (DD-885) in February–March 1964. The destroyer sailed near Hainan Island, a territory of the People's Republic of China, then toward the Vietnamese coast, finally turning back north to Formosa. The North Vietnamese had tracked *Craig* as she swung south of Hainan Island, but had no further reaction even though they knew that *Craig* was a US warship. During the mission, the Naval Security Group (NSG) aboard was responsible for providing tactical intelligence to

Craig's commander, as well as for intercepting specific communications and electronic intelligence in reaction to the destroyer's presence. *Craig* also received support from the navy and air force communications intelligence (COMINT) sites in the Philippines, though no Vietnam-based sites were involved since *Craig's* mission barely touched North Vietnamese territorial waters.

In mid-July 1964, the US Joint Chiefs approved another Desoto mission. However, when the patrol was first proposed, its mission was expanded. Unlike the previous mission, this would concentrate on collecting intelligence regarding North Vietnam's coastal defenses. Additionally, Commander Seventh Fleet (Com7thFlt) wanted the patrol to move in closer than the original 20-mile limit, to operate as close as 12 miles. Eventually, *Maddox* was ordered to operate eight nautical miles from the North Vietnamese coastline but only four miles from any of its islands, including the island of Hon Me, in the Tonkin Gulf; the DRV at the time claimed a seven-mile limit as its coastal waters.

While the Desoto missions had a long-standing history in the region and were well understood by the other side, there were two critical differences between *Maddox's* mission and the previous mission undertaken by *John R. Craig*.

First, the mission was expanded to include a broader collection of "all-source intelligence" – photographic, hydrographic, and meteorological information. This was not purely a passive mission. The Commander in Chief Pacific (CinCPac) order to Captain Herrick was explicit and ambitious: *Maddox* was to locate and identify all coastal radar transmitters, note all DRV navigational aids, and monitor the North Vietnamese junk fleet in the gulf to determine if there was a possible connection to DRV/Viet Cong maritime supply and infiltration routes to the communist forces operating in the Republic of Vietnam. US communications intercept sites in the region were alerted to the real reason for the Desoto mission, which was to stimulate and record North Vietnamese reactions to the ship's presence, in support of the US SIGINT effort.

The second difference was the presence of the OPLAN 34A missions. As *Maddox* sailed into the South China Sea, the politico-military situation in Southeast Asia was moving toward a crisis point due to efforts by the United States to shore up its South Vietnamese ally, though this increased tension was not obvious to the American public back home. While *Maddox* would sail along the entire North Vietnamese coastline, closer than any previous Desoto patrol, OPLAN 34A missions would be occurring at the same time. Importantly, *Maddox* was not informed of these additional operations. By July, the North Vietnamese were reacting aggressively to these raids, pursuing and attacking the seaborne commando units.

In light of increased North Vietnamese activity in the Gulf of Tonkin over recent months, the Seventh Fleet's Task Force 77, composed of the modernized Essex-class aircraft carriers USS *Bon Homme Richard* (CVA-31) and *Ticonderoga (*CVA-14), was operating in the eastern region of the Tonkin Gulf, tasked with providing any air cover needed by *Maddox* during her patrol. Senior Officer Present Afloat (SOPA) and commander of the US naval forces was Captain George S. Morrison, captain of *Bon Homme Richard. Ticonderoga*'s commander was Captain Damon W. Cooper, a universally well-regarded naval aviator who had come aboard in late June after three years in command of *Pine Island*.

Physically, destroyers assigned to the Desoto patrols were unique in having a small mobile van brought aboard and lashed to the midships deck that housed intercept positions operated by the complement of 12–18 officers and men from the NSG. One position was equipped to intercept and record voice and Morse radio communications. A second position intercepted non-communications emissions such as radars, called electronic intelligence (ELINT). A communications position allowed the detachment to send and receive messages from the other monitoring stations in the area, as well as other SIGINT organizations and commands, via the CRITICOMM communications system.

While the 34A commando raids had failed to achieve their objective, the Johnson Administration believed the government should continue to demonstrate US political support for the unsteady regime of General Khanh, who had led the coup against President Diem and had succeeded to the presidency of South Vietnam after his assassination. In the administration, a policy of "doing something," even if it was as ineffective as the raids had proven to be, was seen as essential in maintaining South Vietnamese morale and commitment to continuing the war. In fact, the ARVN had steadily lost ground since Vann's gloomy report the previous summer. Following the

NLF ground campaign of 1963–64 during the monsoon, which took advantage of the bad weather to deprive the ARVN of effective air support, the communist insurgents controlled the majority of the South Vietnamese countryside by the early summer of 1964. The military situation was such that NLF commandos operating in Saigon itself had set mines in the Mekong River and sunk the American aircraft ferry USNS *Core* anchored in the river off Saigon on May 2, 1964, when the old World War II escort carrier arrived with replacement helicopters. The river was shallow enough at this point that the ship now sat at an awkward angle, its keel sunk in the muddy bottom, a constant visual reminder of the enemy's capability. "Doing something," doing anything, constituted the entire US policy to prop up the Saigon government.

Rather than deter the North Vietnamese, the OPLAN 34A maritime raids had only increased their determination to meet the attacks head-on. The National Security Agency (NSA) and US Navy monitoring site at San Miguel in the Philippines reported in June and July that there was increased conflict along the coast of North Vietnam, as the North Vietnamese Navy assumed a more active role in responding to the raiders. Communications were intercepted and reported to the administration in Washington regarding small boat actions, commando landings, and high-speed chases in the Tonkin Gulf. The reports showed a more aggressive North Vietnamese Navy reacting with increased force to incursions by the South Vietnamese commandos. On July 4, the NSA reported that North Vietnamese tactical radio communications had increased by nearly 400 percent during the first week of June as compared to the previous period in May, and that North Vietnamese naval patrols now covered the entire coastline. On July 28, the day *Maddox* rounded Hainan Island and entered the Tonkin Gulf, North Vietnamese Swatow-class gunboats pursued the raiders for 45 nautical miles following an attack on Hon Gio Island before giving up the chase. Two days later, two US Navy jet aircraft flying in international air space off the coast were taken under fire by a patrol boat that claimed a hit on one jet. Whether or not the North Vietnamese believed that the United States was preparing for a larger war was unimportant. What was critically important was that the situation along the North Vietnamese coast was near boiling point. The 34A attacks on these North Vietnamese islands, especially

Hon Me, combined with the proximity of *Maddox* which could give at least the appearance of coordination between the two, would trigger the confrontation.

It is important to note that, while there was interconnection between 34A operations and the Desoto patrols at higher command levels, and the Desoto mission involved collection of intelligence which could be useful to the 34A planners and commanders in Da Nang and the Pentagon, there was not a direct operational connection between the two. They were managed under separate commands and did not coordinate mission planning, except when the Desoto patrol was warned to stay clear of 34A operational areas. The North Vietnamese, however, were not privy to the American organization charts.

On the night of July 30–31, 1964, the Tonkin Gulf boiled over. South Vietnamese commandos struck Hon Me Island, located several miles off the central coast of North Vietnam. The commandos first attempted to land and attack a radar station, but were driven off. The raiding boats then maneuvered offshore and peppered the radar site with machine-gun and small cannon fire. As this went on, two other commando boats opened fire on Hon Ngu Island near the port of Vinh.

Maddox followed her orders to stay well out to sea that night. The next morning, as the destroyer headed for her patrol station eight miles offshore, Captain Herrick saw the retreating commando boats (they were called "nasties" after the boat's manufacturer, "Nast") heading south. At the same time, the navy communications monitoring site at San Miguel intercepted North Vietnamese radio reports of the unsuccessful attempts by their patrol craft to catch the enemy. *Maddox* continued down the coast, collecting ELINT and observing the Vietnamese fishing junks.

At 0700 hours local time on August 1, the Army Security Agency (ASA) communications intercept site at Phu Bai in South Vietnam monitored the North Vietnamese Swatow-class gunboat *T-146* when she radioed tracking data on the *Maddox* to another North Vietnamese Swatow. At the time, the destroyer was steaming northeasterly, nine miles southeast of Hon Me Island. The Swatow-class gunboats were fairly large, displacing 67 tons, with a top speed of 44 knots and a cruising speed of 20 knots, armed with two 37mm antiaircraft (AA) gun mounts, two 20mm AA mounts, and up to eight depth charges. Swatows generally worked with smaller P-4-class torpedo boats, performing communications relay between North Vietnamese naval command centers and the P-4s, which lacked long-distance communications capability. *Maddox* was followed by North Vietnamese patrol craft throughout the day.

Shortly after 2300 hours on the night of August 1, the San Miguel intercept site reported that the North Vietnamese naval base at Ben Thuy had informed an unidentified entity, possibly *T-146*, that it had been "DECIDED TO FIGHT THE ENEMY TONIGHT WHEN YOU RECEIVE DIRECTING ORDERS." The base also questioned if the boat had received the enemy's position change from what was possibly an authority on Hon Matt Island. *Maddox* was informed of this intercept. Thirty minutes later, Captain Herrick informed Commander Patrol Force 7th Fleet (ComPatFor7thFlt), Com7thFlt, and CinCPac that he had terminated the mission and was heading east out of the patrol area at ten knots, due to indications of an imminent attack from interceptions of North Vietnamese communications by the NSG detachment aboard ship and alerts from San Miguel and Phu Bai. Throughout the night, according to the intercepted messages, the North Vietnamese continued to track *Maddox* as she remained 25 miles offshore, east of Hon Me Island. Nothing further happened, and at dawn on August 2 the destroyer returned to the patrol line off the North Vietnamese coast.

During the early morning of August 2, while *Maddox* steamed along the northern track of the patrol area, the tracking stations at San Miguel and Phu Bai notified her that the North Vietnamese torpedo boat squadron stationed at Port Wallut was shadowing her under control of the radar station on Hon Me Island. Later that morning, *Maddox* was warned that the North Vietnamese had ordered several P-4 boats and Swatows to concentrate near Hon Me Island. The Soviet-supplied P-4 was potentially a dangerous adversary, displacing 25 tons with a top speed of 50 knots and cruising speed of 30 knots, armed with two twin 12.7mm machine-gun mounts and two 18-inch torpedo tubes. The communications interceptions were interpreted by the Americans as a prelude to an attack.

At 1002 hours local time, the NSA sent an urgent message to CinCPac, MACV, Com7thFlt, and ComPatFor7thFlt warning of a possible attack. Ironically, *Maddox* was not on the distribution list. The message was simple: repeated attacks by enemy vessels on Hon Me Island "THE INDICATED SENSITIVITY ON PART OF DRV AS WELL AS

THEIR INDICATED PREPARATION TO COUNTER, POSSIBLE THE DRV REACTION TO PATROL MIGHT BE MORE SEVERE THAN WOULD BE OTHERWISE BE [sic] ANTICIPATED."

At 1144 hours, the Marine SIGINT group attached to the ASA site at Phu Bai intercepted a message from *T-142* to the naval base at Port Wallut, stating "WE HAVE RECEIVED THE ORDERS. T146 AND T142 DID USE HIGH SPEED TO GET TOGETHER PARALLEL WITH ENEMY FOLLOWING LAUNCHED TORPEDOES." The Phu Bai station issued a CRITIC (critically important message) alerting all commands, and *Maddox*, of the planned attack, adding that *T-142*, *T-146*, *T-166*, and *T-135* were engaged in tracking and following an "enemy" which "is probably the current mission."

Throughout the day, the listening stations in the Philippines and South Vietnam monitored the North Vietnamese ship-to-ship and ship-to-shore Morse and voice communications nets, intercepting the all-important vectoring information, orders from shore commands, and all tactical communications between the shadowing patrol boats. However, the North Vietnamese made no hostile moves against *Maddox*.

Half an hour after the Marine interception unit at Phu Bai had transmitted its warning, the Marine detachment at San Miguel intercepted the same message. This was not unusual, and meant the North Vietnamese were retransmitting it to ensure its reception. The Americans, however, took the second transmission as a direct order to engage in hostilities.

At the same time, *Maddox*, which was on a northwest heading away from Hon Me Island, visually observed the arrival of the three Swatow boats. Several minutes later, two more Swatows were spotted in the same area as the first three. All five North Vietnamese boats were now concentrated near the island.

Actually, the first three boats *Maddox* had spotted were the P-4 boats *T-333*, *T-336*, and *T-339*, while the two Swatows that had been located later were likely *T-142* and *T-146*, whose orders directing them to shadow the destroyer had been intercepted that morning. The P-4 boats departed Hon Me Island at about 1300 hours, apparently seeking *Maddox*. Over the next hour, conflicting orders were sent to the North Vietnamese boats, all of which were picked up and passed along by the US listening sites. At 1409 hours, Port Wallut notified the two Swatows that the "enemy" was a large ship bearing

125 degrees (from My Duc) at a distance of 19 miles and speed of 11 knots, heading 020. The information put the target on a north-northeast heading, matching that of *Maddox*. The message also included a garbled phrase to "THEN DETERMINE," the meaning of which is unclear. The North Vietnamese later said that the order to attack the destroyer was sent at 1350 hours. Since the file time of the message from Port Wallut was 1400 local, this may have been the "attack" message.

However, six minutes before the Port Wallut "attack" order was intercepted, the San Miguel site intercepted a message from Haiphong to the two Swatows, telling them "ORDER 135 NOT TO MAKE WAR BY DAY." The message also ordered all the boats to head toward shore and then return to Hon Me Island. Although this message was sent shortly after 1400 local time, it contained a file time of 1203 local, which means this message, an order to recall the boats, was originated nearly two hours *before* transmission of the order to attack was sent! A second intercept of the same message contained orders that *T-146* was to order the recall of Squadron 135's torpedo boats. The North Vietnamese had lost command control of the situation. If there was to be an attack, the authorities in Haiphong wanted it at night rather than in daylight when the conditions for surprising *Maddox* were unfavorable. Since the boats continued their attack, it is apparent the recall order was ignored, possibly because the deciding factor for the North Vietnamese commander was the much earlier file time of the recall order than that of the attack message.

At approximately 1400 hours, *Maddox* detected the approach of the three P-4s from the southwest on her radar. Forewarned of the North Vietnamese intention to attack, *Maddox* then commenced a turn to the east, then to the southeast and increased speed from 11 to 25 knots. At 1430 hours, *Maddox*'s captain, Commander Ogier, ordered the crew to general quarters. Ten minutes later, at 1440 hours, *Maddox* sent a flash precedence message to JCS, CinCPac, Com7thFlt, MACV, and ComPatFor7thFlt that she was being approached by high-speed craft with the intention of executing torpedo attacks. At the end of the message, force commander Captain Herrick announced he would fire in self-defense if necessary. Additionally, he requested air cover from *Ticonderoga*, which was at the time 280 miles to the southeast. The ship vectored four F-8E Crusaders led by Commander James B. Stockdale to provide cover and USS *Turner Joy* (DD-951) was ordered to make best speed to assist *Maddox*.

The chase continued for the next 20 minutes, with the North Vietnamese torpedo boats inexorably closing the gap with *Maddox*. At 1500 hours, Captain Herrick gave Commander Ogier permission for the gun crews to open fire if the North Vietnamese boats approached within 10,000 yards. Five minutes later, *Maddox* fired three 5-inch rounds from the aft mount to warn off the North Vietnamese. The fact that *Maddox* had fired first was never reported by the Johnson Administration, which insisted that the North Vietnamese had issued the first fire. Between five and ten minutes later, *Maddox* resumed fire as the North Vietnamese boats moved in through the shellfire in attacks that proved ineffective. Within 15 minutes of *Maddox*'s first salvo, the four *Ticonderoga* F-8Es arrived overhead and attacked the North Vietnamese, leaving one boat dead in the water and the other two damaged. *Maddox* was unscathed other than suffering a single bullet hole from a North Vietnamese machine-gun round.

The North Vietnamese later claimed they had shot down two aircraft. In reality, one of the Crusaders sustained wing damage during the attack and was escorted from the area by its wingman. Since both aircraft departed the area under full power, they were making heavy exhaust trails which could have appeared to the North Vietnamese sailors to be battle damage. The damaged Crusader was forced to land at Da Nang. All three of the attacking North Vietnamese PT boats eventually made it back to their base, despite their damage. *T-339*, the boat thought to be dead in the water and claimed sunk by the Americans, and initially reported sunk by the other North Vietnamese boats, managed to restart her engines and limp back to base, carrying four dead and six wounded from a crew of 12.

Two hours after action was initiated, the patrol boat *T-142* received orders to contact *T-165* north of Hon Me Island, while *T-146* received orders to assist the return of the P-4 boats. Two days later, *T-146* reported the damage received by the P-4s in the action: *T-333* was hit three times, suffering light damage to her water pipes and lifeboat; *T-336* was "heavily damaged with many holes" and one of her deck guns was wrecked, while two crewmen had been wounded.

Reaction to the news of the attack was relatively subdued in Washington, since no Americans had been injured. President

Johnson ordered the event downplayed in the media, while the State Department sent the first diplomatic message ever to the Democratic Republic of Vietnam, strongly protesting the actions of the torpedo boats and insisting on the right of free passage in international waters. The note ended with a statement that any further unprovoked actions would entail "grave consequences." Secretary of State Rusk, who was in New York City for a speaking engagement, spoke to his audience of the day's event in familiar election campaign terms. In response to questions, he observed that "many incidents since 1945 could have led to another world war if sobriety had not exercised a restraining influence."

Now-retired General Maxwell D. Taylor, former Chairman of the Joint Chiefs, World War II paratroop hero as commander of the 101st Airborne at Normandy, and final commander of the Eighth Army in the Korean War, who had become American ambassador to the Republic of Vietnam in June, responded forcefully to the lack of a strong response by the administration. In a message to Rusk, he stated that the absence of retaliation for the attacks would encourage the North Vietnamese into further aggression and lead the South Vietnamese to conclude that America "flinches from direct confrontation." He ended the cable with the recommendation that the president announce that American forces would attack North Vietnamese torpedo boats wherever they were found, conduct overflights of North Vietnam to maintain regular air surveillance of the North Vietnamese PT boat bases and mine the approaches to their harbors, and also increase the capability of the South Vietnamese Navy to attack targets in the North.

After reading the cable, Assistant Secretary of State George C. Ball told Rusk that the ambassador's recommendations were extreme and amounted to a declaration of war, saying that at most there was a need for more defined rules of engagement. McNamara agreed with Ball and suggested they ignore the cable, recommending that the president merely announce American willingness to "attack and destroy any force that attacks us in international waters." The president decided after conferring with McNamara to follow this advice the next day in his planned impromptu White House press conference. Rusk privately assured Taylor that they appreciated his advice, stating "we have no intention of yielding to pressure." This was all in line with the evolving strategic concept for dealing with Vietnam at this time: demonstrate restraint, yet appear determined and steadfast. The administration would not give Senator Goldwater any ammunition to claim American "weakness," while preserving the position of the president as the "peace" candidate.

Secretary McNamara's public statement that the North Vietnamese had fired first was wrong; the North Vietnamese quickly broadcast a report stating that the *Maddox* had fired first. Realizing the situation was "muddled," the secretary said nothing more. In the upper reaches of the administration, there was dismay that they had miscalculated the reaction to the 34A raids, since the North Vietnamese had concluded that the raids were coordinated with the presence of *Maddox*, while the intercepted enemy messages suggested the North Vietnamese had lost control of the situation. In an attempt to defuse the crisis, McNamara stated, "We believed it possible that it had resulted from a miscalculation or an impulsive act of a local commander." Politically, nothing more would come of the events of August 2, and those who had hoped for a North Vietnamese response that might provide an opening for an escalation of US actions were frustrated.

While political Washington attempted to put the incident aside, the Pentagon doubled down rather than allow cooler heads to prevail. Plans were set in motion to replace *Bon Homme Richard* with the new carrier USS *Constellation* (CVA-64) which was then making a port visit at Hong Kong, to operate with *Ticonderoga*, while Pacific Air Forces commander General Emmett "Rosie" O'Donnell, an officer who had been involved in US military affairs in Asia since he led the first formation of B-17s from Hawaii to the Philippines just before the outset of the Pacific War 22 years earlier, and had directed the heavy bombing campaign against North Korea as commander of Far East Air Force Bomber Command, dispatched additional USAF units to Clark Air Force Base (AFB) in the Philippines to reinforce the US presence in the region.

Turner Joy had been dispatched to rendezvous with *Maddox* while the August 2 action was underway. Pacific Fleet commander Admiral Sharp ordered both ships to return to the Desoto patrol area where the attack had taken place, seeing such action as being "in our interest that we assert right of freedom of the seas." New rules of engagement were issued by Commander in Chief Pacific Fleet (CinCPac), authorizing both destroyers to approach the North Vietnamese coast to eight miles and four miles from the islands. They were to commence the daylight patrol one hour before dawn and to retire east one hour before sunset, remaining out to sea during the night.

While the military leadership was anxious to up the ante in the Gulf of Tonkin, Captain Herrick displayed more caution. He dispatched an after-action report on the evening of August 2 that reviewed the attack and the successful American defense, ending with the warning: the "DRV HAS CAST DOWN THE GAUNTLET AND NOW CONSIDERS ITSELF AT WAR WITH US," stating a concern that the North Vietnamese torpedo boats could be far more dangerous at night, when they could hide and approach the destroyers with little warning, and pointing out that *Maddox* and *Turner Joy*, with their 5-inch main armament and top speed of 33 knots, were not able to effectively defend themselves against such an opponent. Herrick suggested that the Desoto patrol would be safe only with a supporting cruiser and continuous air cover. The final item in the report was that *Maddox*'s AN/SPS-40 long-range air search radar was inoperative, and that the AN/SPG-53 fire control radar on *Turner Joy* was out of action indefinitely. Just before dark on August 2, the two destroyers conducted an underway replenishment of ammunition and supplies. Following Herrick's report and despite the noted equipment failures, the destroyers were ordered to return to the North Vietnamese coast at daybreak on August 3.

On August 3, President Johnson announced that he had instructed the Navy to maintain the patrols in the Tonkin Gulf with continuous air cover overhead. He concluded his announcement with the statement that if any US forces were attacked in international waters, they would respond with the intention not merely of driving the attackers off, but of "destroying them." In the words of Assistant Secretary Ball, the president's words "appeared fierce." The administration had demonstrated restraint, while appearing determined and steadfast. The political strategy remained firm.

Despite the increased public awareness domestically of the situation in the Tonkin Gulf and its potential political ramifications, and the increased North Vietnamese vigilance and sensitivity to American and South Vietnamese naval activity in their territorial waters, MACV approved execution of an OPLAN 34A mission against the North Vietnamese radar site at Vinh Son, which had previously been planned for the night of August 3–4. By mid-morning, *Maddox* and *Turner Joy* were approaching their patrol station near Hon Me Island, where North Vietnamese torpedo boats were patrolling, approximately 100 miles northwest of the 34A operating area. They were advised to avoid operating in the area of the Tonkin Gulf bounded by the 17th and 18th parallels in order to remain clear of the 34A operation.

The North Vietnamese naval authorities in Haiphong were still unaware of the status of the torpedo boats that had taken part in the action the day before and sent several messages to the *T-142* and *T-146* requesting information updates. The messages were intercepted by the Marine site at Phu Bai, where this search and salvage activity on the part of the North Vietnamese was misconstrued as a prelude to concentrating the torpedo boats and an increased threat to *Maddox* and *Turner Joy*. Phu Bai issued a CRITIC at 1656 hours that placed six North Vietnamese patrol and torpedo boats near Hon Me Island. In fact, this concentration of resources was not happening.

Once *Maddox* and *Turner Joy* arrived on station south of Hon Me Island at approximately 1330 hours, they were shadowed by a Swatow gun boat that tracked them through the afternoon and into the early evening. Phu Bai picked up communication between the boat and the North Vietnamese naval command in Haiphong exchanging position data on the American ships, which was construed by the intelligence monitors as further proof that the North Vietnamese were concentrating a force for a second attack. At around 1800 hours, Haiphong ordered *T-142* to track the destroyers. The gun boat took up position north of the ships and made several position reports which were intercepted at Phu Bai, where anxiety grew regarding the expected attack. *Maddox* reported at 2252 hours that the destroyers were being followed by a patrol boat 38 miles distant that was tracking them by radar while they headed southeast out of the patrol area as they had been instructed. Thirty minutes later, the North Vietnamese patrol craft sheered off when the destroyers moved out of range.

The four-boat OPLAN 34A mission departed Da Nang at 1510 hours that afternoon and was in position off Vinh Son shortly before 2400 hours, about 40 minutes after the North Vietnamese turned away from tracking *Maddox* and *Turner Joy*. Three of the boats opened fire on the radar station at midnight, while the fourth attacked a nearby security position before the arrival of a North Vietnamese gun boat that chased it off. With that, the OPLAN 34A attackers evaded the North Vietnamese as they withdrew from the area and returned to Da Nang. The North Vietnamese, who were uncertain of the position of the two destroyers at the time of the attack, inferred from their maneuvering during the day that they were the unidentified ships that had fired on the radar site. So far as the North Vietnamese were now concerned, *Maddox* and *Turner Joy* were active participants in the combat happening in the Tonkin Gulf and they stated such when they lodged their formal protest against the raid. Despite this, US authorities still believed that North Vietnam would not take direct action in the matter.

Dawn on August 4 found the two destroyers sailing back toward the North Vietnamese coast, arriving on station off Thanh Hoa around 1300 hours. Air cover in the form of four A-1 Skyraiders from *Ticonderoga* was overhead to the east, remaining in international air space over the gulf as the ships turned southwest. At 1400 hours, *Maddox* reported a shadower 15 miles east, following the Americans on radar. The ships maintained their patrol during the daylight hours without further action by the North Vietnamese other than continuing to shadow the two destroyers.

At 1815 hours, the Marine listening site at Phu Bai sent a CRITIC to the NSG SIGINT detachment aboard *Maddox*, stating "POSS DRV NAVAL OPERATIONS PLANNED AGAINST THE DESOTO PATROL TONITE 04 AUG. AMPLIFYING DATA FOL." At 1840 hours, Phu Bai sent a follow-up that reported "IMMINENT PLANS OF DRV NAVAL ACTION POSSIBLY AGAINST DESOTO MISSION," adding that the unit had intercepted a message that had been sent to *T-142*, *T-146*, and *T-333* at 1627 hours to "make ready for military operations the night of 4 August." Captain Herrick was notified and at 1940 hours he messaged CinCPac, Com7thFlt, ComPatFor7thFlt and MACV that he had received "INFO INDICATING ATTACK BY PGN P-4 IMMINENT. MY POSITION 19-10N 107-00E. PROCEEDING SOUTHEAST." At this time, *Maddox* and *Turner Joy* were 80–85 nautical miles from the nearest point on the North Vietnamese coastline. They increased speed to 20 knots and took a course southeast to put more distance between themselves and North Vietnam.

At 2000 hours, *Maddox* reported radar detection of "two skunks" (surface contacts) and three "bogeys" (air contacts) 40–45 miles northeast of the two destroyers, putting the ships about 100–110 miles away from the North Vietnamese coast, but very close to Hainan Island. In response to this report, *Ticonderoga* launched four F-8 Crusaders led by air group commander (CAG) Stockdale, which arrived over the ships at 2045 hours.

At about the time the Crusaders arrived, Captain Herrick reported the loss of the original surface contacts. In the meantime, *Constellation* had launched three VA-144 A-4C Skyhawks led by squadron operations officer Lieutenant Commander John Nicholson to cover the destroyers. Soon after, *Ticonderoga* launched four VA-56 Skyhawks, led by commanding officer Commander Wesley L. McDonald, as reinforcement. Nicholson recalled that the night was stormy with rain, thunder, and lightning as they manned their planes on the flight deck but that the weather was less harsh when they arrived in the vicinity of the destroyers. The *Constellation* aircraft arrived over the ships at 2108 hours, just as *Maddox* reported she had detected another radar contact that was first identified as one boat, then later thought to be several boats in tight formation, 15 miles southwest of the two destroyers and moving toward them at 30 knots. At 2117 hours the Skyhawks were vectored toward the reported location of the boats. The pilots reported that they could see the wakes of the destroyers clearly but could see no boats at the position indicated by *Maddox*'s radar; she lost the contact at 2131 hours.

Suddenly, at 2134 hours, what appeared to be a single boat suddenly appeared on *Maddox*'s radar screen at a range of 9,800 yards and closing at nearly 40 knots from the east. *Turner Joy* picked up a contact approaching on a different heading, distance, and speed. Three minutes later at 2137 hours, when it had closed to 6,200 yards from the destroyers, *Maddox*'s radar target appeared to make a sharp turn to the south, which was interpreted in *Maddox*'s Combat Information Center (CIC) as a turn after a torpedo launch. If true, this was not in accordance with North Vietnamese tactical specifications for the P-4, which called for torpedo launches under 1,000 yards. A launch at over 6,000 yards at a moving target was unlikely to hit anything. *Maddox*'s chief sonarman detected a noise spike on his gear, but did not report it as a torpedo. *Turner Joy* never detected any torpedoes on her sonar throughout the night. Nicholson later reported hearing "Torpedo!" from the CIC controller.

Herrick informed CinCPac at 2140 hours that *Maddox* had opened fire on the attacking PT boat, immediately after *Turner Joy* opened fire at its radar return. Both destroyers experienced difficulty holding a radar lock on their respective targets. Five minutes later, the return on *Maddox*'s radar that was last seen moving away from the destroyers disappeared from the screen at a distance of approximately 9,000 yards, while *Turner Joy*'s return kept approaching until it disappeared at a range of about 4,000 yards. The radar screens of both ships were blank for the next 15 minutes, until more contacts were suddenly detected coming from the west at 2201 hours.

The two ships maneuvered wildly in the dark waters with *Turner Joy* firing more than 300 rounds at what were reported as being up to 13 North Vietnamese torpedo boats and dodging more than 24 torpedoes. She also fired 24 star shells to illuminate the area and dropped five depth charges to ward off the pursuers. As this went on, *Maddox* vectored the air cover to the reported surface contacts; each time that the aircraft reached the designated location and dropped flares, there was nothing there. Unnoticed in the rush of events at the time, a spot report was issued by the Phu Bai intercept site at almost the precise instant that Herrick ordered *Maddox* and *Turner Joy* to open fire on the approaching radar returns, stating that both *T-336* and *T-333*, which had earlier been reported through intercepts as ready to attack the Desoto patrol, were actually being readied for tow to either Haiphong or Port Wallut, having been damaged on August 2. According to multiple SIGINT intercepts, there were no North Vietnamese torpedo boats at sea in the Gulf of Tonkin that night; they were all involved in bringing the damaged P-4s back for repair.

Throughout the action, the radar returns on the screens of both ships were mostly "flashing returns"; i.e., they appeared on the scope, held for a few sweeps, then disappeared. At other times, targets suddenly appeared a few miles from the destroyers and their returns held for a while, then disappeared. The targets came from all directions. Whenever one of the radar tracks "turned away," this was interpreted as a torpedo launch. The sonar rooms were then alerted to a possible torpedo attack. Both ships engaged in wild evasive maneuvers to avoid the torpedoes they believed had been launched against them.

It was later determined that it was this high-speed maneuvering that created all the additional sonar reports of more torpedoes in the water. Every time either of the destroyers changed course, the sonar operator on the other reported hearing the distinctive high-speed sounds of torpedoes.

The assistant gunnery officer aboard *Turner Joy* later described the confusion of proliferating targets thus: "We were getting blotches on the radar screen – nothing real firm, so we were whacking away at general areas with proximity fuzes, hoping to get something." As *Turner Joy* continued to fire, a target would appear to be hit, then disappear as if it had been incinerated in an explosion; this was contrary to the experience on August 2, when the North Vietnamese PT boats were seen to take several hits but still remain afloat. The fire control technician operating *Maddox*'s main gun director maintained that the ship never acquired any targets during the battle and in fact he refused Captain Herrick's order to open fire three times on grounds that the only target out in the darkness was *Turner Joy*. He later stated that when he did open fire at the outset of the action, he believed he was shooting at the high waves and swells brought on by the nearby storms. For his pains, he was later given a General Court-Martial for "failure to obey a direct order" and broken in rank to E-3.

At one point late in the action, Commander Stockdale, who was flying at approximately 1,500 feet over the destroyers, saw the two ships close at each other in a flash of lightning. Fortunately, while the sailor controlling *Maddox*'s fire control director refused the order to open fire, the assistant gunnery officer aboard *Turner Joy* managed to convince his captain that there was only the *Maddox* in the vicinity and the destroyer did not open fire at *Maddox*. Stockdale reported when he returned to *Ticonderoga* that, "I had the best seat in the house from which to detect boats – if there were any… I could see the destroyers' every move vividly. The edges of the black hole I was flying in were still periodically lit by flashes of lightning – but no wakes or dark shapes other than those of the destroyers were ever visible to me."

Stockdale's account was backed by the report of VA-56's Commander Wesley L. McDonald: "I didn't see anything that night other than the *Maddox* and the *Turner Joy*. And I think the *Maddox*, basically, was in disarray as far as the Combat Information Center controller was concerned in trying to get us to attack PT boats that were imaginary.

I didn't see any wakes; I didn't see anything." VA-144's Lieutenant Commander John Nicholson echoed McDonald's account, adding, "There is no doubt in my mind those two ships were under stress, judging from the voice of the guy at the CIC control… his voice was very tense, he had his headings completely screwed up, and there is no doubt in my mind the crew felt they were under attack."

By 2335 hours, the attack appeared to be over as the returns gradually disappeared from the ships' radar screens. Captain Herrick sent a "flash" to CinCPac, Com7thFlt, ComPatFor7thFlt, and MACV reporting two enemy craft sunk and a third damaged.

Within an hour, Herrick and the other officers aboard *Maddox* realized what had been the cause of the reports that torpedoes were in the water: when the rudders of the two ships were turned, they reflected the turbulence of the ships' own propellers and caused the high-speed returns. With this information and awareness of what had likely occurred, Captain Herrick relayed his doubts about the attack in an after-action report. After reviewing the number of contacts and possible sinkings, he stated, "ENTIRE ACTION LEAVES MANY DOUBTS EXCEPT FOR APPARENT ATTEMPTED AMBUSH AT BEGINNING." He suggested a thorough air reconnaissance of the area in daylight to search for wreckage. In a follow-up message, he added that the Maddox had "NEVER POSITIVELY IDENTIFIED A BOAT AS SUCH."

The captain's doubts were unwelcome in Washington. The first CRITIC warning of a possible attack had arrived at the Pentagon at 0740 hours Eastern Standard Time (EST). Since then, official Washington had closely followed the action in the Gulf of Tonkin. Secretary McNamara had called President Johnson at 0925 hours with news of the imminent attack. The Pentagon received the flash message that the two ships were under attack at 1000 hours EST. At approximately 1400 EST, Admiral Sharp informed Secretary McNamara that "a review of the action makes many reported contacts and torpedoes fired 'appear doubtful.'" The admiral pointed out that this was because of freak weather, over-eager sonar operators, and the absence of visual sightings. Sharp ended with the statement there was "a little doubt on just what exactly went on." *Ticonderoga* transmitted an evaluation based on Stockdale's and McDonald's reports: "REPORT NO VISUAL SIGHTINGS OF ANY VESSELS OR WAKES OTHER

THAN TURNER JOY AND MADDOX. WAKES FROM TURNER
JOY AND MADDOX VISIBLE FROM 2–3000 YARDS."

However, right after Admiral Sharp hung up from his conversation
with McNamara, a translation of a reputed North Vietnamese after-
action report was issued by NSA at 1433 hours. The report quoted
an unidentified North Vietnamese naval authority that had been
intercepted reportedly stating that the DRV had "SHOT DOWN
TWO PLANES IN THE BATTLE AREA," and that "WE HAD
SACRIFICED TWO SHIPS AND ALL THE REST ARE OKAY." It
also added that "THE ENEMY SHIP COULD ALSO HAVE BEEN
DAMAGED." McNamara was quick to take this as direct evidence of
the attack.

Following up the NSA report, Admiral Sharp called McNamara a
second time at 1640 hours EST with more information on the attack.
McNamara and the Joint Chiefs met shortly thereafter at 1700 hours
to evaluate the evidence of the attack. At the end of the meeting, they
concluded it had in fact occurred and that five factors were critical:

1. The *Turner Joy* was illuminated by a searchlight when fired on
   by automatic weapons
2. One of the destroyers observed cockpit bridge lights of one of
   the DRV patrol boats
3. A PGM 142 had shot at two US aircraft
4. A North Vietnamese announcement had stated that two of its
   boats were "sacrificed"
5. Admiral Sharp had determined that there was indeed an attack.

As the leaders in Washington attempted to find the "smoking gun"
they were searching for to justify the action they wanted to take, the
NSA issued a report to cover the discrepancies created by the Phu
Bai intercepts that had the P-4 torpedo boats being towed for repair.
This report stated that though the earlier intercepts had indicated that
T-142, *T-146*, and *T-333* would participate in the attacks, it had been
"determined" they were not involved and that naval units at Quang
Khe were detailed for the attacks. The fact that there were no intercepts
of the North Vietnamese giving such orders, and that the only naval
units at Quang Khe were Swatow-class gun boats which did not carry
torpedoes – thus making it impossible for them to carry out torpedo

attacks as reported by the destroyers – was just another small detail that those who wanted reality to fit their hopes were willing to overlook.

Of the five pieces of "evidence," two were from the same NSA report issued that afternoon. If the two pieces of visual evidence – the searchlight and cockpit light reports – were not that strong, the intercepted North Vietnamese message was, so far as Secretary McNamara, the Joint Chiefs and President Johnson were concerned, the "smoking gun" evidence needed to justify the decision the president had made at 1400 hours that afternoon to order air strikes on North Vietnam.

There was another military operation that took place in the Gulf of Tonkin the night of August 4–5 that was the more likely subject of the original North Vietnamese intercept regarding "military operations." This was another OPLAN 34A mission, planned to shell the island of Hon Matt at around midnight. The attack craft for this mission were moving northward along the North Vietnamese coast at the time *Maddox* and *Turner Joy* were doing battle with the flickering radar returns. At 2316 hours, the Marine unit at Phu Bai intercepted a message from the North Vietnamese naval headquarters at Haiphong to *T-142*, that six enemy vessels had been located south of Thanh Hoa. This North Vietnamese intercept happened only minutes before an urgent recall of the OPLAN 34A mission by CinCPac was approved in Washington by the Joint Chiefs' staff. There was one other intercepted position report interpreted as regarding the Desoto patrol sent from the P-4 boat base at Port Wallut to an unknown vessel at 2246 hours, approximately an hour after the supposed engagement had started. This report located the destroyers 35 nautical miles east of Hon Matt Island, which would place the two ships nearly 80 nautical miles northwest of their actual location – but would be a very likely position for the boats that were to attack Hon Matt Island that night. This OPLAN 34A operation was never mentioned in official Washington. In fact, in classified testimony during secret hearings on the Tonkin Gulf incident held by the US Senate Armed Forces Committee in February 1968, shortly before his resignation as Secretary of Defense, Secretary McNamara claimed that the last OPLAN 34A mission to take place prior to what was now called "the Tonkin Gulf Incident" had happened during the night of August 3–4, and that there were no American or South Vietnamese activities on the night of August 4–5 that might have provoked the North Vietnamese.

There was an additional fact not commented on when the alleged battle happened. During the fight on August 2, the Phu Bai and San Miguel stations had intercepted numerous command and control messages from the North Vietnamese controllers to the three P-4 boats, which was standard operating procedure for the North Vietnamese in order to maintain control of their side of the battle. However, on the night of August 4–5, no American station intercepted any sort of command and control messages during the time of the "battle." When the NSA was directed on August 5 to provide SIGINT proof of the battle, the NSG detachment aboard *Maddox* was asked to provide any communications or evidence of radar surveillance they had intercepted. The unit replied that they had no such communications intelligence or surveillance, though they had collected many communications and evidence of radar tracking during the August 2 event.

Inside the NSA, there was now doubt regarding the accuracy of the account of the August 4-5 events. NSA middle management was generally certain an attack had happened, while the operational analysts were not. The doubters pointed to the fact that the intercept time of the North Vietnamese "after-action report" coincided with the time frame of the reported attack on the destroyers, which would be a difficult report to produce while the "action" was still unfolding. A "coin toss" was made within the agency, and the translation that was interpreted as supporting the validity of the events of August 4–5 was the one put out. Less than six hours after issuing the "after-action" translation, NSA released its initial summary report of the event, using quotes from the "positive" after-action translation. The quotes were placed in the summary in such a way that the collateral radar, sonar, and visual information from the destroyers appeared substantiated. Interestingly, while all the other intercepted North Vietnamese messages later quoted included the original Vietnamese text as well as the translation, this "after-action" report only included the translation, without the supporting Vietnamese text for back-up.

The next day, August 6, the agency released more SIGINT that supported the scenario of a second attack. Thus, publicly and from the very beginning, the NSA supported the Johnson Administration's claim of a second attack despite the doubts raised within the agency over the accuracy of the translation on which the support was based. Even with the agency taking this public position, there were still many in the NSA and the cryptologic community who doubted that the SIGINT quoted was convincing evidence an attack had occurred. Notable among the doubters were the chief of B Group, whose reports expressed skepticism from the morning of August 5 onward, and the NSA Pacific Representative (NSAPAC), who sent a message to the Director of NSA outlining his doubts after he had reviewed a CinCPac study of the incident.

Officially, all parties in Washington supported the conclusion that there had been a second attack the night of August 4–5. In later years, several high-ranking CIA, State Department, and Pentagon officials would claim that at the time they could not see the evidence Secretary McNamara had assembled as proving the attack had happened. These doubters included General Bruce Palmer, Jr., at the time the Army Deputy Chief of Staff for Military Operations; CIA Deputy Director for Intelligence Ray Cline; the heads of the State Department's Intelligence and Far Eastern divisions; and several staffers on the National Security Council and in the Defense Department, most notably Daniel Ellsberg.

As to why these doubts were not more strongly expressed at the time, there was an awareness that President Johnson would brook no uncertainty which could undermine his position. Ray Cline said later that, "we knew it was bum dope that we were getting from the Seventh Fleet, but we were told only to give the facts with no elaboration on the nature of the evidence. Everyone knew how volatile LBJ was. He did not like to deal with uncertainties." Over the following weeks, teams from CinCPac and Seventh Fleet conducted reviews that verified the attack. In mid-August, a team from the Defense Department arrived in the Philippines and conducted interviews with the pilots and the destroyer crewmen, all of which found strong evidence for the attack.

In counterpoint to these official attempts to provide the president with the facts he wanted, the NSG that oversaw manning for the Desoto missions issued several reports on the incidents that were quite reticent regarding the evidence of an attack the night of August 4–5. The report issued by the officer who commanded the NSG detachment aboard *Maddox* contained two-and-a-half pages devoted to SIGINT regarding the August 2 attack, with another half-page regarding the follow-up air strikes on August 5. The summary of SIGINT activity for August 4 is one sentence: "On 4 August information received from USN 414T and USM 262J [Phu Bai] indicated a possible attack on the Desoto ships by the DRV naval vessels." The August 24, 1964 report from the director, Naval Security Group Pacific, was similar, devoting 12 paragraphs to recounting the SIGINT detail of the August 2 attacks while the recounting of the "attack" on August 4 is accomplished in two paragraphs, the first of which refers to "moderately heavy tracking by two DRV tracking sites at Thanh Hoa and Hon En." The second paragraph only mentions the two reports from Phu Bai, stating that they indicated "a possible attack."

One of the strongest pieces of evidence that there was no attack on August 4–5 was the intercepted North Vietnamese naval headquarters reports following the alleged incident. On August 6, the naval headquarters at Port Wallut transmitted a recap of the previous combat with the Americans that summarized the events of August 2, which mentioned their boats being in combat with an "American warship." The report also noted that the naval and air defense forces had shot down American warplanes on August 5, capturing one American pilot alive. However, the report made no mention of anything happening the night of August 4–5. Since the report details the heavy North Vietnamese losses that happened on August 2 and 5, the lack of any statement regarding events on the night of August 4–5 leaves only one possible conclusion: that there was no attack that night. This intercept was never widely circulated among American military commanders or political leaders at the time.

A report issued by the NSA in September 1964 to provide a time-line of the events of the first week of August quoted only six of 53 relevant pieces of SIGINT regarding the events of August 4–5, yet claimed these six pieces were "representative" of the rest, despite the fact that subsequent analysis of the other 47 pieces of evidence demonstrated that the overwhelming majority of them either cast doubt on the event's occurrence, or contradicted the six pieces of evidence used in the report. These unused pieces of evidence included intercepts from the North Vietnamese naval headquarters directing their patrol boats to avoid contact with the Americans after the battle on August 2. While the report provides several examples of North Vietnamese command and control intercepts during the action on August 2, it makes no mention of the complete lack of North Vietnamese command and control message intercepts on August 4–5. Subsequently, throughout the war that followed, this September report was used by the Johnson Administration as the "final official report" on the Tonkin Gulf Incident in response to all congressional attempts to further investigate the incident.

With the "smoking gun" evidence, a retaliatory air strike against the four North Vietnamese torpedo boat bases and an oil storage depot near Vinh was ordered as Operation *Pierce Arrow*. *Ticonderoga* launched four F-8s and 12 A-4s led by CAG Stockdale and VA-56 commanding officer (CO) McDonald at 1043 hours local time on August 5, to hit the oil storage depot at Vinh at 1323 hours. A second mission was launched to hit the PT boat bases at Quang Khe and Ben Thuy. At 1136 hours local time, nearly two hours before *Ticonderoga*'s first strike would hit their target and well before *Constellation* even commenced launch of her strike, President Johnson went on national television to inform the public of his decision to strike North Vietnam in reprisal for the attacks on the *Maddox* and *Turner Joy*. *Constellation* launched A-4 Skyhawks of VA-144 and A-1 Skyraiders of VA-145 shortly after 1330 hours. At approximately 1540 hours, the aircraft hit the PT boat bases at Hon Guy and the nearby Lach Cho Estuary.

Ninety percent of the storage facility at Vinh was destroyed, with three PT boats destroyed at Ben Thuy; one boat was destroyed and three damaged at Qyang Khe. Six boats were destroyed at Hon Gai and five damaged at Hon Me Island near the Lach Cho Estuary. Altogether, 33 of the 34 North Vietnamese PT boats were hit, with seven sunk, ten severely damaged, and 16 suffering lesser damage.

Warned of the attack by President Johnson's address to the nation in which he revealed the coming strike, the North Vietnamese defenders were ready when the aircraft appeared overhead. Lieutenant (jg) Richard C. Sather of VA-145 was killed in the crash of his Skyraider when it was shot down, becoming the first Navy pilot killed in Vietnam, while VA-144's Lieutenant (jg) Everett Alvarez managed to eject from his burning Skyhawk. Alvarez was captured to become the first American prisoner of war (POW) of the coming war.

VA-144's Lieutenant Commander Nicholson later recalled that the squadron pilots were initially surprised by Alvarez' loss to antiaircraft guns. He attributed the loss to prewar training that had emphasized attacking at extremely low altitudes below 500 feet and at less than top speed. Nicholson felt the loss of his wingman so deeply that he would later cut short his assignment to the Naval Post Graduate School at Monterey in 1966 and volunteer for three more tours in Southeast Asia. "Alvarez was sitting in a prison camp; I could not sit still with that on my mind."

Exactly why the president was so eager to engage in military action in Southeast Asia has been the subject of controversy and dispute ever since. In April 1964, he had promised the nation, "We are not about to send American boys nine or ten thousand miles away from home to do what Asian boys ought to be doing for themselves." However, three weeks before the Tonkin Gulf Incident, on July 16, Senator Barry Goldwater made his acceptance speech after receiving the Republican nomination for president at the party's convention in the San Francisco Cow Palace, in which he declared: "I would remind you that extremism in the defense of liberty is no vice! And let me remind you also that moderation in the pursuit of justice is no virtue!" The Johnson re-election campaign had already positioned the president as the "peace candidate" in opposition to the "extremist hawk," as they would define the senator from Arizona throughout the campaign; the famous TV commercial of the little girl plucking a daisy against the backdrop of a countdown to a nuclear explosion, which would run once on national TV on September 7, was already in production. Despite polling that showed him well ahead of his opponent and strong public support for his position of limiting American involvement in Vietnam, the president still feared being called "soft on communism" if he failed to act in the face of "communist aggression." Lyndon Baines Johnson believed, with all the conviction that an American politician who had lived through McCarthyism could believe, that if he was to be the successful "peace candidate" it would only be as the "peace *through strength* candidate."

By dealing with the war decisively this one time at this relatively early point in the election campaign, he hoped to put it behind him so that he could concentrate on becoming president in his own right. Johnson's short-term political goals were contradictory and at some points in opposition to any long-term planning for an escalation of the war that would result in clear US involvement. The president was reluctant to take any additional military action before November 3, while he preserved his options to change the nature of the war after that date when he was safely in office for four years. It would be made clear throughout the campaign that "preventing Communist domination of South Vietnam is of the highest importance to US national security."

Two months before the events in the Tonkin Gulf, Assistant Secretary of State for Far Eastern Affairs McGeorge Bundy had prepared a congressional resolution at President Johnson's request that would give the president the power to commit US military forces to the defense of any nation in Southeast Asia deemed threatened by communist aggression or subversion. It gave the president the discretion to determine the extent of the threat and, by virtue of this evaluation, the leeway to define what forces and actions would be committed to counter the threat. Once drafted, it had been planned to put the resolution before the Senate as soon as possible. At the last minute, the president decided not to do so, out of fear it would ruin the image of moderation in international affairs he had been cultivating in the presidential campaign, and the draft resolution was quietly shelved. With the August 4 incident, the president ordered the draft resolution updated and submitted it, now known in the press as the Tonkin Gulf Resolution, to the Senate where it was passed 98–2; in the House of Representatives it was passed unanimously. The administration publicly portrayed it as a moderating measure "calculated to prevent the spread of war." When President Johnson learned of the resolution's passage by both houses, he laughed and told an aide that it "was like Grandma's nightshirt. It covers everything." The events of the first week of August demonstrated how military strategy and policy would be viewed through the lens of its effect on domestic politics throughout the coming Vietnam War.

Thus, the war that came to be known by the public in later years as "the war of lies" began with a lie, a "stove-piping of intelligence" – as such an effort would later be termed in the run-up to the American decision to invade Iraq in 2003 – of the greatest magnitude. It led to nearly ten years of war that saw the deaths of more than 58,000 American service personnel and at least 1,500,000 Vietnamese as well as perhaps another million in Cambodia and Laos, in addition to promoting political and social division in the United States unseen since the Civil War, with effects that are still felt in American society and politics.

Years after the end of the war, researchers studying the Tonkin Gulf Incident determined that it was highly likely that the "cockpit lights" and the "searchlights" reported by destroyer crewmen at the time were reflections in the moonlight from an enormous school of flying fish transiting the gulf that night. Thus, President Johnson's initial judgment of the whole event, "Hell, those dumb, stupid sailors were just shooting at flying fish," was probably more true than he would ever know.

2

NAVAL AVIATION'S REVOLUTIONARY
NEW SWORD

The years between the end of the Korean War and the outbreak of the Vietnam War saw naval aviation go through some of its most revolutionary changes.

For the United States, the possibility of the Cold War becoming a thermonuclear hot war dominated military decision-making in the 1950s, during which the aircraft that would fight in Vietnam were designed and developed. With the high-altitude jet-powered strategic bomber seen as the delivery system for nuclear weapons, fighter aircraft changed from a mission of air superiority over an enemy air force to a shield against nuclear annihilation. What were still called "fighters" progressively became interceptors, with the goal of destroying the enemy bombers as far from their possible targets as possible. The idea of fighting enemy fighters was seen as less and less likely, since attacking forces would not be coming in massed formations escorted by those enemy fighters, as had been the case in World War II. By the late 1950s, Air Force and Navy leaders actively discouraged fighter pilots from engaging in any form of air combat practice, commonly known as "hassling" in the fighter pilot community. The goal of a fighter was to fly faster, higher and farther, to protect the homeland from nuclear devastation. In naval aviation, this became the fleet defense fighter, whose mission was to destroy attacking nuclear-armed enemy bombers several hundred miles from the fleet.

Supersonic flight was developed in the greatest technological and industrial mobilization on the part of the United States since the Manhattan Project, while the aircraft carrier as a ship was transformed by the introduction of the Forrestal-class "super carriers," ships so large they could not fit through the Panama Canal, forcing them to revert to sailing around South America to transfer from the Atlantic to the Pacific oceans. All this took place in the years between 1950 and 1961, with six entirely new aircraft types developed and brought operational to fly from the decks of these new ships. By the end of the decade, aviators who had begun their flying careers in 80-knot Stearman biplanes were in the cockpits of F-8 Crusaders capable of flying to Mach 1.6 and the newly arrived Mach 2-capable F-4 Phantom had such performance that in 1963 the US Air Force (USAF) would adopt it for front-line service, the first naval aircraft operated by that service since the Boeing F4B became the P-12, 34 years earlier. Night and all-weather operation from aircraft carriers, which had been a lesser part of naval aviation as recently as the Korean War, became the norm during these years.

The supersonic aeronautical revolution began in the years immediately before the outbreak of the Korean War, an event that would speed the revolution's advance. North American Aviation first began thinking about making a supersonic fighter in 1948. At that time, there were two ways to go: a very big fighter powered by a very big engine, or Something Else, only dimly seen at the time. Edgar Schmued and Raymond Rice, the premier fighter designers in the United States, were aesthetically offended by the idea of a big airplane that was unable to match what highly maneuverable, high-performance air superiority fighters like their earlier P-51 Mustang and F-86 Sabre were capable of doing.

The key to the design would be the engine. Had the project proceeded then, it would have probably been powered by the big General Electric J53, which later provided 23,000 pounds of thrust with afterburner. At the time, North American believed the best alternative lightweight engine would be the afterburning J40; fortunately, they never pursued this option, since this Navy-developed design ultimately became one of the major disappointments of early jet engine development. Everything changed in early 1949, when Pratt & Whitney let them know about the JT3, the engine that would prove to be the most significant gas turbine engine since Whittle's W1.

The JT3 was a turbojet development of what had begun life as the PT4 turboprop, the planned powerplant for the first design of the B-52. In its developed form as the J57, it would power the F-100, the F8U Crusader, and the F4D Skyray, as well as the Boeing 707 and Douglas DC-8 jetliners. It was light, yet as strong as anything ever made by Pratt & Whitney; its reliability record would be second to none. North American formally proposed a supersonic fighter powered by the JT3 in January 1949. The Air Force gave quick approval and the program became official on February 3, 1949, though it was still essentially company-funded.

In April 1949, North American used company funds to build the first supersonic wind tunnel. A development based on the German Kochel system (Edgar Schmued, who was conversant with all prewar German aerodynamic research, and who didn't have to wait for translations of what the company found in Germany in 1945, has to qualify as the single most cost-effective aircraft designer in history), the tunnel had a sphere of dry air exhausting through the working section into a vacuum chamber, with a peak attainable Mach number of 5.25. The result of these wind tunnel tests was a radical redesign of the initial idea, with the very fortunate result that the horizontal stabilizer was pulled off the vertical fin and put low on the fuselage, where it belongs on a supersonic airplane. At the same time, Pratt & Whitney developed the variable nozzle for an afterburner. The result was a reliable engine with an afterburner that never failed to ignite. By June 1949, wind tunnel tests had determined that the optimum sweepback was 45 degrees, and the project became known within North American as the "Sabre-45."

Designated "F-100" by the Air Force, the airplane was the first beneficiary of a mobilization between industry and government that provided more financial support for more basic aerodynamic research and advanced machine tool development than had been spent in the 50 years since the Wright Brothers first flew, in the quest to create operational supersonic flight. Such an effort was only possible in the country which in 1950 produced 52 percent of the planetary Gross Economic Product while at the same time taking the German autobahns to their penultimate development in the Interstate Highway System, not to mention creating the modern American middle class through the GI Bill.

It would have been impossible to develop the Super Sabre and the following supersonic aircraft developed by both the Air Force and Navy without this government-funded effort to create the industrial wherewithal to build supersonic airplanes. Creating what came to be known as "the Century Series," as well as the Navy's Crusader and Phantom II, was only possible with major advances in structures, materials and techniques, propulsion, systems, and aerodynamics that eclipsed everything that had gone before. The bill for aerodynamic research, which included the cost of the X-1 series, the X-2, X-3, and D-558-2 Skyrocket, was $375 million, while the cost of engine research and development was $280 million, all in 1950s dollars.

The Air Force spent $397 million between 1950 and 1954 on a program to create heavy presses capable of squeezing large light-alloy forgings which would have been otherwise sculptured from a solid slab by "hogging" or constructed from many separate parts. The result of this was the industrial ability to pop out lightweight single-piece aircraft skins in minutes. Radical new machine tools that could remove vast amounts of metal at high speed with extreme precision were created at a cost of $180 million. Automatic precision machinery capable of drilling, countersinking, dimpling, riveting, reaming, bolting, and sealing, and doing all these operations in sequence, was created – all before computers. A brand-new industry capable of creating 500–600 tons of wrought titanium a month was created; it was the metal that made supersonic fighters possible. Further hundreds of millions were spent on developing electrical and hydraulic systems able to operate reliably after soaking in temperatures up to 300 degrees Celsius. This was in addition to a range of reliable miniaturized electronic devices that still used fragile vacuum tubes, since this was before the transistor revolution.

Between 1950 and 1955, the United States spent over $200 billion in 2021 dollars, just to acquire the industrial capability to produce supersonic fighters. When the cost of aeronautical research is added in, the creation of supersonic flight cost approximately $300 billion. This industrial mobilization was only exceeded in cost by the Manhattan Project. While the F-100 did not use all this infrastructure, it paved the way for all others.

The Navy's first supersonic fighter, Chance-Vought's F8U-1 Crusader, is proof of the old saying that "it's better to be lucky than good." The

F-8 Crusader series was not only lucky, but good to boot. As the last all-gun US Navy fighter to achieve production, the Crusader ranks as one of the "greats," a carrier-based fighter that was the equal of its land-based opponents, in the tradition of the F6F Hellcat and F4U Corsair.

The airplane was lucky from the beginning. In 1952, as a result of US government legal action, the holding company United Aircraft – of which Vought Aircraft was a component company – was broken up, with Vought left to fend for itself right after making an expensive move at government request from its original Connecticut factory to Dallas, Texas. Vought had always been on the cutting edge in the development and production of naval aircraft, going back to the VE-7, the first US Navy carrier-based airplane. The F4U Corsair was a serious contender for the title of "best piston-engine fighter ever built," and at the time was still in production, though the end was in sight. In any case, the Corsair was "yesterday's technology," and Vought had not been able to create a successful follow-on design. The F6U-1 Pirate had proven to be underpowered, while the F7U-3 Cutlass was both underpowered and difficult to mate to a carrier. Vought was in need of success if the company was to remain a viable business.

By 1952, the US Navy was well aware that its current jet fighters were outclassed by the opposition; the F9F Panther could only barely hold its own in an aerial battle against Soviet-flown MiG-15s due to pilot quality. The admirals were so desperate to get an airplane that could match the MiG-15 that they went and bought a navalized version of the MiG-killing F-86 Sabre, which they called the "Fury." The first generation of what were supposed to be supersonic fighters – the Douglas F4D Skyray and the McDonnell F3H Demon – were saddled with the awful Westinghouse J40 engine, which didn't deliver the promised power, and for which Westinghouse seemed unable to find a fix. The F4D was only saved when Douglas redesigned it to use the J57, while McDonnell never quite found the replacement needed to let the Demon live up to its potential. The Navy needed the next design to be a "winner," to put the service back in the leading position it had held with the Grumman Hellcat and Vought Corsair during World War II.

Vought's submission, which would become known as the F8U-1 Crusader, was lucky from the beginning. Freed of the requirement to use the dreadful J40, Vought was able to use the J57, which provided both high power and great fuel economy. With a new afterburner, the engine that powered the first fighter capable of supersonic speed in level flight, the F-100 Super Sabre, Vought started with a proven powerplant capable of providing the desired performance. The design continued to be lucky; Vought's design team created their airplane prior to Dr. Richard Whitcomb's publication of the "area rule" in 1954, which describes how an airframe must be as long as possible to mitigate abrupt airflow discontinuities at the juncture of the flying surfaces that bring on abrupt drag rise. It turned out Vought's team had independently managed to follow the then-unknown rule and get things so right that the F-8 became the first fully supersonic fighter that didn't look funny with a "coke-bottle fuselage" or a "wasp waist," design excrescences which were forced on other designers to "lengthen" their existing designs once the aerodynamic rules for supersonic flight were known. The result was that the Crusader, powered by the exact same engine as the F-100 (the only successful supersonic airplane ever built that did not conform to the area rule), ended up 300 miles per hour faster and with greater range than its Air Force competitor. The entire wing other than the folding outer section and the control surfaces was a gas tank, while other tanks were provided throughout the long fuselage. The Crusader's wing was also the first supersonic wing to have the needed "dog-tooth" in the design from the beginning. The wing-body shape of the Crusader was so right that the airplane ended up a generation ahead of all its competition, world-wide.

Mating a high-performance fighter like the Crusader to a carrier deck was the big problem, and Vought's solution was truly elegant: the first variable-incidence wing, which increased the angle of attack at low speed by moving the wing rather than the entire airframe. Coupled with full-span leading edge slats and drooping ailerons the movable wing allowed the fuselage to remain at an angle that provided the pilot with sufficient visibility for a carrier landing, while not forcing such loads onto the landing gear that would result in the usual weight escalation for naval aircraft in this area. The mechanism for operating the wing weighed in at 500 pounds, while the gear was 500 pounds lighter than would have been the case with any other airframe configuration, which meant the wing was "free." Of the eight designs submitted to the Navy, the Crusader was the only one which could provide such performance while still exhibiting the docile flying qualities the Navy needed.

The first XF8U-1 flew on March 25, 1955, powered by the Air Force version of the J57, the P-11, which provided less power than the definitive Navy version, the P-12. Even thus "underpowered," Vought Chief Test Pilot John Konrad easily took the Crusader supersonic in level flight, achieving Mach 1.2 on the first flight. Further tests demonstrated that in comparison with the F-100, the Crusader had longer range, faster climb, more rapid rate of roll, and a smaller turning circle at all speeds and heights, as well as lower landing speed and a shorter landing run. In fact, de-navalizing the Crusader would have resulted in a world-beating land-based fighter. So few changes were found necessary that the third Crusader delivered was the first full-production aircraft, with the only visible change being the addition of a flight refueling probe on the left side of the forward fuselage that retracted into a "bulge" that actually added to aerodynamic smoothness. Outside of that, the other major change was putting in the necessary wiring to allow the Crusader to use the Sidewinder missile from the outset.

On August 31, 1956, Commander R.W. "Duke" Windsor took one of the first production F8U-1s up to 36,000 feet over China Lake, California, pushed the throttle forward as he entered a 15-kilometer (9.3-mile) course, and set a national speed record of 1,015 miles per hour. It was the first time a non-experimental airplane had flown this fast, an achievement for which he was awarded the 1956 Thompson Trophy. In April 1956, the Crusader made its first carrier landing aboard the brand-new "super carrier" USS *Forrestal*, followed within six months by successful operation from a 27-Charlie conversion of a World War II-era Essex-class carrier.

On July 16, 1957, the Crusader burst onto the newspaper front pages when an F8U-1P was flown from Los Angeles to New York in 3 hours, 23 minutes, 8.4 seconds, for an average transcontinental speed of 726 miles per hour, or Mach 1.1. In fact, the Crusader, which had to come down from 35,000 feet to 25,000 feet and slow down to 320 miles per hour to refuel three times from AJ-2 Savage tanker aircraft, was actually flying in full afterburner at Mach 1.7 for the majority of the mission. The Marine aviator who won the Distinguished Flying Cross for this feat would become far better known when Lieutenant Colonel John H. Glenn, Jr., became the first American to fly in orbit in February 1962. Like almost everyone who ever flew a Crusader, he was often quoted saying it was the best airplane he ever flew. Vought topped a winning year that December when they won the Collier Trophy for having designed the airplane.

The completion of 318 F8U-1s and 144 F8U-1P photo-reconnaissance planes was followed by 130 F8U-1Es, which had full all-weather capability with addition of the APS-67 radar. The 187 F8U-2s received the more powerful J57-P-16 engine, which required the addition of two ram air intakes in the extreme rear fuselage to cool the hot afterburner, as well as ventral fins for supersonic stability. The fastest of all Crusaders were the 152 F8U-2Ns, which appeared in 1960 with a new APQ-83 radar and the J57-P-20 engine, which provided a level speed of 1,230 miles per hour. The 296 F8U-2NEs were equipped with a new APQ-94 radar which required a slightly larger nose, and an infrared-seeker; they took Crusader production over 1,000 aircraft. Introduced as the F-8E following the 1962 change in aircraft designations, the F8U-2NE's heavier weight gave it a speed of only 987 miles per hour, but it also had ground-attack capability built in, the first Crusader to become a "mud-mover."

In 1962, Vought began remanufacturing the original F8U-1 (F-8A) aircraft. This updating process would provide the F-8H (rebuilt F8U-2N/F-8D), F-8J (rebuilt F-8E), F-8K (F8U-1N/F-8B) and F-8L (F8U-2/F-8C); the latter two were employed as advanced trainers and used by a number of US Navy/US Marine Corps Reserve squadrons as well as by several composite squadrons. The F-8H, which was only slightly slower in its rebuilt version than the F8U-2N, was the first re-built Crusader to go to war in 1967, and was the leading MiG-killer in Vietnam, with more than twice as many kills as the F-4 Phantom II.

Despite its being known as "the last gunfighter," only four of the 18 F-8 MiG victories in Vietnam were achieved using the guns and only two were actual gunfights from the start. The Colt Mark 12 20mm cannon that was the primary weapon of the F-8 was an advanced derivative of the World War II Hispano HS 404 that had been used on British and some American fighter aircraft. It used a lighter projectile with a bigger charge for better muzzle velocity and higher rate of fire, at the cost of hitting power. In service, the Mark 12 proved less than satisfactory. Although its muzzle velocity and rate of fire were acceptable, it was inaccurate and frequently unreliable, a function of the squadron armament shop, since the stresses of catapult launches, arrested landings, and salt water corrosion all had an effect on the weapon. In air combat over North

Vietnam, jams and stoppages were common, especially following hard dogfighting maneuvers. Fortunately, the F-8 had been designed to use the Sidewinder from the outset, and put the superior AIM-9D version to good use.

In 1953, as the F8U Crusader neared its first flight, McDonnell Aircraft began work on revising its F3H Demon naval fighter, seeking expanded capabilities and better performance. The company developed several projects, including a variant powered by a single Wright J67 engine and variants powered by two Wright J65 engines, or two General Electric J79 engines. The J79-powered version promised a top speed of Mach 1.97. On September 19, 1953, McDonnell approached the United States Navy with a proposal for the "Super Demon." Uniquely, the aircraft was to be modular, able to be fitted with one- or two-seat noses for different missions, with different nose cones to accommodate radar, photo cameras, four 20mm cannon, or 56 unguided folding fin air rockets (FFARs) in addition to the nine hardpoints under the wings and the fuselage. The Navy was sufficiently interested to order a full-scale mock-up of the F3H-G/H, but felt that the upcoming Grumman XF9F-9 (later F11F-1) Tiger and Vought XF8U-1 Crusader already satisfied the need for a supersonic fighter.

McDonnell therefore reworked the design into an all-weather fighter-bomber with 11 external hardpoints for weapons and on October 18, 1954, the company received a letter of intent for two YAH-1 prototypes. On May 26, 1955, four Navy officers from the Bureau of Aeronautics "fighter desk" arrived at the McDonnell offices and, within an hour, presented the company with an entirely new set of requirements. Because the Navy already had the Douglas A-4 Skyhawk for ground attack and F-8 Crusader for dogfighting, the project now had to fulfill the need for an all-weather fleet defense interceptor. A second crewman was added to operate the powerful radar.

The XF4H-1 was designed to be powered by two J79-GE-8 engines and carry four semi-recessed AAM-N-6 Sparrow III radar-guided missiles. The engines sat low in the fuselage to maximize internal fuel capacity and ingested air through fixed geometry intakes equipped with variable geometry ramps to regulate airflow to the engines at supersonic speeds. The thin-section wing had a leading edge sweep of 45 degrees and was equipped with blown flaps for better low-speed handling. Wind tunnel testing revealed lateral instability requiring the addition of 5 degrees of dihedral to the wings. To avoid redesigning the titanium central section of the aircraft, McDonnell engineers angled the outer portions of the wings at 12 degrees, which averaged to the required 5 degrees over the entire wingspan. The wings also received the distinctive "dogtooth" for improved control at high angles of attack. The all-moving tailplane was given 23 degrees of anhedral to improve control at high angles of attack while still keeping the tailplane clear of the engine exhaust. All-weather intercept capability was provided by the AN/APQ-50 radar. To accommodate carrier operations, the landing gear was designed to withstand landings with a sink rate of 23 feet per second, while the nose strut could extend 20 inches to increase the angle of attack at takeoff. No thought was given to creating a maneuverable airplane capable of engaging in close-in air combat with enemy fighters, as was the case with the Crusader. The final result was, to many who saw it for the first time, a big and remarkably ugly airplane. It would later gain the nickname "Rhino," a term of respect, for its look.

On July 25, 1955, the year the Crusader went public with its many new records, the Navy ordered two XF4H-1 test aircraft and five YF4H-1 pre-production examples, with the emotive name "Phantom II" carrying on the McDonnell tradition of naming their fighters for supernatural entities, and honoring McDonnell's first jet fighter, the FH-1 Phantom. The airplane made its maiden flight on May 27, 1958 with Robert C. Little at the controls. A hydraulic problem precluded retraction of the landing gear but subsequent flights went more smoothly. Early testing resulted in redesign of the air intakes, including the distinctive addition of 12,500 holes to "bleed off" the slow-moving boundary layer air from the surface of each intake ramp. Series production aircraft also featured splitter plates to divert the boundary layer away from the engine intakes. The aircraft competed with the XF8U-3 Crusader III for a production contract as a fleet defense interceptor; on December 17, 1958, the F4H was declared the winner. Delays with the J79-GE-8 engines meant that the first production aircraft were fitted with J79-GE-2 and -2A engines, each having 16,100 pounds of force of afterburning thrust. In 1959, the Phantom II began carrier suitability trials with the first complete launch-recovery cycle performed on February 15, 1960, from USS *Independence* (CVA-62). As a result of these tests, the canopy line was raised some ten inches to increase pilot visibility during carrier landings, and the airplane was so modified as the F4H-2 after 45

Phantom IIs essentially similar to the prototypes were produced as the F4H-1 (F-4A). The F4H-2 (later F-4B) also changed the radar to the Westinghouse AN/APQ-72, an AN/APG-50 with a larger radar antenna that necessitated the bulbous nose. A total of 649 F-4Bs were built with deliveries beginning in 1961. VF-121 Pacemakers became the first operational squadron at Naval Air Station (NAS) Miramar. The Phantom would go on to a total production run of more than 5,000 in all versions, being used by the US Air Force as well as numerous foreign air forces, with the last not taken off first-line operations until the end of the century.

Shortly after the initial deliveries, a series of unexplained in-flight engine emergencies resulted in the loss over the course of a month of three aircraft due to engine failure, with fires on relight attempts forcing crews to eject. The aircraft crashed at sea, taking the secret of the problem to the bottom of the Pacific off the California coast with them. The Navy was faced with having to ground its newest fighter, with program cancelation looming if the problem could not be discovered and fixed. All that was known was that the airplanes had been involved in air combat maneuvering just before their loss.

VF-121 commanding officer Commander E. Royce Williams, Jr., the Navy pilot who had shot down four of seven Soviet MiG-15s while flying an F9F Panther in an air battle off Vladivostok on November 18, 1952, was the next pilot to experience the emergency. While engaging in combat maneuvers, both engines suddenly shut down. When Williams attempted to get an air start, one engine caught fire while the other refused to start. With the burning engine producing only idle power, Williams was able to stay in the air by lighting off the afterburner of the flaming J79! Determined to try to bring the plane back to Miramar, he ordered his radar intercept officer (RIO) to eject, but the order was refused. Williams was able to land the burning Phantom on the main Miramar runway, shutting down as soon as the wheels touched ground. Firefighters were able to extinguish the blaze before the airplane exploded. Post-accident analysis revealed a design anomaly in the curvature of the intake duct, which at higher angles of attack than had been achieved in initial tests resulted in air starvation to the engines. McDonnell was able to fix the problem and the Phantom program was saved.

Despite its imposing dimensions and a maximum takeoff weight over 60,000 pounds, the F-4 was capable of reaching a top speed of

Mach 2.23 and had an initial climb rate of over 41,000 feet per minute. As had been done with the Crusader, the Navy decided to publicize its new fighter by setting new speed and altitude records. These record-setting flights began on December 6, 1959, when the second XF4H-1 was flown in a zoom climb by Commander Lawrence E. Flint, Jr., to a world record 98,557 feet in Operation *Top Flight*, beating the previous record of 94,658 feet set by a Soviet Sukhoi T-43-1. Commander Flint accelerated his aircraft to Mach 2.5 at 47,000 feet, then climbed at a 45-degree angle to 90,000 feet, where he shut down the engines and glided to the peak altitude. As the Phantom fell through 70,000 feet altitude, he restarted the engines and resumed normal flight. On September 5, 1960, an F4H-1 averaged 1,216.78 miles per hour over a 500-kilometer (311-mile) closed-circuit course. Twenty days later, on September 25, another F4H-1 averaged 1,390.21 miles per hour over a 100-kilometer (62-mile) closed-circuit course.

To celebrate the 50th anniversary of Naval Aviation on May 24, 1961, three F4H-2 Phantoms set a transcontinental speed record, despite having to slow down for tanker refuelings. The fastest airplane of the trio, flown by Lieutenant Richard Gordon and RIO Lieutenant Bobbie Long, averaged 869.74 miles per hour and completed the trip in 2 hours 47 minutes, earning Gordon the 1961 Bendix trophy.

Operation *Sageburner* saw an attempt on the world sea level speed record, which required the airplane to fly a three-mile course at an altitude under 125 feet at the Salton Sea in southern California. During the first attempt on May 18, 1961, Commander J.J. Felsman was killed when his Phantom disintegrated in mid-air after suffering pitch damper failure. On August 28, a second Phantom averaged 902.769 miles per hour over the course for a new world record. On December 22, 1961, a Phantom modified with water-methanol injection set an absolute world record speed of 1,606.342 miles per hour in Operation *Skyburner*. On December 5, another Phantom set a sustained flight altitude record of 66,443.8 feet.

1962 saw Operation *High Jump* set a series of time-to-altitude records: 34.523 seconds to 3,000 meters (9,840 feet), 48.787 seconds to 6,000 meters (19,680 feet), 61.629 seconds to 9,000 meters (29,530 feet), 77.156 seconds to 12,000 meters (39,370 feet), 114.548 seconds to 15,000 meters (49,210 feet), 178.5 seconds to 20,000 meters (65,600 feet), 230.44 seconds to 25,000 meters (82,000 feet), and

371.43 seconds to 30,000 meters (98,400 feet). Although the feat was not officially recognized, the Phantom in the final flight zoom-climbed to over 100,000 feet.

Over the three years between 1959 and 1962, the Phantom set 16 world records. With the exception of Operation *Skyburner*, these records were all achieved in unmodified production aircraft. Five of the speed records were not broken until the F-15 Eagle appeared in 1975.

Following production of the F-4B, 522 F-4J Phantoms, with improved air-to-air and ground-attack capability, commenced delivery in 1966, ending in 1972. Powered by J79-GE-10 engines with 17,844 pounds of afterburning thrust, the F-4J used the Westinghouse AN/AWG-10 fire control system, which was the first operational radar system with look-down/shoot-down capability.

The first Phantom-equipped squadron to deploy aboard a carrier was VF-74 "Be-Devilers," based at NAS Oceana, Virginia, which received its F4H-1s on July 8, 1961 and became carrier-qualified that November. The squadron went aboard USS *Forrestal* (CVA-59) for a Mediterranean cruise from August 1962 to March 1963. The first Pacific Fleet squadron to equip with the F-4B was VF-114 "Aardvarks," which deployed to WestPac aboard USS *Kitty Hawk* (CVA-63) in September 1962. By the time of the Tonkin Gulf incident in August 1964, 13 of 31 carrier-based fighter squadrons were flying Phantoms, and the first combat mission was flown from USS *Constellation* on August 5, flying escort in Operation *Pierce Arrow*.

While many will state that the F-4 Phantom was one of the great fighters of history, in fact by definition it was hardly a fighter at all. With its large size and poor air combat maneuverability, it exhibited few of the fighting qualities normally associated with an air superiority fighter. It was never designed for the air superiority role, with its design optimized for the role of long-range bomber interceptor. The Phantom's design emphasized speed over maneuverability, since getting to the interception point before a bomber could release its warload was its goal.

In combat, one of the biggest problems was that the J79 engines produced so much black smoke at military power that the airplane could be seen as far away as 30 miles on a clear day. The only immediate solution was to use afterburner, but this compromised fuel efficiency. The problem was finally solved by the Navy-initiated refurbishment program Project Bee Line in 1972. The F-4B was updated as the F-4N with J79-GE-15 smokeless engines, with 228 updated by 1978, while 265 F-4J Phantoms became the F-4S when equipped with J79-GE-17 smokeless engines at the same time.

The biggest combat weakness of the Phantom was the lack of an internal gun. This was due to two factors: the first was that, as a fleet defense fighter in a nuclear war environment, the Phantom was only expected to engage Soviet bombers, since the Soviet Navy lacked aircraft carriers, and these would be dispatched at long range with the Sparrow. Contemporary 1950s air combat doctrine held that turning combat would be impossible at supersonic speeds. No one foresaw that most jet air combat would occur at subsonic speeds, and there was no expectation of the United States becoming involved in another limited war like Korea, where an air war similar to that which occurred in "MiG Alley" between 1951 and 1953 would be repeated. The rules of engagement in Vietnam required that pilots make a visual identification of the potential target, which negated the advantage of the long-range Sparrow. Once a visual ID was made, many pilots found themselves too close to the opposing fighter to fire their short-range Sidewinders. The second reason was that there was no place to put an internal gun in the carrier-based Phantom; when the F-4E was finally equipped with an internal gun mounted beneath the nose ahead of the nose gear, the airplane was not capable of raising its nose high enough to "take a cut" and land on a carrier deck without stalling. The belief that the Phantom would not have to engage in air combat led to gunnery training and air combat maneuvering training being halted outside of the F-8 Crusader community in the year before the outbreak of war in Vietnam. Looking back at his experience in Vietnam, retired Rear Admiral H. Denny Wisely wrote in his memoir *Green Ink* that the only reason he was successful in air combat flying the Phantom was that he had been fortunate to learn the rules of air combat maneuvering when he flew the F4D Skyray in his first squadron assignment after flight school and engaged in "hassling" with other aircraft in the years before the war began.

Vietnam saw the first widespread use of guided missiles as a primary fighter weapon. While initial enthusiasm for missile armament was such that the F-4 was the first fighter developed without an integral gun (after this was removed in the AH-1 initial development that became the Phantom), operational experience over North Vietnam would demonstrate that this enthusiasm was premature.

The first US missile developed was the infrared-seeking AIM-9, known as the Sidewinder. This was based on wartime German research in developing an infrared heat-seeking anti-shipping missile, the Blohm und Voss BV-143 glide bomb. Development of what eventually became the Sidewinder began at the Naval Ordnance Test Station (NOTS), now the Naval Air Weapons Station China Lake, in 1946, as an in-house research project conceived by William B. McLean. The research finally received official funding which continued until 1951 when an operational heat seeker was shown to Admiral William Parsons, Deputy Chief of the Bureau of Ordnance, and received designation as a program in 1952. With the seeker head mounted on a Zuni unguided rocket, the Sidewinder was simpler and much more reliable than the Air Force AIM-4 Falcon infrared-seeker that was under development during the same period. The missile was first fired live on September 13, 1952 and intercepted a drone for the first time on September 11, 1953. The program carried out 51 successful guided flights in 1954, and production was authorized in 1955. The AIM-9B was first fitted to Navy F9F-8 Cougar and FJ-3 Fury fighters in 1956.

The Sidewinder was first used in combat by F-86 Sabres flown by the Republic of China Air Force against People's Liberation Army Air Force (PLAAF) MiG-17s during the Taiwan Straits Crisis of 1958, with the first combat launch on September 24, 1958, when four MiG-17s were ambushed and shot down with the missiles. In a later combat, a MiG 17 was hit by an AIM-9B that did not explode. With the missile lodged in the MiG's airframe, the pilot returned to base, where it was eventually sent to the Soviet Union. Soviet engineers were later quoted as saying the captured Sidewinder served as a "university course" in missile design. The missile was reverse-engineered so closely it had the exact same number of parts. This became the Vympel K-13/R-3S missile, with the NATO reporting name AA-2 Atoll.

The AIM-9B was generally less effective than expected in air combat starting in 1965. As a result, the Navy contracted for development of what became the AIM-9D, which was introduced into combat in June 1966. It was a significant improvement over the AIM-9B, with a new rocket motor that increased its speed and gave it longer range. The infrared-seeker head was cooled with liquid nitrogen to increase its sensitivity; the seeker head in the AIM-9B operated in frequencies that allowed it to be pulled off target by clouds and by the countryside at the low altitudes at which combat was taking place, as opposed to the high altitudes at which it had been tested. The AIM-9D sensor detected infrared radiation in a spectrum that made it less vulnerable to clouds and landscape. The improvements meant the usage envelope for the new Sidewinder was double what was the case for the AIM-9B. In combat, the AIM-9D/F-8 Crusader combination resulted in the F-8 having the highest kill-per-engagement ratio of any fighter during the war.

Unfortunately, the Air Force listened to Hughes Aircraft extol the virtues of the AIM-4 Falcon, and decided not to replace the AIM-9B with the "Navy missile," using the inferior AIM-9B throughout the Vietnam War, and introducing the AIM-4 in 1966; the Falcon proved to be the least successful US missile and its failure in one particular combat was responsible for Colonel Robin Olds failing to achieve his fifth victory and become the first US ace of the war.

The major US aerial missile program was the radar-directed long-range Sparrow. What became the Sparrow began as a Navy program after World War II to create a guided rocket weapon for air-to-air use. The Navy contracted Sperry in 1947 to build a radar beam-riding version of a standard 5-inch HVAR, under Project Hotshot, with Douglas aircraft responsible for designing the airframe. The weapon was initially designated KAS-1, then AAM-2, and AAM-N-2 in 1948. The diameter of the HVAR proved inadequate for the electronics and Douglas enlarged the missile's airframe to 8-inch diameter. Following unpowered tests in 1947, leading to powered tests commencing in 1949, the prototype successfully made its first aerial interception in 1952.

The initial AAM-N-2 Sparrow began limited operational service in 1954, carried by specially modified F3D-2M Skyknight all-weather fighters. In 1956, the F3H-2M Demon and F7U-3M Cutlass became operational with the Sparrow. The Sparrow I was limited and primitive, with the beam-riding guidance only successful against large targets flying a straight course. Since the main threat at the time was seen as enemy bombers, this was acceptable. The need to receive a strong reflected radar signal was difficult with smaller, maneuvering targets since the launching aircraft's radar had to be aimed at the target throughout the engagement.

In 1951, Raytheon began development of a semi-active radar homing version, the AAM-N-6 Sparrow III, which became operational in 1958. The AAM-N-6a was similar, but used a new Thiokol liquid-fuel rocket engine for improved performance. Rocketdyne developed a solid-fuel motor for the AAM-N-6b, which entered production in 1963. This new motor increased maximum range to 22 miles for head-on attacks. In 1963, the Sparrows became the AIM-7 series.

Unfortunately for their later service, both missiles were originally designed to intercept bombers. Prewar testing of both missiles had indicated that the AIM-7 would hit the target 71 percent of the time while the AIM-9 would be successful 65 percent of the time. This was due to the fact that during tests both the Air Force and Navy operated on the assumption that the missile would work. Thus, failure was ascribed either to poor missile maintenance or to an improperly executed test. Test managers thus made sure that the missiles were carefully handled and that the target maneuvers were as benign as possible to maximize the opportunity for a hit. When the missiles entered combat, the success rates were far below what had been expected, since they were being used in ways that the testing had not dealt with. Aboard carriers or at airfields ashore, the weapons were treated like any other piece of ordnance, and were not cared for as they had been in tests. Southeast Asian humidity affected operating systems. Most importantly, they were being used against maneuvering targets, which completely skewed the "book" envelopes for successful operation. When this was coupled with the decision to reduce or drop air combat maneuvering training for F-4 aircrews by both services, because air combat maneuvering between fighters was no longer seen as being relevant to modern air warfare where the target was a bomber with an A-bomb, it was no wonder that results of air-to-air combat were as poor as they were during *Rolling Thunder*, the US bombing campaign over North Vietnam that occurred between April 1965 and November 1968.

Reviews of the missiles' performance during *Rolling Thunder* demonstrated that they and the aircrews using them had a long way to go before they lived up to their prewar expectations. During the *Rolling Thunder* campaign between April 1965 and November 1968, 330 AIM-7s were fired for 27 hits, an eight percent success rate. Ninety-nine Sparrows fired were a miss, for a 29 percent failure-in-combat rate; worst of all, 214 were mechanical failures: either they did not leave the rail when launched for various reasons or their engine did not fire when launched, for a mechanical failure rate of 63 percent. Comparing the real world statistics with the original test results demonstrated that it was impossible under normal operating conditions ashore or afloat to keep the missiles in the pristine condition they had been used in during those long-ago tests. Also, the time it took the missile to lock on and allow firing was five seconds, an eternity in air combat. The missiles were being fired against maneuvering targets they had not been designed for, and used by F-4 crews in both services who lacked the experience and knowledge from training to use them properly in an air combat environment.

The Sidewinder was more popular, due to its ease of use and reliability. However, real world results were wildly different from earlier test results. Of 187 Sidewinders fired during *Rolling Thunder*, 29 resulted in kills, a success rate of 15 percent. A total of 53 were misses, a combat failure rate of 28 percent, while the overwhelming majority were the 105 mechanical or technical failures, for a 56 percent failure rate. One major problem was that in a maneuvering air combat scenario, the firing envelope for the Sidewinder was significantly smaller than had been the case in the original tests against non-maneuvering targets. A target in a 3G turn shrank the AIM-9B firing envelope 50 percent. Against a target pulling more than 5Gs – not unusual in a turning combat – the AIM-9B was completely unusable. If the missile was fired against an enemy with a background of ground, clouds, or sun, it was more likely to home in on one of those choices than the target it was fired at. The AIM-9D with its vastly superior seeker head solved many of these problems, but Air Force aircraft couldn't use this missile until the late 1970s.

Both the Navy and Air Force had high initial expectations of the F-4 Phantom In the belief that the two different missiles plus the best available on-board radar of any fighter of its time, coupled with the highest speed and acceleration properties, would give the Phantom a decisive edge over the MiGs. Such was not the case. The Phantom proved unable to engage in close-in air combat maneuvering against the lighter MiG-21, while both the radar-guided Sparrow and the infrared heat-seeking Sidewinder proved to be less capable than expected. This, along with the adoption by the North Vietnamese of the tactic of engaging in air combat at close range, which put them "outside the envelope" for successful use of the missiles, meant that F-4s suffered unexpected losses.

Had US designers had a more realistic understanding of the true capabilities of the missiles that armed the aircraft they produced, both they and the services they were working with would have been less likely to abandon the on-board cannon as they did, which only came back into use on Air Force F-4s after the hard-earned lessons of combat, while the Navy never did adopt a gun package for its Phantoms.

The Douglas A-4 Skyhawk was as revolutionary as the Crusader and the Phantom, albeit in a very different way from these two fighters. The Skyhawk, along with the A-20 Havoc, SBD Dauntless, B-26 Invader, AD Skyraider, F4D Skyray, and A3D Skywarrior, was the product of one of the few truly genius aircraft designers: Ed Heinemann. Heinemann began work in the 1930s, employed by the visionary Jack K. Northrop, for whom he created the BT-1 dive bomber; when Northrop's company was absorbed by Douglas Aircraft and became the Douglas El Segundo Division, the best thing Donald Douglas acquired was Northrop's young designer. The BT-1 went on to become the SBD Dauntless, the greatest ship-killer of the Pacific War.

By the early 1950s, Heinemann, along with every other aircraft designer, was dismayed by the growth in weight and technical complexity that jet power had brought to aviation. Where other designers chafed at this and then created an airframe that could carry the weight, Heinemann fought back. When the Bureau of Aeronautics began looking for a jet-powered replacement for the Skyraider, they expected an airplane about the size of today's A-10. What they got from Heinemann was a proposal for an airplane so small that it wouldn't need folding wings to fit on a standard carrier elevator and would go on to hold the record as the smallest operational aircraft in its class ever used by the Navy. It was immediately dubbed "Heinemann's Hotrod." While some doubted, many looked at Heinemann's record and gave the proposal serious thought. When the Navy's review of the design came up with the answer that the airplane should do what Mr. Heinemann said it would, a contract was let on June 21, 1950, for the XA4D-1, which first flew on June 22, 1954.

Powered by a Wright J65 Sapphire providing 7,200 pounds of thrust and armed with two 20mm cannon, the "Skyhawk," as it was by then known, had a Low Altitude Bombing System (LABS) provision for a Mark 7 nuclear store on the centerline, with wing racks for either drop tanks or conventional bombs. The A4D-1 entered service in September 1956 with VA-72. The Skyhawk was used in day attack, capable of dive bombing, interdiction, and close support missions; when the requirement of carrying a (then heavy) nuclear weapon was added to the specification, Heinemann's answer was "no problem." As of 2021, Skyhawks are still flying off the Brazilian aircraft carrier *São Paulo* after serving with the US Navy and Marines, the Australian Navy, the New Zealand, Singaporean, and Israeli air forces, most of that service involving combat; Argentinian-flown Skyhawks gave the Royal Navy fits during the Falklands War, 20 years after it first went to war in Southeast Asia.

The A4D-2N, the third version of the Skyhawk to enter service, featured limited all-weather capability, with the addition of an APG-53 terrain-clearance radar, the AJB-3 all-attitude reference and loft-bombing system, a TPQ-10 ground control blind bombing system, an angle-of-attack indicator, an improved gunsight, and an automatic flight control system. The first flight of the A4D-2N was August 21, 1958, with introduction into service commencing in March 1960 with Marine Attack Squadron 225 (VMA-225) at Marine Corps Air Station (MCAS) Cherry Point. This was the first Skyhawk produced in substantial numbers, with a total production run of 638. The A4D-2N was powered – as were the A4D-1 and A4D-2 – by the Wright J65, a license-built version of the Armstrong-Siddeley Sapphire. By then redesignated A-4C under the new tri-service designation system, the Skyhawk first faced the possibility of going to war in the Cuban Missile Crisis of October 1962 and did go to war two years later in the Tonkin Gulf Incident and the retaliatory air strike flown in response. On June 12, 1961, the A4D-5 first flew with a Pratt & Whitney J52-P-6A giving 8,500 pounds of thrust. The armament was augmented with multiple ejector racks (MERs) on a total of five stations, allowing the airplane to carry up to 9,155 pounds of bombs, missiles, rockets, or drop tanks. The A4D-5 went into production as the A-4E, with 500 delivered by April 1966.

Vietnam combat experience brought forth the A-4F, first flown on August 31, 1966, with a J52-P-8A that increased power to 9,300 pounds of thrust. The main visual difference at the time was an avionics "hump" aft of the cockpit, though this was later retrofitted to the surviving A-4Es. Between August 3, 1964 and the bombing halt of March 31, 1968, the little Skyhawk was the principal Navy attack aircraft used over North Vietnam, as well as the main close air support aircraft in South Vietnam for the Marines. The final version to serve in combat with US units, the A-4M, was specifically developed to meet requirements of the Marines for a close-support aircraft after the Navy adopted the A-7 Corsair II; it served the Marines in front-line service from 1969 to 1985, and flew as an "aggressor" in air combat training until the early 1990s. All in all, the Skyhawk series was perhaps the most successful single-purpose postwar aircraft. As a close support light attack aircraft, it had no equal, and it was produced in greater quantities than any of its would-be multi-role competitors. During the Vietnam War, the aircraft was so reliable that Skyhawk squadrons regularly reported 85–100 percent availability day in and day out at Yankee Station.

While the Skyhawk revealed itself as amenable to further development to maintain its viability as a light attack aircraft, by 1960 the US Navy could see the Skyhawk was near the end of its development and that a more capable aircraft capable of carrying greater loads with greater range was needed.

On May 29, 1963, a Request for Proposals for the new requirement, known as VAL (Heavier-than-air, Attack, Light), was issued. All proposals submitted were to be based on existing designs in order to minimize development cost. Vought, Douglas, Grumman, and North American submitted proposals by September, with the Vought proposal based on the F-8 Crusader fighter with which it shared a similar configuration. The evaluation process was completed by November and funding for VAL was approved by Congress on February 8, 1964. On February 11, Vought was declared the winner, receiving an initial contract on March 19 for an aircraft designated A-7, which received the name "Corsair II" in June, an emotive reminder of Vought's World War II fighter-bomber.

The A-7A first flew on September 27, 1965. Chief Test Pilot John Conrad demonstrated the Corsair II's ability to perform rapid rolls carrying an ordnance load of six 250-pound and 12 500-pound bombs on November 2. Further tests demonstrated that the A-7 could carry twice the bomb load of the A-4E the same distance, or the same bomb load as the A-4E for twice the Skyhawk's range. A total of 199 A-7As were produced, but these aircraft were found to be underpowered, and the A-7B, powered by a Pratt & Whitney TF30-8 turbofan, quickly replaced the earlier sub-type on the production line. Use of the turbofan dramatically increased fuel efficiency in comparison to a standard turbojet. The Corsair II first entered squadron service in the spring of 1967, and the first combat deployment was made to Southeast Asia that fall.

A-7A/B aircraft powered by the TF30 had difficulty operating in the high-humidity Southeast Asian environment, though overall combat experience was so good that the Air Force adopted the aircraft as the A-7D, powered by an even more powerful TF41-A-2, a license-built version of the Rolls-Royce Spey engine, to replace the A-1 Skyraiders it was using. The A-7D's performance was so much improved that the Navy adopted the new engine for the A-7E that appeared on operations in 1970, though the first 30 were powered by the TF30-8 and received the designation A-7C.

By 1971, 27 Navy attack squadrons were operating the type in both the Atlantic and Pacific fleets. On October 6, 1972, four A-7Cs from VA-82 – two carrying two 2,000-pound Walleye guided bombs each while the others carried two 2,000-pound Mark 84 "dumb" bombs each – attacked the Thanh Hoa Bridge that had seemed to be impervious to air attack since 1965. The bombs all hit the center piling on the bridge's west side, which broke the span in half and finally permanently destroyed a target against which both the Navy and Air Force had flown multiple missions with high casualties throughout the air campaign.

The Korean War had demonstrated the value of carriers having a night-attack capability, with the small number of night fighter-bomber detachments aboard Task Force 77 carriers achieving greater results against enemy truck and train transportation than the larger units operating in daylight did. Following the good performance of the propeller-driven Skyraider in the night attack role during the Korean War, the Bureau of Aeronautics issued preliminary requirements in 1955 for a jet-powered all-weather carrier-based attack aircraft, publishing an operational requirement document in October 1956 and releasing a Request for Proposals in February 1957. Bell, Boeing, Douglas, Grumman, Lockheed, Martin, North American, and Vought responded with proposals. Following evaluation of these proposals, the Navy announced the selection of Grumman on January 2, 1958, awarding a contract for development of the A2F-1 in February 1958. The design team was led by Lawrence Mead, Jr., who later played a leading role in the design of the Lunar Excursion Module and the F-14 Tomcat.

The first prototype YA2F-1, now named the "Intruder," which lacked radar and the navigational and attack avionics, made its first flight on April 19, 1960, with the second prototype flying on July 28. Development flying went well, with the major problem encountered being handling problems associated with the aircraft's air brakes mounted on the rear fuselage. In an attempt to solve this, the third prototype had its horizontal tailplane moved rearwards by 16 inches, but this did not completely solve the handling problems, which were finally resolved by fitting split-hinged speed-brakes on the aircraft's wing-tips. Early production aircraft were fitted with both the fuselage and wingtip air brakes, although the fuselage-mounted items were soon bolted shut, and were removed from later aircraft.

For its day, the Intruder had surprisingly sophisticated avionics, with a high degree of integration. It was felt that this could lead to extraordinary maintenance requirements to identify and isolate equipment malfunctions. Hence, the aircraft was provided with automatic diagnostic systems, some of the earliest computer-based analytic equipment developed for aircraft. These were known as basic automated checkout equipment, or BACE (pronounced "base"). There were two levels, known as "Line BACE" to identify specific malfunctioning systems in the aircraft, while in the hangar or on the flight line; and "Shop BACE," to exercise and analyze individual malfunctioning systems in the maintenance shop. This equipment was manufactured by Litton Industries. Together, the BACE systems greatly reduced the Maintenance Man-Hours per Flight Hour, a key index of the cost and effort needed to keep military aircraft operating.

Designated the A-6A in 1962, the Intruder became operational with squadrons beginning in 1963, and first entered combat in 1965.

With the post-World War II emphasis on nuclear strike capability, the Navy first introduced the AJ-1 Savage, a bomber powered by two R-2800 piston engines with a J35 jet in the rear fuselage to provide "sprint speed" over the target. The airplane was about the size of the B-25 medium bomber of World War II and was the largest aircraft operated on an aircraft carrier at the time of its introduction. The Navy then proceeded to develop a jet-powered strategic nuclear bomber, which would operate from the new Forrestal-class carriers that had been approved in 1951 after the opening rounds in Korea had demonstrated that aircraft carriers had value that no other weapon system could provide. These ships replaced the planned United States-class carriers, the first of which had been canceled during construction in 1949.

What became the A-3 Skywarrior began development in January 1948, when the Bureau of Aeronautics issued a requirement for a long-range, carrier-based attack plane that could deliver a 10,000-pound bomb load; the specification set a target-loaded weight of 100,000 pounds. Ed Heinemann, who feared that the new United States-class carriers were vulnerable to cancelation, proposed a significantly smaller aircraft of 68,000 pounds loaded weight, capable of operating from existing carriers. The Navy awarded a development contract on September 29, 1949, some eight months after cancelation of the *United States*. The prototype XA3D-1 first flew on October 28, 1952.

The Skywarrior had a 36-degree swept wing and the production aircraft was powered by two of Pratt & Whitney's wonderful J57 turbojets after the prototypes had used the intended Westinghouse J40, which was subsequently canceled. The three-man crew were in a forward cockpit and were not provided with ejection seats; escape was rather by a tunnel below the cockpit which proved difficult to use when the time came; a standard joke among crews was that "A3D" stood for "All Three Dead." The A3D-1 and A3D-2 had a defensive armament of two radar-directed 20mm cannon in the tail.

Eventually, the strategic nuclear bombing requirement that the aircraft was created to perform was taken over by the Polaris submarine-launched intermediate-range ballistic missile that first entered service in 1960. From that point on, the Skywarrior, with its large bomb bay, was converted into reconnaissance platforms with special operators of the recon systems housed in the bomb bay. The A-3 designation changed to RA-3B for photographic reconnaissance, EA-3B for electronic reconnaissance, and ERA-3B for electronic warfare. As the KA-3B, the plane was used as a flying tanker with fuel in the bomb bay, transferred through the probe-and-drogue system. Electronic jamming equipment was added without removing tanker capability, allowing the EKA-3B to jam enemy radar while waiting to refuel tactical aircraft. The Skywarrior flew off carriers until the early 1990s, and was known by its crews and the flight deck crews that handled it aboard ship as the "Whale." The four-plane A-3 detachments that operated from US carriers provided electronic warfare capability as well as aerial tanking. Tanking allowed aircraft to launch from a carrier with a maximum bomb load that would be too great if the aircraft was also fully fueled; with the tankers, the strike aircraft could "top off" on their way to the target, and also refuel on the way back to their carrier if they had engaged in combat and were low on fuel.

The year after the Skywarrior first flew, North American Aviation commenced a private study for a carrier-based, long-range, supersonic, all-weather nuclear strike bomber. Two years later in 1955, the North American General Purpose Attack Weapon concept was presented to the Navy, which accepted it with some revisions, and a development contract was awarded on August 29, 1956, as the XA3J-1. The prototype made its first flight almost two years later to the day in Columbus, Ohio, on August 31, 1958, and received the name "Vigilante."

At the time of its introduction to the fleet in 1960, the Vigilante was one of the largest and by far the most complex aircraft to operate from an aircraft carrier. Its high-mounted swept wing used blown flaps in a boundary-layer control system to improve low-speed lift. There were no ailerons; roll control was provided by spoilers in conjunction with differential deflection of the all-moving tail surfaces. Directional control was provided by a single large all-moving vertical stabilizer, and the wings, vertical stabilizer, and nose radome folded for stowage aboard ship. The wing skins were made of aluminum-lithium alloy, while critical structures were made of titanium. The aircraft was powered by two General Electric J79 turbojets, fed by intake ramps. The crew of pilot and bombardier-navigator (B/N) were seated on North American HS-1A ejection seats in tandem cockpits in the extreme nose. The nuclear weapon was carried in a novel "linear bomb bay" between the engines, and was ejected to the rear; the system was not reliable and no weapons were ever carried. All variants of the Vigilante were built at North American Aviation's facility at Port Columbus Airport in Columbus, Ohio.

Despite its size and weight, the Vigilante, by now designated A-5A, was surprisingly agile; escorting fighters found that the clean airframe and powerful engines made the Vigilante very fast at both high and low altitudes; it was capable of speeds in excess of Mach 2 at altitude and could fly supersonic at extremely low altitudes. However, its high approach speed and high angle of attack in the landing configuration made returning to the aircraft carrier a challenge for inexperienced or unwary pilots.

With the problems associated with the linear bomb bay limiting its role as a bomber, and with the strategic nuclear strike role taken over by the Polaris missile shortly after the A-5A became operational, North American needed to find other employment for the Vigilante. Its high speed at all altitudes and long range in the A3J-2 (A-5B) sub-type, which had internal tanks for an additional 460 gallons of fuel in a pronounced dorsal "hump" behind the cockpits, along with blown slats on the wing leading edge and sturdier landing gear, made it an obvious candidate for development into a high-speed reconnaissance aircraft.

The reconnaissance version, at first designated A3J-3P and after September 1962 RA-5C, had a slightly greater wing area and added a long canoe-shaped fairing under the fuselage for a multi-sensor reconnaissance pack that included an APD-7 side-looking airborne radar (SLAR), AAS-21 infrared line scanner, and camera packs, as well as improved electronic countermeasures (ECM). Additionally, an AN/ALQ-61 electronic intelligence system could be carried. The RA-5C retained the AN/ASB-12 bombing system, and could carry weapons, though it never did in service. Late-production RA-5Cs had more powerful J79-10 engines with afterburning thrust of 17,900 pounds. The RA-5C weighed almost 10,000 pounds more than the A-5A with almost the same power and only a modestly enlarged wing. While the changes cost it acceleration and climb rate, it remained very fast in level flight.

The A3J-1 strike aircraft first entered service with Heavy Attack Squadron 3 (VAH-3), replacing the A3D-2, in June 1961. Early service proved troublesome, with many teething problems involved with its advanced systems. While these systems were highly sophisticated, the technology was in its infancy, and reliability was poor. Although maintenance personnel gained greater experience supporting these systems, the aircraft tended to remain a maintenance-intensive platform throughout its career. With the Polaris system now operational, production of the Vigilante ended in 1963. The A3J-2s were returned to the factory where they were converted to the RA-5C. The first RA-5Cs were delivered to VAH-3, at NAS Sanford, Florida, in July 1963. As the heavy attack squadrons operating the Vigilante transitioned to the reconnaissance role, they were redesignated as Reconnaissance Attack Squadron (changing from VAH to RVAH). A total of ten RA-5C squadrons were ultimately established. Eight of the ten squadrons saw extensive service in the Vietnam War, carrying out hazardous medium-level post-strike reconnaissance missions. Although it proved fast and agile, 18 RA-5Cs were lost in combat: 14 to antiaircraft fire, three to surface-to-air missiles (SAMs), and one to a MiG-21 during Operation *Linebacker II*. Nine other RA-5Cs were lost in operational accidents with Task Force 77; with these losses, 36 additional RA-5C aircraft were built between 1968 and 1970 to make up attrition.

The carriers from which these aircraft would operate were equally revolutionary. Popularly known as "super carriers" once they appeared, they were the largest movable structures on earth, being the first ships over 1,000 feet in length, and only exceeded in the 21st century by super-large container ships.

The development of USS *Forrestal* CVA-59), the US Navy's first super carrier, represented many significant improvements over previous carrier designs. *Forrestal*, named for former Secretary of the Navy and first Secretary of Defense James Forrestal, who fought to keep naval aviation on the cutting edge in the late 1940s, was the first carrier designed specifically to operate jet aircraft, and included an angled deck which permitted simultaneous takeoffs and landings. The revolutionary design became the basis for all US Navy aircraft carriers that followed. The flight deck of *Forrestal* had a different layout than those that followed, with the island placed closer to the bow and a different starboard elevator configuration – one forward of the island and two aft. The No. 4 elevator on the port side was forward of the two waist catapults. *Forrestal* and her sister ships had twice the displacement tonnage of the original Essex-class carriers and carried 70 percent more ship's fuel and 300 percent more aviation fuel, as well as two-and-a-half times the amount of ordnance. (The limited ordnance capacity of the Essex-class carriers had been a problem in Korea, where the A-1 Skyraider squadron aboard ship was capable of emptying the ship's magazine in three days of high-level operations.) With their additional size, these new carriers were more stable in heavy seas and could operate their air wing 95 percent of the time in even the roughest seas, while the smaller Essex-class carriers could only do so about 65 percent of the time.

Originally, the Navy planned eight Forrestal-class carriers. In the event, the class was composed of three in addition to *Forrestal*: USS *Saratoga* (CVA-60), *Ranger* (CVA-61), and *Independence* (CVA-62). Changes introduced in USS *Kitty Hawk* (CVA-63) resulted in the final four being termed the Kitty Hawk class: *Kitty Hawk* herself, *Constellation* (CVA-64), *America* (CVA-66), and *John F. Kennedy* (CVA-67). These ships differed from the Forrestals by having greater length, with the island moved so that the elevators were changed to two ahead of the island and one aft, the port elevator being moved to the rear of the waist catapults. Additionally, their antiaircraft guns were replaced by Talos surface-to-air guided missiles.

The real revolution in aircraft carriers came with USS *Enterprise* (CVAN-65), the first nuclear-powered aircraft carrier. The largest aircraft carrier ever built with an overall length of 1,123 feet, she was "overpowered" with eight nuclear reactors and was capable of a top speed in excess of 40 knots. *Enterprise* was planned as the first of a class of six nuclear-powered ships, but massive cost-overruns resulted in the other five being canceled. Commissioned in 1961, *Enterprise* would be one of a kind, with the later nuclear-powered carriers of the Nimitz class having a significantly different propulsion system.

The three postwar Midway carriers, and many of the sturdy Essex-class fleet carriers that had been at the forefront of the Pacific War, where they provided the backbone of victory once the Navy went over to offense in 1943, and which had held the line in the Sea of Japan during the Korean War, were given major updates in the years after the end of the Korean War. The traditional straight flight decks of these carriers were replaced with the angled deck first developed by the Royal Navy and tested by the US Navy with the modification of USS *Antietam* (CVA-36) in 1953. The angled deck allowed an aircraft to execute a missed approach to landing without endangering the other aircraft spotted ahead of the landing area on the flight deck. The SBC-27 modification known as "27-Charlie" saw the Essex carriers equipped with angled flight decks and steam catapults that allowed operation of larger and heavier aircraft even up to the A-3 Skywarrior; the Essex carriers operated every Navy jet other than the F-4 Phantom, A-6 Intruder, and RA-5C Vigilante, which were restricted to the larger Midway and Forrestal carriers.

Regardless of the carrier, a naval air wing at this time consisted of two fighter squadrons and two or three attack squadrons, with detachments of early-warning and photo-reconnaissance aircraft, and a helicopter detachment. The F-4 Phantom equipped the large carrier fighter squadrons, while the F-8 Crusader operated from the Essex carriers. Both the Forrestal and Midway carriers operated the A-6 Intruder in one of the attack squadrons. The fleet's airborne early-warning capability was met initially with the EA-1E Skyraider until it was replaced in 1957 with the Grumman E-1 Tracer, a development of the S-2 Tracker twin-engine antisubmarine aircraft. The Grumman E-2 Hawkeye, which was designed as an airborne early warning aircraft from the outset and first flew in 1960, entered service aboard ship in January 1964; although the ability to operate from the smaller Essex carriers had been part of the initial design requirements, the E-2 never operated from these ships. The E-1 Tracers continued to operate from the Essex carriers until both they and it were retired from service in 1977. The A-3 Skywarriors provided a tanker detachment on the Essex carriers, which also operated an RF-8 photo-recon Crusader detachment for reconnaissance. All carriers operated the A-4 Skyhawk in two of the attack squadrons, while the Essex carriers operated a squadron of A-1 Skyraiders until they were withdrawn from naval service in 1967.

The Vietnam War, like the Korean War, was not a naval war in which there was an opposing enemy fleet. As in Korea, the carriers would be used for power projection ashore, with the ships acting as mobile airfields located off the enemy's coastline.

3

OPPONENTS

Five fighters would dominate the battle for air supremacy over North Vietnam in the Navy's air war. They were the F-8 Crusader and the F-4 Phantom for the US Navy, and the MiG-17, MiG-19, and MiG-21 for the North Vietnam Air Force, known officially as the Vietnam People's Air Force (VPAF).

The most numerous fighter used by the North Vietnamese was the MiG-17, which began production in 1952 as an advanced development from the MiG-15, the first Soviet fighter competitive with Western designs, which had been heavily involved in combat over Korea. The Mikoyan-Gurevich design bureau had begun theoretical development of the aircraft as a follow-on replacement for the MiG-15 in 1949 and the design was the result of feedback from operational experience with the MiG-15 in Korea. The primary emphasis in the new design was to maximize high-speed controllability, which was the major defect of the MiG-15.

The MiG-17 fuselage was extended approximately three feet, since the short fuselage of the MiG-15 had resulted in loss of control in extended high-speed high-G combat turns. The forward fuselage, cockpit, and armament arrangement of the MiG-15 was kept in the new design. The entirely new, thinner wing and tailplane were more highly swept for speeds approaching Mach 1, though the horizontal stabilizer was kept in its high position to position it as far aft as possible on the highly swept vertical fin to maintain pitch control. This had limited the MiG-15 to subsonic speeds only, and the MiG-17 only became supersonic when it was fitted with an afterburner; lacking the "all-flying" tailplane that improved controllability near and through Mach 1, the MiG-17 was still inferior to the F-86 Sabre, the first fighter equipped with an "all-flying" tail and which crucially had its horizontal stabilizer mounted low on the fuselage, the proper position for supersonic pitch control.

The MiG-17's wing was significantly different from its predecessor, with a "crescent" compound shape in which the inner wing was swept at 45 degrees while the outer wing was swept at 42 degrees. This reduced the tendency of the wing to pitch up when approaching a high-speed stall, and maintained a constant critical mach across the wing, reducing wave drag and increasing top speed. Additionally, the stiffer wing resisted the tendency to bend the wingtips and lose aerodynamic symmetry unexpectedly at high speeds and wing loads, which was experienced with a "straight" swept wing. While the MiG-17 was initially equipped with the same VK-1 turbojet developed from the British Nene engine used by the MiG-15, the definitive MiG-17F day fighter used a VK-1F engine which had a longer TBO than the MiG-15's powerplant, and was equipped with an afterburner that increased thrust from the normal 6,000 pounds to 7,600 pounds. Although the MiG-17 was not designed to fly supersonic, a skilled pilot could manage the progressive loss of control above .93 Mach due to the lack of a properly positioned "all-flying" tail and go supersonic in a shallow dive, though the aircraft would often pitch up just short of Mach 1; this was similar to the ability of the F-86A without an all-flying tail to exceed Mach 1, with the MiG-17 powering through to a top speed of around 711 miles per hour at 10,000 feet. The primary value of the afterburner was that it doubled the climb rate.

The MiG-17 was highly maneuverable at speeds below 575 knots, and the design solved the controllability problems of the MiG-15 in high altitude maneuvers after the wings had been stiffened to avoid aileron reversal that had been found in initial flight testing of the early prototypes. Though the first prototype had flown in the fall of 1951, production was delayed to maximize production of the MiG-15 during the Korean War, and the MiG-17 did not enter initial service until late 1952. Like the earlier fighter, it was primarily designed to climb to high altitude and shoot down enemy bombers flying straight and level, not for air-to-air combat, using the same heavy cannon armament of an N-37D 37mm cannon and two NS-23KM 23mm cannons carried by the MiG-15. The fighter was equipped with a gunsight that had been reverse-engineered from the gunsight on Bud Mahurin's F-86E that had been recovered after his crash in May 1952 and taken to the Soviet Union where the optical gunsight and SRD-3 gun ranging radar were copied, to become the ASP-4N gunsight and SRC-3 radar.

The MiG-17 would prove a nasty surprise to American flyers in Vietnam, who initially underestimated it as being "old technology" not much improved over the Korean War MiG-15. It was highly effective against heavily loaded US fighter bombers, and could outmaneuver the F-4 Phantom at subsonic air combat speeds and stay even with the F-8 Crusader in such a situation. American pilots in Vietnam found, as had their forebears in Korea, that one hit from the 37mm cannon was sufficient to knock off a wing or blow up an engine. Due to its small size, the MiG-17 was difficult to spot at combat distances, a problem made more difficult when the North Vietnamese began camouflaging their airplanes for the low-altitude combat in which they typically engaged. While the F-8 Crusader could successfully engage in traditional air combat maneuvers with the MiG-17, the heavier and larger Phantom was at a distinct disadvantage unless the pilot fought the MiG in the vertical plane where the F-4's superior power allowed it to outmaneuver the enemy fighter.

When the XF-100 went supersonic in level flight 20 minutes after its first takeoff on May 25, 1953, no one knew that, two weeks before this event, the Soviet Union had flown the prototype of what would be known as the MiG-19, which also went supersonic in level flight on its first test flight. The unexpected Soviet achievement, which was created in a country still climbing out of the wreckage of its industrial base in World War II, was based on much of the same German theoretical research as that used by North American. In the case of the Soviets, resources also included a large number of German aeronautical experts who had been forcibly relocated to the Soviet Union in 1946.

Among the spoils of war brought back from Germany was a half-finished rocket-powered aircraft, the DFS-346, which had been found at the Siebel factory by the Red Army. Designed as a reconnaissance aircraft, the DFS-346 was to be carried aloft by a larger aircraft and launched at high altitude, where the two Walter HWK 109 liquid rocket engines would accelerate it to supersonic speeds after it was dropped. The design featured highly swept wings and tail surfaces with the pilot prone in a cockpit sited in the extreme nose.

The DFS-346 and its German technicians were moved to a location in the Urals to complete development. Renamed "Samolyot 346," or "Aircraft 346," it was completed in late 1946 and was used in various ground tests, including wind tunnel tests. In 1947, a second one was completed as an unpowered glider for launch and slow-speed flight tests conducted by German test pilot Wolfgang Ziese, with the aircraft launched from an American B-29 which had made an emergency landing in Siberia during the war and been repaired. These successful flights resulted in construction of the 346-1, 346-2, and 346-3, which was the first fully functional version with an operational propulsion system. Tests continued through 1951, when 346-3 was destroyed after losing control in its second flight. Since the 346-3 was lost on its second flight, it is doubtful that supersonic speed was achieved.

Mikoyan and Gurevich had just completed initial design of the follow-on MiG-17 when they were tasked in 1950 with developing a supersonic fighter. Their initial design looked very similar to the DFS-346, with highly swept wings and tailplanes. It would be powered by two new Mikulin AM-5 turbojets which had been developed as smaller and lighter versions of the AM-3 which would power the Tu-16, the first "strategic" Soviet jet bomber. A MiG-17F was allotted for research, with its VK-1 turbojet replaced with two AM-5s. The resulting testbed was designated the SM-1; it first flew in late November 1951.

Construction of the SM-2, which was the actual prototype of what would become the MiG-19, was authorized on August 10, 1951. The wings were swept at an extreme 55 degrees and a T-tail was fitted. The first SM-2, the SM-2/1, first flew on May 24, 1952, piloted by G.A. Sedov. With un-reheated AM-5A engines, the SM-2 was not supersonic in level flight; afterburning AM-5F engines were substituted, but subsequent flight tests revealed handling problems, particularly at high angles of attack, with the aircraft prone to spinning. The design profited by the knowledge gained from the Mahurin F-86E Sabre recovered in North Korea after being shot down that May, which was brought to the TsAGI (Central Aerodynamic Research Institute) where its "all-flying" tail was thoroughly examined. As a result, the SM-2 was redesigned with its horizontal stabilizer turned into an "all-flying" tail and positioned low on the rear fuselage. Now redesignated SM-2B and with the tail finally in the right place and operating correctly, the airplane went supersonic in level flight in March 1953, five weeks before the

US XF-100. While it was capable of supersonic level flight, the engines were deemed inadequate, and over the summer of 1953, it was rebuilt with the AM-9B which provided 5,700 pounds of dry thrust and 7,600 pounds in reheat. With these engines, the SM-2 became the SM-9, which first flew on January 5, 1954 and was ordered into production the following month, four months after the delivery of the first production F-100. Unknown to the United States, the Soviet Union had matched aircraft development within a matter of months, as had happened with the F-86 and the MiG-15. However, the Soviets were never able to match the industrial development the United States had undertaken simultaneously with the development of the F-100, which meant that all Soviet supersonic aircraft would be much more primitive in terms of construction than their US opposite numbers, forcing them to rely on simplicity of design and construction.

The MiG-19 was only taken into the North Vietnamese Air Force in 1969 after the end of the *Rolling Thunder* campaign; 100 Chinese-built MiG-19s, known as the J-6, were delivered at a time when deliveries of MiG-21s were delayed. Following the initial success of the MiG-19 in 1954, the Voyenno-Vozdushnye Sily Rossii (the Russian Air force, shortened to V-VS) became more interested in the MiG-21, the follow-on to the MiG-19, despite the fact that the fighter was the first outside the United States capable of supersonic speed in level flight; the V-VS lost confidence in the design when severe control and hydraulics issues caused a high number of crashes once it entered operational service in 1955. By the time the MiG design bureau solved these issues with the MiG-19S (*Stabilizator*) in 1957, the USSR was supplying the aircraft to Soviet satellite states and Third World allies while development was concentrated on the MiG-21. This was despite the fact that the MiG-19S as developed was an excellent day fighter with better maneuverability than the MiG-21 and a heavy gun armament.

The People's Republic of China was among the allied states that were given MiG-19s, and license production began just as the Sino-Soviet split became public. Once that split had happened and Soviet military aid was ended, the Chinese put considerable effort into refining the MiG-19, which would serve in PLAAF front-line units until the late 1980s. US pilots who were able to fly MiG-19s supplied to Pakistan in the late 1960s found that the airplane was capable of out-turning the F-4 Phantom; in slow and medium-speed engagements; when set to 15 degrees, the "maneuvering flaps" increased rate of turn below 460 knots. Unlike the MiG-17, the MiG-19 had excellent acceleration; it could out-accelerate the F-4 to Mach 1.2, and its top speed of Mach 1.6, while slower than that of the MiG-21 and the F-4, was still sufficient to make it a formidable adversary. Additionally, the airplane had a better view out of the cockpit than either the MiG-17 or MiG-21. The major shortcomings were its short range and the fact that it was more difficult to maintain than the other two MiG fighters. However, when the MiG-19 was supplied to the VPAF in 1969, the fact that it operated as a point defense interceptor under positive control mitigated this problem to an extent.

The MiG-19 equipped a third VPAF fighter unit, the 925th Fighter Regiment. By April 1969, nine Chinese-trained MiG-19 pilots reported to the unit, which was based at Yen Bai. Chinese deliveries were sporadic, and there were seldom more than 54 of the aircraft in North Vietnam. Despite their small numbers, the 925th Regiment's MiG-19s were involved in extensive combat operations in 1972 during Operations *Linebacker* and *Linebacker II*. The VPAF claimed 12 enemy aircraft – including seven F-4s – shot down by MiG-19s for a loss of eight, while the US admitted a loss of six Phantoms for ten MiG-19s. All six US aircraft were lost in gun fights, a tribute to the three 30mm cannon that the MiG-19s was armed with, which had 90 rounds per gun, allowing approximately six seconds of firing time. A two-second burst of 90 rounds could hit a US opponent with 81 pounds of metal; this was considerably more than the US Vulcan 20mm cannon, which would put out 39 pounds of metal in a two-second burst.

The most important fighter fielded by the VNAF during both *Rolling Thunder* and the battles of 1972 was the MiG-21, known as the *En bac*, or "Silver Swallow," in Vietnamese.

The Mikoyan-Gurevich Opytnoye Konstruktorskoye Byuro (Experimental Design Bureau – OKB) commenced development of what would become the MiG-21 with the completion of a preliminary design study for an experimental supersonic prototype designated Ye-1 in 1954. Soon after, the project was completely revised when it became clear that the planned engine did not produce sufficient power. The redesign became a second experimental prototype, the Ye-2. Both designs featured highly swept wings similar to what was used on the MiG-19. The Ye-4, the first prototype with delta wings, made its first flight on June 16, 1955 and was first displayed publicly during the

Soviet Aviation Day display held at Tushino airfield outside Moscow in July 1956.

Given the NATO reporting name "Fishbed" following its public display, early details of what was now called the MiG-21 were often confused with similar Soviet designs of the period. *Jane's All the World's Aircraft 1960–1961* had the Fishbed listed as a Sukhoi design with an illustration of the Su-9 Fishpot.

Tests revealed that the MiG-21 was the first successful Soviet design to combine fighter and interceptor characteristics in one airframe. As a lightweight fighter capable of flying at Mach 2 with a relatively low-powered afterburning turbojet, it was comparable to the Lockheed F-104 Starfighter and Northrop F-5 Freedom Fighter, and the French Dassault Mirage III. The "tailed delta" layout did not find acceptance in the West but was used for several other Soviet designs including the Su-9 interceptor and the MiG E-150 prototype. The use of a movable shock cone and air intake at the front of the fuselage was not used outside the Soviet Union due to the fact that this configuration left only a very small space available for the radar. Use of a horizontal stabilizer with the delta wing improved stability and control at the extremes of the flight envelope, which made such maneuvering safer for lower-skilled pilots; this was of particular importance to the VPAF when it first received the MiG-21. In air combat, with a skilled pilot using the Atoll missile, the early MiG-21 could give a good account of itself against the Crusader and Phantom, being capable of pulling +7G in air combat maneuvers.

Thirteen VPAF pilots attained ace status with five or more aerial victories flying the MiG-21. Nguyen Van Coc was the VPAF ace of aces with 11 victories in the MiG-21. Twelve other VPAF pilots were credited with five or more aerial victories while flying the MiG-21: Pham Thanh Ngan, Nguyen Hong Nhi, and Mai Van Cuong with eight each; Dang Ngoc Ngu with seven; Vu Ngoc Dinh, Nguyen Ngoc Do, Nguyen Nhat Chieu, Le Thanh Dao, Nguyen Dang Dinh, Nguyen Duc Soat, and Nguyen Tien Sam with six each; and Nguyen Van Nghia with five. Pham Ngoc Lan and ace Nguyen Nhit Chieu – who both scored victories in the MiG-17 and MiG-21 – declared that they preferred the faster speed of the MiG-21 and its two Atoll missiles. Pham Ngoc Lan stated, "The MiG-21 was much faster, and it had two Atoll missiles which were very accurate and reliable when fired between

1,000 and 1,200 yards." Chieu preferred the MiG-21 "because it was superior in all specifications in climb, speed, and armament. The Atoll missile was very accurate and I scored four kills with it. In general combat conditions I was always confident of a kill over a F-4 Phantom when flying a MiG-21."

Between 1966 and 1972, the primary versions of the MiG-21 flown by the VPAF were:

MiG-21-F13 (NATO reporting name "Fishbed-C," known to US pilots as "MiG-21C"). "F" in the designation stands for *Forsirovannyy* (Uprated), while "13" referred to the K-13 infrared-seeking missile system known in the West as the "Atoll." The MiG-21F-13 was the first MiG-21 sub-type produced in large numbers and had one NR-30 30mm cannon mounted in the starboard fuselage below the cockpit, with 60 rounds; it carried two Atoll missiles on a hardpoint under each wing. The F-13 had an improved ASP-5ND optical gunsight and an upgraded SRD-5ND ranging radar. The MiG-21F-13 was also built under license in China as the Chengdu J-7 or F-7 for export, and some Chinese F-7s were provided to North Vietnam.

MiG-21PF (NATO designation "Fishbed-D," known to US pilots as "MiG-21D"). "P" in the designation stands for *Perekhvatchik* (Interceptor), while "F" designated *Forsirovannyy* (Uprated). This was the first all-weather interceptor version of the MiG-21. These were powered by the R11F2-300 turbojet and were fitted with the RP-21 radar with a much larger cone than the MiG-21F. The MiG-21PF featured a modified weapons control system that allowed use of the RS-2US (K-5MS) beam-riding missile in addition to the infrared-seeking K-13. The NR-30 integral cannon was removed, leaving the fighter with only missile armament.

MiG-21PFM (NATO reporting name "Fishbed-F," known to US pilots as the "MiG-21F"). In the designation "P" designates *Perekhvatchik* (Interceptor), "F" *Forsirovannyy* (Uprated), and M *Modernizirovannyy* (Modernized). This was the production version of the Ye-7M, modernized with an upgraded RP-21M radar, SRZO-2 Khrom-Nikkel IFF (identify friend or foe) transponder, and newer avionics. Late-production PFMs were able to carry a GSh-23 cannon and 200 rounds in an underbelly pod.

The MiG-21's primary deficiency was its short range, which was exacerbated by the internal fuel tanks being placed in the fuselage ahead of the center of gravity; this meant that as the internal fuel was consumed, the center of gravity shifted to the rear, which had the effect of making the aircraft statically unstable to the point that it was difficult to control, leaving the airplane with only a 45-minute endurance in clean condition. This was changed with the second-generation Soviet MiG-21s and on the Chinese J-7 copy of the original MiG-21F. An additional problem was that when the fuel state was at 50 percent, violent maneuvers could prevent fuel reaching the engine, causing it to shut down in flight and risking tank implosions since the fuel tanks were pressurized by air from the engine compressor. This affected the MiG-21F, PF, PFM, S/SM, and M/MF variants, the primary types used by the VNAF during the war. The aircraft was designed to be used in very short ground-controlled interception (GCI) missions, for which it became well known during the air war over North Vietnam.

As regarded combat capability, the delta wing was an excellent choice for a fast-climbing bomber interceptor, and the MiG-21bis was capable of a phenomenal climb rate of 45,250 feet per minute. However, in fighter vs. fighter combat where turning ability was important, the delta wing at a high angle of attack would lead to a rapid loss of speed. The Tumansky R-25 jet engine had a second fuel pump in the afterburning stage; this allowed the engine to develop an emergency maximum thrust of 21,896 pounds of force at altitudes under 13,000 feet. This could be used for a maximum of one minute in air combat, and three minutes in a wartime emergency, before the engine would overheat. With this temporary power, the MiG-21bis had a thrust-to-weight ratio slightly better than 1:1. Using this war emergency power provided the amazing sight of a blowtorch exhaust 15 feet long with six or seven "shock diamonds" visible inside the flame, which gave the name "diamond regime" to the war emergency power setting.

The MiG-21s first arrived in North Vietnam in April 1966. They were issued to the oldest fighter unit in the VPAF, the 921st "Sao Do" (Red Star) Fighter Regiment, which had come into existence on February 3, 1964, and had flown the MiG-17 in combat longer than any other unit. Following the conversion of the 921st to the MiG-21F-13, the less experienced 923rd Fighter Regiment continued to use their MiG-17s, while the 925th Fighter Regiment was organized in 1969 to use the

Shenyang J-6 version of the MiG-19S that was provided by China. The 923rd Fighter Regiment had been created on February 3, 1964 as a MiG-17 unit. Just before the 1972 offensive, a fourth unit, the 927th Fighter Regiment, was created to use the newly arrived MiG-21PFM.

Following Soviet practice, the VPAF operated its fighters under active guidance from ground controllers using radar to position the MiGs for an ambush of the American aircraft, using what was known to the US pilots as the "one pass, then haul ass" attack. While MiG-17s generally engaged in head-on attacks due to being slower than their opponents, the MiG-21s attacked from the rear, using their Atoll missiles which allowed them to attack from distances greater than a mile. The primary objective was to get the enemy fliers to drop their bombs prematurely with aerial victories entirely secondary. Once they had made their attack on the formation, the North Vietnamese disengaged rapidly, not waiting for retaliation. What the Vietnamese termed "guerilla warfare in the air" was generally successful throughout the war; over half of US strike forces intercepted by the VPAF were forced to jettison bombs without reaching their target owing to the hit-and-run MiG attacks. The tactic was perfectly suited to the MiGs, both of which were much smaller than their American opponents and far more difficult to spot and engage at combat ranges. When these aircraft and their active radar-guided ground control were combined with the SA-2 Guideline SAM and the vast numbers of AAA under the control of the North Vietnamese, the US forces were confronted with what was at the time the most formidable air defense system in the world, one in which the perceived US technological advantages were not that much greater than those of the defense.

The North Vietnamese, who were using a missile that was essentially a clone of the AIM-9B, did not experience many of the problems encountered by US pilots due to the fact that the majority of their interceptions were against non-maneuvering bomb-carrying aircraft. In air combat against US fighters, their success rate was likely similar to that experienced by the Americans.

Organizationally, the VPAF arose from very humble beginnings in ways similar to the PLAAF and the North Korean People's Air Force (NKPAF). Throughout the Vietnam War, the VPAF as an organization was far less experienced than its opponents in the US Air Force and US Navy.

OPPONENTS

Though the Vietnam People's Army (VPA) had become a credible offensive force on the ground in combat with the French armed forces during the First Indochina War, the insurgents had been nearly powerless against the French Expeditionary Air Force.

The first aircraft used by what became the VPAF were a DeHavilland Tiger Moth and a Morane-Saulnier M.S.223, which had been abandoned by their French owners when they fled the country in 1945 and had become the possessions of Emperor Bao Dai when he came to Vietnam that year. Later that year, Bao Dai offered the airplanes to the Viet Minh, who accepted them with the idea of using them as trainers for a new air arm. The two were dismantled and shipped by train from Hue to Hanoi by Phan Phac, head of the Department of Military Training and a veteran of the French Colonial Army. In early 1946, the two aircraft – still in their packing crates – arrived at Tong airfield, where mechanic Tran Dong led a team assigned to assemble them. While some thought was given to using them in combat, they eventually ended up at Chiem Hoa, where an airfield was created from a cornfield.

On March 9, 1949, Ho Chi Minh directed General Vo Nguyen Giap to establish the Air Force Research Committee (Ban Nghien Cuu Khong quan) under the leadership of Ha Dong, a member of the General Staff, to study how the army could establish an air force. The first task was to organize flight training, and 29 would-be pilots and ground crew were in the first class. Flight training was given by former Japanese POWs, as had been the case with the PLAAF. After a few hours of ground school, the first group of trainees moved to the airfield at Chiem Hoa, where they trained with the Morane-Saulnier and the Tiger Moth.

On August 15, 1949, Nguyen Duc Viet, a German soldier whose mother was German and father Vietnamese, who had been raised in Germany and come to Vietnam in 1946 as a member of the French *Légion Étrangère* where he had deserted and joined the Viet Minh in 1947, made the first flight for the Vietnamese air force. Taking off in the Tiger Moth that afternoon with mechanic Tran Dong as passenger, Viet reached an altitude of 3,000 feet. On return to the airfield, the Tiger Moth experienced engine problems as he descended. He managed to make a crash-landing on a sand bar and the aircraft was a total write-off, though both men emerged from the crash unharmed.

Though there were to be no formal navy or air force organizations in either North or South Vietnam according to the 1954 Geneva

Agreement, the North Vietnamese government did establish small navy and air force elements within the Army. At the same time, the government of South Vietnam established the Vietnam Air Force with personnel who had been trained by the French during the First Indochina War. In the North, formal development of an air arm began in March 1956, when 110 students were sent abroad for training. Thirty went to the USSR and 80 to China, where 50 commanded by Pham Dung began training to become fighter pilots, being trained on the Yak-17UTI and then the MiG-15. The other 30, led by Dao Dinh, began multi-engine training on the Lisunov Li-2, a Soviet-built license version of the Douglas DC-3. The 30 students sent to the USSR trained on the Li-2 and the Ilyushin Il-14 (known in the west as the Crate).

On May 1, 1959, the 919th Transport Regiment was officially organized for service, operating the Antonov An-2 (Colt), the Li-2, and the Il-14 cargo and passenger transport aircraft. Later that year the 910th Training Regiment was established at Cat Bi airfield with Yak-18 trainers to provide initial primary flight training in Vietnam before flying school candidates were sent abroad for advanced training. Reorganization in 1963 saw the separate Air Force and Air Defense Force merged into the unitary Air and Air Defense Force of the People's Army of Vietnam. The force was commanded by Colonel General Phung The Tai. His deputy was Colonel General Dang Tinh.

By 1960, 85 pilots had been trained at Cat Bi. Thirty-five were sent to China to receive advanced training on jets after the DRV had concluded a Mutual Defense Agreement with the Soviet Union, which promised to provide MiG-17 fighters for the new air force. A problem nearly all Vietnamese pilots had with the Soviet aircraft they flew was the fact that the airplanes were designed for pilots of average European size. The Vietnamese were on average smaller, with many too small for the ejection seats the aircraft were equipped with, and they had difficulty operating the controls due to their small size.

In September 1963, Lieutenant Chert Saibory, a pilot of the Royal Lao Air Force, defected to North Vietnam, providing his armed North American T-28 Trojan as the VPAF's first combat aircraft. With US aircraft now penetrating North Vietnamese airspace by night on clandestine supply missions for South Vietnamese commando units, the air force command decided to use it as a night fighter after repairs were finished. Lieutenant Saibory, who had been imprisoned after his defection, was released and assigned to teach VPAF pilots to fly the T-28.

At 2330 hours on February 15, 1964, an American aircraft was picked up on radar as it approached Con Cuong in Nghe An Province and tracked as it flew over Truong Son, on the Ho Chi Minh Trail, and headed north toward Hoi Xuan. Nguyen Van Ba took off in the T-28 at 0107 hours on February 16 with orders to intercept if possible. In the moonlight, he saw a black spot against a white cloud. Closing on the unknown aircraft, he recognized it from a distance of 500 yards as an American C-123 provider and fired two bursts. The aircraft caught fire and crashed in a forest near the North Vietnam–Laos border. One crewman – a member of the South Vietnamese air force – was pulled alive from the wreckage. It was the VPAF's first victory of the Second Indochina War.

On February 3, 1964, the 921st "Sao Do" Fighter Regiment, commanded by Lieutenant Colonel Dao Dinh Luyen, was commissioned when Lieutenant General Hoang Van Thai, Deputy Minister of Defense, signed order 18/QD to establish the unit. The air force took delivery of 36 MiG-17s from the Soviet Union. These were used in China for advanced training along with the previously provided MiG-15s. Training continued for the next six months until August 6, 1964, the day following the Tonkin Gulf Incident that would lead to war with the United States, when the pilots flew their MiG-15s and MiG-17s to Phuc Yen airfield outside Hanoi. By the end of 1964, there were 34 MiG-15s and MiG-17s based at Phuc Yen, the only one of the 21 airfields in North Vietnam that was capable of operating jets.

In the summer of 1965, another 30 trained jet pilots returned from China and on September 7, 1965, the 923rd Fighter Regiment, was formed, known as the "Yen The Squadron" and commanded by Lieutenant Colonel Nguyen Phuc Trach. By now, the MiG-15s had been removed from operational service and were being used as trainers by the 910th Training Regiment, thus allowing pilots to be completely trained in Vietnam as well as sent abroad.

In the summer of 1965, the best pilots of the 921st Fighter Regiment were selected for training to fly the supersonic MiG-21 that the Soviet Union had agreed to supply the VPAF. These pilots were sent to the USSR where they trained in Kazakhstan with other trainees from the Warsaw Pact and other allied nations. Initial fast-jet training was accomplished with the then-new Czech L-29 Delfin trainer, on which they were trained in all-weather jet flying as well as advanced aerobatics. From there, they moved to the MiG-17 with which they were already familiar for more experience-building before they progressed to the MiG-21UTI two-seat trainer. The Vietnamese pilots, on average, had fewer flying hours than their Warsaw Pact comrades, which was why they were provided "remedial" fast-jet training before moving to the MiG-21. When they returned that winter with the first shipments of the MiG-21F-13 fighters in December 1965, the 921st Fighter Regiment became the unit that would fly the MiG-21 in combat. More pilots were sent to the USSR in early 1967 to train on the MiG-21. The unit was fully equipped with MiG-21s and pilots trained to fly it by the summer of 1966.

Between April 1965 and November 1968, the VPAF claimed 244 US aircraft shot down, while admitting to the loss of 85 MiGs. Of these, 46 air combats occurred between F-4s and MiG-21s, with 27 F-4 Phantoms – 12 Navy and 15 Air Force – claimed shot down, for a VPAF loss of 20 MiGs.

Since gaining air superiority over US forces was out of the question, the North Vietnamese leadership decided to implement a policy of "air deniability." At the beginning of the campaign, North Vietnam possessed approximately 1,500 antiaircraft weapons, most of which were light 37mm and 57mm weapons. Within one year, however, the US estimated that the number had grown to over 5,000 guns, including 85mm and 100mm radar-directed weapons. During *Rolling Thunder*, 80 percent of US aircraft losses were attributed to antiaircraft fire.

Backing up the guns were the fighter aircraft of the VPAF, which originally consisted of only a few MiG-17 fighter aircraft. They were fast enough for hit and run ambush operations and they were also maneuverable enough to shock the American fighter community by shooting down more advanced F-8 Crusaders and F-105 Thunderchiefs, which had to quickly develop new tactics. The simple appearance of MiGs could often accomplish their mission by causing American pilots to jettison their bomb loads as a defensive measure.

In 1965, the NVAF had only 36 MiG-17s and a similar number of qualified pilots, which increased to 180 MiGs and 72 pilots by 1968. The Americans had at least 200 USAF F-4s and 140 USAF F-105s, plus 300 US Navy F-8s, A-4s, and F-4s flying from the aircraft carriers that operated three at a time in the Gulf of Tonkin, as well as scores of other support aircraft available at any given time.

Although most US aircraft losses continued to be inflicted by antiaircraft fire, USAF F-105s and Navy A-4 Skyhawks increasingly encountered SAMs and MiGs. North Vietnamese fighters also became a particular problem because of the lack of radar coverage in the Red River Delta region, which allowed the MiGs to surprise the strike forces. Airborne early warning aircraft had difficulty detecting the fighters at low altitudes and the aircraft themselves were difficult to see visually due to their relatively small size.

The VPAF flew its interceptors with guidance from ground controllers, who positioned the MiGs in ambush positions. The MiGs made fast and devastating attacks against US formations from several directions; usually the MiG-17s performed head-on attacks, while the MiG-21s attacked from the rear. After shooting down a few American planes and forcing the others to drop their bombs prematurely, the MiGs did not wait for retaliation, but disengaged rapidly. This "guerilla warfare in the air" proved very successful.

In late 1967, the US launched its most intense and sustained attempt to force North Vietnam into peace negotiations. Almost all of the targets on the Joint Chiefs' list were authorized for attack, including airfields that had been previously off limits. Only central Hanoi, Haiphong, and the Chinese border area remained prohibited from attack. A major effort was made to isolate the urban areas by downing bridges. Also struck were the Thai Nguyen steel complex, thermal and electrical power plants, ship and rail repair facilities, and warehouses. VPAF MiGs entered the battle en masse, as their capital was threatened, and kill ratios fell to one US aircraft lost for every two MiGs.

By 1968, the pilots of the VPAF had gained sufficient experience to allow them to meet the enemy on more favorable terms. During the period August–November 1968, prior to the bombing halt, MiGs accounted for 22 percent of the 184 American aircraft lost over the north: 75 Air Force, 59 Navy, and five Marine Corps.

4

THE RULES OF ENGAGEMENT

The air war fought over North Vietnam during the eight-and-a-half years between the Tonkin Gulf Incident in August 1964 and the end of US direct combat involvement in the war in January 1973 was fought under rules unlike any imposed on US combat forces before. The restrictions imposed during Operation *Rolling Thunder* in 1965–68 by the Johnson Administration would lead to much frustration on the part of the Navy and Air Force aircrews tasked with carrying out the missions and to much later finger-pointing at senior naval and air force leadership for not making a stronger effort to change the politically imposed policy of "limited escalation of force." The political aim of the policy was enunciated by Secretary of Defense Robert S. McNamara in Senate testimony regarding the policy: "total bombing would violate America's limited aims in the war."

Writing three years after the onset of the all-out bombing campaign, former State Department Far East specialist and White House advisor James Thomson ascribed much of the policy-making as it involved the bombing campaign and its "rules of engagement" to what he termed "wishful thinking." As Thomson recalled, "there were those who actually thought that after six weeks of air strikes, the North Vietnamese would come crawling to us to ask for peace talks. And what, someone asked in one of the meetings of the time, if they don't? The answer was that we would bomb for another four weeks, and that would do the trick." He concluded, "And finally, there was the recurrent wishful thinking that sustained many of us through the trying months of 1965–1966 after the air strikes had begun: that surely, somehow, one way or another, we would 'be in a conference in six months,' and the escalatory spiral would be suspended. The basis of our hope: 'It simply can't go on.'" Additionally, there was a bureaucratic detachment that further obscured reality. "In Washington the semantics of the military muted the reality of war for the civilian policy-makers. In quiet, air-conditioned, thick-carpeted rooms, such terms as 'systematic pressure,' 'armed reconnaissance,' 'targets of opportunity,' and even 'body count' seemed to breed a sort of games-theory detachment." With such lack of clarity of purpose at the policy-setting level, it is no surprise that the strategy and rules the campaign would follow would be so singularly unsuccessful.

The lessons learned in the Korean War had been lost, if they had ever been truly learned. The one thing that was obvious from the air campaign carried out against North Korea by the Navy and Air Force was that "limited escalation" didn't work. Originally, the communist targets had been railroad lines, marshaling yards, and roads – the infrastructure needed to bring supplies to the invading North Korean Army; this had little effect, with the only application of air power that did have a long-term effect being the battlefield close air support provided by the Marines flying from the escort carriers *Badoeng Strait* and *Sicily*, and the attacks carried out against rear area storage dumps by Navy squadrons flying from the fleet carrier *Valley Forge*, reinforced by *Philippine Sea* just toward the end of the fighting in the Pusan Perimeter. The result of this effort was to preserve the United Nations (UN) position on the Korean peninsula.

The Air Force had begun the Korean War by bombing "industrial" targets – such as they were in a non-industrialized country – with the B-29s able to bomb from 12,000 feet since there were virtually no antiaircraft defenses, in the expectation that such destruction of the North Korean state would force the enemy to stop their aggression. Strategic Air Command's General Curtis LeMay had advocated fire raids against the five largest cities in North Korea; this was turned down by President Truman, who believed that burning down more Asian cities five years after having burned out urban Japan would do more harm than good as regarded world opinion. Initially, bombing infrastructure such as the electric system and dams was prohibited since the UN command planned an invasion of the North in which they would need those facilities. After the Chinese intervention drove UN forces out of North Korea, the electric plants and dams were bombed in 1952, with no effect on the enemy's conduct of the war.

Bombing North Korean targets after the commencement of peace negotiations in the summer of 1951 was done primarily in order to find a "pain level" that would bring the enemy to the negotiating table prepared to accept the UN conditions. That never happened, even when the bombers attacked the North Korean agricultural dams in the spring of 1953, as well as the Suiho Dam hydroelectric complex which also provided power to Manchuria. James Michener's character of Admiral Tarrant in the novel *The Bridges At Toko-ri* declared his belief – which gave voice to the belief of UN air commanders – that the war would end on the day the communist negotiators were informed "They have even bombed the bridges at Toko-ri," as evidence that the United States would never stop until the opposition gave in. Despite everything, it never happened.

The US bombing campaign in the Korean War eventually escalated to the point that, as one participant described it, "We bombed every building there that was bigger than an outhouse, then we bombed the rubble, then we bombed the outhouses." The North Korean rail and road transport system was bombed repeatedly, and yet the necessary supplies got through to the front-line units; the capital at Pyongyang was flattened, but the political leadership of North Korea remained firm throughout. The power stations were bombed and finally the irrigation dams supporting North Korean agriculture that fed the population were bombed. The result was the total destruction of North Korea and the death of nearly ten percent of the civilian population, facts the American public was unaware of at the time and has remained unaware of since, but that are known by every North Korean and are the reason relations between the United States and North Korea have remained at a stalemate since 1953. Seventh Fleet commander Vice Admiral J.J. "Jocko" Clark declared, "the interdiction campaign didn't interdict." Escalation to the point of unlimited air warfare did nothing to affect the final outcome. The North Koreans and Chinese eventually brought things to an end following the death of Soviet dictator Joseph Stalin in March 1953 and the subsequent uncertainty of support by the Soviet leadership that replaced him; without that support, the war could not continue.

None of this experience had become the kind of necessary "institutional knowledge" that would have affected decision-making about Vietnam ten years later. In Thomson's view, underlying all this was something none of the civil rights warriors of the Kennedy–Johnson administrations would have ever admitted to:

> There is an unprovable factor that relates to bureaucratic detachment: the ingredient of cryptoracism. I do not mean to imply any conscious contempt for Asian loss of life on the part of Washington officials. But I *do* mean to imply that bureaucratic detachment may well be compounded by a traditional Western sense that there are so many Asians, after all; that Asians have a fatalism about life and a disregard for its loss; that they are cruel and barbaric to their own people; and that they are very different from us (and all look alike?). And I *do* mean to imply that the upshot of such subliminal views is a subliminal question whether Asians, and particularly Asian peasants, and most particularly Asian Communists, are really people – like you and me. To put the matter another way: would we have pursued quite such policies – and quite such military tactics – if the Vietnamese were white? Crucial throughout the process of Vietnam decision-making was a conviction among many policy-makers: that Vietnam posed a fundamental test of America's national will. Time and again I was told by men reared in the tradition of Henry L. Stimson that all we needed was the will, and we would then prevail. Implicit in such a view, it seemed to me, was a curious assumption that Asians lacked will, or at least that in a contest between Asian and Anglo-Saxon wills, the non-Asians must prevail.

The senior ranks of Naval Aviation by the early 1960s were dominated by veterans of the Pacific War, in which naval aviation had played a leading role in the defeat of Japan as the ultimate power in naval warfare, who had seen combat in Korea in senior positions as squadron commanders and air group commanders. Most of the squadron and air group leaders had flown as junior officers in the naval air campaign against North Korea. If the Korean War proved anything, it proved that air power was unable to break a committed opponent who had no strategic targets the destruction of which would impair or prevent further military action. The Navy's leadership had experienced this first-hand, yet at no time during the planning for intervention in Vietnam did this experience lead to any dissent against the political decision to use air power in an even more controlled escalation of force against a similar opponent.

The central event of the Korean War that seared the consciousness of every American involved at the time, staying with them as they rose in power and influence in the military and the government in the years following, was the intervention of the People's Republic of China in the war in the fall of 1950. At the time, Secretary of Defense Dean Acheson had called the Chinese intervention "the greatest defeat of American arms since the Second Battle of Bull Run." British historian Sir Martin Gilbert later described it as "the most thorough defeat of a previously-victorious army in recorded history." The US Army had been forced into the longest and most difficult retreat in its history, one in which the majority of American Korean War POWs were captured by the enemy; the Marines had survived their retreat in better order, but the casualties inflicted in that legendary "advance in a different direction" left a lasting impression on the officers who experienced it. Carrier aviators had operated "all out" in terrible conditions to support their comrades ashore and all remembered those terrible weeks of November and December, 1950.

Many of the middle-level politicians and government leaders who had counseled the invasion of North Korea to "roll back communism," who had declared that the Chinese were no threat to UN forces, were the senior leaders when a "second round" of possible conflict on the Asian mainland presented itself. Most prominent of these men was Secretary of State Dean Rusk, who as Undersecretary of State for Asian Affairs in 1950 had been the most prominent State Department advocate of "rolling back communism"; despite his experience ten years before, he voiced no concerns over the possible difficulties stemming from American intervention in Vietnam.

However, if the US was to become involved in Vietnam, Rusk and the others who had been in government in 1950 were committed to never again taking an action that might lead to another confrontation with China. Simply applying the "lesson" of Korea was not enough because they failed to understand that while the Chinese had intervened in Korea because of their long and close political history of supporting and protecting that country from the regional powers who would use the peninsula as a route of invasion to China, and their close cultural connections with the Korean people, the situation vis-a-vis China and Vietnam was the polar opposite; the contentious history between China and Vietnam stretched back thousands of years to the Chinese expulsion of what would become the Vietnamese people from southern China during the expansion of the Han civilization. The Chinese Communist leadership was not so disturbed by the thought of their ancient Vietnamese enemies being humbled by an enemy. Support was provided sparingly and grudgingly out of a need to maintain ideological unity and the reputation of China as the main regional communist power. Only an American invasion of North Vietnam could have changed the Chinese view of the war, and then only due to the threat such an action would pose to China itself. Unfortunately, the US decision-makers were not aware of this history and political background, with the result that their military decisions as to how they would fight a war with North Vietnam proceeded from faulty assumptions and resulted in actions not taken that might otherwise have led to a different outcome. Indeed, the Vietnamese were far more dependent on military and political support for their war from the Soviet Union than from the People's Republic; in any case, the years of what is more accurately the Second Indochina War coincided with the Cultural Revolution in China, an event that left the country nearly prostrate from self-inflicted wounds throughout Chinese society. After Richard Nixon's China visit in 1971, there was at least a tacit understanding that the Chinese would not fully support the North Vietnamese struggle to unify the country while the United States negotiated its departure from the war.

Thus tactics and the rules of engagement in Vietnam differed in detail from those in force during the Korean War, but the result was exactly the same until the final eight months of war in 1972, when President Nixon largely "took the gloves off" in response to the North Vietnamese offensive in South Vietnam.

From the outset of the air campaign against North Vietnam until Operation *Linebacker* in 1972, the North Vietnamese capital of Hanoi and the main port of Haiphong were largely off limits according to the Rules of Engagement. At Haiphong, a four-nautical-mile radius from the center of the port in all directions constituted the zone where all bombing was prohibited regardless, while a restricted zone in which targets could only be struck with the express approval of the Pentagon or White House extended another six nautical miles in all directions beyond the prohibited zone. There was a ten-nautical-mile radius prohibited zone from the center of Hanoi, with a restricted zone extending an additional 20 nautical miles beyond that. Additionally, there was a buffer zone in which bombing was prohibited within 30 miles of the Chinese border.

All third-party shipping in Haiphong was off limits to attack, even if those ships fired on US aircraft. This included ships from the Soviet Union and its allied states bringing war materiel, as well as Chinese ships. By the convoluted logic of the rules of engagement, supplies coming off a ship at the Haiphong docks could not be touched, but those same supplies in the back of a truck (so long as it was a truck specifically identified as being operated by the North Vietnamese military, despite the fact that all vehicles, civilian and military, were under military control) on the Ho Chi Minh trail was a legitimate target. It was right and proper to attack a bicycle loaded with supplies being pushed down the trail, but until 1967 it was prohibited to attack the factory in Hanoi that produced the bicycles.

The central concept in these rules of engagement was to minimize civilian casualties. Initially, bombing of North Vietnam was only allowed south of the 20th parallel, with the bomb line gradually moved north to eventually encompass the entire country by the end of 1965.

Targets that were allowed were initially restricted to petroleum–oil–lubricant (POL) storage sites and communication networks – roads, canals, and bridges. Strikes against airfields were banned until April 1967; while a MiG being flown in combat was a legitimate target, that same airplane sitting on an airfield being serviced for its next mission, or taking off and landing, was not to be attacked. One explanation offered for this policy was that if the VPAF airfields were attacked, the MiGs would be transferred to bases in China where they would be safe, as had been the case with Manchurian bases in the Korean War. No one noted that in Korea, the US Air Force had maintained patrols south of the Yalu River border with Manchuria that effectively kept the communist air forces based there from ever appearing over the main battlefield, and limited their ability to attack UN aircraft striking targets south of the Chongchon River in North Korea. Had the VPAF been forced to move to China, barrier patrols along the border would have restricted its ability to attack American strikes, with much of the country effectively out of range for its MiGs.

Similarly, when SAM sites were under construction, no strikes could be flown against them. Commander W.A. Franke, commanding officer of VF-21 aboard USS *Midway* (CVA-41), recalled on his return from the Hanoi Hilton in February 1973 that he spent much of the summer of 1965 watching construction of the SAM site that eventually fired the missile that shot him down that fall, unable under the rules of engagement to lead a mission to destroy the site before it became operational. There were other similar examples. By 1966, there were approximately 100 SAM sites around Hanoi, with some 30–40 located inside the prohibited zone, where they could not be attacked, but could fire on US aircraft attacking targets in the restricted zone surrounding the prohibited zone. The policy was changed in 1968 to allow a site that fired on US aircraft to be struck – so long as such strikes posed no likelihood of harm to civilians.

Coupled with the restrictions on what could be attacked were the bad tactics used by the attackers. Although studies after the Korean War had shown that over 500 carrier aircraft had been shot down over North Korea by antiaircraft guns, prewar planners had determined that modern jets were too fast to be tracked by ground gunners and that the real threat to aircraft was the surface-to-air missile, which was seen as a major threat to high-altitude aircraft. Francis Gary Powers' U-2 had been shot down over Sverdlovsk in May 1960 while flying at 70,000 feet, and Major Rudolf Anderson had been shot down over Cuba in the midst of the Cuban Missile Crisis on October 27, 1962, while his U-2 was at a similar altitude. Both planes were the victims of the SA-2 Guideline SAM. The SA-2's envelope was known to be from a minimum altitude of 3,500 feet to the altitude the two U-2s had been at when shot down. As a result, in order to protect attacking aircraft from the major threat posed by the SA-2 missile, strike tactics were changed to have the aircraft come in low, below the SA-2's minimum effective altitude. When making low-level attacks, the attackers have to spread out so that the bombs dropped by one aircraft do not explode under the one following. The result is that the strike force stays over the target longer than would be the case in a high-altitude dive-bombing attack. Bringing the aircraft down to under 3,000 feet over the target brought them in range of every antiaircraft weapon the enemy had, from the 23mm to the 37mm cannons and on up; many of these were the same types of weapons that had been employed in Korea. Although it had been determined after Korea that the higher speeds that attacking aircraft were capable of rendered the antiaircraft gun obsolete since the gun crew could not track the speedy attackers, this proved irrelevant in practice. The gunners didn't need to track individual aircraft, they only had to fill the air between the attacker and the target with as many bullets and shells as possible. It was the lesson the Eighth Air Force had learned over Germany in 1944–45, when the fighter groups were sent to strafe German airfields, resulting in the overwhelming majority of air losses in that final year of World War II happening at low level over the airfields. Once pilots were low, flying into a barrage of fire, the law of probability took over. During the years of *Rolling Thunder*, the major cause of aircraft loss was gunfire, as pilots were forced to fly extended distances well within range of hundreds of guns. A hit was inevitable, and a hit that put an airplane down was only slightly less inevitable. As Chuck Yeager once said when asked about his World War II experience, "going down on those airfields wasn't a fight – it was a crapshoot." Things hadn't changed in the following 20 years.

The first year of strikes following the Tonkin Gulf Incident saw the greatest losses-per-sortie of the war, as the attackers used the low-level strike tactics that had been learned during the Cuban confrontation in October 1962, where it had been discovered that flying at the lowest possible altitude was the best defense against SAMs when there was no means of detecting a launch. During the first three months of *Rolling Thunder*, the Navy's loss rate was 15–30 losses per 1,000 sorties. By late 1965 and early 1966, as the bombing reached further north and tactics became more realistic (no more treetop pullouts), losses dropped to seven per thousand, and over the course of the remainder of *Rolling Thunder*, when new technology was put to use to protect aircraft from SAMs and tactics were further changed to deal with flak, the loss rate stabilized at less than four per thousand. By late 1967, flak suppression tactics managed to bring losses below three per thousand sorties. This, while the number of guns in North Vietnam grew from fewer than 1,000 medium-to-heavy-caliber guns in spring 1965 to more than 3,000 over the course of that summer to between 6,000 and 7,000 guns after the end of 1966 through the end of the campaign two years later. The sector fire of North Vietnamese gunners became so good that they could fill a five-mile-square airspace from 3,500 feet to 20,000 feet with enough ordnance to make every airplane flying through that space statistically vulnerable. Every gun in the target area opened up simultaneously at peak intensity, and remained at that firing rate for the duration of the raid. Even small arms fire was added to the cacophony. Enemy guns were responsible for 68 percent of naval air losses over North Vietnam.

In the expectation of a coming US attack in the months following the Tonkin Gulf Incident, the Soviets had agreed to supply North Vietnam with a missile defense system and provide Soviet technicians to train the North Vietnamese crews in their operation. Operationally, this meant that the initial SAM sites were actually manned by Soviet personnel who actively took part in combat operations. The US military expected this development as a result of the experience in Cuba. The first SAM sites were spotted under construction in North Vietnam in April 1965. Both the Navy and Air Force commanders requested permission to strike the sites before they became operational, but the requests were turned down in Washington out of fear that any strike might result in Soviet personnel being harmed. As a result, while construction of the sites was observed, nothing was done to prevent their becoming operational; on June 24, 1965, an Air Force F-4 became the first victim of a SAM fired by a Soviet "training" crew.

5

ROLLING THUNDER, 1965–68

Lieutenant John Miles, a Skyhawk pilot in VA-163 "Saints" from USS *Oriskany* (CVA-34), later wrote of his experience aboard the carrier during their 1966 deployment:

> Max effort, of course, but within "guidelines" prescribed – no body punching, no uppercuts to the chin; only thrust and parry. Keep dancing, boys. When we were in the thick of it and losing Jim Dooley and Ralph Bisz and the rest, I could only think of some faceless policy maker saying "Gentlemen, we must accept two facts in this war: limited objectives and unlimited losses." It was a time filled with excitement and personal pride – and filled with sadness. Thrills and pride fade with time, but the sadness lives on – missing squadron mates, killed or captured. Fate. Luck. Providence. Timing.

Miles could as well have been writing of the experience of all naval aviators over North Vietnam during the years 1965–68 when they flew in Operation *Rolling Thunder*.

The unexpected outbreak of a conventional war in Southeast Asia demonstrated how unprepared both the Navy and the Air Force were to fight a non-nuclear war such as that they had engaged in ten years earlier in Korea. The lessons learned had been quickly forgotten as the services got back to their "real" mission: preparing to fight World War III with the Soviet Union. Outside of the F-8 Crusader, the aircraft of both services that had come into service since Korea had been designed and their pilots trained for strategic operations against the Soviet Union. The new war exposed years of neglect of training in conventional tactics, while the capabilities of the aircraft and their armament were ill-suited to the fighting they would face; particularly, Vietnam exposed that air-to-air missiles were not really ready to be the complete replacement for an on-board gun.

Naval Aviation was on the whole better prepared to operate in the Vietnam environment than the Air Force; the F-4 was so much better than what the Air Force operated that the service was forced to order the aircraft for its own use, and had nothing on hand or even in design that could equal the new A-6. Indeed, the Navy's ancient warhorse, the Korean-veteran A-1 Skyraider, was still so good at battlefield close air support that the Air Force grabbed every one as the Navy dropped them from the active inventory. When the A-7 Corsair II appeared, the Air Force was already involved in adapting it for their now-demonstrated needs. With the exception of the A-7, the Air Force leadership consistently refused to develop aircraft and weapons appropriate to the conflict in the belief that Vietnam was a temporary aberration.

An issue few had considered before the war that compounded the difficulty of maintaining a long-term air campaign was the one-year tour of duty policy adopted by the Pentagon for combat in Southeast Asia, with any further tour of duty strictly voluntary on the part of the individual. For the Air Force, while the first aircrews that arrived in-theater were highly experienced, the rapidly growing tempo and ever-expanding length of the operation demanded ever more personnel. The USAF rotation policy caused its own set of peculiar problems. A tour of duty was 100 missions over North Vietnam. The policy also required that no pilot would serve twice until everyone had served once. The result was that many pilots who had never flown a tactical aircraft or understood the tactical mission, as well as many pilots who had not been in a cockpit for years, were suddenly given orders rushing them through an abbreviated course of refresher training and sent to war in Southeast Asia. Too often, due to their rank, these inexperienced, unqualified officers were placed in combat leadership roles for which they had no background or experience. The result was a growing lack of experienced aircrews in mid-level and senior positions; and a resulting division between leaders who often avoided combat missions they knew themselves unqualified to lead, and younger, lower-ranking pilots who did have the experience and who were thus alienated from their leadership.

The issue was different for the Navy, which stopped the "generalist" policy at the outset of World War II, since maintaining a policy of specialization for its aircrews through service in the same "community" – fighter, attack, patrol, etc. – for the duration of their careers with rare exception, a policy that both retains and expands particular expertise.

There was no limit to the number of combat missions a naval aviator could fly over North Vietnam as there was with the Air Force. A typical tour of duty for a pilot in a squadron was three years. In that time, it was not abnormal to make two or three deployments to the Tonkin Gulf, with aviators typically flying 60–70 missions over North Vietnam during each period on station. Thus, in a single squadron assignment, a naval aviator could fly well over double the 100-mission limit that sent an Air Force pilot home with no expectation of ever having to return. Navy fliers could expect to be sent back again at least once more and possibly a third time before their time in a squadron was over. These policies ensured continued combat exposure in multiple deployments; surviving naval aviators became highly experienced. Surviving pilots flew even more combat tours as the supply of new aviators tightened. The result was that the same group of pilots flew the missions over North Vietnam – and took the majority of the losses. The combination of rising combat losses with the increasing unpopularity of the war resulted in serious morale problems within the naval aviation community. By 1966, there were severe personnel problems, particularly with pilots and naval flight officers (NFOs) as junior officers decided not to make the service a career and departed when they had completed their service obligation.

As well as a shortage of aircrew, the Navy faced a shortage in aircraft, as combat and operational loss rates far exceeded prewar planning estimates. In 1966, A-4 Skyhawks were being lost at a rate of six a month. However, with procurement contracts still at peacetime levels, only ten Skyhawks a month were coming off the production line, for distribution to both Atlantic and Pacific fleet squadrons and the Marines. Short-term relief came from depleting stateside and Atlantic Fleet units of aircraft, while the technicians in squadrons on the line at Yankee Station were forced to scavenge damaged aircraft for parts due to shortages in the supply line.

Another complicating factor was the weather. The cyclical monsoon patterns meant that the weather was deplorable for flight operations over North Vietnam from late September/early October to late March/ early April, during which rain and fog tended to conceal targets. Lack of adequate all-weather and night-bombing capability necessitated that the majority of US missions be conducted during daylight hours, thereby easing the burden on the North Vietnamese air defense forces.

Claims of damage per sortie inflicted on North Vietnam became as inflated as similar claims on the battlefield in South Vietnam where the "body count" was the statistical measure of professional success. VA-164 Skyhawk pilot Lieutenant Frank Elkins wrote in his journal shortly before his loss in October 1966:

> There's an incredible overestimation on the damage we do. It's mostly imagination or propaganda. Radio Hanoi yells about the numbers of aircraft shot down in a given day, and we laugh and call them crazy, wild propagandists. Then we tell about the bridges, trucks, barges, and POL storage areas which we've blown to hell every day, and our releases read worse than the Hanoi crap. Hell, if you took the combined estimated BDA [bomb damage assessment] reports from just the time we've been here, a total like that would cripple the little nation. As Norris [another pilot in the squadron] says, "I'd hate to be an aviator's mother back in the States reading Hanoi's evaluation of antiaircraft successes, but I'd hate worse to be a truck driver's mother in Hanoi reading the American estimates of trucks blown up – it reads like a Detroit production figure!"

The obsession with numbers on the part of the Pentagon leadership blinded them to the actual goals of the air campaign. Sorties were flown for the sake of flying sorties, with strikes sometimes launched in which all the aircraft in the flight carried between them fewer bombs than was the maximum load each individual airplane was capable of, to pad the sortie and bomb drop rate. Stories of missions that bombed empty jungle listed as "suspected truck parks" became common as each carrier and air wing sought to produce results that reflected well on them and on the Navy in its comparison to the Air Force. The result in the front-line squadrons was universal cynicism on the part of those called on to fly the missions from which the statistics were created.

The operation of the air war was also complicated by domestic US politics and the additional fear of committing some act that would bring formal involvement in the war on the part of the Soviet Union and China, despite firm intelligence throughout the period that neither country was in a position to do so, with the Soviets experiencing a major change in leadership and the Chinese suffering from the excesses of Mao's "Cultural Revolution." It was not until mid-1966 that many targets that had been on the forbidden list at the outset of *Rolling Thunder* were taken off that list and attacked. Throughout the war until the end of 1967, President Johnson doled out sensitive targets one by one in response to entreaties from the military leadership, while simultaneously trying to placate the doves in Congress and within his own administration with periodic cutbacks and holiday halts in the bombing, combined with half-hearted peace initiatives made following any escalation in the hopes that the event had finally convinced the enemy it was time to end the war. In the end, this erratic course satisfied no one and only resulted in continuing failure to resolve the war while the enemy increased in strength and ability.

The initial bombing of North Vietnam was undertaken in Operation *Pierce Arrow*, the retaliation strike for the North Vietnamese "attacks" in the Tonkin Gulf Incident, on August 5, 1964. Sixty-four sorties were flown by aircraft from the carriers *Ticonderoga* and *Constellation* against the North Vietnamese torpedo boat bases of Hon Gai, Loc Chao, Quang Khe, and Phuc Loi, and the oil storage depot at Vinh. Skyraider pilot Lieutenant Richard Sather was killed, while Skyhawk pilot Lieutenant (jg) Everett Alvarez, Jr., successfully bailed out and was captured. Following these strikes, no further military action was taken during the fall election campaign, in which Lyndon Johnson ran as the "peace" candidate.

Throughout late 1964, US forces were gathered in the western Pacific to support the launch of "Level Four" operations. USAF units moved into Royal Thai Air Force bases in Thailand, while the Navy increased the number of aircraft carriers assigned to the Seventh Fleet and Task Force 77. Once President Johnson had secured election as president in his own right on November 3, 1964, planning for the attacks moved into higher gear. The four objectives of the coming campaign were to boost the sagging morale of the Republic of Vietnam; to persuade North Vietnam to cease its support for the communist insurgency in South Vietnam without sending ground forces into communist North

Vietnam; to destroy North Vietnam's transportation system, industrial base, and air defenses; and to halt the flow of men and materiel into South Vietnam. As late as February 8, 1965, in a cable to Ambassador Maxwell Taylor, President Johnson stressed that the paramount goal of a bombing campaign would be to boost Saigon's morale, not to influence Hanoi. The president expressed the hope "that the building of a minimum government will benefit by... assurances from us to the highest levels of the South Vietnamese government that we... intend to take continuing action." The South Vietnamese government created by the November 1963 military coup was completely unstable, with various factions coalescing around different military leaders and conspiring against each other; during the first six months of 1965 there would be four extra-legal changes of government leadership. Under the doctrine of "gradualism," threatening increasing destruction would serve as a more influential signal of American determination than destruction itself; it was thought better to hold important targets "hostage" by bombing trivial ones.

President Johnson later wrote about why he made the decision to fight a limited campaign of escalation, rather than an all-out aerial assault on North Vietnam:

> By keeping a lid on all the designated targets, I knew I could keep the control of the war in my own hands. If China reacted to our slow escalation by threatening to retaliate, we'd have plenty of time to ease off the bombing. But this control – so essential for preventing World War III – would be lost the moment we unleashed a total assault on the North, for that would be rape rather than seduction, and then there would be no turning back. The Chinese reaction would be instant and total.

Lyndon Johnson, who had been in the Senate in 1950, remembered the crisis following the Chinese intervention in North Korea, which had led to the Democrats losing their majority in Congress during the off-year elections held the month the intervention began, and had no intention of seeing that happen in the 1966 elections. A further refinement of the action plan was developed by William and McGeorge Bundy on November 29, 1964, with a shorter target list that the Joint Chiefs opposed.

In January 1965, the political and military structure of South Vietnam was deteriorating, due to pervasive corruption on all levels of the South Vietnamese government that alienated the rural population and many of those in the cities, and the success of communist guerilla activity throughout the country outside of the cities. In December 1964, the ARVN had suffered two major defeats at the hands of the guerillas; by early January, it was near to collapse. The United States was faced with two options: withdraw from South Vietnam or enter the war as an active participant.

Matters came to a head with the Viet Cong attack on Camp Holloway in Pleiku on February 7, 1965, which destroyed or damaged several B-57 air force bombers as well as killing ten and injuring 100 US personnel. The attack demanded immediate action, and resulted in a reprisal raid known as Operation *Flaming Dart*. This involved strikes by the three carriers on station in the Tonkin Gulf: *Ranger* (CVA-61), *Coral Sea* (CVA-43), and *Hancock* (CVA-19). *Ranger*'s strike against a North Vietnamese army camp north of the demilitarized zone (DMZ) was recalled due to bad weather, while the *Coral Sea* and *Hancock* strikes against Dong Hoi and Vinh succeeded in knocking down 16 buildings at a cost of eight A-4s damaged by flak and Lieutenant Edward A. Dickson becoming the second American pilot killed in the war when his Skyhawk exploded. A sapper raid against an American enlisted men's billet at Qui Nhon on the night of February 10 killed 23 and wounded 21 US military personnel, and led to *Flaming Dart II* the next day by the three carriers against the port of Chanh Hoa. Lieutenant Commander Robert H. Shumaker of VA-154 was captured when he ejected from his Skyhawk after it was damaged by blast from his own bombs, to become the second POW after Alvarez. These attacks were small-scale operations launched against the southern region of North Vietnam, where the majority of the bases for the People's Army of Vietnam (PAVN) and its supply dumps were located.

Neither strike had any effect on the enemy; they were flown in response to President Johnson's exclamation, "I've had enough of this!" when informed of the Pleiku attack. At their conclusion, Secretary of Defense McNamara held a press conference at the Pentagon where he declared the missions satisfactory because "Our primary objective, of course, was to communicate our political resolve." After three months of indecision following the Kennedy assassination, the decision had been made: the United States was willing to commit itself to direct involvement in the war.

At this point, most American military personnel were enthusiastic about the possibility of engaging in the war. Belief in the goals was high. As VA-94's CO, Commander Paul Peck, remembered, "Everybody was very enthusiastic. The pace was exciting; something most of us had been training to do for years and now we were doing it. I think everyone was pitching in and working real hard, and I really didn't have much time to stand around and hold pep talks, nor did I need to."

What would become Operation *Rolling Thunder* began life as "Step Four" of Operations Plan (OPLAN) 34A-64, the planned escalation of military action against North Vietnam to cause the communists to cease fighting in South Vietnam that had been approved in January 1964, as a program of selective intrusions and attacks against the North Vietnamese of graduated intensity.

Step Four of the OPLAN was the commencement of an American-led aerial bombing campaign to damage North Vietnam's capacity to support the actions of the NLF in the south, or cripple the North Vietnamese economy sufficiently to make the North Vietnamese leadership decide that the extent of the losses was not worth continued support of the war in the South. By early 1964, most of the civilians surrounding President Johnson shared the Joint Chiefs of Staff's collective faith in the efficacy of strategic bombing to one degree or another, reasoning that a small nation like North Vietnam, with a tiny industrial base that was just emerging after the First Indochina War, would be reluctant to risk its new-found economic viability to support the insurgency in the South. Any slight study of Vietnamese history would have demonstrated how mistaken this belief was. In March 1964 CinCPac commenced development of plans for a sustained eight-week air campaign that would escalate in three stages. This was published at the end of August as CinCPac OPLAN 37-64, which included the "98 targets list" developed for "Level Four" operations in OPLAN 34A.

Bridges, rail yards, docks, barracks, and supply dumps were all targeted, with selection based on a criterion system with the goal of: (a) reducing North Vietnamese support of communist operations in Laos and South Vietnam, (b) limiting North Vietnamese capabilities to take direct action against Laos and South Vietnam, and finally (c) impairing North Vietnam's capacity to continue as an industrially viable state.

Fears of possible counter moves or outright intervention by the Soviet Union, China, or both, affected the planning, since the leadership of the Johnson Administration contained several senior members who had been chastened by the Chinese intervention in that war and the near-disaster to US forces that had resulted.

Plans for an air campaign were re-examined and revised. On February 13, a new plan merging targets and priorities from the lists produced by the Bundys and the JCS was approved and given the name *Rolling Thunder*. The campaign was not planned as a reply to specific actions by the North Vietnamese, but was rather intended as a larger response to the growing hostilities as a whole. While some within the administration believed the campaign would be costly and might not work, they agreed with Secretary McNamara, who reasoned that it was "an acceptable risk, especially when considered against the alternative of introducing American combat troops." The *Rolling Thunder* plan called for an eight-week air campaign consistent with the restrictions imposed by Johnson and Secretary of Defense Robert S. McNamara and would be aimed at targets in the North Vietnamese "panhandle" south of the 19th parallel (so called because the geographic shape of the country was reminiscent of a profile view of a cooking pan), each of which would have to be cleared individually by the President and McNamara. If at the end of that period the insurgency continued in the south with DRV support, strikes against the DRV would be extended with intensified efforts against targets north of the 19th parallel. The US strategy was based on the belief that selective pressure, controlled by Washington, combined with diplomatic overtures, would prevail and compel Hanoi to end its aggression.

Despite the hopes that initiation of an air campaign against the north would obviate any need to introduce American combat troops, NLF actions against the air base at Da Nang, the northernmost airfield in South Vietnam and the only one other than Bien Hoa and Tan Son Nhut outside Saigon capable of supporting jet operations, resulted in a decision to send in Marines to defend the airfield. F-100s of the 3rd Tactical Fighter Wing had deployed there from Clark AFB in the Philippines in early February, followed at the end of the month by F-105s of the 35th Tactical Fighter Wing. These aircraft had participated in the first attacks of *Rolling Thunder* on March 2. With the base overcrowded by the arrival of new squadrons, a major expansion was approved. It was crucial that the area surrounding the airfield be cleared of the enemy.

On March 8, the 9th Marine Regiment executed an amphibious landing at Red Beach north of Da Nang, while the 1st Battalion, 3rd Marines, arrived at Da Nang Air Base by air from Naha Air Base on Okinawa. This marked the first deployment of American combat troops to South Vietnam. The 9th Marine Expeditionary Brigade was tasked with defending the airfield while overall responsibility for defending the Da Nang area remained with the ARVN. Initiation of *Rolling Thunder* had changed the American commitment to the war irrevocably.

Following *Flaming Dart II*, Operation *Rolling Thunder* was scheduled to begin on February 20, ten days later. The instability of South Vietnam was, however, demonstrated by a failed coup that week, while bad weather afterwards forced several postponements of the initial strike. The first *Rolling Thunder* strikes, involving USAF and VNAF aircraft striking north of the DMZ, was finally flown on March 2. Aircraft from *Ranger* and *Hancock* flew the Navy's first *Rolling Thunder* missions on March 15. Preceded by eight F-8C Crusaders from *Hancock* which went after AAA positions, 64 A-4s and A-1s hit the ammunition depot at Phu Qui, halfway between Vinh and Thanh Hoa, with two RF-8As following to take bomb damage assessment photos. Even with the Crusaders attacking the defensive gun sites, the Skyhawks and Skyraiders were still met with heavy defensive fire when they went in to drop their Mark 81 250-pound bombs and fire their Zuni rockets. An A-1H from *Ranger* was badly hit by AAA and ditched after leaving the target area. Lieutenant (jg) Charles F. Clydesdale was lost when he was unable to exit the sinking airplane, to become the first casualty of *Rolling Thunder*. This first Navy *Rolling Thunder* raid was considered a limited success.

From the beginning of the air campaign, political leaders in Washington dictated which targets would be struck, the day and hour of the attack, the number, types of aircraft and the tonnages and types of ordnance utilized, and sometimes even the direction of the attack. In addition to the restrictions on air strikes against Hanoi and Haiphong, there was an additional 30-mile buffer zone also extended along the length of the Chinese frontier. Targeting bore little resemblance to reality, in that the sequence of attacks was uncoordinated and the targets were approved randomly – even illogically. Airfields, which, according to any rational targeting policy, should have been hit first, were off limits. There was little consultation between President Johnson and the military chiefs during the target selection process, which was usually held over lunch in the White House on Tuesdays. Even the chairman of the Joint Chiefs, General Earl G. Wheeler, was not present for most of the critical discussions of 1965 and participated only occasionally thereafter. Until 1967, no senior military leader was allowed to attend the target selection meetings and thus the military leadership had no input in the target selection process. CinCPac Admiral Ulysses S. Grant Sharp, Jr., later stated, "The omission, whether by deliberate intent or with the indifferent acquiescence of Secretary McNamara, was in my view a grave and flagrant example of his [McNamara's] persistent refusal to accept the civilian-military partnership in the conduct of our military operations." The president and his Tuesday lunch group never received information from the military that would allow them to make informed decisions. They had little knowledge of the capabilities of military equipment or of realities, such as the weather over North Vietnam, that affected operations. When targets were finally approved, the operational aircrews were never given more than two weeks to destroy targets before they were taken off the approved list.

In the fall of 1965, North Vietnam was divided into six "route packages" for targeting and mission planning. Route Package 6, which included Hanoi and Haiphong, was the most dangerous and was divided in half, with Route 6A covering Hanoi and the area west and north of the capital, while 6B was centered on the port of Haiphong. On April 1, 1966, operational control of air operations over the North was regularized, with the Air Force assigned responsibility for strikes in Route Packages 5 and 6A, the closest areas to that service's airfields in Thailand, while Air Force and Marine units based in South Vietnam were assigned operations in Route Package 1 just north of the DMZ. The Navy assumed control of operations in Route Packages 2, 3, 4, and 6B, which covered the heavily populated coastal region of North Vietnam.

Over the course of 1965, the naval air campaign in Southeast Asia gradually grew in scope and intensity. The specific objectives of the *Rolling Thunder* bombing program against North Vietnam were to (1) interdict the enemy's lines of communication into Laos and South Vietnam, (2) destroy his physical ability to support the war in Southeast Asia, and (3) deprive him of external military assistance without triggering Soviet or Chinese Communist military intervention. This last point was the major lesson of Korea, and it hampered operations in Vietnam as much as it had in the earlier war.

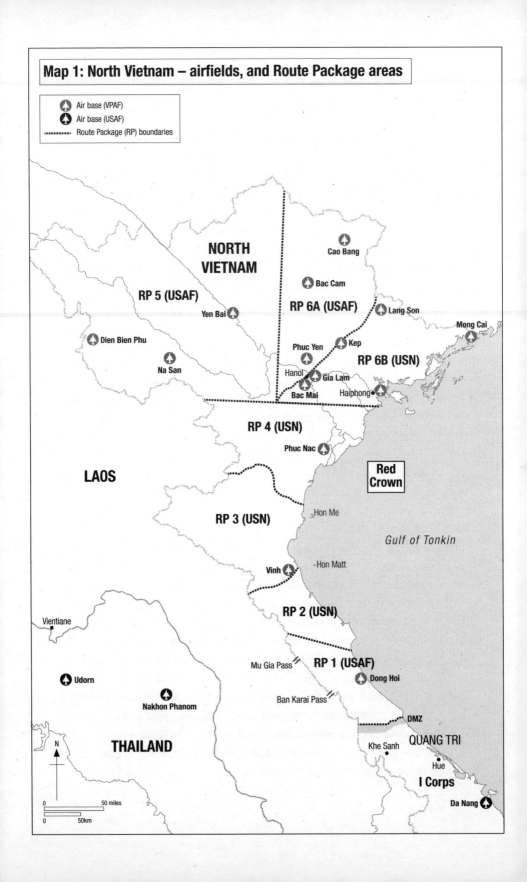

Map 1: North Vietnam – airfields, and Route Package areas

- Air base (VPAF)
- Air base (USAF)
- Route Package (RP) boundaries

NORTH VIETNAM

Cao Bang

Bac Cam

RP 5 (USAF)

Yen Bai

RP 6A (USAF)

Lang Son

Mong Cai

Dien Bien Phu

Phuc Yen

Kep

RP 6B (USN)

Na San

Hanoi

Gia Lam

Bac Mai

Haiphong

Red Crown

RP 4 (USN)

Phuc Nac

LAOS

RP 3 (USN)

Hon Me

Gulf of Tonkin

Hon Matt

Vinh

RP 2 (USN)

Vientiane

RP 1 (USAF)

Udorn

Mu Gia Pass

Dong Hoi

Nakhon Phanom

Ban Karai Pass

DMZ

THAILAND

Khe Sanh

QUANG TRI

Hue

I Corps

Da Nang

N

0   50 miles
0   50km

Operations over South Vietnam had first priority for the Navy's air resources. Due to the scarcity of the airfields in South Vietnam capable of sustaining jet operations, one-third of the sorties flown in South Vietnam were by carrier-based aircraft operating from Dixie Station, a point in the Tonkin Gulf some 100 miles off the coast, east of Qui Nhon. This assignment was generally carried out by newly arrived air wings, to prepare them for the more dangerous environment over the North.

The majority of *Rolling Thunder* missions were flown by the Air Force, with units operating from four Royal Thai Air Force (RTAF) bases in Thailand. Navy strikes were launched from the aircraft carriers of Task Force 77, cruising off the North Vietnamese coast at Yankee Station, approximately 100 miles east of Haiphong in the Tonkin Gulf. Naval aircraft, which had shorter ranges and carried lighter bomb loads than their air force counterparts, flew the majority of their strikes against coastal targets.

When *Rolling Thunder* first began, air strikes were limited to targets south of the 20th parallel. By the summer, it was clear the North Vietnamese were not going to respond politically to the air campaign. Authorized strikes gradually progressed northward toward Hanoi and then northwest of the capital, while observing the prior restrictions regarding Hanoi, Haiphong, and the Chinese border. Between the outset of *Rolling Thunder* on March 2 and December 24, 1965, when a temporary bombing halt was ordered by President Johnson to allow the North Vietnamese the opportunity to respond politically, Task Force 77's aircraft flew 31,000 combat and combat support sorties, dropped 64,000 bombs, and fired 128,500 rockets in the effort to interdict the enemy's lines of communication to the South. While these statistics appeared important and were used by McNamara's analysts at the Pentagon in their assessments of progress, in truth they had little connection to the operational question that mattered the most: was the enemy reducing his activities as a result of these attacks?

The Vietnam People's Air Force first appeared in combat on April 3, 1965, when two flights of four MiG-17s were launched from No Bai airbase against a large Navy attack on the Thanh Hoa Bridge. They claimed an F-8 Crusader shot down, while losing one of their own, written off when it landed on a riverbed after running short of fuel. Early on in the campaign, sorties flown and tonnages of bombs dropped became the statistical measurement of progress. There would be times during the campaign when there were shortages of bombs as domestic production ramped up, most notoriously in the fall of 1966, when shortages were such that bombs from World War II that had been untouched in 20 years were taken out of storage and sent on to the carriers and air bases in Thailand for use. Many were duds, which led to a lowering of morale as pilots began to wonder why they were risking their lives to drop bombs that were known to be defective. The drive for high sortie rates led to ludicrous situations where aircraft were launched on missions with as few as a single bomb each, to add to the sortie rate. As of December 24, 1965, 180 US aircraft had been lost during the campaign: 85 Air Force, 94 Navy, and one Marine. Air Force aircrews had flown 25,971 sorties and dropped 32,063 tons of bombs. Naval aviators had flown 28,168 sorties and dropped 11,144 tons. By the middle of 1966, many pilots began to look on the sortie rate with the same kind of cynicism that their infantry brethren in-country held for the "body count" used by their Army superiors as the measurement of battlefield success.

Political control of the bombing irked the men in the cockpits. Commander Harry Jenkins, CO of VA-163 "Saints," aboard USS *Oriskany*, remembered a mission he flew in late August 1965:

> I took a route to the target that took me nearly to the Chinese border by way of a railroad. I came south down the railroad tracks to the target and passed two trains sitting on the rails. I could have chewed them up with the CBUs [cluster bomb units] I was carrying, but you just didn't touch anything unless it had been cleared.

In the spring of 1965, aerial reconnaissance spotted the construction of launch sites for SA-2 antiaircraft missiles. Throughout the rest of the campaign, the number of missiles and sites would constantly increase, while more and more conventional antiaircraft artillery was deployed by the North Vietnamese and their air force was strengthened with the supply of MiG-19 (F-6) fighters by China and advanced MiG-21s by the Soviet Union. In 1964, the USSR had supplied North Vietnam with approximately $25 million in aid. The next year, when the bombing campaign began, this jumped to $240 million, and $670 million in 1966. In 1966, 122 Russian ships arrived in the main port of Haiphong with military supplies. By the following year the total was 185, one arrival every other day. In 1966, a year after the first SAM sites were built, US intelligence counted 200 sites; not all of these mounted SAMs all the time, but they provided alternative locations for the missiles to be moved around ahead of US strikes against them. By 1967, the North Vietnamese air defense system included nearly 8,000 gun sites, with weapons ranging from 37mm to 57mm to 85mm.

The North Vietnamese air defenses were organized with the cooperation and active participation of Soviet military advisors. The first such advisors arrived in 1965 to establish both the antiaircraft artillery units and the missile (SAM) units. Throughout 1965–66, the SAM sites in North Vietnam were manned and operated by Soviet personnel assigned from the PVO/Strany, the air defense forces of the Soviet Union. There was no official admission by any party to this Soviet military role, which was similar to the Soviet role in the Korean War. One of these officers, then-Senior Lieutenant Vadim Petrovich Shcherbakov, a fire control operator who served with the 260th "Bryansky" Antiaircraft Missile Regiment, arrived in Vietnam with the regiment in March 1966. The unit's assignment was to establish operational SAM batteries and train the North Vietnamese 274th Antiaircraft Missile Regiment for combat duty. Shcherbakov was credited by both the Soviets and the VPAF with ten air-to-air engagements and six shootdowns in 1966–67, the only Soviet officer to be so credited officially during the war. Upon his return to the Soviet Union in 1967, Shcherbakov received the Order of Lenin, the highest Soviet decoration, for his service.

Between March 2, 1965, when the campaign began, and March 31, 1968, when President Johnson announced a "bombing halt" in his attempt to bring a negotiated end to the war, Operation *Rolling Thunder* became the most intense air/ground battle waged during the Cold War. It was the most difficult aerial campaign fought by the United States since the bombardment of Germany during World War II. Supported by its communist allies, North Vietnam eventually fielded a potent mixture of sophisticated air-to-air and surface-to-air weapons, creating one of the most effective air defenses ever faced by American fliers. During this time frame, the US Navy lost 382 aircraft, of which 57 were shot down by SAMs and the rest by AAA. American military commanders, who had pushed for permission to strike the SAM sites when the first ones were discovered under construction in April 1965, were not allowed to hit the sites until after they became operational and several aircraft had already been lost.

The first Navy loss to SAMs occurred on the night of August 11–12, 1965, when Lieutenant Commander Francis D. Roberge and Lieutenant (jg) Donald H. Brown, flying A-4Es from VA-23 aboard USS *Midway*, were attacked by SAMs while on a road recce 60 miles south of Hanoi. Brown's Skyhawk was lost with the pilot, while Roberge's was damaged; he managed to bring it back aboard the carrier. The reaction was ill-conceived and costly. Seventy-six Skyhawks were launched from the carriers on August 13 to seek out and destroy SAM sites. AAA shot down five planes with two pilots killed while the other three managed to get their damaged aircraft over water before they ejected. Seven other Skyhawks were damaged, while no SAM sites were found. One of the two pilots killed was Commander Harry Thomas, CO of VA-153 "Blue-Tailed Flies." The Navy never hunted for SAMs that way again.

Thomas was succeeded in command of VA-153 by executive officer (XO) Commander Davie Leue. Both were veterans of the Korean War, where Thomas had gained experience in night attack, and was a believer in the value of night operations even by a squadron operating an airplane without radar like the Skyhawk. He had already demonstrated the ability of a small number of airplanes to have an outsized effect in attacking convoys traveling at night after initiating night flying training in the squadron when he succeeded to command following the promotion of Commander Peter Mongilardi to CAG of Air Wing 15. Following Thomas's loss, Leue continued the night work. "We taught young, first-tour aviators to hit trucks at night underneath a flare. They embraced the tactic… and became very good at it. We were the boss at night… and when we caught the enemy, we killed him." Leue remained in command of the squadron for their 1966 deployment aboard *Constellation*, where he honed the night operation.

During the 1966 deployment, Leue and his wingman got incredibly lucky one night when they came upon a truck convoy moving a SAM battery.

I coasted in and hit the lead truck while my wingman hit the back one, got it burning, and trapped the convoy. We ate 'em up. There was exploding ordnance, fuel running down a hill and exploding, and the scene was visible for a hundred miles. The two of us eventually ran out of ammo and called in the A-6s to finish it up.

While the A-6 Intruders were designed for night and all-weather operation, VA-153 found that the Intruders were better against hard targets that could be picked up by radar; trucks were a target best found visually. Leue described his main tactic:

> I'd put my wingman at 4,000 feet, lights out. I'd get on Route 1 at 500 feet, and rocket down the road with my wing down a little bit, and just like that, I'd see trucks... Once the flares were released, then underneath it was VFR. We'd operate at 100, 200 feet, dropping snake eyes and cluster bombs, eating up a lot of trucks.

Leue was able to interest the commander of fellow Skyhawk squadron VA-155 in night missions and the *Constellation* Skyhawks became noted for their interdiction operations at night. Leue later described their success: "Our squadron successfully attacked trucks in two cruises and I'm convinced that's the most good we did."

Unfortunately, despite the demonstrated success, Leue was never able to convince any Skyhawk squadron commander other than VA-155's Commander Edmund "Bud" Ingley to adopt the tactic. "They all thought it was a foolhardy mission. They really did, though we lost more dearly in the daytime than we did at night." Leue flew 235 missions over the two VA-153 tours, the majority at night.

One major problem confronting the naval air war until 1968, when losses were such that the rules about how much combat time a pilot could accrue were dropped, was that most of the air wing commanders in the early years did not have combat experience prior to taking their pilots into combat. There were few Korean veterans. At the time, the squadron commanders who returned from a deployment with experience were not allowed to "fleet up" (be promoted) to CAG and return to lead wings in Vietnam. The problem was they had by then accumulated too much combat time. Dave Leue was one who wanted to go back as a CAG and couldn't. "I felt like I was an expert in keeping guys alive in combat. I had a Ph.D. in how to get into tough places without being killed, without getting equipment hurt, and that's why I wanted to go back to Vietnam as an air wing commander." However, according to the rules of the time, the experienced and proficient pilots didn't go back to combat until later, when losses among naval aviators required that men return for multiple tours.

Following the end of the Christmas 1965 bombing pause on January 30, 1966, air strikes resumed in North Vietnam. The Navy and Air Force were directed by the Joint Chiefs of Staff to concentrate on the enemy's vital petroleum storage and distribution system. These were the first attacks that could be considered "strategic" in *Rolling Thunder*. CinCPac and the JCS had pleaded with the Johnson Administration since the outset of *Rolling Thunder* to approve attacks on these targets, which it was believed would put a serious crimp in the enemy's ability to get supplies to the South. Pacific commander Admiral Sharp later stated that the publicity over these arguments, which had gone on for a year, gave the enemy the opportunity to disperse their POL storage, with much of it going into 55-gallon drums stored in villages, where the fuel was protected by the rules of engagement that forbade bombing populated areas intentionally.

The possibility that the mission would be flown had been leaked to newspapers in the United States, which caused the first strikes to be set back from June 23 to June 29, 1966. The carriers *Ranger* and *Constellation* carried out the first attacks, with *Ranger*'s Skyhawks from VA-146 and VA-55 dropping 19 tons of bombs on the main storage facility in Haiphong over an eight-minute attack, while *Constellation*'s Skyhawks and Intruders went after the Do Son POL storage facility on the peninsula forming the southeast arm of the harbor. *Constellation* was joined by *Hancock* on June 30 to hit the POL site at Bac Giang. On July 1, bombers from the two ships hit Dong Nham, 13 miles northwest of Haiphong.

These initial strikes were credited with destroying 80 percent of Haiphong's POL storage capacity. The strikes that continued through the month of July against the Hanoi storage facilities were credited with destroying 70 percent of the country's total storage capacity. However, 26,000 metric tonnes (28,660 US tons) survived the attacks in dispersed sites. The CIA estimated that the country only needed 32,000 metric tonnes (35,273 US tons) to meet its annual needs, an amount that could be covered by what remained and what was brought into Haiphong on Soviet ships the Navy was not allowed to attack. POL strikes continued for the rest of the year into early 1967.

On July 1, 1966, in what seemed like a replay of the August 1964 attack on *Maddox*, a Phantom pilot on combat air patrol spotted three North Vietnamese torpedo boats headed for the guided missile frigate

USS *Coontz* (DLG 8) and destroyer USS *Rogers* (DD 876), located at the North Search and Rescue (SAR) Station 55 miles east of Haiphong in the Tonkin Gulf. Thirty minutes later, around 1600 hours local time, F-4s from *Constellation* attacked the boats with rockets and bombs. The boats launched torpedoes against the ships, then ten miles away, before turning for home. Aircraft from *Hancock* joined the fight and all three were sunk. The destroyers proceeded to rescue 19 North Vietnamese Navy survivors, taking them to Da Nang where they were held until returned to North Vietnam in 1967 and 1968 in exchange for US prisoners.

The second half of 1966 saw the first high-level questioning of the way the war was being fought and its overall success. Earlier in the year, Secretary McNamara had commissioned a study by a committee of scientists from the Jason Division of the Institute for Defense Analysis regarding the effectiveness of the *Rolling Thunder* campaign. On August 29, 1966, the committee submitted what became known as "The Jason Report." Their report evaluating the results of the *Rolling Thunder* campaign began:

> As of July 1966 the US bombing of North Vietnam (NVN) had had no measurable direct effect on Hanoi's ability to mount and support military operations in the South at the current level. Although the political constraints seem clearly to have reduced the effectiveness of the bombing program, its limited effect on Hanoi's ability to provide such support cannot be explained solely on that basis. The countermeasures introduced by Hanoi effectively reduced the impact of US bombing. More fundamentally, however, North Vietnam has basically a subsistence agricultural economy that presents a difficult and unrewarding target system for air attack.

The political response in Washington to this report and further statements by Secretary McNamara about the campaign's effectiveness resulted in the Senate Armed Services Committee, chaired by long-time "hawk" Senator John Stennis, setting a series of hearings into the war's conduct that finally began in the summer of 1967. Military leaders were set to testify about the political restrictions under which they fought. In response, President Johnson made a political decision to expand the air war. On August 9, the first day of the Stennis Committee Hearings as they became known, the president announced he had added 16 new targets to the approved target list and expanded armed reconnaissance missions over North Vietnam, and that he was removing the bombing restrictions surrounding Hanoi and Haiphong and the buffer zone along the Chinese border. The war had already heated up that spring with permission given to finally attack the VPAF's airfields, and would do so even more after the president's announcement.

By 1967, North Vietnam had formed an estimated 25 SAM battalions, with six missile launchers each, which rotated among approximately 150–200 sites. With the assistance of the Soviet Union, the North Vietnamese had also quickly integrated an early warning radar system of more than 200 sites that covered the entire country, tracking incoming US raids, and then coordinating SAMs, antiaircraft batteries, and MiGs to attack them.

Between March 1965 and April 1968, aircraft of the Navy and Marine Corps flew 152,399 sorties in support of *Rolling Thunder*. On December 31, 1967, the Department of Defense announced that 864,000 tons of American bombs had been dropped on North Vietnam during *Rolling Thunder*, compared with 653,000 tons dropped during the entire Korean War and 503,000 tons in the Pacific Theater during World War II.

During the bombing halts over the 1966–67 Christmas and New Year period, and the Tet holiday in late January 1967, air strikes by the Navy and Air Force were concentrated in the Laotian Panhandle. These attacks were designated *Steel Tiger* and *Tiger Hound*, while strikes further north in Laos were designated *Barrel Roll*. The attacks were aimed at supplies rushed down the Ho Chi Minh Trail during the bombing halt.

Following the Tet halt at the end of January 1967, Task Force 77 was authorized to attack the North Vietnamese industrial heartland in the northeastern region. Carrier attacks hit iron and steel plants, thermal power plants, cement factories, ship and rail repair shops, ammunition depots, and warehouses. Finally, in April, the airfields at Kep and Hoa Lac were attacked. During this new phase, railroad yards, highway and railroad bridges, and rolling stock were bombed in an attempt to stem the flow of military supplies from China. Transportation routes out of Hanoi were also struck.

In February 1967, approval was finally given to dropping 1,000-pound Mark 52 magnetic mines in the mouths of key North Vietnamese rivers, with further missions to lay mines in inland waterways later in the year, in an attempt to decrease the growing use of coastal and inland waterways for movement south, while the ongoing armed route reconnaissance missions against road traffic, antiaircraft sites, and other targets of opportunity continued. The year also saw limited strikes in the prohibited areas within ten miles of the center of either Hanoi or Haiphong and 20 miles from the Chinese border. The Hanoi electrical power plant was among those targets, hit in May by aircraft from USS *Bon Homme Richard*.

In August, the Hanoi thermal power plant was bombed by aircraft from *Oriskany*. August also saw an attack on Long Son rail and highway bridge eight miles from the Chinese border that dropped the bridge's center span. At the end of the month, the naval base at Van Hoa was hit for the first time, causing extensive damage. In September, aircraft from *Oriskany*, *Constellation*, *Coral Sea*, and *Intrepid* struck previously off-limits areas in Haiphong and in the smaller ports of Hon Gai and Cam Pha. Overall during 1967, carrier-based forces flew 77,000 sorties.

In 1968, the Tet Offensive began on January 30 throughout South Vietnam. The North Vietnamese attacked the isolated Marine outpost at Khe Sanh in the Central Highlands on January 21. With Route 9 cut by the PAVN forces, there was no way to supply the base overland, and aerial supply would become necessary, as well as a high level of air support to prevent the expected main attack. The northwest monsoon was at its height, shrouding the mountains of the Central Highlands in low clouds, fog, and frequent rain, which severely affected air operations. General Westmoreland was determined that Khe Sanh would not become the "American Dien Bien Phu," and both the Air Force and Navy were ordered to ensure this did not happen. The battle was considered so important that, at one point, Westmoreland was ready to request authorization to use a tactical nuclear weapon on the enemy.

For the only time in the Vietnam War, air operations by all services were placed under a single command, that being Seventh Air Force. Operation *Niagara II* became the most concentrated application of aerial firepower in the history of aerial warfare. Daily air operations saw an average of 350 sorties by Air Force, Navy, and Marine tactical fighter-bombers and 60 B-52 sorties, while 30 Marine observation aircraft of VO-67 operated near the base. The B-52 strikes were initially limited to no closer than two miles, which allowed the North Vietnamese to closely engage the Marines. By the end of February, B-52s were regularly striking the enemy within three-quarters of a mile from Khe Sanh. At the end of March, the PAVN forces began to withdraw and the battle came to a halt. During the campaign, the Air Force flew 9,691 sorties and dropped 14,223 tons of bombs. The Marines flew 7,098 sorties and dropped 17,015 tons of mixed munitions. Naval Aviation – which was concurrently flying the majority of *Rolling Thunder* missions over the north – still managed to fly 5,337 sorties and drop 7,941 tons of bombs.

The Tet Offensive crisis in South Vietnam and the worst flying weather over the North since *Rolling Thunder* began, severely limited operations between January and March. The carriers *Coral Sea, Kitty Hawk, Enterprise, Ticonderoga, Ranger, Bon Homme Richard*, and *Oriskany* operated from Yankee Station with as many as five carriers "on station" at one time. The main offensive activity involved dropping more mines in river mouths and vital choke points south of Vinh north of the DMZ, and mounting attacks against targets of opportunity along the Ho Chi Minh Trail.

During this period, Task Force 77 A-4 and A-6 squadrons hit rail and highway bridges along Route 1 at Long Ngoc, Thanh Hoa, Dong Phong, Haiphong, and Kien An, as well as the airfields at Vinh, Ke Sat, Cat Bi, and Bai Thuong. Power plants, railroad yards, naval facilities, barracks, and heavy industrial plants at Hanoi, Haiphong, Nam Dinh, Hai Duong, Hon Gai, and Cam Pha were also hit by March 31. On March 31, a break in the weather exposed a major enemy truck convoy headed south. Carrier attack aircraft pounced quickly and destroyed or damaged 98 of the 100-plus enemy trucks.

On March 31, President Johnson surprised the world by removing himself from consideration for re-election in the 1968 presidential election and halted bombing of North Vietnam north of the 20th parallel in an effort to jump-start peace negotiations. *Rolling Thunder*, now limited to the southern third of North Vietnam, continued until shortly before the US elections in November in an attempt to interdict supplies moving south. Task Force 77 mounted a concentrated interdiction effort over these seven months between the 18th and 19th parallels north of the DMZ. Carrier aircraft mined and bombed traffic control points, including ferry crossings, railway and highway bridges, storage areas, truck parks, fuel dumps, inland waterways, and roads that were constricted by the surrounding geography. Cruisers and destroyers participating in Operation *Sea Dragon* steamed along the coast shelling many of the same targets, as well as coastal defenses south of the 19th parallel.

In a concentrated campaign in May, three areas in the vicinity of Ha Tinh, Vinh, and south of Phu Dien Chau, which contained the most important choke points in the region, were each assigned as targets of separate carrier task groups, which carried out round-the-clock strikes. In August, the entire weight of Task Force 77 was concentrated against the southern traffic area around Ha Tinh. These strikes finally saw the turning point of the campaign. Continuous day and night air strikes, route reconnaissance, and shore bombardment resulted in backing up North Vietnamese truck traffic so it became the target of further attack. Over 600 trucks were destroyed or damaged in August, the highest monthly total of the campaign, which forced the enemy to rely on coastal and inland waterway transport. At the same time, air and surface naval forces destroyed or damaged nearly 1,000 waterborne logistic craft in September, a record for the six-month interdiction operation.

By the time all bombing of North Vietnam ceased on November 1, 1968, the logistic flow through the panhandle and along the coast had been reduced to a trickle. The post-Tet offensive in South Vietnam attempted that fall was weak and of short duration due to the success of the interdiction campaign by Seventh Fleet. However, the entire *Rolling Thunder* anti-infiltration program was only partially successful. Heavy weather, operational restrictions, and communist determination to win in the South made prosecution of the air campaign difficult.

Fifteen years earlier, writing about the interdiction campaign against North Korea, then-Seventh Fleet commander Vice Admiral J.J. "Jocko" Clark had concluded that the campaign did not accomplish the goal of interdicting enemy supplies. The same was true with *Rolling Thunder*, and for the same reasons. The enemy demonstrated an astonishing ability to make good damage to the transportation infrastructure. North Vietnamese citizens were drafted into brigades to repair and rebuild roads, bridges, and railroads that had been bombed. By 1967, US intelligence estimated that 97,000 North Vietnamese worked full time at this, while another 370,000–500,000 worked several days a month in such activity. It was no surprise that the North Vietnamese were advised in organizing this work by North Korean veterans of the earlier war. The ingenuity that had been shown in North Korea was transferred to the Vietnamese, who could use more than half a dozen ways to move a truck across a river after the bridge had been bombed, from finding a simple ford to constructing temporary bridges using lashed-together boats, to constructing sunken spans with rocks that a truck could drive across but which could not be seen from the air by a photo-reconnaissance airplane.

The primary fault in *Rolling Thunder* was the decision at the highest levels not to bomb the port of Haiphong out of fear of sinking or damaging Soviet shipping or ships from US allies like Britain that came to the port. Royce Williams, who served three tours in Vietnam as an air wing commander, explained: "One or two bombs dropped on a ship tied up at a pier in Haiphong, which would destroy an entire shipment of military equipment wasn't allowed, but we were cleared to destroy that shipload of equipment one truckload at a time after it was ashore."

Ultimately, the strategy promulgated in Washington and the tactics that were approved as a result had as corrosive an effect on the morale of naval aviators as did the strategy and tactics allowed in the war on the ground in South Vietnam on front-line infantrymen. The Project Jason report included a comment from a naval aviator who wished to remain anonymous in order to speak freely of the situation at the time:

> By 1967, the aircrews had largely decided that the war couldn't be won under the rules of engagement by which they had to fight. Outside of the hard-heads, the rest of us had determined that no amount of "carry on regardless" would change things. And that meant we put far more effort into surviving our tour than to pressing an attack on the enemy that wasn't going to have a result worth the cost of a guy going down. I was a division leader on my second tour, and I can tell you I put every effort into coming up with ways to get my guys through a mission and bring them back to the ship alive. It didn't matter whether the target was knocked out or not, since they were going to rebuild it and we were going to come back and hit it again, and probably again. Getting through alive was what mattered. None of it was worth the loss of one of my guys. That was what made the losses that happened anyway so damned hard to accept – that they were so useless. We flew the sorties and the bean-counters got their statistics, and the politicians in Washington used those to claim we were winning, and in the end none of it mattered.

On November 1, 1968, when the bombing campaign was halted, none of the four objectives established in 1964 as the goal of an aerial bombing campaign against the north – to boost the sagging morale of the Republic of Vietnam; to persuade North Vietnam to cease its support for the communist insurgency in South Vietnam without sending in ground forces; to destroy North Vietnam's transportation system, industrial base, and air defenses; and to halt the flow of men and materiel into South Vietnam – had been achieved. When *Rolling Thunder* ended after three-and-a-half years of effort, the North Vietnamese were better positioned to support their forces in the South than they had been in 1965. The CIA estimated that *Rolling Thunder* cost the United States $6.60 to render $1.00 worth of damage in 1965, and $9.60 by 1966. The estimated $600 million of damage inflicted by *Rolling Thunder* during the campaign was dwarfed by the $6 billion it cost to replace the aircraft lost during those three-and-a-half years of the longest air campaign ever flown by either the Air Force or the Navy.

6

AIR COMBAT, 1964–66

During the years of *Rolling Thunder*, VPAF pilots claimed three F-8 Crusaders shot down in aerial combat. In return, F-8 Crusader pilots claimed 15 MiG-17s and four MiG-21s shot down. Despite their "last gunfighter" nickname, F-8 only gained four victories using their four 20mm cannon armament, due to the propensity of the ammunition feeding mechanism of these Colt Mark 12 weapons to jam under G-loads during high-speed dogfight maneuvering.

Air combat over North Vietnam began on April 3, 1965. A strike group from USS *Hancock*, composed of three A-4Cs from VA-216 and three A-4Es from VA-212, escorted by four F-8E Crusaders from VF-211 to provide flak suppression, was tasked with bombing the Dong Phong Thong Bridge south of the soon-to-be-infamous Thanh Hoa Bridge. The four Crusaders carried a full load of 450 rounds of 20mm each, and eight Zuni rockets mounted on the missile rails to either side of the fuselage aft of the cockpit, for use against the defending antiaircraft sites around the bridge. The monsoonal weather lowered visibility, which became progressively worse with increased haze, mist, and fog below 5,000 feet as they approached the target.

Unknown to the strike force, a flight of four VF-96 F-4B Phantoms had been launched from USS *Ranger* as protection should the enemy send up any of their small force of MiG-17s to oppose the mission. Each formation was operating on its own radio frequency and didn't know the frequency being used by the others. The Phantom crews knew the air defense mission they'd been briefed for, but had no way of knowing if the strike force got into trouble.

The Crusader division was led by Lieutenant Commander Spence Thomas, who was shepherding a new ensign as wingman on his first mission, with Lieutenants Jerry Unruh and Bobby Hulse at the second section. As they neared the target, Thomas and his wingman accelerated ahead of the first section of Skyhawks, diving to strafe and rocket the antiaircraft positions as they revealed themselves when they opened fire. However, the haze was such that the two pilots lost track of their targets as they pulled off their first run firing Zunis. Spence zoom-climbed to 10,000 feet back into clearer air, and orbited until his wingman joined up, but his inexperienced wingman lost sight of him in the haze and became separated. The attacking Skyhawks also had difficulty spotting their target.

Unruh and Hulse then dived on the flak sites to cover the second Skyhawk section. Coming off their attack run, they heard the new pilot calling for help. They were able to find him with their radio direction finders. As the three F-8s began climbing to rejoin Thomas, he suddenly called that he was taking fire. While the US pilots at first assumed they were under fire from the ground, it was soon apparent that the VPAF was making its first combat appearance, as two MiG-17s closed on Thomas.

The two MiGs, flown by Lieutenant Pham Ngoc Lan and his wingman, Lieutenant Phan Van Tuc, had approached the US strike at 1,000 feet after taking off from Gia Lam airfield, east of Hanoi, and mixed in with the attacking Skyhawks in the haze. They were quickly joined by Lieutenants Ho Van Quy and Tran Minh Phuong, all members of the 921st Fighter Regiment. Pham Ngoc Lan opened fire on Thomas and scored several hits in the Crusader's canopy, wings, and tail with the MiG's two 23mm cannon. The F-8 appeared to explode as it dropped away, and Phan Van Tuc opened fire on a second F-8. Thomas struggled to maintain control of his F-8 as it fell to the right with the loss of its utility hydraulic system.

Lan closed for a second firing pass, but had to pull off when his panel light flashed on, indicating he was running low on fuel. In fact, he was so low on fuel that he had to execute a forced landing on the banks of the Duong River. Convinced he had shot down the Crusader, Lan claimed the victory on return to Gia Lam. When his MiG was recovered, the gun camera film appeared to support his claim and he was recognized as the first VPAF pilot to shoot down an enemy plane.

In fact, the gun camera only recorded while the trigger was pulled, and thus the results of his final burst of fire were not recorded; this had been a problem with Soviet pilot victory claims in the Korean War where F-86s that appeared fatally damaged on the limited film in fact survived. Wingman Tuc's claim of a second Crusader shot down, which was also supported by gun camera film that failed to show the final hits, was actually Thomas's airplane, which he, due to his lack of experience, had misidentified when it fell away from where he first sighted it.

In reality, Thomas had been unable to return to *Hancock* and land due to the loss of his utility hydraulics, so he diverted to Da Nang, escorted by the other members of the division, where he blew down his landing gear with the emergency air system and landed successfully. The Crusader was a mess, but it would be recovered and repaired, and would serve throughout the rest of the war until the end of the Crusader's career on carrier decks.

Through all of this, the VF-96 Phantoms never heard a word, since *Ranger* herself was not listening to *Hancock*'s frequency, while those in *Hancock*'s CIC didn't know there was a force available that they could call on for reinforcement. The F-4s returned to the carrier, where all learned later of the fight they had missed.

This first combat was the confused beginning of what would be a confusing air war. Six days after this first combat between the two opponents, an F-4 Phantom crew claimed the type's first aerial victory – in a fight in which the victorious crew also became the first Phantom crew claimed shot down by their opponents. The fight was not between the Navy and the VPAF, but rather with the People's Liberation Army Air Force of China, and was not reported for several years. At the time of the event, it was feared this was an indication that China would intervene in the Vietnam War as had happened in Korea.

USS *Ranger* and her Carrier Air Wing-9 (CVW-9) were already veterans of combat over North Vietnam, having flown the pre-strike "Blue Tree" reconnaissance flights that happened before the commencement of *Rolling Thunder* in December 1964, with F-4s from VF-92 and VF-96 flying top cover for the *Flaming Dart I* strikes against Vit Thu Lu on February 7 and the *Flaming Dart II* strikes against the Chanh Hoa barracks on February 11.

At 0803 hours on April 9, *Ranger* began launching a four-plane Barrier Combat Air Patrol (BARCAP) to patrol off the North Vietnamese port of Haiphong. The first section of two F-4s was led by VF-96 squadron CO, Commander William F. Fraser and RIO Lieutenant (jg) Christopher Billingsley, with wingman Lieutenant Don Watkins and RIO Lieutenant (jg) Charles R Hayes. Both Phantoms carried two AIM-7D Sparrow IIIs and two AIM-9B Sidewinders.

Second section leader Lieutenant Commander William E. Greer and RIO Lieutenant (jg) Richard R. Bruning experienced an engine failure two-thirds of the way through the catapult stroke. The two ejected as the Phantom crashed into the gulf. The second F-4 of the section, crewed by Lieutenant (jg) Terry M. Murphy and RIO Ronald J. Fegan, launched as replacement section leader. The standby Phantom, which was manned but not in position to take an immediate catapult shot, was crewed by Lieutenant Howard B. Watkins, Jr., and RIO Lieutenant (jg) John T. Mueller. Both of these aircraft carried four Sparrows only. The two sections were communicating on different radio frequencies.

Launched several minutes late, Howard Watkins' and Mueller's Phantom went to full power to catch up with Murphy and Fegan as they flew north in answer to commands received minutes after launch from Ranger's CIC to investigate a radar contact headed toward the ship from Hainan Island, a nearby territory of China. As they climbed after their section leader, Howard Watkins and Mueller heard Murphy call "Three in the con" (contrails). Murphy and Fegan soon identified these as three MiG-17s carrying Chinese markings. Howard Watkins and Mueller were still out of visual contact with Murphy and Fegan when they were then jumped by a fourth MiG-17. At the same time they were bounced, Murphy reported that a MiG had fired on him. The two Phantoms of the second section would now have to fight separate battles alone, until Fraser and Don Watkins could arrive after being hastily redirected from their station to join in.

Fraser and Don Watkins showed up at 0855 hours. Fraser obtained a boresight on one of the MiGs at a range of six miles as it passed from left to right. At five miles, Fraser illuminated the MiG with the Phantom's radar; RIO Billingsley was able to secure a missile lock quickly and switched to Multiple Aim Point (MAP) mode to obtain auto track. Fraser banked 30 degrees right, establishing a lead on the MiG, then put the steering dot in the Allowable Steering Error (ASE) circle. With the MiG three miles in front, he fired an AIM-7. Although the Sparrow maintained lock-on, it failed to track and went ballistic, flying wide of and below the MiG.

Still keeping the original lock, Fraser reported that he "switched to heat and tracked the MiG optically with 3.5 miles lead and received tone." He fired the Sidewinder at a range of 1.5 miles. It initially tracked the MiG, which was in a shallow left bank, but then the target broke hard left and slightly nose down, a maneuver that caused the Sidewinder to lose track and miss the plane by 50 feet. In their after-action debrief, both Fraser and Billingsley reported that "This missile should have been able to intercept the target, but the missile did not appear to be turning as sharply as it was capable of, even at that high altitude."

Fraser continued after the MiG and prepared for another shot with the MiG maneuvering at 47,000 feet. He obtained a lock-on at 12 miles, then lost it, and re-acquired it at a range of seven miles. At three-and-a-half miles, he fired his second Sparrow with the MiG flying straight and level; however, the Sparrow's rocket motor failed to ignite and it dropped harmlessly into the sea below.

Don Watkins and Hayes experienced frustrations as they pursued their MiG-17. Watkins later reported:

Our first run commenced as soon as the MiGs were spotted visually in the contrails. We acquired them on radar about 45 degrees left, 18 miles, and made a port turn to put them on a collision course. At this time the arm-safe switch was placed to "arm." The starboard missile armed since the port select light had blinked off. The MiGs appeared to turn into us, and a forward quarter run developed. We switched to "ten-mile" scale. We were at "in range" at eight miles with maximum blossoming at five miles, at which time we fired the Sparrow III missile on number seven fuselage station. The pilot felt a thud, but the missile was not observed, even after sharply banking the aircraft left and right. Apparently, the missile motor did not fire.

Don Watkins then made a second run at the MiG, acquiring it at ten degrees left and a range of six miles, in a starboard turn. Pulling hard to the right to match the MiG's turn, Watkins fired his second Sparrow at the MiG at a range of three-and-a-half miles, but it, too, dropped when the motor failed to fire. Undaunted, Watkins then managed to close on the MiG's seven o'clock position. He obtained a good tone at a mile-and-a-half and fired the starboard Sidewinder. Frustration went sky-high when it failed to fire. Quickly switching to the second

Sidewinder, Watkins fired into the MiG's now-ignited afterburner; it failed to track and missed wide. He made a final attempt with the starboard AIM-9B, but it again failed to fire.

While Fraser and Don Watkins tried to down the MiGs they engaged, Murphy radioed "Out of missiles, RTB" (Returning to Base). Howard Watkins and Mueller had engaged the MiG that attacked them. When it disengaged its afterburner and turned back for a second run, Watkins lit his afterburner and disengaged. As Watkins and Mueller dove away, they saw what they identified as a silver MiG-17 explode and crash and called out "Good shooting, who got him?"

The fight was over by 0905 hours. The VF-96 crews were directed by *Ranger*'s GCI to rendezvous with nearby A-3B tankers that had been diverted from the morning's strike. Only three Phantoms showed up at the rendezvous; Murphy and Fegan were missing. Despite repeated radio calls, Murphy and Fegan didn't respond and were posted missing in action. At around the same time Murphy's call about returning to base was heard, the GCI controller in *Ranger*'s CIC had noticed Murphy's F-4 turn away from Hainan, with a second blip behind it. Moments later, the Phantom disappeared from the radar plot. *Ranger* launched other aircraft and an unsuccessful air search was conducted over an area of 7,500 square miles of the Tonkin Gulf for over two hours.

The Chinese claimed that the Phantom had been destroyed by their Air Force, stating that it had tried to turn with a MiG-17, bled off speed, and "was caught in the gunsight." On the basis of the report by Howard Watkins and John Mueller, Murphy and Fegan were credited with a victory, though there was no public mention of it until after the war to avoid upsetting the Chinese government.

In a 1994 interview, Captain Li Dayun of the PLAAF, the pilot of the number four MiG-17, said that he saw a Phantom fire two Sparrows at his leader from a vertical maneuver, but both missed. According to Captain Dayun, the Phantom was hit by one of the malfunctioning missiles and crashed just offshore, killing the crew. Dayun stated that he and his fellow pilots never received permission to fire, and that all returned to base.

While "the Hainan Island Incident" was officially buried to avoid provoking an international incident, the fight had revealed problems that would arise over and over again in future combats when Phantoms attempted to fight a MiG-17 on its own terms. The failure of all the missiles fired by Fraser and Don Watkins demonstrated what would come to be seen as the inherent unreliability of American air-to-air missiles, which would plague Navy and Air Force crews throughout the war. The mission report by Fraser and Billingsley would be repeated many times in the years to come: "The performances of the missiles was most disappointing and frustrating. Three good runs were made that should have resulted in the missiles intercepting their targets. All indications available to the crew were that the weapons system should have been functioning perfectly."

Skirmishes between US and VPAF aircraft continued throughout the spring, but there was no air-to-air combat until the first two victories over VPAF fighters were scored by two Phantoms from USS *Midway*'s VF-21 "Freelancers" of CVW-2 on June 17, 1965.

Around 1100 hours that morning, a 14-plane strike mission from *Midway* and *Bon Homme Richard* was headed for a strike against the Thanh Hoa Bridge, about 80 miles due south of Hanoi. One of the most important targets in North Vietnam and one of the most-bombed before its final destruction in the fall of 1972, the bridge provided a direct road link between Haiphong and the Mu Gia Pass through which supplies passed into Laos and then into South Vietnam, and was thus a primary target in the battle to block the Ho Chi Minh Trail.

The two VF-21 Phantoms in the six-plane Target Combat Air Patrol (TARCAP) were flown by VF-21 XO Commander Lou Page and RIO Lieutenant John C. Smith in NE-101, with wingman Lieutenant Jack E.D. Batson and RIO Lieutenant Commander Robert Doremus in NE-102. Both F-4s were armed with two Sidewinders and three Sparrows each.

Lieutenant Batson later recalled. "About half of the missions we were flying at this time were *Rolling Thunder* strikes. Briefing was in the Air Intelligence Center as usual about two hours before launch. It was a large strike on a military target south of Than Hoa." Secretary of the Navy Paul Nitze, one of the authors of NSC 68, the 1950 document that created the blueprint for the militarization of the Cold War from Korea in 1950 to the collapse of the Soviet Union in 1991, was present at the briefing while traveling to visit Navy units in Southeast Asia. Batson remembered, "Lou Page told him we would shoot down MiGs." *Midway*'s aircraft launched, joined up with those from *Bon Homme Richard*, then made a running rendezvous with the KA-3 tankers 75 miles off the coast of North Vietnam. "We then proceeded to our search area in the vicinity of Ninh Dinh, north-west of Than Hoa. We began patrolling in a north-south pattern in basic search formation – one mile abeam of each other so that we could provide each other with protection from someone sneaking up on our tail." The Phantoms maintained position while the Skyhawks executed their strike against the bridge.

"As the strike group called 'feet wet,' Lou called for one more sweep north." Up to that point, there had been no indication of enemy aerial activity other than dealing with AAA from Ninh Dinh. "As we rolled out of the turn, J.C. Smith spotted two radar contacts about 45 miles north. Rob Doremus spotted them almost immediately, also." The fliers had seen MiGs appear late in missions when fuel was getting low; all were suspicious of the contacts. "Lou called for me to move from the search position to the attack position – a three-mile trail and slightly below. We accelerated to approximately 500 knots for better maneuverability." Page and Smith would set up a head-on attack after making a positive visual ID, while Batson was to maneuver for a head-on Sparrow shot in the event they made contact with the enemy.

"J.C. and Rob talked to each other regarding which radar targets to lock on to. J.C. took the farther target, creating a slight offset to the head-on attack." At closer distance, the contacts were two sections of two enemy fighters each, which were soon identified when they banked and exposed the distinctive wing plan of the MiG-17 as the first section turned in toward the lead Phantom. "Lou fired at close to minimum range while shouting 'It's MiGs!' I saw his missile fire, guide towards the formation and the warhead detonate. At first, I thought it had missed, but then the outer half of the right wing came completely off the MiG and it started rolling out of control."

Batson put his full attention to the steering information on the radar scope, and fired a Sparrow at the leader of the second section at minimum range:

The missile fired and swerved under the nose of the MiG. I lost sight of it, but Rob saw it guide to a direct hit. One of the MiGs flew right by me. I think my missile hit either the number one or number two aircraft. The next phase of Lou's tactics was for us to disengage quickly. He was very concerned about trying to turn with a MiG-17 – our most likely foe – or MiG-19. We disengaged by lighting afterburner, climbing up through an overcast and rendezvousing.

The two F-4s reversed their heading, went back into search formation and dived back through the clouds in search of the remaining two MiGs. "We saw smoke trails from our missiles, but no MiGs and one parachute. By this time we were below bingo fuel, so we headed back to Midway."

The two Phantoms were offered an opportunity to refuel from a tanker. Batson explained:

> We declined because if something went wrong we might not make it – we had just enough fuel to land. I was actually showing 400 pounds, sufficient fuel for just three minutes of flying, at the top of the glide slope. After landing, I taxied by our CO, Commander Bill Franke, who was jumping up and down with his hands over his head. After shutdown, Rob came up from the back seat, shook my hand, and said "Four more to go!"

Commander Page was escorted up to the flag bridge where he was congratulated by Secretary Nitze. The others headed below. "To get to our ready room, we had to pass through the VF-111 ready room, where they were yelling and cheering. Our own ready room was packed." Batson was handed a coffee cup, which he quickly discovered was full of scotch. He still had the "coffee" when the two crews were taken to Air Intelligence where they told the task group commander and captain what had happened.

The four fliers were put on a C-1A Carrier Onboard Delivery (COD) transport and flown to Tan Son Nhut, then driven to MACV headquarters in Saigon to participate in the daily press briefing, already known as "the Five O'Clock Follies" to the reporters present. That night, they stayed as guests of General Westmoreland at his private quarters. All four were awarded the Silver Star for the mission. Unfortunately, a little over two months later on August 24, Lieutenant Commander Doremus, flying in NE-112 flown by skipper Commander Franke, was hit by a SAM during another attack on the Thanh Hoa Bridge; they were VF-21's only combat loss during the deployment. Doremus managed to eject and was captured, spending the rest of the war as a POW. RIO John C. Smith would later become one of the first instructors at Top Gun, which he later commanded.

While much was made of the first two F-4 kills of the war, they prolonged the belief that the F-4 could be successfully employed against the MiG-17 without dogfighting, since the fight had been a classic non-maneuvering intercept, for which the early Phantom II crews had trained.

After the fight, Batson maintained that a second MiG-17 had been damaged from ingesting debris from the MiG he had shot down. In 1999, following the declassification of other documents relating to the June 17, 1965 battle and the backing of then-CAG Commander Bob Moore, Batson was finally awarded a second confirmed victory.

Following the 1965 deployment, VF-21 was considered by many to be the premier West Coast F-4 unit regarding air-to-air tactics. The squadron developed and authored the first written fighter tactics doctrine manual for the Phantom, in which they summed up the fighter squadron's mission over North Vietnam: "The primary function of Navy BAR/TARCAP and escort units is to provide warning of the approach of enemy aircraft. Secondarily, the fighter units provide protection as necessary until the attack aircraft can safely retire. Air superiority is not the aim of the fighter units."

The final Navy aerial victory of the first year of the war came on October 6, when Lieutenant Commander Dan MacIntyre and RIO Lieutenant (jg) Alan Johnson of VF-151 in *Coral Sea*'s CVW-15 were covering a strike by the air wing against a bridge near the VPAF base at Kep airfield. Orbiting at 2,500 feet with clouds above at 3,000 and 4,400 feet, RIO Johnson picked up multiple radar contacts 18 miles distant. At first he thought they might be F-8s, which he had spotted earlier. As they closed to visual range, the three-plane line-astern formation was a dead-ringer for MiGs.

Johnson obtained a missile lock on the second MiG at eight miles. At three miles, MacIntyre made a visual ID, calling "Three MiG-17s on the nose," as the enemy fighters crossed from right to left 1,000 feet above. MacIntyre then slid in behind the trailing MiG and fired a Sparrow that hit the enemy fighter and sent it down streaming smoke. He then spotted the leader off to his left turn behind him for a shot. The second enemy fighter was nearly dead in front of him. Knowing the leader would not open fire with one of his own just ahead of his target, MacIntyre closed on the MiG as he rolled directly over the enemy's canopy in full afterburner, pulling a tight barrel roll to the left, converging on the lead MiG inside his turn. Startled by this, the number two MiG turned away, headed for Phuc Yen.

Completing his turn, MacIntyre rolled out behind the second MiG and prepared to score a second victory. Before he could fire, the lead MiG turned in pursuit of MacIntyre's wingman and opened fire as the Phantom turned to evade the attack. With his wingman in trouble, MacIntyre turned to confront the enemy leader. From his position above the MiG, Johnson was unable to break through the ground-clutter for a lock. As MacIntyre turned toward the MiG, now at the same altitude, Johnson obtained a Sparrow lock, but the enemy pilot broke off and headed for China. MacIntyre followed for a few minutes but was unable to secure a missile lock. Breaking off the pursuit, he joined up on his wingman who was headed back to *Coral Sea*.

Four VPAF MiG-17s were officially shot down in 1965, three by Phantom crews and one by a *Midway* Skyraider pilot, for no Navy losses to the Vietnamese fighters.

1966 saw more air action, with the F-8 Crusader taking the lead role from the Phantom in downing MiGs, with three MiG-17s and the first MiG-21 downed by US fighters being scored by Crusaders to one MiG-17 and two AN-2 "Colt" biplane transports shot down by F-4s, and one MiG-17 shot down by a VA-176 A-1 Skyraider.

The first MiG-21F-13 fighters (NATO code name "Fishbed-C") arrived direct from the Soviet Union in late 1965. The aircraft were assigned to the first fighter regiment formed in the VPAF, the 921st "Sao Do" Regiment, which had the most experienced pilots in the air force and was based at Noi Bai airfield northwest of Hanoi, commanded by Tran Hanh. Among the pilots of the regiment were future ranking aces Nguyen Van Coc, Pham Thanh Ngan, Nguyen Hong Nhi, Pham Ngoc Lan, Nguyen Ngoc Do, Nguyen Nhat Chieu, Dao Dinh Luyen, and Tran Hanh, who had all trained on the MiG-21 in the Soviet Union prior to the aircraft's arrival in Vietnam, but even with this training, the aircraft represented a major "step up" for the relatively inexperienced pilots of the VPAF. After shooting down two unmanned Ryan Firebee reconnaissance drones in March 1966, two MiG-21s attempted to engage a flight of Air Force F-4s on April 23. However, the pilots could not get a positive radar lock to fire their R-3S (NATO code name "Atoll") guided missiles. Over the rest of April and May, there were three more engagements in which 14 missiles were fired without success. Several pilots were forced to eject from their fighters when they ran out of fuel after extended attempted interception missions. The first Fishbed was lost in combat when an Air Force F-4C crew from the 480th Tactical Fighter Squadron, 35th Tactical Fighter Wing shot it down on April 26.

Potentially, the MiG-21 had the power to change the air war, since it was fast enough to overtake US fighter-bombers like the Republic F-105 Thunderchief from the rear, which was advantageous to the defenders due to the poor rearward visibility from the F-105's cockpit. To this point, the MiG-17 was only able to intercept these high-speed aircraft in head-on attacks where they could be spotted before opening fire, allowing the bombers to salvo their bombloads in order to evade the defenders.

The VPAF's MiG-21s claimed their first success on June 7, 1966, an F-105 shot down by a fusillade of unguided S-5M rockets. During the same period, the MiG-17s of the 923rd Regiment were becoming more successful as they engaged American aircraft more frequently and their pilots gained further combat experience.

The first MiG kill by an F-8 was scored by *Hancock*'s VF-211 "Checkmates" skipper Commander Harold L. Marr on June 12, 1966. Marr and wingman Lieutenant (jg) Phil Vampatella were escorting a strike by A-4s of VA-212 and 216, in company with a section of VF-24 "Renegades" Crusaders led by Lieutenant Commander Fred Richardson, just under a cloud deck at 1,500 feet. As the Skyhawks came off their runs, Vampatella spotted four MiG-17s closing behind the F-8s. Marr and Vampatella turned into the first pair and each opened fire on the enemy jets with their 20mm cannon as they passed, without effect. Both F-8s turned back on the enemy and made a further gun pass without scoring. Marr saw the MiG he had chosen. With the MiG below him at 1,500 feet, Marr fired his first Sidewinder, but it failed to track on the MiG and spiraled to the ground. The MiG was in afterburner when he turned and headed back for his base. Marr got behind him and caught up easily, pulling into the enemy's six o'clock. "At half a mile, I fired my last 'Winder, and it chopped off his tail and right wing. It tumbled end of end and the poor pilot had no chance to eject."

Richardson and his wingman engaged the other MiG, each firing both their Sidewinders, all four failing to track. Marr spotted the second pair orbiting above him and engaged one of them with his guns, firing

30 rounds before his gun jammed. Pieces flew off the enemy fighter, which he claimed as a probable.

Nine days after Marr's victory, Phil Vampatella shot down the third MiG-17 to fall to a Crusader. Lieutenant Commander Cole Black, Lieutenant Gene Chancy, and Vampatella were escorting six A-4s, while second section leader Lieutenant Dick Smith escorted the RF-8A trailing the strike force to obtain bomb damage assessment photos. As the A-4s dove for their target, word came that the RF-8A had been shot down and its pilot, Lieutenant L.C. Eastman, had ejected. The three Crusaders quickly joined Smith, who was now the on-scene SAR commander, and orbited over the area where Eastman had gone down. Soon, the Skyhawks began calling that there were SAMs and MiGs. The Crusaders came under heavy AAA fire and Vampatella took a hit. Black and Chancy climbed to get better radio reception with the incoming rescue helicopter and Black ordered Smith and Vampatella to find a tanker and top off.

Suddenly, Black spotted two MiG-17s as they popped out of the clouds half a mile to the south. Black led a break into the enemy fighters and opened fire at them. Chancy fired at the wingman as the two MiGs flew past, and knocked off the enemy fighter's wing. He later recalled, "He was so close, I could have counted his teeth." Chancy had also fired a Sidewinder, but it failed to guide. While his victory has been listed as a missile kill, Chancy always maintained that it was his burst of fire that brought down the MiG. Initially, his claim was recorded as a probable, being changed to a definite victory several months later when intelligence was able to confirm the loss of the enemy fighter.

In the heat of the moment, Chancy lost contact with Black, realizing moments after the MiG went down that the other MiG had gotten Black, who had ejected. Unfortunately, the rescue chopper experienced an equipment failure and both Black and Eastman were captured and became POWs.

When Black called out the MiGs, Smith and Vampatella turned around and returned, despite the damage to Vampatella's Crusader. As they neared the fight, Smith called two MiG-17s diving on the other Crusaders and opening fire on one that burst into flames, which turned out to be Black. An instant later, two other MiGs attacked Smith and Vampatella. Smith tried to open fire on one, but his guns jammed in the high-G turn. In the meantime, the other fastened on Vampatella, who could only pull 5-G turns to try to get away, due to his previous damage. Finally, despite being low on fuel, he went into afterburner and pulled away to the east. The F-8 was getting hard to fly, but he saw the enemy fighter turn away. Seizing the opportunity, he turned back after the departing MiG. His first Sidewinder failed to track, but the second guided straight to the target and exploded behind it, damaging the tail so that it went out of control and crashed.

Chancy was able to take 300 pounds of fuel from the KA-3B tanker, but Vampatella was only able to take on a minimum. Fortunately, he made it the 60 miles back to *Hancock*, where his jet was examined. It had taken a 37mm hit in the vertical fin that peppered the rear fuselage, creating more than 80 holes. Black's Crusader was one of only three lost in air combat during the war, with the pilots of the other two being picked up and returned to their carriers.

On July 7, a month after their first claimed success, two MiG-21s flown by Nguyen Nhat Chieu and Tran Ngoc Xiu attacked a formation of F-105s and Xiu claimed one shot down with an Atoll missile, though US records recorded no loss that day. Four days later on July 11, Vu Ngoc Dinh and Dong Van Song shot down an F-105D of the 355th Tactical Fighter Wing, flown by Major W.L. McClelland over Son Duong, though the Air Force claimed the loss was due to fuel exhaustion after an engagement with a MiG-21. F-4Cs of the 35th Tactical Fighter Wing's 480th Tactical Fighter Squadron claimed two MiG-21s shot down on July 14, giving the squadron a score of three Fishbeds. The 921st claimed an F-105 on September 21, a loss the US Air Force credited to a SAM. The Air Force admitted the loss of an F-4C to a MiG-21 on October 5, though the VPAF records show no claim. The first VPAF claim for an F-4 was made on October 9, a Navy F-4B of VF-154, flown by Lieutenant Commander Charles Tanner and RIO Lieutenant Ross R. Terry, who were captured and spent the rest of the war as POWs. Tanner and Terry claimed they were shot down by a well-aimed burst of flak, but were tortured by their North Vietnamese captors until they agreed they had indeed been shot down by a MiG-21.

To distinguish between the two North Vietnamese fighters over the radio, the MiG-17 became the "Red Bandit," while the new MiG-21 became the "Blue Bandit." As the radar operators on the Red Crown air warning ships became more proficient in understanding the difference in tactics and flight performance and were able to distinguish between the two, it was important to be able to alert the aircrews whenever possible as to the identity of their opponents, since the two fighters had such different performance parameters and attack strategies, and required different air combat strategies from the US aircrews.

The F-8E Crusaders of VF-162 "Hunters" arrived for their third Southeast Asian deployment and second wartime deployment on June 30 aboard USS *Oriskany*. After missions over South Vietnam flown from Dixie Station, the carrier had moved to Yankee Station and the squadron flew their first mission into North Vietnam on July 8. During her three deployments to Vietnam between 1965 and 1968, *Oriskany's* CVW-16 suffered the highest losses of the war of any carrier air wing, accounting for 20 percent of total Navy air losses during *Rolling Thunder*. In part, these losses were the result of *Oriskany's* deployment schedules, which coincided with the most dangerous phases of *Rolling Thunder*. The gradual escalation of operations during *Rolling Thunder* each year came in the spring, since the summer monsoon weather pattern saw the clearest skies over North Vietnam, which allowed increased air attacks to take advantage of the newly allowed attacks on previously untouched targets. The result for CVW-16 was that the missions flown took pilots into heavily defended areas previously declared off limits, with the numbers of sorties flown dramatically increased.

Fortunately for "The Hunters," as the pilots of VF-162 had named themselves, they had Commander Richard M. Bellinger for an XO. Bellinger was one of the most unique characters in naval aviation history. Going by the call sign "Belly One," "Belly," as his pilots affectionately called him, was something of a "dinosaur" by the 1960s. At age 42, he was a decade older than the next-oldest man in the squadron, and was older than the CO. A USAAF veteran who had flown bombers in World War II, he had joined the Navy after the war and flown combat in Korea. He was known throughout the naval aviation community as a one-of-a-kind fighter pilot, a real throwback to an earlier time of air combat, with a notorious reputation as a raging bull, who was often seen by his superiors as out of control; he was a well-known hell-raiser ashore. Then-Lieutenant (jg) Bud Flagg, a member of the squadron on the 1966 deployment, recalled Bellinger as a "colorful" character. "He flew the F-8 well and commanded the squadron well. He was always there to do the job. He was tops." Lieutenant James R. "Flap" Andrews agreed with Flagg's assessment:

> Belly was wonderful as a CO and very colorful to boot. He did not sweat the small stuff – at all! – and he was very difficult to keep up with. During a squadron party after his victory at the Subic Bay Officer's Club, which was a much more formal place than the Cubi Point Officer's Club where most aviators went, Belly ended up walking down the table tops, shooting champagne corks at the Admiral's dinner party across the room. I have many, many fond memories of him.

VF-162 began suffering losses quickly. On July 11, Lieutenant (jg) Richard Adams, flying as wingman for Bellinger, was heavily damaged by a nearby SAM explosion; aiming for the water, Adams ended up ejecting through the fireball when his Crusader finally exploded just after crossing the beach, and he was quickly picked up by helicopter. This was his second ejection and pickup, his first having occurred during the previous tour, when he went into the water offshore. Three days later on July 14, it was Bellinger's turn when his F-8E was damaged chasing a MiG-17 over Hanoi. Unable to land on the carrier due to damage, he tried to make it to Da Nang before his fuel ran out. Halfway to Da Nang and 40 miles out over the Tonkin Gulf, the fuel gauge read empty and he was forced to eject, being recovered by a rescue helicopter and returned to *Oriskany*. Five days later, Lieutenant Terry Dennison was shot down southeast of Hanoi. A rescue was mounted but he had already been captured. The Hunters' last loss occurred on October 6, when an F-8E was hit by antiaircraft fire. The pilot was able to successfully eject over the Tonkin Gulf and was rescued.

October 9, 1966 saw the F-8 Crusader finally engage in combat with the MiG-21, the fighter that had long been seen as its natural enemy. The fight again involved VF-162's XO; Bellinger was flying F-8E BuNo 149159, AH 210, as division lead for three F-8s escorting A-4s from USS *Intrepid*. They went "feet dry" as they crossed ashore near the mouth of the Red River, heading for a target near Hanoi. Warned by an E-1B Tracer flying air control that there were enemy aircraft in the area, Bellinger soon spotted four strange shapes that became silver delta-winged silhouettes. Bellinger recognized them as MiG-21s as they flashed past and accelerated after number four. Pushing the throttle forward, the Crusader passed through Mach 1 and closed with the MiG. The enemy pilot spotted Bellinger gaining on him and accelerated as he tried to turn away but Bellinger easily curved onto his tail inside the turn. With a good "tone," he fired two of his four Sidewinders, which both tracked on the target. When the first hit the MiG-21 in its rear fuselage, the enemy fighter erupted in a fireball that the second missile passed through, exploding just as it came out on the far side. The pilot failed to eject. Bellinger and his Crusader had just become the victors in the first supersonic air combat. He was awarded the Silver Star, which was pinned on him by Secretary of Defense Robert McNamara a week later during the Secretary's tour of Southeast Asia.

The night of December 19–20, 1966, the crew of pilot Lieutenant H. Denny Wisely and RIO Lieutenant (jg) Dave L. Jordan of *Kitty Hawk*'s VF-114 "Aardvarks" were in the cockpit of F-4B NH-215 standing what was known as "Condition One CAP," positioned at the waist catapult ready for immediate launch. Wisely later recalled that he and Jordan were keeping themselves awake by reading World War II fighter pilot novels, since there were normally no alerts in the middle of the night out in the Tonkin Gulf. Suddenly, at 0200 hours on December 20, *Kitty Hawk* made a sharp turn into the wind and the order blared over the ship's 1MC public announcement system: "Stand by to launch Condition One CAP!" The Phantom was surrounded by the deck crew as Wisely went through his start-up, and by the time the carrier had steadied on course into the wind he was ready for launch. Two seconds later, the fighter cleared the deck, climbing away at 160 knots.

As Wisely cleaned up the airplane and continued climbing, GCI told him, "Your bogies bear 310 at 110 miles, cleared to arm, cleared to fire!" Wisely climbed through the low overcast and broke into the clear moonlit night at 3,000 feet while he and Jordan armed the Sparrow missiles. While the Phantom headed toward North Vietnam, there was momentary disagreement between the carrier and Red Crown, the nuclear-powered cruiser USS *Long Beach*, operating as the air defense ship off the North Vietnamese coast, over whether they were cleared to fire without a visual identification. This was settled when the carrier division commander gave the order at 0220 hours that they were "cleared to fire."

GCI informed Wisely "Your bogey bears 295 at 20 miles, speed 120." Jordan was painting two targets on the radar as Wisely realized they were headed toward Than Hoa, a "hot" area. Due to the reported low speed, Wisely was worried the bogeys were a North Vietnamese trap to entice a US plane into range of the SAMs. On the radar, it was clear the bogeys knew of the Phantom's presence; as the two headed south along the coast, they turned right and headed inland. Wisely continued closing. At eight miles, Jordan got a lock on the second, and at three miles, Wisely fired a Sparrow. He later recalled, "It followed the bogey into the overcast at 2,500 feet. When it got to where they were, it exploded as advertised and a large fireball glowed through the clouds. I tried to fire a second missile at Number One, but it didn't leave the rails. I remember yelling in excitement to Dave 'We got the bastard!'" The target was recorded as destroyed at 0230 hours, December 20.

Wisely turned back for the carrier. VF-213's Lieutenant Dave McRae, with RIO Ensign Dave Nichols, had been launched soon after Wisely and was vectored to go after the remaining target. "I made it quite clear to them who I was and what my heading was so there could be no mistaking us for the enemy. As we headed on back, we heard him call a lock and watched his missile launch and track to the target and explode as ours had done. I rolled the airplane a couple of times in sheer joy!" The two Phantoms had demonstrated the performance of the Sparrow III when used in the beyond-visual-range (BVR) role for which it had been originally designed.

Back on *Kitty Hawk*, the victorious crews went to Strike Ops, where they debriefed VF-114 skipper Hank Halleland and VF-213 CO Jim Wilson, and received congratulations from *Kitty Hawk*'s commanding officer, Captain Paul Pugh, who as an exchange pilot with the USAF 4th Fighter Wing in Korea had been the second F-86 Sabre pilot to down a MiG-15 in December 1950, and a leading contender to become the first US ace of that war in the spring of 1951.

Due to the targets' speed, it was clear the two Phantoms had not shot down enemy fighters. It was later determined that their victims were two Antonov An-2 "Annushkas," the largest single-engine cargo-carrying biplane ever built, used by the Soviets and North Vietnamese as utility aircraft. These particular An-2s had been maneuvering to attack South Vietnamese naval units at the time they were spotted.

While the *Rolling Thunder* air war was going on, back home comedian Bill Cosby had a routine that parodied the rules of engagement under which the aircrews fought over North Vietnam. Cosby used the traditional football meeting of the captains of the opposing sides at the outset of a game to receive pre-game instruction from the referee, transposing that to the American Revolution and using Revolutionary War tactics as an analogy to the war the United States was fighting in Vietnam:

> Cap'n Washington meet Cap'n Cornwallis. Cap'n Cornwallis meet Cap'n Washington. Cap'n Cornwallis, your team gets to wear bright red coats, stand in nice straight lines, and march around in the open. Cap'n Washington, your team gets to hide behind trees, shoot from behind rocks, and run away if the red coats get too close. Good luck to both of you.

While it has been both easy and convenient to blame President Johnson, Secretary McNamara, and others in the Johnson Administration for the failure of Operation *Rolling Thunder* to achieve its goal of convincing the North Vietnamese to end their war in the south, blame for the overall failure also rests on the shoulders of the top leadership of the armed forces who continually promised government leaders they could achieve decisive results against a country that was a poor target for a strategic bombing campaign. In seeking to find a middle ground, and using the campaign purely for political objectives, the results were inevitable failure.

It is resoundingly true that Robert Strange McNamara was exactly the wrong man to hold the office of Secretary of Defense, and perhaps the perfect demonstration that what works in the world of business makes no sense in the world of government and most particularly in military operations. However, President Johnson was determined not to be forced to choose between the expenditures for the domestic social improvements he was dedicated to in his Great Society and the expenditure necessary to fight the war in Southeast Asia, proclaiming that the United States was rich enough to afford both "guns and butter." McNamara's "reforms" in military operations gave the president the kind of "facts" that would allow him to believe his claim.

At his heart, McNamara was an accountant, and was perhaps the best example ever of the criticism of that profession, that its practitioners know "the price of everything and the value of nothing." With his accounting background and experience as chief executive officer of the Ford Motor Company, he was able to reel off statistics on any subject he was called upon to discuss, astonishing his subordinates and leaving the stenographers struggling to keep pace. In this, he was perhaps also the quintessential "New Frontiersman," dedicated to the belief that there was no activity that could not be dealt with through the rational application of pure analysis to determine the right course.

As Secretary of Defense, McNamara's reforms were founded on the introduction of quantifiable accounting and control methods into upper management of the Pentagon. As an accountant and former chief executive officer, McNamara himself would have been the first to agree that the first step of such management was in the choice of what information to quantify, and whether that was the information which would provide an accurate portrayal of reality, to form the basis of such rational decision-making. Unfortunately, information relevant for the production of widgets is of use in military affairs only in discovering if the production of weapons is adequate to the needs at hand. It has nothing to do with the question of whether the right weapons are being produced, or whether they are being used in an effective manner. McNamara's failure was that he did not understand that he had violated this fundamental truth.

With regard to Operation *Rolling Thunder*, McNamara's "whiz kids" who performed his information gathering and analysis – none of whom had any experience in air warfare – determined that they would quantify "success" using statistics regarding expected sortie rates for the different aircraft types in use. Sortie rates were essentially chosen due to the lack of any other quantifiable criteria. Essentially, the top decision makers were operating on the belief that if US forces flew enough sorties and dropped enough ordnance, the North Vietnamese would be forced to quit as a result of the power of mathematics. It was data similar to – and equally as useless as – the "body count" that formed the basis of determining success on the battlefields of South Vietnam. Success or failure in war is not capable of reduction to such simplistic "facts." There is no method available to quantify such things as "national commitment" and "individual fighting spirit."

With the war being fought "on the cheap" in order to allow the president to concentrate on the domestic reforms that he had championed throughout his political career, many decisions were made that adversely affected the conduct of the air war over North Vietnam. One of the most important of these was the lack of aircraft carriers. By mid-1965 the pace of operations for Pacific Fleet carriers was such that carriers from the Atlantic Fleet were deployed to Southeast Asia. Naval navigators and ship handlers became familiar with rounding the Cape of Good Hope and the vagaries of the weather in the Indian Ocean, where US ships had not normally seen large-scale operation previously.

Compensating for the carrier shortage resulted in the line period for carriers and their supporting ships on Yankee Station being extended past the normal three weeks and the total length of the overseas deployments beyond the standard six months to terms of seven to ten months at a time. Such extensions resulted in increased wear and tear on a navy for which 60 percent of its combat ships dated from World War II, were reaching the end of their effective lives and were in need of major overhaul to meet such demands, with consequent increases in maintenance costs and deterioration of service of worn-out ships.

In the meantime, the extension of overseas deployments adversely affected crews, leading to a loss of morale and a loss of trained personnel as both officers and enlisted men who might have made a career of the Navy opted to return to civilian life at the expiration of their terms of service. With active tours on Yankee Station of 25–35 days and even longer, and line periods 150–200 percent more than originally planned, combined with reduced turnaround time in the United States between deployments, which was traditionally used for equipment repair and training, overall efficiency declined throughout the war. A fire on *Oriskany* in the fall of 1966 and another aboard USS *Forrestal* nine months later contributed to the degradation of the carrier fleet.

What was worst was the internal rot in the fighting force in terms of morale, as those tasked with doing the fighting and dying dealt with the inability to fight the war by any rational rules of combat and the impossibility of striking targets like supplies at a choke point where the strike might have an effect on enemy operations. This, along with the wastage of aircrews in piecemeal attacks on transportation targets with small returns, led to men deciding that they would concentrate more on surviving their tour than on risking their lives by fighting the war in a way that exposed them to maximum danger for minimal return.

As was pointed out many times during the war by many Americans in the forefront of the fighting, one side was fighting for their country and the other was fighting to survive their tour of duty and return home. The difference in those two levels of commitment cannot be quantified, but they are blindingly obvious in the study of the war and its outcome.

7

AIR COMBAT, 1967–68

After claiming 11 air-to-air victories against the VPAF in 1966, the next air battle between the Navy and the VPAF came on April 24, 1967, after the weather improved at the end of the monsoon, when permission was granted to attack airfields in North Vietnam. Kep airfield was located 37 miles northeast of Hanoi and was one of five major MiG bases in North Vietnam, capable of operating both the MiG-17 and MiG-21. The air battle that erupted over the airfield that day was the biggest aerial engagement of the war to date. Once again *Kitty Hawk*'s "Aardvarks" were involved as they covered the attack by Intruders from VA-112 and Skyhawks of VA-144. VF-213 CO Commander Jim Wilson led the strike.

The "Aardvarks" had the assignment of MiG Combat Air Patrol (MIGCAP), led by skipper Commander Hank Urban. Once again, Lieutenant Denny Wisely was part of the strike, flying with his regular RIO, Lieutenant (jg) Gareth L. Anderson, as wingman to division leader Lieutenant Commander John Holm. Wisely was concerned by the fact that his Phantom was only carrying one Sidewinder, due to technical problems with the other three launch stations. Also on the mission was Lieutenant Charles Southwick with RIO Ensign James W. Liang. The squadron's assignment was to arrive over Kep ahead of the strike force and provide cover should any MiGs attempt to interfere. Wisely remembered the mission as one of the hottest he flew over Vietnam:

We flew low up through the Ha Long Bay area east of Haiphong. By the time we crossed the beach near Cam Pha, we were at 10,000 feet and they opened up with 85mm guns. The AAA stopped firing and we could hear talk over the radio about SAMs being fired. As we came out of the hills north of Haiphong into the Red River Valley, they started shooting at us with everything from BB guns to SAMs. This was probably the most intense ground fire I had seen. Finally, up ahead, we could see Kep Airfield.

Wisely's division took up an orbit over a small mountain east of the airfield. In doing so, they got too close to the main railroad from Hanoi to China. Wisely's APR-27 gave warning that they were being tracked by a Fan Song radar, and soon two SAMs were launched which the Phantoms were able to evade. "The red tracer rounds from the AAA were so thick I couldn't believe we were not getting hit."

Wisely and Anderson saw an A-6 take a hit and catch fire, with the crew ejecting near the airfield. "Immediately after that, Charlie Plumb, our skipper's wingman, got hit in the starboard engine and one of his missiles caught fire. I remember thinking I was watching a movie." Commander Urban ordered his wingman to head for home. "It wasn't long before Charlie started yelling he had MiGs on his tail. With only one engine, he was in no position to take them on by himself." Division leader Holm turned to give help with Wisely in "Loose Deuce." Minutes later, they received word that Plumb had eluded his pursuers. "We turned around and headed back to protect the departing strike force."

The two Phantoms had just returned to the Red River Valley when they were warned there were MiGs approaching up the valley:

John and I made a 360-degree turn and suddenly there were MiG-17s everywhere. I saw an A-6 and an A-4 come through with MiGs chasing them. A MiG cut across left to right in front of me and headed for the deck. I rolled left and pulled hard, completing a barrel roll and came out right behind him at treetop level. However, I was too close to do anything without guns. I looked back and saw another MiG in a left turn. I pulled around hard and passed another MiG canopy to canopy. I told Gary our chances of a radar lock were minimal and he should loosen his straps and spend his time being a tight wingman in the back seat with his head on a swivel.

While Wisely had gotten past the AAA unhit, Southwick and Liang felt a "thud" but dismissed it since the Phantom kept flying as though all was well. While the strike aircraft dropped their bombs, they heard the call that MiGs were coming down the Red River Valley. With the strike aircraft departing, Southwick had turned east, intending to return to *Kitty Hawk*, but he turned around at the call and immediately spotted several MiG-17s headed straight at him. As they roared past, he radioed "Tally Ho" and started a horizontal turn, then pulled the Phantom up into a climbing vertical loop and dropped down on the MiGs, which had taken up their new low-altitude "wagon wheel" maneuver. There was one on his right, then a second flashed by on his left and exposed its belly as it turned. The North Vietnamese pilots' maneuver was new, and Southwick then entered the wheel after the MiG, which was actually what the enemy wanted him to do. He got a good tone and launched an AIM-9D that hit the second MiG in its right wing. The enemy fighter smoked as it spewed fuel, then fell off and dived into the ground.

Wisely spotted the MiGs in the "wagon wheel," attempting to entice Southwick into a fight on their terms down low. He pulled the vertical climbing loop maneuver several times in an attempt to get position on one of the MiGs. "Another MiG appeared ahead of me in a left turn. Either he didn't see me or was a poor pilot because I should not have been able to out-turn him. I got a good tone on my only Sidewinder, but we were too close! I rolled to the right, checked my six, and gave the MiG some separation." Wisely punched afterburner and went vertical, coming over the top and aiming at the enemy fighter. He suddenly saw two Sidewinders pass ahead, fired by Holm. "I really don't know how many MiGs there were, but they were everywhere."

Wisely turned to go after the last MiG he had seen when another passed very close to his left, having overshot. "He was in afterburner, which looked like a Sterno can with flames lapping out in an irregular pattern behind the aircraft. Here I was, again in a great position for a gun, but too close for a missile." He rolled again and pulled down to go after the MiG again. "I found him about a mile in front of me in a port turn. With him approaching almost head-on at that range, it did not give us time to lock up and get off a Sparrow. As he came by canopy to canopy, I gave him the international signal for 'I love you very much.'"

Wisely then saw another MiG roll in below and to his right. The first MiG was at his four o'clock with 40 degrees to go in his turn before he would pull in on Wisely's tail. "I rolled in on the MiG behind the F-4 and got a great tone. I fired!" For a moment, it looked to Wisely as if the Sidewinder was homing on Southwick. "I called 'Linfield pull up!' and he did. What was happening was the Sidewinder was giving itself some lead. The MiG on my tail must have seen me fire the missile because the MiG I was shooting at suddenly reversed his turn to the right, the wrong way." Wisely knew the MiG-17 didn't turn well at high speed. "It was like watching in slow motion. He put his tailpipe directly in front of the missile, sweetening the shot. The 'Winder went right up his tailpipe and a large piece of his horizontal tail came off. He trailed black smoke as he continued in a right turn down to the ground." Wisely had just become the first Navy fighter pilot to score more than one aerial victory in the Vietnam War. He would hold the position of leading "MiG killer" for five years, until Operation *Linebacker* in 1972.

With the MiG that had been pursuing them shot down, Southwick rolled out and lit the afterburner to climb away from the enemy. At that moment, RIO Liang noticed the low fuel warning light flash on and realized that the "thud" they had felt must have been shrapnel from an exploding AAA shell. Apparently, the hit had severed the fuel lines since he was unable to transfer fuel from the still-full wing tanks.

Wisely had also turned east to return to *Kitty Hawk*. Just then he spotted Southwick's F-4 and moved to join up. As he closed, he spotted another MiG-17 circling above the fight and considered attempting to shoot it with a Sparrow. "Before I could, Southwick said he couldn't transfer his wing fuel because of damage and only had 500 pounds useable. We throttled back and stayed with him."

Liang called for a tanker to meet them as close to the beach as possible, since they only had a few minutes' fuel available as Wisely weaved behind the damaged F-4 to provide cover. He recalled:

We coasted out between Cam Pha and Hon Gay, two very hot areas. Fortunately, we didn't draw fire. Then another Phantom that was running out of gas hooked up with the tanker just as one engine quit. We were about four miles south of the off-shore islands when they ran out of fuel. Andy and I had already alerted Search and Rescue. They punched out and we watched them land in the water. We circled till the helo [helicopter] showed up 30 minutes later, then went back to the ship. What an incredible flight! This was the wildest one I had ever flown from a sheer excitement perspective.

The 923rd Fighter Regiment's Mai Duc Toai, Le Hai, Luu Huy Chao, and Hoang Van Ky claimed to have shot down Southwick's F-4 and were credited with a shared victory.

Wisely and Anderson, with strike leader Wilson, were flown to Saigon with a stopover on *Ticonderoga* where they met Admiral Damon W. Cooper, Task Force 77 commander at the time. Flown on to Saigon for "five minutes of fame with the world press corps," as Wisely described it, they were taken for drinks at the top of the Hotel Continental. "We were exhausted and had not slept in a day-and-a-half. It was now dark and in the distance, we could see flares being dropped and shortly after hear the bombs going off." When they got to the Bachelor Officer Quarters at Bien Hoa Air Base, they found their quarters were a tent. "I started putting up my mosquito net and the army guy in the next bunk says 'Why bother? If you get malaria they send you home.'" *Kitty Hawk* put in at Subic Bay until May 8, when the ship and its air wing returned to Yankee Station.

The air war continued to escalate in intensity through the spring and summer of 1967. In the two weeks following their return to Yankee Station, several of the aviators who had seen action over Kep on April 24 would experience reversals of fortune. Each flying with a different crewman, Wisely, Liang, Southwick, and Anderson were all shot down in that period with vastly differing outcomes.

Southwick, flying with RIO Lieutenant J.D. Rollins, went down on May 14. Rollins, a former enlisted man, asked the squadron commander for a flight as lead in a major attack. He was assigned to fly with Southwick in an attack on the Thanh Hoa Bridge. Southwick's F-4 was carrying six Zuni packs with a total of 24 rockets, as lead flak suppressor. He rolled in on the gun emplacements and salvoed all 24 rockets. Their exhaust gases and debris caused an idle engine stall in both engines. While Southwick attempted a relight, they were hit by AAA in both engines. After Southwick and Rollins ejected, with both being captured quickly, the damaged Phantom II flew on without power and finally came to rest upright on the riverbank where the two had been captured. *Kitty Hawk* launched three Alpha strikes ("Alpha strike" is a Navy term denoting a large air attack by multiple squadrons of a carrier air wing, equivalent to the Air Force term "strike package") in an unsuccessful effort to destroy the aircraft that was hampered by bad weather before it was recovered by the

North Vietnamese. The remains of this Phantom can be found today in a museum outside Hanoi.

Anderson, who had been Wisely's RIO on April 24, flew with pilot Charlie Plumb, who had been hit in his engine by AAA over Kep that day, on a strike against the Van Diem POL storage facility near Hanoi on May 19, assigned as TARCAP. Over the target, numerous SAMs were fired and they were hit by one while dodging another. With the Phantom badly damaged, they headed east in an attempt to reach the water, but the plane started shedding parts and they were forced to eject. Again, both were captured and spent the rest of the war as POWs.

Denny Wisely and Jim Liang, who had been Southwick's RIO on April 24, were luckier when they were shot down by AAA on May 21. Wisely remembered, "We were due to leave the line for Subic Bay in two days. We again were going on a major strike against the Van Diem storage area south of Hanoi, where Charlie and Andy had gotten it." As with Plumb and Anderson, Wisely was flying wing in the third section of the two divisions assigned as TARCAP. The formation had just crossed inland when the right generator kicked off line and wouldn't reset. Wisely and Liang debated aborting, but decided to continue on. "We had decided to come out of the mountains very low to avoid the radar and hopefully the SAMs." Wisely's section had just turned north to take station west of the target when the first SAM launches came. "Linfield 213" dodged two SAMs. "I turned to the right and there ahead of us was a wall of automatic weapons fire coming from a small town." At that moment, the APR-27 started warbling, a warning they were being tracked by a Fan Song radar controlling a SAM.

"I pulled the airplane for all it was worth and got down very low to the ground to avoid the SAM. I ended up flying over that village and they opened up on me. I felt a thump well behind the cockpit." A moment later, the Phantom was hit again and Wisely knew it was bad when the controls went "mushy." "I told Jim we might have to get out." Neither wanted to go down where they were, so they decided to stick with the airplane as long as possible. "I called out, 'I just took a second hit and think we are going to have to get out.'" Wisely's flight leader alerted SAR and requested assistance from Red Crown. "The controls were responding so poorly that I decided to climb. I lit the afterburners figuring I would make a rocket out of it and put as much distance between us and Hanoi as possible."

A minute later, Lieutenant John Nash pulled his F-4 alongside Wisely and took a look. The left engine was on fire! He told Wisely to take it out of afterburner:

The afterburner had ignited fuel streaming from holes in my wings and fuselage. I shut the engine down. When the fire went out, I re-lit it but stayed out of afterburner and was able to level off about 7,000 feet.

Then I completely lost my number two hydraulic system. I had already lost the utility system when we were hit. I told Jim we had no chance of making it to the coast. The airplane wouldn't turn south anyway, and it was all I could do to keep it heading west. We were over the mountains, but still in a very bad area. The aircraft became very hard to control and the stick was almost useless. Then I lost my number one hydraulic system and had nothing. Luckily, the stabilator had frozen in neutral. I flew it that way for about 20 miles, using brute force on the left rudder pedal to stay level.

Finally, Wisely lost control. As the Phantom started to roll to the right, he signaled Liang to get out:

After he ejected, I ejected at 425 knots about 800 feet above the mountains. I held onto the face curtain with all my strength and my elbows flailed in the slipstream until I could pull them back. When my 'chute opened it took a few seconds to adjust my helmet to where I could see. I could see a village and the fireball from my airplane not far away, but fortunately the wind was blowing us away from both.

Overhead, Lieutenant Nash orbited the crash. He contacted Wisely on the rescue radio and told him SAR was coming. Wisely spotted Liang's parachute and maneuvered his to get closer. When he went into the jungle canopy, he pulled his visor down to protect his face as he fell through the branches, head down. He dropped the radio, but fortunately it was on a line and came to rest in the crotch of a branch he could reach when he finally was able to break his fall. He was 125 feet from the ground, with his parachute in the next tree. "I informed Nash I was OK. I was actually in the best possible hiding place available. The jungle was so thick the only way someone could spot me would be to find my tree and look straight up to see me."

Liang and Wisely were down in the jungle-covered mountains west of Hanoi, toward the Laotian border. Unknown to them at the time, they were in Laos, near Sai Koun, 85 miles southwest of Hanoi. "While it was debatable if we'd survive if we were captured here, the chances of a pickup were much better than they had been back where we got hit." Ten minutes later, he heard a burst of 20mm cannon fire that announced the arrival of the Air Force "Sandy" A-1 rescue cover aircraft. "Sandy Lead" informed him they had both his position and Liang's and that a helicopter would arrive in 20 minutes. "After about three hours, the twenty minutes finally passed. I heard more Skyraiders overhead. The Navy helicopter finally arrived, to discover their hoist wouldn't work, having been damaged by AAA when they came inland from the gulf." Thirty minutes later, an Air Force Jolly Green Giant arrived:

> He came in about fifteen feet above me. The rotor downwash was so great it almost blew me out of my nest. The part I was sitting on all but blew away. I thought about waving them away, but then I saw the penetrator and reached for it. I managed to slip my head in and then pull down a prong and sit on it and up I went. What a feeling it was to get into that helo!

Exhausted, Wisely dropped to the cabin floor and lay there.

The helicopter moved over to Liang's position. He had landed on the ground, which took 150 feet of cable to reach him. On the way up, the cable began unraveling. "When he got to the helo, he was spinning like a top. His arm was broken above the elbow and he was in a lot of pain, but he was smiling." As they flew off, they learned over the radio that the first helicopter had made a forced landing in North Vietnam from the damage suffered. Fortunately a second Navy helicopter was able to rescue them. Wisely, Liang, and their would-be rescuers all met at the forward base in Laos where they were then airlifted to Bangkok. Liang went to the hospital, while Wisely was flown to Da Nang the next day, where he was picked up by a COD and delivered back to *Kitty Hawk* the day before they left the line for Subic Bay for turnover to *Constellation* and Air Wing 14. Following his recovery from his injuries, Jim Liang went on to become an instructor at VF-121 before becoming one of the "Original Bros" who founded Top Gun, as an air combat maneuvering (ACM) radar operation and RIO training instructor.

While the Air Force worked throughout the war to find answers to problems of the air war in technology development, the Navy did not treat the issue with the same effort. As the North Vietnamese air defenses grew stronger in 1966–67, they made increased use of radar to control AAA as well as SAMs. Both the Air Force and Navy realized there was a need for on-board electronic jammers to defeat the expanding threat. The Navy's Project Shoehorn mounted the ALQ-51 deception jammer in its tactical aircraft. The ALQ-51 was small and had a low power output. Rather than use excess power to block the opponent's radars, the ALQ-51 operated as a deception jammer, sending a false return signal to the interrogating enemy radar, on the operating premise that the radar operator would be confused by the return and unable to determine which return on his screen to fire on.

Initially, the reliability of the ALQ-51 was poor. During 1965, the Navy had no worthwhile self-protection jammer. Captain Julian Lake, the officer in charge of the Project Shoehorn program, recalled:

> The program was deficient as hell – spares, test equipment, training and equipment. The guys didn't have any training in the U.S. because we didn't have any equipment back here. Everything was out there, but they couldn't support it, couldn't use it properly, couldn't maintain it properly, couldn't test it properly. Also, the commanders failed to understand the importance of EW [electronic warfare] at first. When they were about to launch a plane they wouldn't send it if they couldn't start an engine, they wouldn't send it if the wings wouldn't spread, they wouldn't send it if the radio didn't work. We had to convince them not to send it if the EW equipment didn't work.

Initially, aircrew flew with their ALQ-51 in standby mode. After they detected a missile site about to engage them, they would turn it on, which lessened the system's effect. During 1966, the glitches were worked out and the ALQ-51 started to make significant problems for North Vietnamese missile crews. The SAM loss rate fell to one aircraft per 50 missiles fired, compared to one plane per ten missiles without the ALQ-51.

However, after careful study, the missile crews developed a technique by which they could differentiate between the ALQ-51's false returns and actual targets. They had become so proficient against the ALQ-51 that on August 31, 1967, two A-4 *Oriskany* Skyhawks were destroyed by a single SA-2. Throughout the conflict, the Air Force upgraded its jammers, but the Navy did not further modify the ALQ-51. Naval air wings flew missions over North Vietnam in the heart of "SA-2 country" ignorant of the fact the North Vietnamese had defeated their jammers. While the Air Force SAM loss rate continued to fall, Navy losses steadily increased. In 1967, SAMs were responsible for half the Navy's losses.

Eventually, the main weapons used against SAMs were A-4s and A-6s armed with anti-radiation missiles (ARMs) that homed on the controlling radars. The first was the AGM-45 Shrike, which was followed by the larger and faster AGM-78. The Shrike was developed by the US Navy at NOTS China Lake, California, as the world's first operational ARM, entering combat with A-4E squadron VA-23 in 1965. A relatively simple weapon, the Shrike was also adopted by the US Air Force's nascent Wild Weasel force. The mission in both services was called "Iron Hand," symbolic of a mailed fist smashing the SAMs.

Operationally, use of the Shrike required selection of a specific passive seeker-head, with a limited frequency range and target radar, prior to launch. Once airborne, it could not be changed. The Shrike was also short-ranged, having an endurance that was considerably less than the SA-2s being fired at the Iron Hand aircraft. As famously stated, using the Shrike to duel with SAMs was "like trying to fight a rattlesnake with a BBQ fork." The weapon's warhead was not particularly large either, and it did not take the North Vietnamese SAM operators (who were by now the most proficient in the world) long to realize that merely shutting off their radar would usually defeat the missile. What the Shrike could do, however, was "suppress" the site, which provided space and time to strikers while the SAM or AAA sites were otherwise occupied.

The AGM-78 Standard ARM was a totally different animal. Another US Navy-developed weapon, the STARM, gave the A-6B greater standoff range, placing it outside the SA-2's reach. The missile also had wider frequency coverage and could be programmed for a specific target prior to launch – something the Shrike could not do. It was also very expensive, and crews were instructed to wait for a "high percentage" shot before sending it down range. The weapon went on to give sterling service through the war with the A-6B, as well as with the US Air Force's much better-known F-105G Wild Weasels.

April and May 1967 saw the heaviest air fighting over North Vietnam until May 1972. Eight of the 38 kills claimed over North Vietnam in the period were by naval aviators, five by Crusaders, two by Phantoms, and one by a Skyhawk. The high point of the Crusader's combat with enemy fighters came in May and June 1967 and again involved VF-211 and VF-24, this time operating from *Bon Homme Richard*. On May 1, VF-211's Lieutenant Commander Marshall O. "Mo" Wright shot down a MiG-17 while escorting Iron Hand Skyhawks. Spotting the enemy fighter as it got on the tail of a Skyhawk, he pulled behind it and fired a Sidewinder. His wingman, USAF exchange officer Captain Ron Lord, called the kill "Beautiful – it just came apart at the seams when the missile exploded."

On May 19, six F-8s led by VF-211's skipper, Commander Paul H. Speer, and wingman Lieutenant (jg) Joseph M. Shea provided cover for an Iron Hand mission against heavy concentrations of SAMs and AAA near Hanoi. Section leader Lieutenant Commander Kay Russell's Crusader was shot down and Russell was captured. While the two VA-212 Iron Hand A-4s fired their Walleyes at a SAM site, Speer spotted MiGs coming in. He engaged a MiG in prolonged air combat maneuvering before the enemy showed his tail and Speer hit him with his second Sidewinder after the first one failed. Wingman Shea then spotted another MiG coming in and Speer told him to take it, which he did. Both of his Sidewinders hit the MiG and sent it spinning into the Hanoi suburbs below.

VF-24's Lieutenant Commander Bobby C. Lee and Lieutenant Phillip R. Wood were escorting A-6 Intruders when they spotted MiGs attacking a *Kitty Hawk* Intruder. Wood fired a Sidewinder at one, but it missed and the enemy dived away. A second MiG dived on Wood but he turned into it, then hit the MiG with his second Sidewinder. The enemy pilot ejected, but his parachute streamed and did not open. Wood's F-8 was damaged in the fight and after taking on a limited amount of fuel, he landed aboard *Kitty Hawk*, where the damaged Crusader was declared a total loss; in 1985, he would return to the carrier as her captain. Lee and his wingman Lieutenant (jg) Kit Smith attacked a radar site with Zunis. As they pulled out of their run, a MiG-17 crossed in front of them. Lee's Sidewinder cut it in half. The day's missions had seen more MiG-17s shot down in one engagement than in all the rest of *Rolling Thunder.*

When *Kitty Hawk* handed over to *Constellation* in Subic Bay, Wisely ran across two old friends from his early days when he flew F4D Skyrays in VU-3 and learned air combat maneuvering, who were now members of VF-142 "Ghostriders." The pilots laughed about the old days and the hassling that had given Wisely the edge to survive. *Kitty Hawk* headed for Yokosuka, while *Constellation* headed to Yankee Station. The next month would see the air war die down since many of the VPAF's fighters had fled to China following their losses.

The "Checkmates" and the "Renegades" got into it again with the "Red Bandits" on July 21, when an escort by VF-211 and 24 ran into a pack of MiG-17s. VF-211's Lieutenant Commander Tim Hubbard was carrying three Zuni packs and one Sidewinder as he flew escort for the Iron Hand A-4s. When the MiGs attacked, he fired the Sidewinder and several Zunis and finally used his guns on the MiG he shot down. VF-24's brand new XO, Lieutenant Commander Marion I. Isaaks, got behind one. His F-8 was carrying a full load of four Sidewinders, and he finally shot the enemy fighter down with his third missile after the first two failed. Isaacks was paying so much attention to the falling enemy that he failed to see another MiG until it came at him head-on, firing, turning aside at the last moment.

Lieutenant Commander Robert L. Kirkwood fired at one MiG that crossed in front of him but he was out of position and the Sidewinder went ballistic. He then shot a Sidewinder at the MiG Isaacks fired at, but the XO's missile arrived first. Kirkwood then turned on another MiG and fired a Sidewinder that missed. He closed and opened fire with his cannon, becoming the only "Gunfighter" pilot to be officially credited with actually shooting down an enemy fighter with his guns. This was the last big fight with MiG-17s in which Crusaders scored multiple kills. With these victories bringing CVW-21's total score to 12, they became the leading MiG-killing air wing of the war. At the end of July, there were only seven MiG-21s and 28 MiG-17s in North Vietnam, based at Phuc Yen and Giaudo Lam airfields which were still off limits for attacks. The rest of the enemy's fighters returned to their bases from China over the first week of August.

At 1145 hours on August 10, 1967, two "Ghostrider" F-4Bs were launched from *Constellation* to fly BARCAP for a two-carrier

Alpha strike against the Phu Ly transhipment point. Lieutenant Guy Freeborn and RIO Lieutenant (jg) Robert Elliot were flying wing to Lieutenant Commanders Robert C. Davis and RIO Gayle O. Elie. The two Phantoms took on fuel from a KA-3B and took up their BARCAP station west of Nam Dinh, flying a left orbit at approximately 22,000 feet rather than the normal 15,000–18,000 feet. The two "Ghostriders" were the first to try a new tactic in which the BARCAP were under greater GCI control from the Red Crown ship off North Vietnam. With the weather forecast of thin cloud layers at 22,000 feet, they hoped to catch any attacking enemy fighters as they broke through the cloud layers since a typical VPAF attack strategy was to dive through the cloud after being brought into position by North Vietnamese GCI control. As Freeborn later explained, "the surprise element worked just as we had planned."

The *Constellation* strike group made their attack and exited the target area. As the two Phantoms turned left to engage following a warning from Red Crown of enemy jets in the area, Freeborn looked up just as two silver MiG-21s appeared out the clouds directly above. Navy fliers had rarely seen these fighters, since they were primarily used at this point of the war against Air Force formations, which flew faster than the Navy formations. The enemy fighters were heading north at 400 knots and did not see the Navy fighters.

The two F-4s moved into position behind the MiGs, ready to shoot. Davis and Elie went after the "Blue Bandit" on the right, but the two Sparrows they triggered refused to fire. Davis quickly went to the Sidewinders, got a tone and fired one that missed. Frustrated, he armed a second, got the tone and fired, but it failed to acquire the target and went ballistic. At that same moment, Freeborn, in pursuit of the MiG on the left, got a tone and fired a Sidewinder that tracked and exploded just left of the enemy fighter, which streamed smoke and fuel. Davis quickly executed a high yo-yo maneuver that brought him in behind the MiG Freeborn had winged, which was now in a left bank at 14,000 feet. Davis fired a third Sidewinder that failed to track, then shot his final AIM-9D, which went up the enemy's tailpipe and exploded, destroying the Fishbed-C.

When Freeborn saw the MiG explode, he exclaimed, "The bastard shot my MiG!" to his RIO. He turned on Davis's original target, which was directly ahead and a thousand feet beneath him. Pulling onto the enemy's tail, he got a good heat tone and squeezed off a second Sidewinder, which misfired and stayed on the rail. Quickly, he positioned himself again and squeezed off a third AIM-9D, which wiggled for a moment before it tracked and hit the MiG, which exploded in a huge fireball.

The two crews had just scored the first Navy F-4 victories against the MiG-21. While both pilots had scored with nearly textbook engagements, the fact that it took nine missiles to shoot down two MiGs was a disturbing example of the fact that poor weapons reliability was robbing aircrews of opportunities for the quick kills the missiles were supposed to achieve, placing the heavy F-4 in jeopardy in an extended dogfight with the lighter and more maneuverable enemy fighters. Guy Freeborn said afterwards, "What we really wanted were built-in guns like in the Air Force F-4Es."

The VPAF had taken heavy losses over the first seven months of 1967, with 12 kills credited to the Navy, of which nine were achieved with the new AIM-9D, which demonstrated its clear superiority over the AIM-9B. Despite these losses, the enemy showed up in strength over the last five months of the year. Their new "aerial guerilla war" harassing tactics that were introduced in September succeeded in drastically increasing the number of missions aborted due to "forced jettisons" of bombs before the strike reached its intended target. As a result of the increase in air activity, President Johnson finally took Phuc Yen off the prohibited list, leaving only Hanoi International Airport on the list of targets not to be touched. Phuc Yen was attacked twice on October 24–25, with one MiG-21 destroyed in the air and another eight on the ground.

In response to the increased activity by the VPAF during 1967, Navy fighter tactics had changed from "Target Combat Air Patrol" (TARCAP) to "MiG Combat Air Patrol" (MiGCAP), with the MiGCAP operating on a different frequency from the strike frequency, so that they could operate under under close GCI control of the Red Crown surface ship which operated advanced ECM and electronic interrogation gear that could pinpoint enemy IFF signals. The two sections comprising a MiGCAP were assigned to stations "A" and "B" in areas most likely to come into contact with MiGs. During the last half of 1967, VF-143 destroyed three MiG-21s and one MiG-17 under this close GCI control.

The squadron's Monthly Report for October 1967 described the MiGCAP operation in detail:

> The MiGCAP briefed with the main strike force, effected a rendezvous overhead with the tanker, refueled approximately 2,500 to 3,000 pounds, then departed separately for pre-briefed CAP stations. After the rendezvous on departure frequency, the MiGCAP switched to Strike Control, checked their SIF [Selective Identification Facility] gear and then checked in with PIRAZ [Positive Identification Radar Advisory Zone] Control. They then shifted frequency to Primary BARCAP Control, giving the controlling ship their state, weapon and armament status, and the station where they would hold feet dry. The controlling ship would then have the MiGCAP shift to a primary or secondary frequency different from the strike frequencies, thus allowing them to give full control to the fighters without disturbing the strike network. This close control was the first positive movement to make use of the full capabilities of the F-4. It was felt that with MiGCAP on their station, along with TARCAP near the strike force, the MiG threat to the force was minimized to a low degree.

The MiGCAP tactic proved its worth during late October. *Constellation* began her final line period at Yankee Station on October 25. The first day on station saw poor weather, but the next day dawned clear and a strike was launched against the Van Dien army barracks. Orbiting between Hanoi and Thanh Hoa, two VF-143 F-4s on MiGCAP under control from Harbormaster, the SAR ship in the northern Gulf of Tonkin, were vectored toward several contacts that appeared to be MiGs. Clearance was given for the crews to fire without obtaining a visual identification of the targets. Fortunately, section leader Commander D.K. Grosshuesch's RIO, Lieutenant James B. Souder, experienced radar failure just as Grosshuesch was about to launch a Sparrow, while wingman Lieutenant (jg) Robert P. Hickey, Jr., and RIO Lieutenant (jg) Jeremy G. Morris also experienced launch failure after getting a missile lock. Hickey's Sidewinder shot also failed. When the two formations came into visual range, the crews realized the 'MiGs' were other VF-143 Phantoms!

A few moments later, they were vectored to another contact. This time, Grosshuesch and Hickey conducted a visual search while Souder and Morris focused on their radars. Souder's radar failed and Morris took over the intercept, directing Hickey into a firing position. The AIM-9D went ballistic and missed. In the meantime, Souder's radar came back and he resumed control, vectoring the two Phantoms to a position on the enemy's tail. Grosshuesch visually identified the MiG-21 but was unable to fire due to a system malfunction and he ordered Hickey to fire. That Sparrow tracked, striking the enemy's port wing and the MiG pitched over into a flat spin.

Further strikes against Phuc Yen, Kep, and the other MiG bases resulted in the VPAF sending their fighters back to China. By the end of the month, there were only four MiG-21s and 12 MiG-17s still in North Vietnam. Despite this withdrawal, VPAF MiG-17 aces Le Hai and Nguyen Dinh Phuc claimed two Phantoms from *Coral Sea*'s VF-151, flown by Lieutenant Commander C.D. Clower and RIO Lieutenant (jg) W.O. Estes, and Lieutenant (jg)s J.E. Teague and RIO T.G. Stier, who had been vectored to Kien An airfield outside Haiphong to intercept enemy aircraft detected by PIRAZ radar. Although they were jumped by the unseen MiGs, they were shot down by SAMs, though the 923rd Fighter Regiment pilots claimed both and a third in another engagement.

Following the conclusion of the Stennis Committee Hearings in the fall of 1967, the Joint Chiefs came to President Johnson with an urgent request for an expansion of the air war and a list of 27 targets they wanted to hit. Despite a second report from the Jason Division that reported no progress in the air campaign since their first, the president released an additional ten targets from the 27 requested in December 1967. Looking forward to 1968, the military leadership was buoyed by reports from MACV headquarters in Saigon that indicated that the enemy forces in South Vietnam had been pushed back in the countryside, with General Westmoreland predicting that 1968 would be the year the war turned in favor of the United States.

At the outset of 1968, the United States was as divided over the conduct of the Vietnam War as it had been in the years immediately prior to the outset of the Civil War. Domestic politics were taking on a division and partisanship unseen in recent memory. Despite this, President Johnson appeared certain to run for re-election with a strong possibility of remaining in the White House for another four years despite the divisions within his political party. The president had taken steps to give the military more latitude of action in fighting the war, though not as much as the generals and admirals had hoped for. Regardless, in January 1968, the rest of the American military echoed the optimism expressed by General Westmoreland that the enemy now faced defeat.

All of this changed on January 30, 1968, when the National Liberation Front opened offensives inside all the major cities of South Vietnam, even attacking the US Embassy in Saigon itself. In the countryside, NLF guerillas and units of the PAVN attacked US bases throughout the country. Most prominent of these battles was that around the Marine base of Khe Sanh in the Central Highlands. February and March would see the naval air units in Southeast Asia put their primary focus on flying air support for the Marines. By late March, the Khe Sanh crisis had passed and the enemy offensive throughout the country had been pushed back with heavy losses. However, the political landscape was now completely different from what it had been on New Year's Day. The fact that the enemy could mount such an offensive, in the face of official American reports of military success over the previous year, destroyed political support in Washington for continuing the war, with a halt to bombing North Vietnam announced at the end of the month.

Naval air operations were immediately affected by the president's decision. The areas where bombing was still allowed in the southern half of North Vietnam were Route Packs 1, 2, and 3, of which the latter two had been the responsibility of the Navy since 1965. Thus, Naval Aviation would see the most use and action in the seven months before bombing of North Vietnam came to a complete halt on November 1. The fighters of the VPAF had shown increased aggressiveness at the beginning of the year, with attacks made on US ECM aircraft over Laos, where a USAF EB-66 was shot down on January 14, and the Gulf of Tonkin, where a Navy EC-121 *Constellation* was chased by MiG-17s as it left its patrol station on January 17. In February, enemy fighters came within 25 miles of another EB-66 over Laos. These events all happened in areas where the enemy fighters had not appeared previously. While air combat was hampered by bad weather over North Vietnam, the fact that the enemy was appearing in larger formations, with fighters now attempting multiple attacks on the formations, pointed to 1968 being a "hot" year for air combat.

The bombing halt changed everything. In response, the VPAF brought back the fighters it had sent to China in November 1967 to its bases in North Vietnam. It adopted the tactic of positioning the fighters in the airspace above the 20th parallel that was now "off limits" to US fighters, then sending them across the line for a quick attack on a strike group, with the fighters returning to their safe airspace after single passes. The result was that there was limited opportunity for the F-4s and F-8s escorting the strikes to catch the enemy and shoot him down.

To counter this tactic, the Navy adopted a strategy of having strike aircraft quickly withdraw and go "feet wet" over the Tonkin Gulf, out of range of enemy defenses, when warned of enemy air activity, thus giving the defending fighters the chance to go after their opponents without having to make a visual identification before initiating an attack. Additionally, the naval aircraft were now operating within the protection envelope of their own SAMs – Talos missiles carried aboard ships off the coast. USS *Chicago* had shot down a MiG with a Talos on May 23, one of seven that would ultimately be claimed by ship-fired missiles.

For the fighters, continued poor weapons performance kept them from scoring victories. On May 7, five VF-92 F-4Bs from *Enterprise* engaged two MiG-21s, firing two Sparrows that missed. In the ensuing fight, Lieutenant Commander W.M. Christensen and RIO Lieutenant (jg) W.A. Kramer in NG210 were shot down by 921st Fighter Regiment ace Nguyen Van Coc. Both aviators were picked up and returned to the carrier. Two days later, squadron fighters again engaged three MiG-21s. The crews fired four Sparrows and claimed one "probable" and one "possible" kill, though no confirmation was received for either claim. Sister squadron VF-96 also engaged MiGs on May 9, with USAF exchange pilot Captain John P. Heffernan and RIO Lieutenant (jg) Frank A. Schumacher, and Lieutenants Robert H. Clime and RIO Eugene L. Sierras engaging three MiG-21s. In a mixed-up furball, both crews fired Sparrows, with Heffernan's second Sparrow leading to a claim for one shot down. Despite Red Crown confirming that only two targets were left after the fight, Heffernan was never given credit for this kill, with speculation for this lack of credit being that the Phantoms might have engaged PLAAF fighters.

On May 30, USS *America* arrived from the Atlantic Fleet for her first deployment to the war, with Air Wing 6 (CVW-6) flying its first strikes the next day. The carrier would see four line periods on Yankee Station over the next 112 days. Importantly, VF-102 and VF-33 introduced the F-4J Phantom to combat. The "J" model had been developed to address deficiencies in the F-4B that had been revealed in operations during *Rolling Thunder*.

The first production F-4J had flown on May 27, 1966, with VF-101 being the first squadron to re-equip that December. A total of 522 were produced by January 1972. The new Phantom's power was provided by two J79-GE-10s, with 17,900 pounds of thrust in afterburner. The new engines were among the visual differences with the earlier fighter, with their longer afterburner "turkey feathers." Because of increased weight, the F-4J had a beefed-up landing gear and larger mainwheels, resulting in a "bulged" wing similar to that of the USAF F-4s. While the Navy wanted better takeoff and landing performance, the need for speed, climb, and range meant that rather than use the high-drag slatted wing of the F-4E, a slot was added to the stabilator leading edge, creating a miniature inverted slatted wing that gave tremendous downward force at low speeds without stalling. The "J" was equipped with the AN/AJB-7 bombing system which gave better ground attack capability and allowed use of the Bullpup ASM. The AN/AWG-10 fire control system was housed in a larger radome and used the AN/APG-59 pulse-Doppler radar in place of the earlier APQ-72. The new radar was better able to detect and track low-flying aircraft without losing them in sea/ground returns. Visually, the "J" could be distinguished by the deletion of the infrared search and tracking pod under the radome of the F-4B. All-weather performance was improved by the AN/ASW-25 one-way datalink which made automatic carrier landings possible.

Despite flying a superior airplane, the aircrews of VF-102 "Diamondbacks" and VF-33 "Tarsiers" had little opportunity to engage with the enemy. Some two weeks after their combat debut, two VF-102 crews led by skipper Commander W.E. Wilbur and RIO Lieutenant (jg) B.F. Rupinski were vectored to an engagement over Do Luong with two MiG-21s of the 921st Fighter Regiment on June 16. In the engagement, Wilbur and his wingman fired a total of four Sparrows without success. On top of that, Wilbur's radio failed during the engagement, so he didn't hear the wingman's shouted warning when one of the "Blue Bandits" got on his tail and fired an Atoll that hit the Phantom, killing Rupinski, though Wilbur was able to eject. He was soon captured and became a POW. Throughout their deployment, both squadrons would engage the enemy but suffer frustration due to persistent radar, fire control, and missile failures. Over the course of *America's* first Vietnam deployment, VF-102 lost two Phantoms, with one man killed, one captured, and one crew rescued. VF-33 lost three F-4s, with Lieutenant Eric Brice killed on June 4 when his Phantom was hit by AAA; his RIO ejected successfully and was rescued. SAMs shot down an F-4J on July 24, but both crewmen were rescued after successful ejections.

On July 10, 1968, *America* had been back on the line for two days when VF-33's Lieutenants Roy Cash, Jr., and RIO Joseph E. Kain scored the first victory for an Atlantic Fleet squadron and the Phantom's last kill of *Rolling Thunder*.

Roy Cash had joined the Navy for flight training after graduation from college in June 1963. At the time there were no pilot slots open, so he opted for training as a naval aviation observer (NAO) in the F-4. After receiving his NAO wings in February 1964, he went to VF-101 at NAS Oceana for his first assignment. Transferred to VF-41 that July, his first act on arrival was to apply for flight training, which was approved in June 1965. He was the first RIO "retread" to qualify for flight training and won his Wings of Gold on June 23, 1966.

As a pilot, Cash, who gained the aviator's nickname "Outlaw," had flown in VF-101 until January 1967, when he joined VF-33 in time to take part in an eight-and-a-half-month deployment to the Mediterranean, where he became a "double centurion" with 200 carrier landings. When he and Kain launched from *America*, flying wing to Air Force exchange officer Major Charlie Wilson and RIO Lieutenant (jg) Bill William, his famous uncle Johnny Cash's *Live At Folsom Prison* album was topping the charts back home. Among the hits on the record was "I Still Miss Someone," which Roy had co-written with his uncle while he was in college in 1959.

The two Phantoms launched at 1550 hours, assigned as MiGCAP for an Alpha strike in Route III. As they took up position 15 miles off Vinh over the Tonkin Gulf, Bill Williams discovered he had a glitch with the radar. Cash remembered:

It was agreed that if we took a vector for bandits I would assume the lead. We quickly established CAP station, then about 45–60 minutes into the flight, our controller, "Raider" aboard USS *Horne* (CG-30), called us on cipher frequency to alert us to impending MiG activity.

There were MiGs that were about to launch and fly down to attack the A-7s below the "no-bomb" line just north of Vinh. Our ECM and Comms Intel planes had picked up good info on them. "Raider" kept us apprised of the increasing activity and communications, switching us back and forth from clear to cipher frequencies.

We told "Raider" that in the event we were vectored, we wanted to fly a specific attack profile, and they concurred. The profile was that we would vector west at high speed and low altitude to gain a position southwest of the approaching MiGs so as to be able to vector northwest with the afternoon sun over our left shoulders. That might provide surprise, and put us in a position so the bandits could not see us coming out of the sun.

The MiGs finally launched and started south. "Raider" vectored us west and we jettisoned our tanks, armed missiles and hit the deck. We were at 1,500 feet and got to the karst ridgeline just as the MiGs crossed the line. We were vectored northeast, turned, and pointed to the area they were coming from.

Kain immediately got a Pulse-Doppler radar contact at 32 miles. The Phantoms were still low, while the enemy fighters were at approximately 5,000 feet:

We were told on cipher they were two "Blue Bandits," which identified them as MiG-21s, and there were no other known bandits in the area. We were also told the MiGs' communications were being jammed by our EA-3 ECM bird that was sitting just off the coast. That meant they probably would not know we were coming. Great sport!

The two F-4Js stayed low, flying at 550 knots, in combat spread formation with their anti-smoke devices diminishing the smoke emitted by the J79s. "Charlie was at my three o'clock position so that he could look through me at 'bad guy' country. He still had no radar. I asked for clearance to fire." To Cash's amazement "Raider" responded "Roger, contacts are two blue bandits – you are cleared to fire!"

Ed and I were ecstatic, since it was normal to have to gain visual ID. I checked that the switches were armed and ready, and made sure that the missiles indicated good. We were loaded with two

AIM-7E Sparrows and four AIM-9G Sidewinders. I reviewed in my mind procedures for switching from "radar" to "heat," and we kept on tracking. We maintained radar contact continuously, down to 20 miles, and we checked everything again, keeping Charlie up to speed on the situation. He was to maintain visual lookout for other bandits who might be hiding in the weeds.

When they were 12 miles from the enemy, Cash reconfirmed "clear to fire" with "Raider" and started looking for the enemy:

At eight miles I called "Tally ho – two, on the nose." What I really saw were two glints from the bright sun behind us on the silver fuselages of the MiGs, not the aircraft themselves, but from eight miles I never lost sight of them.

I was locked on, dot in the center, MiGs head-on. It looked good for Sparrow shots down the throat. At 5–6 miles, the missile launch circle began to expand, indicating maximum range, expanding to mid or optimum range. At four miles the circle reached its largest diameter, indicating the optimum firing parameters had been met. I fired off two Sparrows and called "Fox one, Fox one." The Sparrows appeared to guide, heading for what looked like an imminent kill.

Suddenly, the range on radar froze at three to four miles, and Cash watched the MiGs, which were now fully in sight and not looking like sun glints, began a lazy left turn away from him and the missiles. The two Sparrows exploded at the wingman's two o'clock position, about 100 yards distant.

"Until the Sparrows exploded, the MiGs did not know we were there." Startled by the explosion of the Sparrows, the wingman broke right, into the explosions, then turned back left to stay with his leader. Realizing that Cash was approaching a good firing position, the wingman again broke hard into him and closed to a firing position inside the Sparrow's minimum range. Cash switched to heat and fired off a Sidewinder. However, the aspect was almost 90 degrees off at less than 1,000 feet, so it missed, but it scared the wingman so he continued his descending right break, pulled out low, and headed north out of the fight.

Cash pulled a high-G left barrel roll to get in behind the leader who was breaking right into him. Wilson broke left over Cash and spotted two more MiG-21s that were down low, approximately three miles distant. Red Crown (USS *Long Beach*, CGN-9) called, "Heads up 'Rootbeers.' You got two more bandits west."

> I was too busy to respond, and Charlie was telling me he saw them too, so I continued turning, and with my energy, combined with the MiG leader's bad position and slow speed, I quickly attained the six o'clock at about 1,500 to 1,800 yards and fired an AIM-9G. I watched it guide and impact the tail area of the MiG, blowing the tail completely off. The pilot obviously knew he was had because almost simultaneously with the impact I saw his 'chute. It appeared he had ejected either just before impact, or as it occurred.

In the meantime, the other two MiG-21s joined the fight. "Charlie called out something to me about breaking. I didn't hear it, but what he said was, 'Outlaw,' break left… I mean RIGHT!'" as one of the second pair of MiGs fired an Atoll. Fortunately the enemy was out of range and the missile did not guide on Cash:

> I broke back to where the other MiGs were coming from and saw them hit the deck about two to three miles away. They turned tail and ran. As soon as they were tail-on they disappeared, vanished. I couldn't find them, visually or on radar, so I called to Charlie, "Unload, unload. Bug out, bug out!" and we headed for the water. We called "feet wet," and "Raider" confirmed, "Splash one blue bandit, Rootbeers." I responded, "You betcha Raider. I got that son of a gun."

The two Phantoms hit the tanker and took on enough gas to get back to *America*, where Cash remembered:

> I performed the best rendition of a victory roll I could imagine. The ship and Air Wing crews swarmed me after landing. It was a neat feeling to be a hero for the day – in fact, hero for the cruise. I gave up smoking as a result of that kill. I had told some of the guys jokingly, "If I shoot down a MiG today I'm going to quit smoking." I suppose God said, "Oh yeah? Let's see if you really mean it." I haven't smoked since.

The engagement was important, since it illustrated the way the Navy's engagement philosophy "should" work when all the tactics that had been developed earlier in the year came together. The jamming played an important role in confusing the MiGs by cutting them off from their ground control guidance. Clearing the area permitted the Phantom to employ the BVR Sparrow III without fear of it inadvertently hitting a friendly. Had Cash's Sparrow functioned properly, it would have been a textbook victory.

Lieutenant Pham Phu Thai, who had successfully ejected when Cash's Sparrow blew the tail off his MiG-21, survived the ejection and soon returned to operations. He remained in the air force for a 30-year career and rose to the rank of Lieutenant General, assigned as deputy commander of the VPAF at the time of his retirement.

The summer of 1968 proved frustrating for the Phantom squadrons. They had managed one unconfirmed hit with the Sparrow after launching dozens of AIM-7Es. The AIM-9D had experienced marginally better success, however, crews still faced problems defining its firing envelope in the heat of combat or a high-G maneuvering environment. Over the course of the first seven months of the year, two Phantoms were lost to MiGs while only being credited with downing one enemy fighter in return. To make matters worse, the pilots of the older F-8 had claimed five MiGs destroyed for no losses in six engagements.

Former Top Gun instructor Jim Ruliffson wrote an analysis of the F-4's weaknesses as a whole during *Rolling Thunder*, which explained many of the failures during 1968:

I've always contended that the F-4 was easy to fly in a mediocre way, but very difficult to fly well in ACM. Contributing to this theory were the following factors. Firstly, early lieutenant and above transition pilots came from the Demon (F3H) community, where they had flown an interceptor instead of a fighter, and been trained with the attendant focus on interception, where 30 degrees of bank was an unusual attitude.

Secondly, the early Navy and Air Force Phantom IIs (F-4B/J and F-4C/D, respectively) had no internally-mounted gun, and the missile envelopes were narrow, hard to recognize visually, and were foreign to previous experience.

Thirdly, no one understood the technical aspects of missile employment. Maneuvering to either AIM-9 or AIM-7 envelopes was WAY more complicated than lining up for a guns kill, although doing this in an F-4 presupposed an unsuspecting and non-maneuvering target.

During three-and-a-half years of *Rolling Thunder* operations, Navy F-4 crews claimed 13 victories – seven MiG-17s and six MiG-21s – and one PLAAF MiG-17 in a fight in which the Chinese in turn claimed an F-4 destroyed, for a loss of five Phantoms in aerial combat. In the four years between the engagements of 1968 and the final air combat round in 1972, the Navy would make many changes in the way Phantom aircrews were trained to make the best use of their airplane and weapons in an aerial engagement.

8

ALPHA STRIKE

Unlike infantrymen fighting in South Vietnam who might go weeks or even months without coming into contact with the enemy, every Air Force or Navy pilot knew that every time he climbed into his cockpit and entered North Vietnamese air space, in the words of VA-164 Skyhawk pilot Lieutenant Commander Bob Arnold, "the moment he went feet dry, he was over a death pit that would lash out with flak, missiles and MiGs, the sole purpose of which was trying to kill *you*." Unlike Army troops who were primarily conscripts whose main motivation was to survive a tour of duty described as "365 days or life, whichever comes first," aircrew were all volunteers, and came to the job with high personal motivation. The pilots who flew the strike aircraft knew that they had only one duty, to attack the target, regardless of the opposition they encountered. As the on-again off-again operation of *Rolling Thunder* allowed the defenses to mature and become truly potent, doing that was a test of personal strength and moral courage every time.

VA-163 Skyhawk pilot Lieutenant Frank Elkins, who flew off USS *Oriskany* during her 1966 deployment, wrote of this internal conflict in his journal after the squadron had lost four pilots:

During the brief in Air Intelligence you know you're going and you listen carefully. Then back in the ready room, you begin to dread it and you go on briefing though, even though you're beginning to look for a way out, to hope that you're really not going out, that the spare will be launched in your place, that you'll be late starting, that you'll have no radio, or a bad ALQ, or something – anything – that'll give you a decent, honorable out of that particular night hop. After the brief, waiting to suit up and man aircraft, you really dread it most then. A cup of coffee and another nervous call to the head, and you're told to man your aircraft for the 0300 launch. Up on the flight deck, you start looking for something wrong; you go all the way around the aircraft, looking for that little gem that'll be reason enough to your conscience and your comrades to refuse to go out. And it doesn't come. You never give up though, first the damned radio works, and the damned ALQ works.

In April 1965, Commander James Stockdale, who would later be awarded the Medal of Honor for his conduct and leadership as a POW, spoke to his pilots about the war they were on their way to fight, and what they would be called on to display as individuals. One point stands out:

Once you go "feet dry" over the beach, there can be nothing limited about your commitment. "Limited war" means to us that our target list has limits, our ordnance loadout has limits, our rules of engagement have limits, but that does *not* mean that there is anything "limited" about our personal obligations as fighting men to carry out assigned missions with all we've got. If you think it is possible for a man, in the heat of battle, to apply something less than total *personal* commitment – equated perhaps to your idea of the proportion of *national* potential being applied, you are wrong.

The A-4 Skyhawk's second experience of combat in Vietnam – after its participation in the retaliatory strikes of August 1964 following the Tonkin Gulf Incident – was in Operation *Flaming Dart*, the mission flown on February 8, 1965, in response to an attack by the NLF on a Special Forces camp at Pleiku the night of February 7/8, which had killed eight Americans, wounded over 100, and destroyed ten aircraft on the Pleiku airfield.

Flaming Dart was immediately ordered by the White House in response to President Johnson's exclamation on being informed of the attack that "I've had enough of this!" Air Wing 9 aboard USS *Ranger*, which had arrived in Southeast Asia the day of the second "incident" on August 5, 1964, launched a 34-plane strike against the Vit Thu

Lu staging area, 15 miles north of the DMZ on the 17th parallel and five miles inland, while *Coral Sea* and *Hancock* sent 49 aircraft to hit the PAVN barracks and the dock facilities at Dong Hoi. Commander Paul Peck led the Skyhawks of VA-94, the "Mighty Shrikes"; a naval aviator since 1948, Peck had missed the Korean War, making this his first combat mission. Halfway to the target, Peck received a message from the carrier: "Your signal is jettison your bombs and return to the ship." Peck couldn't believe his ears. As the formation turned around, Peck saw the strikes from *Coral Sea* at Vinh and radioed, "We're unable to reach our target and plan to divert and hit the barracks Air Wing 15 is hitting." The response amazed him. "Negative. Your signal is jettison your bombs." "I thought, you've got to be kidding me there's a target down there, and I've got more bombs than I ever dropped in my life. But that's what we did. We dumped everything into the ocean. Of all the incidents on that cruise, the one that strikes home the most was dropping those bombs in the ocean."

The reason for the recall was bad weather over the target. During the northeastern monsoon, from November to March, the weather over the Tonkin Gulf and North Vietnam is mostly heavy clouds and rain, with an extreme condition known as "crachin," which can see thick clouds and ceilings as low as 500 feet, combined with fog and heavy drizzle bringing aerial activity to a halt. Peck didn't know it, but he was the first of many American flyers to discover the ill effects of "crachin." At this stage of the war, strike groups were assigned one target; if it was weathered in, there was no alternative to a recall. As the weather systems became better known, tactics changed, with strike groups given primary and alternative targets should weather interfere. As Peck later remembered, "The weather at launch was not good; I'd say the ceiling was 2,000 feet, maybe a little more. When we got to the foothills where the target was, the overcast was right down to the ground. I was at 100 feet and we couldn't make it."

As it turned out, the fliers from *Coral Sea* and *Hancock* were able to strike their target, but achieved little result for their effort, with bomb damage assessment photos allowing credit for 16 destroyed buildings at the cost of the death of the first Skyhawk pilot in Vietnam, VA-155's Lieutenant Edward A. Dickson, and eight A-4Es damaged by flak.

Two nights later, NLF commandos blew up a US enlisted barracks at Qui Nhon, killing 23 and wounding 21 Americans. The next day,

February 11, *Flaming Dart II* saw 100 aircraft from *Ranger*, *Coral Sea*, and *Hancock* bomb and strafe a PAVN barracks at Chan Hoa, destroying or damaging 23 of 76 buildings in the camp, at a cost of three aircraft shot down and VF-154's Lieutenant Commander Robert H. Shumaker captured after shooting himself down, the victim of his own bombs' fragmentation pattern, to become the war's second American POW.

After *Flaming Dart II*, a decision was made to mount a stronger and more effective air interdiction campaign against North Vietnam. As Secretary of Defense McNamara had put it at the press conference following those two missions, "Communications of resolve will carry a hollow ring unless we accomplish more military damage than we have to date." Aboard *Ranger*, VA-94 was equipped with 14 A-4C Skyhawks and had 14 pilots. Commander Peck recalled, "We ran 100 percent availability for 45 days on the line at one point, and had no trouble with the A-4C. Our planes were still relatively new and all in damned good shape. We flew everything they would let us fly, and two or three missions a day were not unheard of."

The A-4C flown by Commander Peck's squadron and others in Task Force 77 had been originally developed as the night/all-weather A4D-2N, powered by the Wright J65-W-20 engine providing 8,200 pounds of thrust. First flown in 1958 and appearing in fleet squadrons in 1960, the aircraft had three racks that could carry bombs. However, when two 300-gallon drop tanks were carried on the wing positions, only the centerline rack could carry a maximum of six 500-pound bombs. Improvements over the A4D-2 (A-4B) included an all-attitude gyro system and auto-pilot; terrain clearance radar in a longer nose; and a low-altitude bombing system. Production of the aircraft, which was redesignated A-4C in 1962, was 638. At the time the US entered the war in Vietnam, it was the version in most widespread use in fleet squadrons.

The A4D-5 (A-4E after 1962) first flew in 1961, with deliveries to fleet squadrons commencing in 1963. The result of a 1959 Douglas proposal for a major upgrade in the Skyhawk, the A-4E's improvements included the lighter weight, 8,500-pound thrust Pratt & Whitney J52-P6A engine, with the fuselage center section and inlet ducting redesigned for the increased air needed. The addition of two wing station "hard points" outboard of the inner pylons allowed the airplane to carry drop tanks and up to 12 500-pound bombs, or two Bullpup attack missiles. The aircraft carried improved electronic navigation gear including Doppler navigation radar, a radar altimeter that was extremely useful in night operations over North Vietnam, and an AJB-3A low-altitude bombing system. Beginning in 1966, many A-4Es were upgraded with the J52-P8 engine providing 9,300 pounds of thrust that came as original equipment on the A-4F; these aircraft were identifiable by the same avionics hump of the A-4F, though eventually all A-4Es were retrofitted with the hump, regardless of what engine they used. Production totaled 499, and was completed in 1965. By the time *Rolling Thunder* began, the A-4E was the primary Skyhawk in the attack squadrons on carriers at Yankee Station.

Ordered in 1965, the A-4F was essentially an upgraded A-4E; the A-4F prototype, BuNo 152101, started down the El Segundo production line as an A-4E, with its first flight on August 31, 1966. Production A-4Fs were first delivered in January 1967, and a total of 147 were produced. Primary changes were the addition of nose wheel steering, wing lift spoilers, and the upgraded Escapac 1-C3 ejection seat. The A-4F was initially distinguishable from the A-4E with the avionics hump on the upper fuselage aft of the cockpit and ahead of the vertical fin, and by a refueling probe that was "bent" just ahead of the cockpit in order to move the probe away from the nose to allow use of forward-looking avionics, which also allowed the pilot to better steer the probe into the refueling basket since he could see it better. The A-4F was powered by the J52-P8 engine with 9,300 pounds of thrust. One hundred A-4Fs were retrofitted with the 11,200-pound thrust Pratt & Whitney J52-P408 engine and had enlarged intakes to allow the engine to provide full power in all flight regimes.

The three main "combat" Skyhawks did not replace each other; rather all three sub-types operated throughout the war. The lighter A-4Cs were the primary light-attack aircraft aboard the 27-Charlie Essex-class carriers, while the A-4E and A-4F served aboard the larger attack carriers. There were exceptions to this, as with the air group that USS *Enterprise* brought to the war on her first deployment in December 1965, which included four A-4C-equipped Skyhawk squadrons: VA-26, 76, 93, and 94, in addition to two F-4 squadrons and an A-6 squadron, while *Oriskany*'s VA-163 flew A-4Es during her 1966 deployment. By 1968, losses were such that all versions of the Skyhawk operated from every carrier at Yankee Station.

One of the most incredible Skyhawk missions happened on July 23, 1966, during the POL campaign. Commander Wynn F. Foster, skipper of *Oriskany's* VA-163, who had been Commander James Stockdale's wingman when he was shot down in November 1965, was flying his 238th combat mission, an attack on storage facilities in Haiphong. Foster was one of the few Korean War veterans, having flown 75 sorties in F9F Panthers with VF-33 off USS *Kearsarge* (CVA-33). Shortly after going "feet dry," Foster's division dived toward the target and ran into a barrage of flak. Foster's wingman, Lieutenant (jg) Tom Spitzer, had just checked into the squadron and was flying his first mission:

> I called the flak to my wingman's attention and told him to keep jinking. A few seconds later I heard a loud "bang" followed by a "whoosh" and I felt a stinging sensation in my right elbow. I realized I had been hit and looked down at my right arm. The arm was missing from the elbow down and half my right forearm was lying on the starboard console.

Foster had taken a hit from a 57mm shell; the shrapnel had severed his forearm. He took the stick in his left hand and turned back over the water as he called "Mayday" and told Spitzer to keep jinking. His airspeed was dropping, so he pushed over in a shallow dive, leveling off when he reached 220 knots:

> The burst had blown out most of my cockpit canopy, and the cockpit was littered with shrapnel and blood. The wind noise was terrible as I tried to communicate with Spitzer. My arm didn't hurt but I was bleeding quite badly. I momentarily considered trying to make it back to the ship but realized I would probably pass out before I got there. The nearest "friendly" was the SAR destroyer which was stationed about 30 miles from the coast-in point.

Descending to 2,500 feet, Foster realized he was flying at 70 percent power. Pushing the throttle forward, the engine immediately spooled up, undamaged. Climbing back to 4,000 feet, he contacted USS *Reeves* (DLG-24), informing them he and Spitzer were 15 miles away, approaching from the southwest. Leveling off at 3,000 feet, he saw the ship turn toward him. He felt light-headed from blood loss and shock, and was experiencing tunnel vision. When he was three miles from the ship, he pulled the seat face curtain with his left hand. The ejection sequence went "as advertised," and he found himself suspended under the canopy, drifting toward the water below. "My oxygen mask was still on and my visor was down. I removed the oxygen mask and dropped it. I looked around. The view was beautiful – blue ocean, white clouds above and the destroyer steaming down below. The war seemed a million miles away."

Foster was only in the water a few minutes before he was picked up by *Reeves*' whaleboat and returned to the ship. Once aboard he was taken to sick bay and transferred back to *Oriskany* two days later. Since she was scheduled to return to Cubi Point within a week, he remained aboard in sick bay.

Once ashore in treatment, Foster was in recuperation and therapy for many months, all the while fighting to remain on active duty. His request was eventually approved and he remained on active duty until retiring as a captain in 1972. Foster was awarded the Silver Star and Purple Heart for the mission and also received the Distinguished Flying Cross (DFC) for leading a POL strike a few days earlier. Sadly, wingman Tom Spitzer was killed in the fire that struck *Oriskany* that October.

There was a division between naval aviators by "community," and there were few times when a flier changed from one to another. The "fighter community" was divided between the F-8 Crusader and F-4 Phantom, while the "attack community" was divided between the A-1 Skyraider and the A-4 Skyhawk until the Skyraider was taken off operations in 1968. One pilot did make a change between communities. Lieutenant Commander Ted "T.R." Swartz, an F-8 Crusader pilot, made the decision in 1966 to request transfer to attack aviation, as he later explained it:

> because the attack guys were doing most of the work. They were going over the beach and getting all the action, while the fighter guys were out in the BARCAP once or twice a day not doing a damn thing except flying in circles. Basically, what I wanted to do was go where the action was… The job was going in and stirring up the enemy, making them burn, bleed and blow up.

That fall, Swartz was returning to flight duty after a tour as a landing signal officer (LSO). "I asked my detailer to do me a favor and send me to Lemoore. I didn't care where or who, just send me to Lemoore. If you went to a Lemoore squadron, you were going west." He ended up in VA-76 "Spirits," part of CVW 21, which went aboard USS *Bon Homme Richard* in November 1966 and arrived in Southeast Asia in January 1967. They were just in time to take part in strikes on previously off-limits targets in Hanoi and Haiphong. With the air war heating up, the VPAF made more appearances. Over the course of 1967, naval aviators shot down 17 MiGs, of which ten fell victim to pilots of CVW-21.

For Swartz, the difference between air-to-air and air-to-mud was one of emotion:

> When you're in a no-shit dogfight with somebody else – who can put a weapon on you and blow you out of the sky – it's kind of like just before you go out on the ballfield or get in the ring with somebody, whereas I never got apprehensive flying over the beach. I would feel more comfortable once the guns started or the SAMs came up because you knew they were worried and awake and you knew where they were. I was always worried when nothing happened, and was always waiting for something to happen because then it was time for action, the adrenaline ran, and you were ready and working.

On May 1, 1967, Swartz drew the assignment of flak suppression for an Alpha strike against Kep airfield, which had finally been placed on the list of allowed targets the previous month. His wingman was Lieutenant John Waples:

> Our specific job was to pound some flak sites on the north side of the runway while the bombers took the middle of the runway. We all rolled in together and Waples and I saw a couple of MiGs taking to the runway. We shot at them as well as the flak sites. Just as we pulled off, my eye caught a pair of MiG-17s coming in from right to left. There wasn't anything we could do about it, because our paths were going to cross, and I was going to cross right in front of them. If I turned right to meet them head-on, I'd run into the whole strike group, and if I turned left, which I had to do to stay the hell out of the way of the strike group, I had to accept them on the inside of my turn on the left hand side.

Swartz had three Zuni rockets left in the pack under his starboard wing. "The Zuni package carries four rockets that can be fired in single or ripple, and the book says fire all of them at once. I put one package on single and saved three; I felt naked there with nothing and the MiGs around." He accepted the fight with the MiGs inside his turn. "I looked back over my shoulder and saw the two of them shooting – a 37-millimeter, that really gets your attention." He maneuvered into a high-G barrel roll at 425 knots.

> This is very difficult to follow, and as the airplane came over the top, the MiGs were off my right shoulder. I poked one Zuni at the wingman and missed, poked another one and missed, and then poked the third. Blind-ass fucking luck because all the skill and science about the gunsight was garbage. After getting the one guy I went after the leader with my 20-millimeter, which had just a few bullets because the space had been used for the electronic warfare stuff. The gun kept jamming, and you're not supposed to recharge it, but I recharged it about four times. Then I realized how incredibly dumb it was to continue this because I could get shot down over a field where I shot down a guy, and they'd come after me with pitchforks. So I turned right and got the hell out of there.

Swartz's accomplishment did not meet with universal acclaim. "My ass was chewed out and the captain of the boat damn near wanted to court-martial me for saving the Zunis." Other attack pilots believed that by not firing all his Zunis at the flak sites, and taking out a gun, he was putting the bombers in danger. In the end, however, T.R. Swartz was awarded a Silver Star as the only Skyhawk pilot to shoot down a MiG-17.

Swartz almost scored a second on July 21 during an Alpha strike on the Ta Xa POL site. Swartz was one of four Skyhawks flying Iron Hand SAM suppression, carrying a Shrike anti-radiation missile under one wing and a Zuni pack under the other. Eight MiG-17s attacked the VA-76 and VA-212 A-4s, which had cover from F-8 Crusaders of VF-24 and VF-211. VF-24's Commander Marion H. "Red" Issaks got one with a Sidewinder while Lieutenant Commander Robert L. Kirkwood made one of the rare gun kills of the second with his four 20mm cannon. Lieutenant Commander Ray "Timmy" Hubbard, whose Crusader was armed with Zuni rockets for flak suppression, fired his Zunis and guns and knocked down the third, while Kirkwood's wingman, Lieutenant (jg) Philip W. Dempewolf, got the fourth with a Sidewinder.

Swartz recalled the fight:

I was lead Iron Hand, out in front of the strike with Timmy Hubbard flying cover for me, trolling for SAMs. Incredibly, a flight of eight MiG-17s flew up between me and Timmy, and the strike group. Waples called me that I had two MiGs on my tail – I looked around and I had eight on my tail! Issaks came in and nailed one with a 'winder. Timmy fired his Zunis at the next one and fired off all his ammo at it, but it wouldn't go down. He called he was out of ammo and leaving, just then the MiG caught fire and went in right after the pilot ejected.

At that point, the other four MiG-17s were still in the fight. One chewed up Issaks and set his wing on fire. The fight was getting close to the Chinese border. Swartz called to Issaks to turn right, away from the border, that he would cover him. "I poked two Zunis at these two MiGs, damn near head-on, they whizzed past and scared the hell out of them, and they got off Red's ass." Swartz also saw Kirkwood and Dempewolf:

Kirkwood fired a 'winder and hit a MiG, then Dempewolf fired one and it tracked on Kirkwood! Just as the goddamn thing approaches his tailpipe, he launches another Sidewinder and the one headed for him takes after that one and lops off part of his starboard stabilizer and puts marks under his wing, then one hits the fourth MiG and blows it up and the other flies through the debris.

When all had returned to the carrier, Swartz reported what had happened to Kirkwood's airplane. "Kirkwood about shit and Dempewolf claimed a half a kill and was later credited with number four. It was funnier than hell."

The "World Famous Golden Dragons" of VA-192 had gained their name when the squadron's F9F-5 Panthers starred in two Hollywood Korean War movies, *Men of the Fighting Lady* and *The Bridges at Toko-ri*. Switching from fighter to attack squadron in 1956, the "Golden Dragons" arrived in Southeast Asia aboard *Ticonderoga* in early 1967, and were in the thick of things quickly. The squadron experienced some truly memorable events that spring.

The mission of April 26 would see two high-level medals awarded, including the only Medal of Honor awarded to a fixed-wing naval aviator in the Vietnam War.

That day, Lieutenant (jg) John W. Cain launched in the squadron's CAG bird, NM-200, call sign "Jury 200." As he made his attack run on the POL site outside Haiphong that was the target of the Alpha strike, the Skyhawk was hit and the cockpit filled with smoke. Cain continued his attack but the airplane began to roll uncontrollably. He disconnected the hydraulic controls in order to fly on manual, but the emergency procedure did not work. Finding himself at 2,000 feet and barely making 205 knots with an engine that did not respond to throttle inputs, he ejected and came down just offshore, 15 miles south of the city, near the harbor entrance.

Losing his personal survival radio during the ejection, Cain was unable to call for help. However, his squadron mates saw his ejection and called for help. Eventually, a full-blown SAR developed, with 20 aircraft involved, 19 fixed-wing and one helicopter, an SH-3A Sea King from USS *Hornet*'s HS-2, on SAR duty aboard USS *Mahan* (DLG-11). Orbiting F-8s and A-1s provided much-needed Rescue Combat Air Patrol (RESCAP) cover.

Lieutenant Steve Millikin and his crew in SH-3A "Chink 69" were orbiting outside the harbor entrance as *Ticonderoga*'s strike group passed over. They had been having a little fun by engaging in "Tonkin Gulf plinking," shooting at debris in the harbor. When he got word of an aviator in the water, Millikin immediately headed in at his top speed of 125 knots. When they arrived on the scene, Cain was only 250 yards offshore of a small island. Enemy troops were firing at Cain, who hadn't inflated his life raft since it would have been too much of a target as he drifted in the water, well within range of the enemy.

Suddenly, over the sound of the gunfire, while thinking his prospects looked bleak, Cain heard the beat of rotors as "Chink 69" approached. In the helicopter, Millikin ordered Petty Officer Peter Sorokin to lower the horse collar for the rescue. Fire from the island increased as Millikin hovered over Cain; the water erupted in geysers as rounds came perilously close. Thinking the fire was coming from the A-1s giving cover, Millikin soon realized they were North Vietnamese mortar rounds. Petty Officer

Charles Sather returned the fire with his door-mounted M-60 machine gun, while co-pilot Lieutenant (jg) Tom Pettis opened his window and stuck a submachine gun out, adding to the small barrage coming from the helicopter.

As the engagement intensified, Cain was finally in the sling. Before he could be pulled inside, Millikin turned around and headed out of the harbor as fast as he could. Chancing a glance back to the island, he watched an A-4 drop four bombs right atop the enemy.

Later that day, "Chink 69" delivered Cain back to *Ticonderoga*. For their actions in the rescue, Millikin received the Silver Star, Pettis the DFC, and the two enlisted crewmen Air Medals. Sadly, Lieutenant (jg) Pettis and "Chink 69" would be lost at sea several weeks later.

Flying Iron Hand support for the mission was VF-192's Lieutenant Commander Mike Estocin, a serious, focused man who had always wanted to fly. He was the squadron's Iron Hand specialist, a pilot willing to fly down the throat of an SA-2 battery before firing his Shrike missile. In 1967, the Shrike was not a dependable weapon, and often a pilot would be forced to fire his second weapon to kill the SAM, its crew, and the support radar. With tactics and equipment to fight the ever-increasing number of SAMs constantly evolving, it took a special kind of aviator to fly the mission.

Six days before this mission, Estocin had flown as Iron Hand support for an Alpha strike to hit two thermal powerplants near Haiphong. The three Iron Hand A-4s had successfully attacked three SAM sites. Estocin's Skyhawk sustained severe damage when a SAM detonated beneath him during the second attack. After checking for control problems, he attacked the third site. As the A-4s headed out over the Tonkin Gulf in search of a tanker, Estocin's airplane was streaming jet fuel. Finally, with an estimated five minutes of fuel remaining, he found the orbiting KA-3B and plugged in. It was quickly apparent the Skyhawk was losing fuel faster than it could be pumped in. The Skywarrior then towed the A-4 back to *Ticonderoga*, three miles from the ship and with fuel for one pass, Estocin unplugged and headed for the deck. Listening to the LSO, he made a "roger" pass and caught the three wire as the A-4 caught fire. Estocin remained in the cockpit and waited as the fire-fighting crew smothered the fire with foam. *Ticonderoga*'s CAG wrote him up for a Silver Star for the mission.

VPAF pilots of 923rd Fighter Regiment with their MiG-17 fighters. (VPAF Official)

MiG-21PFM fighters of 921st Fighter Regiment in 1972. MiG-21PFM "5015" is thought to have been the mount of VPAF top ace Nguyen Van Coc (9 victories). (VPAF Official)

USS *Maddox* in the Tonkin Gulf. The "Maddox Incident" on August 4, 1964 set the stage for direct US involvement in the Vietnam War. (USN Official)

The E-1B Tracer, known as "Willy Fudd" provided airborne early warning for carriers at Yankee Station, 1965. (USN Official)

An F-8C Crusader lands aboard *Coral Sea* in 1965. (USN Official)

The Kaman SH-2 Seasprite operated primarily from destroyers and was used in several pilot rescues in North Vietnam. (USN Official)

An A-1H Skyraider launches from *Coral Sea* on an interdiction strike during the 1966 bomb shortage. (USN Official)

Coral Sea and a Forrest Sherman-class destroyer take on fuel at Yankee Station in 1966. (USN Official)

A-4C Skyhawks, RA-5C Vigilantes, and an E-1B Tracer of Carrier Air Wing 9 aboard USS *Enterprise* in 1966. (USN Official)

F-4Bs of VF-113 were given an experimental camouflage of two shades of green in 1966 and temporarily designated F-4Gs. (USN Official)

F-4B Phantoms (left) of VF-112 "Aardvarks" aboard USS *Kitty Hawk* in 1966. Two of the VF-113 camouflaged F-4Gs can be seen on the right. (USN Official)

USS *Oriskany* on fire in the Tonkin Gulf, October 26, 1966. This was the first of three such incidents involving US aircraft carriers in the Tonkin Gulf during the Vietnam War. (USN Official)

A KA-3B Skywarrior is catapulted from *Coral Sea* as an EA-1F Skyraider ECM aircraft awaits launch, January 1967. (USN Official)

The explosion and fire that occurred aboard USS *Forrestal* on July 29, 1967 put the carrier out of action for the next two years. (USN Official)

An RF-8G photo reconnnaissance Crusader prepares to launch from *Coral Sea*, October 1967. (USN Official)

Above An F-5 "Aggressor" used by Top Gun for dissimilar air combat training. (USN Official via Fred Johnsen) *Right* Captain Dan Pedersen, who founded Top Gun in 1968. (USN Official)

A-6A Intruders of VA-196 drop Mark 82 bombs over North Vietnam on December 20, 1968. (USN Official)

Left to Right Enterprise, *Hancock,* and *Coral Sea* at Alameda NAS in 1969. (USN Official)

Above VPAF pilots Le Xuan Di and Nguyen Van Bay, the pilots who attacked USS *Higbee* on April 19, 1972. (VPAF Official)
Right Senior Lieutenant Le Xuan Di's bombs hit *Higbee* and destroyed the aft 5-inch gun mount. (VPAF Official)

Higbee under repair from the damage inflicted by the VPAF pilots. (USN Official)

An A-4F Skyhawk armed with Mark 81 and Mark 82 bombs taxies past other A-4Fs of VA-44 aboard *Hancock* during Operation *Linebacker*, May 25, 1972. (USN Official)

A VF-96 F-4J in flight over *Constellation* in 1972. VF-96 was a top-scoring Navy fighter squadron during Operation *Linebacker*. (USN Official)

On April 26, Estocin was again Iron Hand Lead. As the strike force swept across the tank farm, Estocin and F-8 pilot Lieutenant Commander John Nichols, his escort, remained in orbit as he watched for signs of SAMs. Finally, their radar warning receivers lit up as the Fan Song radars that controlled the SAMs reached out for them. Getting word from the radar controller on the duty air control ship that the strike force was heading for home, Estocin and Nichols both suddenly spotted the flash of a launch 12,000 feet below. Nichols waited for Estocin to turn and take evasive action, but Estocin bored in, intent on getting the site. A moment later, the SAM exploded near the A-4, which began shedding pieces as it burned and spun toward the ground. Somehow, Estocin managed to right his plane at 2,000 feet. Nichols slid in for a closer look at the Skyhawk. Both were flying at 160 knots, barely above stalling speed. Nichols could see Estocin slumped over in the shattered cockpit of the A-4. There was no response to his repeated calls as the shredded Skyhawk staggered through the sky. Finally, the airplane rolled inverted and the two Shrike missiles launched themselves as it dived into the ground and exploded on impact. He called off the incoming rescue force and went "feet wet" back to the ship. There was initial confusion over Estocin's fate, since his death was not confirmed, and there were confusing reports he had ejected and survived. In 1973, the North Vietnamese confirmed his body had been found in the cockpit of his crashed Skyhawk.

At first, the wing wrote a citation for a Navy Cross, but both the task group commander and ComTF-77 sent the write-up back, stating they would "support an upgrade." There was only one award higher than a Navy Cross. Mike Estocin's family received his posthumous Medal of Honor in 1978, which was awarded for his actions on April 20 and 26, 1967. Nineteen fliers received this award during the Vietnam War: ten USAF, five Army, two Navy, and one Marine. Lieutenant Commander Michael J. Estocin was the only naval aviator to receive the award for bravery in the cockpit of a jet. (Commander James Stockdale was awarded the medal for his service while a POW in Hanoi.) Estocin died the day before his 36th birthday. In 1981, USS *Estocin* (FFG-15) was named in his honor, serving until it was decommissioned and sold to Turkey in 2003.

On August 21, 1967, *Oriskany*'s CVW-16 struck Hanoi's thermal power plant in one of the most effective strike missions flown in *Rolling Thunder*. Previous attacks on this important target had been flown against strong opposition from SAMs, with consequent high losses. VA-163's skipper Commander Bryan Compton was able to convince *Oriskany*'s captain to obtain permission to use the new AGM-62 Walleye, a television-guided glide bomb with a 250-pound warhead, arguing that the increased accuracy of this weapon might allow them to knock out the plant with one strike. Because not all the squadron's A-4s were able to carry this weapon, once permission was received for the missile's use, *Coral Sea* transferred four Walleye-capable Skyhawks. Compton led five other pilots, each of whom had a different aim point on the generator that they attacked from a different direction. Two A-4s were hit by the intense AAA, with Lieutenant Commander Dean Cramer forced to abort; he returned to the carrier on fire with more than 50 shrapnel holes including one in the left wing that was 18-by-38 inches. The other badly hit A-4 was flown by squadron XO Lieutenant Commander James Busey; he made the attack and landed on fire, with more than 125 holes and one horizontal stabilizer shot off. Three of the remaining five put their Walleyes into the generator hall while the other two hit the boiler house. After making his attack, Compton flew two more passes, taking pictures of the bomb damage so the air wing would not have to re-attack the target. For his courage and leadership, Compton received the Navy Cross, as did Busey. It was later determined the strike had survived 30 SAMs and the attention of more than 60 guns ranging from 37mm to 85mm.

The naval air campaign received a significant increase in attack capability when USS *Independence*, the first Atlantic Fleet carrier to deploy to Southeast Asia, arrived in-theater on June 5, 1965. The ship's Air Group 7 included the Navy's first true all-weather day or night attack aircraft, the A6A Intruders of VA-75 "Sunday Punchers," led by Commander "Swoose" Snead. The A-6 was capable of carrying an incredible 18,000 pounds – nine tons! – of ordnance and its combat debut was eagerly awaited by the Navy's attack aviation community. Combat flights began on June 27, with strikes launched from Dixie Station. The first missions in North Vietnam were flown on July 3.

However, all was not well with the first Intruders to enter combat. Lieutenant Donald D. "D-D" Smith, an A-4E pilot in VA-72, recalled:

the A-6 had some interesting missions. I envied them and the idea of taking a lone plane in at night, properly equipped, doing deep interdiction work, and then coming out. That had a lot of appeal. But the A-6 back then wasn't equipped for the mission, and was really lucky to pull something off. CINCPAC sent them in, but they couldn't do the job. The mission was there and the capability was supposedly there, but the squadron really had problems. Their gear wouldn't work; it was really unreliable.

VA-75 lost their first Intruder on July 14 while flying a *Barrel Roll* mission over Laos, when Lieutenants Don Boecker and Don Eaton were forced to eject from Flying Ace 507 after a Mark 82 bomb detonated under the right wing immediately after release. The two were rescued by Air America helicopters after spending a night and most of a morning avoiding capture. On July 18, Commander Jeremiah Denton and Lieutenant (jg) Bill Tschudy were forced to eject from Flying Ace 500 when they too suffered the same kind of premature detonation near Thanh Hoa, in North Vietnam. Both became POWs.

Premature bomb detonation was the culprit again on July 24 when AG-511, with Lieutenant Commander "Deke" Bordone and Lieutenant (jg) Pete Moffett, suffered severe damage from an underwing blast on their third pass over a target in southern Laos while flying a Steel Tiger mission. Both survived and were soon picked up and back on "*Indy*" the next day. It was now obvious that something had to be done to correct the situation. Modified ejector racks were quickly installed and improved fuzes were obtained. These solved the problem and VA-75 continued on operations.

The squadron's final loss of the cruise occurred on September 17, when new skipper Commander Fred Vogt and Lieutenant Robert Barber attacked torpedo boats near Bach Long Island at night, using flares. Working under the flares at low altitude, the Intruder hit the water and both were killed.

Independence was relieved on November 15 by USS *Kitty Hawk*. Air Wing 11's VA-85 "Black Falcons" became the second Intruder squadron to enter combat; their tour would be even costlier than that of VA-75. The first loss happened the night of December 21, when squadron CO Commander Billie Jack Cartwright and B/N Lieutenant Ed Gold in Buckeye 801 were lost on a strike north of Haiphong. The reason for the loss was listed "unknown," though there had been reported SAM activity.

Two months later on February 18, 1966, Lieutenant (jg)s Joe Murray and Tom Schroeffel were both killed when NH-812 hit the ground after attacking a group of trucks during a day of armed reconnaissance west of Hanoi. Target fixation and a late pull-up from a bombing run in mountainous terrain was the likely cause. The next "Black Falcon" loss came on April 17, when Lieutenant Commanders Sam Sayers and Charles Hawkins were flying NH-814 off the North Vietnamese coast near Vinh and were hit by AAA that set the Intruder on fire. Both crewmen ejected and were recovered by USAF search and rescue forces.

The next day, two "Black Falcons" – squadron XO Commander Ron Hays, with B/N Lieutenant Ted Been and wingmen Lieutenant Bud Roemish and Lieutenant Commander Bill Yarbrough – flew a night attack against the Uong Bi powerplant, located some 12 miles north of Haiphong. Launched in radio silence at 0100 hours on February 19 with an E-2A Hawkeye from Carrier Airborne Early Warning Squadron 11 (VAW-11) Detachment C for communications, the Intruders went "feet dry," flying at 500 feet or less, until they were 25 miles from the target, at which point they began a slow climb to a safe bomb-release altitude of 1800 feet. Hays and Been dropped 13 Mark 83 1000-pound bombs using the Litton APS-61 digitally integrated attack and navigation equipment (DIANE) that was the heart of the Intruder, while Roemish and Yarbrough bombed manually after suffering a failure of the DIANE system. The two Intruders caught the North Vietnamese flat-footed; AAA didn't open up until after they had turned for home. The post-strike bomb damage assessment showed 25 bomb craters visible within the target area. The next day, Hanoi issued a shrill press release denouncing what was called "a major escalation by the Yankees through the introduction of the B-52 Stratofortress into the North."

Within days of this success, the squadron lost two more aircraft and their crews. On the night of April 21, Commander Jack Keller, who had assumed command of VA-85 following the loss of Commander Cartwright in December, was flying Buckeye 805 with his B/N, Lieutenant Commander Ellis Austin, on a night strike near Vinh. Keller's wingman, who was unable to make his bomb run due to aircraft problems, saw a flash of light that was probably Keller's aircraft hitting the ground near the target. Both Keller and Austin were killed, making him the second squadron CO lost on this deployment. XO Hays immediately assumed command. Keller's loss was followed the next day by the deaths of Lieutenant Commander Bob Weimorts and Lieutenant (jg) Bill Nickerson, who apparently flew their A-6 into the water off Vinh while flying an Iron Hand anti-SAM mission.

Five days later, on April 27, when A-6A NH-811 attacked barges north of Vinh, pilot Lieutenant Bill Westerman was seriously wounded when he was hit by a small-caliber bullet. His B/N, Lieutenant (jg) Brian Westin, reached immediately across the cockpit and took the control stick, pointing the Intruder out to sea. With Westerman lapsing in and out of consciousness, landing was completely out of the question. Once over the water, Westin jettisoned the canopy, then reached over and pulled Westerman's ejection handle, then his own. A Seasprite SAR helicopter was soon overhead and quickly hoisted Westin aboard. He then directed the pilot down the Intruder's track till they spotted Westerman floating in the water. The chopper didn't have a swimmer aboard, and it was obvious the pilot would need help getting into a rescue sling. Westin immediately jumped back in the water and hooked up his pilot, waving the helicopter away to take the wounded Westerman to the carrier. Five minutes later, a second helicopter arrived to rescue him again. Westin was the first of 14 Intruder crewmen during the war to be awarded the Navy Cross for his bravery.

VA-85 suffered their seventh and final loss in an operational accident on May 15, when a returning Intruder suffered a fuel transfer problem that caused engine failure due to fuel starvation. Both crewmen were recovered. *Kitty Hawk* departed on May 23 and arrived back in San Diego on June 13, nearly eight months away, six of which had been on the line in Vietnam, during which CVW-11 lost 25 aircraft, with 20 the result of enemy action. VA-85 had lost seven Intruders, along with eight aircrewmen. To date, the Intruder had not lived up to the Navy's hopes.

In theory, the Intruder's weapon control system was a technological leap from what had been before with its radar mapping capability and the Moving Target Indicator in its bombing system, which allowed it to destroy whole convoys of trucks traveling along a road without any warning. However, the realities of the strain of continuous carrier operations on new equipment led to lower-than-expected readiness rates. The DIANE serviceability rates initially ran at a disheartening 30–35 percent, forcing Navy technicians and Grumman tech reps to spend upwards of 70 hours a week in the hangar bay in an effort to keep aircraft in "up" status. DIANE was called "digital," but it was in reality more of an analog system, with its computer "guts" made up primarily by gears and linkages that could stick or stop working. The common B/N "emergency" procedure to restore operation involved kicking the side of the control pedestal to try to get components to move again. Most obvious was the fact that the complex weapon delivery system required constant special care if it was to achieve the advertised level of capability.

Given that sortie count and total bomb tonnage was the primary data used to measure the wing leadership's professional effectiveness, many Intruders were launched in daylight with inoperative systems to bomb visually "like a very large and expensive double-breasted Skyhawk," in the words of one Intruder pilot. Additionally, the flight deck crew disliked the Intruder being used on night operations, since it was difficult to run small numbers of the aircraft after normal operations had been shut down and the deck respotted for morning launch. Also, at the outset, the A-6 was not as accurate a dive bomber as either the A-4 or F-4, since the initial training for the crews emphasized system release rather than visual drops using a bombsight. One senior B/N commented, "When you miss the target with 28 bombs, people tend to notice."

Constellation arrived for her 1966 deployment in May to relieve *Kitty Hawk*. Air Wing 15 included VA-65 "Tigers"; the third Intruder squadron was initially led by Commander Bill Small, who was relieved mid-cruise when his tour as CO was completed by Commander Robert E. "Bob" Mandeville. In a deployment that lasted until December 3, 1966, VA-65 would be credited with the destruction of four bridges at night, the Hanoi–Haiphong thermal powerplant, many POL storage sites, PT boat bases, and barges. The squadron was responsible for half the bomb tonnage dropped by the air wing, which included 24 F-4 Phantoms and 24 A-4 Skyhawks. As Mandeville later said, "Our deployment was do-or-die for the A-6."

With the support of *Constellation*'s commanding officer, Captain Bill Houser, VA-65's airplanes received deck elevator priority, enabling them to be sent below for additional work as necessary. The operations department planners picked targets appropriate for night attack and A-6 delivery. Finally, the Air Department scheduled one- and two-Intruder missions late into the night outside the standard cyclic operation schedule. The North Vietnamese had become adept at hiding vehicles during the day and moving at night, knowing they could only be attacked by aircraft using flares for visual attacks. The Intruder, attacking without warning out of the night, changed the situation drastically in favor of the truck hunters.

One of the most notable single aircraft missions was flown by pilot Lieutenant Commander Bernie Diebert and B/N Lieutenant Commander Dale Purdy, who dropped the center span of the Hai Duong Bridge with five 2,000-pound bombs. During Constellation's last line period in November 1966, as the northeast monsoon gathered sufficient strength to create weather bad enough to keep the Phantoms and Skyhawks on deck, the Intruders flew 73 percent of the missions flown during that period; on four days, VA-65's Intruders accounted for all Yankee Station missions flown. The A-6s were so effective at night that the VPAF attempted to launch night MiG intercept missions, while the defenses fired SAM barrages in an attempt to down one of the planes.

VA-65's performance was so good that the squadron literally saved the A-6 program. By the conclusion of the deployment, VA-65 had dropped over 5,000 tons of bombs in 1,239 sorties, with no losses at night. During its tour, VA-65 suffered only two Intruder losses. The first, on June 25, was the victim of AAA during a daylight attack on the Hoi Thoung barracks near Vinh in which pilot Lieutenant Richard Weber was recovered but B/N Lieutenant (jg) Charles Marik was killed. The second was lost to AAA during a daylight strike near Vinh on August 27, with both pilot Lieutenant Commander Jack Fellows and B/N Lieutenant (jg) George Coker captured and made POWs. CVW-11 had participated in an experimental program to camouflage many aircraft in the wing. The fact that both Intruder losses involved camouflaged aircraft was determinative in the decision not to use an Air Force-type camouflage on naval aircraft since it appeared that the camouflaged planes were easier for enemy gunners to track in daylight.

With VA-65's success, the Intruder was now seen as the airplane the Navy had wanted when the specifications were first drawn up. The squadron would return in July 1967 for an unfortunately aborted combat tour aboard USS Forrestal.

In December, 1966 VA-35 "Panthers," the fourth Oceana-based Intruder squadron, arrived as part of CVW-9 embarked in the nuclear-powered USS Enterprise. The squadron functionally replaced two of the four A-4C squadrons the ship had operated during her first combat deployment the year before. The squadron's most notable mission was laying mines in the Song Giang and Song Ca rivers on February 26, 1967. While Air Wing 9 lost 14 aircraft to enemy action during the six-month deployment, only one Intruder was lost. The airplane and its crews were coming of age.

The Intruder's worst day of the war was August 21, 1967. The unlucky squadron was VA-196 "Main Battery," the first Pacific Fleet A-6 squadron to deploy to Southeast Asia, which arrived aboard *Constellation* in mid-May.

That day, VA-196 skipper Commander Leo Profilet led four A-6As on his 59th mission, headed for a day attack on the Duc Noi railway marshaling yard north of Hanoi. En route to the target, SAM and AAA activity increased and NK-400, flown by Lieutenant Commander Jim Buckley and B/N Lieutenant Bob Flynn, was damaged by flak; nevertheless, they flew on. In addition to the enemy's actions, the Intruders found the weather challenging as heavy clouds and thunderstorms built throughout North Vietnam. There was rising chaos on all fronts, with two F-105Ds from the Takhli-based 355th Tactical Fighter Wing shot down at a nearby target. The emergency radio traffic made coordination of the Intruder formation all the more difficult.

Finally arriving at the target, the Intruders' warning systems alerted that SAM radars were guiding on the airplanes as they initiated their dives. Profilet's NK-410 took a SAM hit that separated a wing and set the remainder of the airplane on fire. Profilet and B/N Lieutenant. Commander Bill Hardman ejected and were quickly captured on landing. They would spend the next five-and-a-half years in prison. The three surviving A-6s departed the target area, but the heavy weather separated the Intruders as they headed for the coast. Only one A-6 returned to trap aboard *Constellation*.

It did not take long to discover the fate of the two missing airplanes. The official Chinese government radio soon announced that two US Navy aircraft had been shot down well inside the border by J-6 fighters (license-built MiG-19s). Lieutenant (jg)s J. Forrest Trembley and Dain Scott, who had been flying NK-402, as well as pilot Jim Buckley of NK-400, were missing in action (MIA). Buckley's B/N, Bob Flynn, was the only survivor. He was captured and imprisoned by the Chinese, spending the next five-and-a-half years mostly in solitary confinement, before being released in March 1973 along with the POWs held by North Vietnam. Navy radar tracking indicated that both Intruders had flown 11 miles into Chinese airspace, though Flynn maintained after his release that they had been well south of the border and the Chinese MiGs had crossed into North Vietnam to attack them. NK-400 and NK-402 were the only Intruders lost to enemy aircraft during the war.

Commander Profilet was popular with his men and the loss of three A-6s on one mission hit the squadron hard. XO Commander Ed Bauer immediately fleeted up to squadron command. The next senior man, Commander Bob Blackwood, then announced to crews in the squadron ready room that he was now second in command, and would take the position of XO. However, Blackwood was a naval flight officer; at that time, NFOs were not eligible for command, which meant they could not hold either of the top two spots in a squadron. Through sheer strength of personality, Blackwood was accepted by all in the unit as Exec, even if his position was "not quite legal" as it was described at the time. Blackwood's performance as XO was such that his example led to a change in the rules in 1970, allowing NFOs to occupy command positions in both a squadron and an air wing.

VA-196 also had the opportunity to fly a mission that perfectly demonstrated the value of the Intruder and its superiority over other attack aircraft. Following the terrific losses on August 21, replacements were quickly sent, including four Intruders, six aircrew, and 49 maintenance crewmen from VA-65. Pilot Lieutenant Commander Charlie Hunter and B/N Lieutenant Lyle Bull, instructors in Intruder training squadron VA-128 at NAS Whidbey Island, who each had more than 600 hours in type, both immediately volunteered when the word went out of what had happened to VA-196. They had the most experience of anyone in the squadron and remained a crew after arrival.

One of the most important targets in North Vietnam was the Hanoi Rail Ferry on the Red River. It had been on the "high priority" list since being taken off the "prohibited" list and approved for attack. Several attempts had been made to hit the target with air wing Alpha strikes that had failed due to the high number of defending SAM and AAA sites in the area. Lieutenant Commander Blackwood had long maintained that a single Intruder could hit the target by going in at very low altitude at night, stating strongly that the rail ferry was the exact mission the Intruder had been built to do.

On the night of October 30–31, 1967, Hunter and Bull were assigned the mission. After going "feet dry" north of Vinh, they flew toward Hanoi at an altitude of 500 feet, carrying 13 1,000-pound Mark 83 Snake Eye retarded bombs hanging on five MERs. Hunter took advantage of the terrain, running down parallel rocky ridges known as karsts so as to stay inside the radar shadow of the ridgelines. There was no enemy reaction until they were 18 miles from the target, when their PRC-68 radar warning receiver told them they were being tracked by Fan Song SAM radar. Moments later, they spotted the launch of the first SAM.

Flying at 500 feet, Hunter expected to avoid the missile, since it was believed the SAM could not track a target at an altitude lower than 1,500 feet. When Bull reported that the SAM appeared to be tracking them, Hunter began a high-G barrel roll to throw it off. The SAM went behind them and exploded on impact with the ground at the moment the Intruder was halfway through the roll, inverted at 500 feet. Instantly, the darkness below was lit by the launch of five more SAMs as tracers from multiple AAA positions split the night sky. Hunter finished with a snap roll to upright and dove to 100 feet as he accelerated to 450 knots while jinking wildly and they flew on toward the ferry. Bull saw the radar altimeter read 50 feet three times as they headed in, but he had complete faith in Hunter's flying ability. At that altitude, the SAMs had no chance of catching them.

Moments later, the target appeared on the radar. Hunter pulled up to 200 feet and Bull salvoed the Snake Eyes when the DIANE showed they were in position. All 13 bombs landed on the ferry, knocking it out. Hunter immediately turned east to avoid Gia Lam Airport, which was just ahead. He jinked as much as possible while he headed for the Tonkin Gulf, with the Intruder followed by AAA tracers and large-caliber aerial explosions. One 85mm round exploded so close it shook the plane, but they were soon out to sea. Hunter executed a normal night recovery aboard *Constellation* after a memorable 1.9 hours in the air.

Hunter and Bull each were awarded the Navy Cross. Their flight was publicized for years after as the textbook example of how to use a single A-6 in its designed role. Both later became admirals.

VA-75 returned to the war in early 1968, again aboard *Independence*. This time, the "Sunday Punchers" brought with them a new Intruder, three A-6B "defense suppression" aircraft.

The Bravo Intruder had electronic receivers that covered parts of the radio frequency spectrum from C- to F-bands, with specific threats like the SA-2's Fan Song and Fire Can AAA radar systems being high on the list of targets. The initial versions also required the deletion of the DIANE and related bombing systems, making them dedicated to the Iron Hand mission. The B-model would be sequentially developed into four subvariants, each better than the other in terms of frequency coverage and crew displays, while also eventually returning traditional weapons delivery capability to the airframe.

After initially looking at establishing three 12-aircraft A-6B squadrons dedicated to the SAM suppression Iron Hand mission (much as the US Air Force would do), the US Navy decided that it could not afford such a luxury and instead dealt with the requirement from within its existing attack force. Intruder squadrons that were assigned A-6Bs usually only had a small number of aircrew who were actually trained in the system and remained proficient in its use. This would include B/Ns who had some knowledge of the electronic "beeps and squeaks" that the system provided to analyze the electronic environment.

The A-6B provided a sophisticated ARM capability for the US Navy that would not be substantially improved upon in the fleet until the AGM-88 High-speed Anti-Radiation Missile (HARM) entered service with EA-6B Prowler squadrons in the mid-1980s.

The largest airplane found on a carrier deck at Yankee Station was the Douglas A-3 Skywarrior, a twin-engine three-seat medium bomber originally designed to put the Navy in the strategic nuclear war business, before it was replaced by the submarine-launched Polaris missile in 1964. Up to the summer of 1967, A-3s participated as part of the strike force against targets in North Vietnam since it could carry up to 10,000 pounds of internal ordnance. An Essex-class carrier modernized through the 27-Charlie program could carry a detachment of four to six A-3s, while the larger Forrestal-class carriers could carry up to a squadron. By 1966, even the Forrestals carried only squadron detachments of four A-3s to free their decks for other aircraft.

The Skywarrior was first used in a conventional bombing role on March 3, 1965, when six A-3s of VAH-2 based on *Coral Sea* took part in a strike against Bach Long Vi Island in the Gulf of Tonkin. Then Lieutenant (jg) David Mason, a junior pilot in VAH-4 based on the USS *Constellation* in 1967, recalled that when the carrier first arrived in Southeast Asia, "We operated from Dixie Station and the A-3s engaged in dive bombing and close air support, which was pretty amazing because they didn't have a gunsight or bombsight that was capable of putting the ordnance on target. But we had a reputation as being the most accurate dive bombers around." This lasted until General William Westmoreland, commander of US forces in Vietnam, saw an A-3 dive-bombing mission and was told the aircraft didn't have bombsights. "It didn't matter how accurate we were; Westmoreland wasn't about to allow any reporter to announce that the Navy was bombing by gosh and by guess. They tried fitting some A-3s with gunsights from A-4s, but it was a lash-up effort. A-3s weren't allowed to bomb visual targets in north or south Vietnam again." Since the A-6 Intruder had not yet arrived in the fleet in large numbers, A-3s did perform radar bombing missions over both North and South Vietnam at night and in bad weather.

The last combat mission flown by the Skywarrior involved the Navy's first attempt to mine the river approaches to Haiphong Harbor in May 1967. US military planners pleaded throughout the war to be allowed to choke off Haiphong, the main port for supply of war equipment sent to North Vietnam by the Soviet Union and other Warsaw Pact countries, and were finally given the go-ahead by President Johnson in the spring of 1967, when it was sold to the president as a way to bring the enemy to the negotiating table. *Constellation*'s VAH-4 detachment was given the assignment. They planned a night mission using two waves of two Skywarriors each, with each A-3 carrying ten 1,000-pound Mark 52 magnetic mines, which they would drop into the two river entrances to the harbor from an altitude of 50 feet above the water.

Mason recalled:

I was number two in the second group. Just before we were set to launch, they lost contact with one of the two aircraft in the first wave. No one knew what happened, whether the NVAs got it, or what. But with the possibility that the NVAs had downed the plane and now knew about the mission, our strike was scrubbed.

It was later determined that the missing A-3 had most likely hit the water and suffered a catastrophic breakup of its airframe. When

Operation *Pocket Money* was given the go-ahead in May, 1972, following the North Vietnamese assault on South Vietnam, the plans made by VAH-4 were dusted off and the mission was carried out by Grumman A-6 Intruders.

There were two reasons that the A-3 was cut from the strike force: the first was that the Grumman A-6 Intruder – half the size of the A-3 but capable of carrying a similar offensive load – had equipped sufficient attack squadrons to be a fleet-wide presence by 1967. The second was that the A-3 was no longer fast enough to survive in the highly threatening defensive environment of North Vietnam.

Fortunately, beginning with the 178th A-3 produced, all subsequent aircraft were delivered with a tanker package to facilitate their conversion into in-flight tankers. The value of this development was first shown in May, 1961, when three F4H-1 Phantoms flying in the Bendix Trophy Race established a transcontinental speed record of 2 hours and 47 minutes at an average speed of 870mph, an achievement that would not have been possible without the three refuelings by A-3s.

Flying in the aerial tanker role, the A-3 could carry 34,178 pounds of jet fuel, of which two-thirds could be transferred to other aircraft using the probe-and-drogue system. The tactical strike aircraft that the Navy used to fight the strategic air war over the North could never have carried a load useful for the task had they not had the air-to-air refueling capability of the A-3s regularly available to them. Usually, the A-4s and A-6s would launch from the carriers with a maximum bomb load and minimum fuel load, then take on fuel from the KA-3B tankers while en route to their targets in North Vietnam. The A-3s would then orbit off the North Vietnamese coast to offer fuel to aircraft returning from the strike if needed.

One of the most amazing tanker missions was flown by Lieutenant Commander Don Alberg of the VAH-4 detachment aboard USS *Enterprise*, the first nuclear-powered aircraft carrier, in mid-May, 1967, at the height of Operation *Rolling Thunder*. The four KA-3Bs – call signs "Hollygreen" 896, 897, 898, and 899 respectively and led by Lieutenant Commander John Wunsch in 896 – were tasked with supporting a strike on Hanoi by 16 A-4 Skyhawks of VA-212 "Rampant Raiders." With the Skyhawks fully fueled, the four Skywarriors took up a racecourse pattern off the coast to await their return.

Ten minutes later, Lieutenant Commander Arvin Chauncey's A-4 took a hit and he ejected 50 miles from Hanoi. Four F-8 Crusaders from VF-24 "Red Checkertails" assumed RESCAP for him. Alberg recalled:

> Wunsch notified Hollygreen 898 and 899, numbers three and four of our flight, that they would assume responsibility for tanking the strike on egress and that he and I – Hollygreen 896 and 897, respectively – would cover the RESCAP. Everything was standard procedure. All that was now needed was for the SH-2 Seasprite launched from the duty SAR destroyer to arrive and pick up Chauncey.

Regardless of how "routine" any military mission may be, the vagaries of weather and the mechanical reliability of equipment can always change the routine into the memorable. "About fifteen minutes later, we heard that our chopper had a mechanical abort and they were launching a backup." Soon, Alberg and Wunsch were the only US airplanes in the vicinity when they learned the second helicopter had also aborted. "We kept calling the task force about the chopper but didn't get a solid answer. The RESCAP leader detached two F-8s to tank with us. At last, the third helicopter they launched was reported inbound." This helicopter was launched from *Enterprise* herself, rather than from an escort ship, which was more than 100 miles out at sea. Arrival was a good hour away at best speed. In any rescue, time is of the essence; this one was beginning to look very iffy.

The two Skywarriors again provided fuel for the thirsty F-8s and maintained their position. As the two F-8s went "feet dry" inbound to the site of the rescue, Alberg watched his own fuel status with increasing anxiety. "We were close to 'bingo' for our internal fuel, but the helo was nowhere in sight, and the F-8s weren't going to make it back to the carrier without another hook-up."

Finally, after what seemed like much longer than an hour, the Sea King hove into view and headed inland. At this point, Alberg had ten minutes' fuel, and Wunsch six. The tankers needed tanking – fast! "I called on all the tanker frequencies, and a KC-135 reported he was nearby. I asked his altitude, and he was at 28,000 feet. We were at 1,500 feet, so no way would we have enough gas to climb up to him. He said he'd come down."

When the big Air Force tanker arrived, Wunsch made the first hookup and took on 30 minutes of fuel, then Alberg followed:

He got his fuel and I moved in. I had trouble hooking up because the Air Force system with the basket was different from that of the Navy. With the Navy, if you hit the basket and put the tip in with a push, you'll screw up the hose and it won't feed. With the Air Force, it's just the opposite. I probed three times for maybe five minutes and was really sweating a flameout and a crash because I couldn't get a hookup, and then they got around to telling me this.

With connection made at last, Alberg breathed more easily as his fuel-gauge indicators moved upwards. Meanwhile, the rescue mission failed in the most heartbreaking manner when the North Vietnamese captured Lieutenant Commander Chauncey while the rescue helicopter was still five minutes away. The F-8s had remained on station longer than they should have; when they went "feet wet" coming out of North Vietnam, each had less than ten minutes' fuel remaining.

Having just solved the difficulty of hooking into the basket, Alberg was only beginning to take on fuel:

I had about seven or eight minutes' fuel on board and couldn't unhook. They couldn't wait. I deployed my hose, and the F-8s came in one at a time and took on fuel from me while the KC-135 fueled us. Fortunately, our intake system was faster than our delivery system, so we brought in more than we needed to keep flying.

The complicated aerial ballet took place within sight of the enemy coastline.

With the F-8s fueled and on their way home, Alberg dropped back so that Wunsch could take on enough fuel to get back to *Enterprise*, and the two crews thanked the KC-135 crew for their help. The Air Force tanker had burned so much fuel at low altitude that it could not return to Thailand and had to make an emergency recovery at Da Nang:

Several weeks later, we got word that the crew of the KC-135 had been brought up by Seventh Air Force on charges of abandoning their assigned post and were going to be court-martialed. We let the

Air Force know these guys had saved two A-3s and four F-8s – ten aircrew, who would definitely not have made it home feet dry had the Air Force not saved us. So, instead of a court-martial, they were each awarded a Distinguished Flying Cross! We got a pat on the back and a "Well done" from the Task Force Commander.

In July 1967, Alberg saved an A-4 Skyhawk that had been hit heavily in its wing and was streaming fuel almost as fast as it was using it:

I got him connected, and he was able to keep it going as long as we were hooked up, but he wouldn't have more than 30 seconds of flight time when we had to cut him loose to land. There was no way we could take him back to the carrier, so I flew him down to Da Nang. I kept him hooked all the way through the landing pattern until he was 10 seconds from touchdown, and then I disconnected and pulled away. He put it on the runway safely, but the engine died before he reached the first taxiway.

The A-3 excelled in another mission about which little has been disclosed: electronic warfare. After the heavy attack squadrons had been reorganized in 1968, Alberg was assigned to the squadron that was redesignated VQ-2:

When I brought the detachment aboard a carrier, most of the time, the CAG was an old fighter type who had no idea what the A-3 could do other than take up valuable space on his flight deck. Once they discovered what we could do to the bad guys – listen in to everything they said, tell the strike force what was ahead, the kind of attack they would face – most of them came around to the view that we were pretty useful.

By 1968, the Skyhawk was on its way out of Navy squadrons, though it would soldier on through the end of the war while the LTV A-7 Corsair II replaced it in the squadrons. Development and operational use of the aircraft was very rapid, with the prototype first taking flight on September 26, 1965; VF-174, the first squadron, was re-equipped on October 14, 1966, with VA-147 "Argonauts" declared operationally ready in February, 1967; the squadron's nickname honored the mythological group of adventurers, with their call sign "Jason." The Corsair II carried a payload 80 percent that of the A-6 Intruder, with a longer range/loiter capability than the Skyhawk due to the turbofan powerplant being more economical in fuel consumption than a turbojet engine. However, both the A-7A with the Pratt & Whitney TF30-P-6 turbofan engine producing 11,345 pounds of thrust, and the A-7B with the more powerful Pratt & Whitney TF30-8 engine producing 12,190 pounds of thrust, were underpowered. For the Navy, the definitive Corsair II would be the A-7E that entered service in 1970, powered by the Allison TF41-A-2 engine, a licensed version of the Rolls-Royce Spey engine that corrected issues in the earlier versions, such as severe compressor stalls and low thrust.

USS *Ranger*, veteran of two combat deployments to Southeast Asia, departed San Diego with CVW-2 (which included the "Argonauts") on November 20, 1967, arriving on Yankee Station on December 3.

The squadron wasted no time, flying their first combat mission the following day. Led by Commander James C. Hill, the A-7As hit flak and SAM sites, railway and highway bridges, and other targets, demonstrating the value of their load-carrying capacity and accuracy. XO Commander W. Scott Gray led a flight of Corsair IIs against a train discovered 35 miles southeast of Hanoi on December 14, in company with a strike force from USS *Oriskany*. Gray recalled, "We rolled in and literally cut the train in half."

Lieutenant Jack Connor credited the A-7 with "pinpoint accuracy" during a bombing attack, but also remembered that the airplane "smoked like a locomotive," and "could be seen coming before we got feet dry, and maybe right off the cat." This was an exaggeration, but the A-7A did leave a noticeable trail. A quick fix was found using a five-gallon tank filled with bleach. Approaching the target, pilots would open the bleach tank, which removed the smoke from the exhaust!

The squadron took its first loss on December 22. Lieutenant Commander James M. Hickerson, who had been involved with the initial A-7 test program at NAS Patuxent River, was flying an Iron Hand mission with wingman Lieutenant (jg) Dave Carroll. Each carried two AGM-45 Shrike ARMs. They were to team up with an Air Force crew and "troll" for Fan Song SAM radar sites. When the Air Force plane failed to appear, the two flew toward Haiphong alone. Once there, they were lit up by a Fan Song. While Carroll remained high, Hickerson launched a Shrike that quickly stopped functioning. The site launched a missile before his second missile took out the radar, but now he was above a layer of clouds that prevented his seeing another SAM, which exploded beneath his A-7, knocking him unconscious. Hickerson came to from bumping around in the cockpit, to discover that the plane was in a spin and that he was no longer attached to his ejection seat. He managed to strap back in as the wounded Corsair II dove for the ground. At what he thought was the last minute, he pulled his face curtain and ejected, landing right at the water's edge where he was quickly captured. The mission was his 13th, and the A-7's side number was "313." Hickerson was the first of five A-7 pilots to become a POW, two of whom died during their captivity.

The air war heated up with the new year. On March 21 and 22, VA-147 flew missions in support of the Marines at Khe Sanh in company with A-4Cs of VA-22 and A-6As of VA-165 to hit enemy bunkers, artillery sites, and storage caves. On April 28, Commander Hill flew a mission just before sunrise and got secondary explosions at a supply area near Dong Hoi. The squadron had proved its night attack credentials on April 25 when Lieutenant Commander John B. Streit found a truck convoy. He reported, "After I put the bombs down, there was a big ball of fire, and it kept mushrooming up." VA-147's deployment ended with its return to the United States in May. The Navy was happy with the A-7 based on their success over 1,500 sorties.

Other squadrons followed. By the end of *Rolling Thunder* in November, VA-82, VA-86, VA-27, VA-97, VA-105, and VA-37 had flown from Yankee Station. Next up after the "Argonauts" was VA-86 "Sidewinders," flying from USS *America*. Skipper Commander Jack E. Russ was awarded the DFC for leading a strike against the Binh Thuy thermal power plant on July 20, 1968. The strike group faced intense flak, but the A-7s went in and hit the target.

A month later on August 24, Lieutenant James R. Lee of VA-27, part of CVW-14 aboard *Constellation*, was hit by small arms fire just as he rolled in to attack a flak site near Vinh. With his A-7 on fire, Lee headed for the water where he ejected, coming down near a small island. While North Vietnamese troops ashore attempted to launch a boat with which to capture him, fellow pilots Lieutenant (jg)s Dave Hollis and Roger Stroup kept them at bay, attacking with rockets and gunfire that forced the North Vietnamese to abandon the boat. An SH-3 from the HC-7 detachment aboard the duty SAR ship USS *Sterett* (DDG-104) pulled Lee out. For their efforts to cover their squadron mate, Hollis received the DFC and Stroup the Air Medal.

On September 18, VA-82's Lieutenant Commander Fred Hueber and Lieutenant (jg) James Counter gave cover for the rescue of Lieutenant Don Wright, a Skyhawk pilot from *Hancock's* VA-55, who had been hit by ground fire during a bridge-busting mission near Vinh. Wright had managed to eject and was in his life raft near Hon Ngu Island, where he was coming under enemy fire. As his squadronmates ran low on fuel, Hueber and Counter fortuitously appeared just in time to keep the enemy down long enough for a Sea King to pick Wright up. Counter later commented, "It was one of those things that happen out there that make you feel good."

Rolling Thunder ended six weeks later. The A-7s would reappear in the skies over North Vietnam three-and-a-half years later, where they would leave an even stronger mark on the war.

9

SPADS vs. MIGS

In a naval air force composed of jets, one anachronism stood out, seemingly a throwback to naval aviation of World War II; it was so old technologically that pilots called it the "Spad," after the well-known World War I fighter. The piston-engined Douglas Skyraider began life as a 1944 Navy proposal for an airplane to replace the SB2C Helldiver dive bomber and TBF Avenger torpedo bomber, a single-seat aircraft equally capable in either role. Designed by the legendary Ed Heinemann, the prototype was ordered as the XBT2D-1 on July 6, 1944, with its first flight on March 18, 1945. The airplane was "right from the beginning" and passed manufacturer's tests by the following April, at which time the Navy began testing it over the next year. It was ordered into production in April 1945 as the BT2D-1, with a production run of 548 aircraft. This was reduced to 277 in September 1945. In 1946 the aircraft was redesignated AD-1 (Attack, Douglas, first model). VA-1B took the first AD-1s aboard USS *Midway* in November 1947. Named the Skyraider, it was the first navy attack aircraft capable of lifting its own weight in ordnance. The AD-1s were followed by AD-2 and AD-3 sub-types, with a night-attack version introduced at the end of the AD-1 production which carried two electronics technicians in the fuselage just aft of the wing to operate the on-board radar; in subsequent production these aircraft were identified by an "N" in the designator (i.e., AD-3N). An airborne early warning version with a bulbous radome under the fuselage designated with a "W" (i.e., AD-2W) was also developed and saw extensive carrier service.

The Korean War saved the Skyraider, which was set to go out of production in 1950 following completion of the order for AD-3s. However, the turboprop-powered A2D Skyshark was delayed and then found unable to proceed with development. With no other aircraft capable of taking the Skyraider's role aboard ship, the AD-4 that first appeared in mid-1950 increased armament from two to four 20mm cannon in the wings and later added significant armor protection as the result of combat experience.

The Skyraider first saw combat immediately following the outbreak of the Korean War when USS *Valley Forge* struck Pyongyang on July 3–4, 1950, and provided the medium attack squadron for Navy carriers throughout the conflict. One notable Skyraider operation was breaching the Hwachon Dam in 1951. Conventional bombing was unable to breach the dam, so the pilots of VA-196 came up with the idea of using the aerial torpedoes discovered in the ship's magazine. The mission was the first (and last) use of aerial torpedoes in combat by the Navy since World War II. Rear Admiral John W. Hoskins, commanding Task Force 77 stated "I am convinced the Skyraider is the most effective close-support aircraft in the world!"

Production continued through the 1950s, as no other design was able to replace the piston-engined Skyraider in terms of capability and dependability. The AD-6 appeared in 1953, produced in parallel with the multi-seat AD-5, with 713 AD-6s off the line by 1956. The AD-7 entered production shortly thereafter and the last Skyraider came off the production line on February 18, 1957, by which time 3,180 had been produced. The aircraft was redesignated the A-1E (AD-5), A-1H (AD-6), and A-1J (AD-7) when the tri-service designation system was adopted in 1962. During its naval career, the A-1 fulfilled every task from close air support to low-level nuclear strike, night attack, airborne early warning and electronic countermeasures, antisubmarine warfare, troop-carrying, and target towing, and would engage successfully in air combat against jet-powered opponents in Vietnam. No other basic airframe has ever fulfilled such a multitude of roles in Navy service, and the last Skyraiders to see combat were flown by the French in Africa in 1984.

The Skyraider continued to fly on as the heart of naval attack aviation after the end of the Korean War, while the Navy cycled through two generations of jet fighters on its carriers. "Heinemann's Hotrod," the

AD-4 (later A-4) Skyhawk couldn't come close to matching the big prop bomber for payload and battlefield air support. However, the lessons learned in Korea regarding the need for all-weather/night-strike capability were at work throughout the postwar period as the Navy sought to come up with an aircraft that could exceed the Skyraider in capability. By 1965, the appearance of the Grumman A-6 Intruder in the attack squadrons meant the days of Skyraider operations from the fleet carriers were now numbered.

With the deactivation of the Air Task Groups (ad hoc air groups first created during the Korean War to meet operational demand without exceeding the formally authorized Carrier Air Groups) in 1957, there were only 14 operational Skyraider squadrons in the naval air force. The airplane was considered to be old and obsolete, and technologically "out of step" with the rest of the carrier force. With the arrival of the A-6 in squadron service beginning in 1963, the number of Skyraider squadrons further declined. By the time Operation *Rolling Thunder* began in early 1965, there were only ten Skyraider squadrons still flying off flight decks, with only VA-176 "Thunderbolts" still part of the Atlantic Fleet.

As the need for Skyraiders decreased in the Navy, 25 AD-6s were transferred to the VNAF of the Republic of Vietnam in 1960 to replace aging F8F-1B Bearcats, and the Skyraider entered its second war. With range, load-carrying capability, and a loiter time measured in hours, the airplane was an unbeatable combination and was so good at what it did that when the Air Force realized in 1964 that the service had a crying need for an effective battlefield close air support aircraft to support US forces in Vietnam, it turned to the supply of mothballed Skyraiders.

Despite Navy plans to finally get rid of the Skyraider, when American involvement in Vietnam began, the old prop bomber was still the medium attack aircraft in all carrier air wings. Skyraiders from the carriers *Constellation* and *Ticonderoga* participated in the first US Navy strikes against North Vietnam on August 5, 1964 as part of Operation *Pierce Arrow* in response to the Gulf of Tonkin Incident, with one Skyraider from *Ticonderoga* damaged by antiaircraft fire, and a second from *Constellation* shot down, killing its pilot, Lieutenant (jg) Richard C. Sather, who became the first naval aviator killed in action in Vietnam.

When Operation *Rolling Thunder* began, the Skyraider was the best aircraft for "road recce" missions, since its relatively low speed allowed a pilot flying at low altitude to see enemy vehicles hidden under trees off the road that would be missed by a jet flying at twice that speed with the ground close to a blur at that altitude. The initial lack of enemy air defenses over North Vietnam meant the A-1 was operating in a "benign" combat environment. This situation would begin to change over the summer of 1965, with the result that in 1966 and 1967 the A-1's operating area in the north was significantly reduced with the expanded number of light antiaircraft guns and the introduction of SAMs.

While Skyraider attack bombers were the majority of the type found on carrier flight decks, the "Electric Spad" was of equal importance if found aboard in smaller numbers. The Pacific Fleet electronic countermeasures squadron was VAW-13, based at NAS Cubi Point in the Philippines, from which it operated four-plane detachments aboard the carriers at Yankee Station. Designated EA-1F and modified from the multi-seat A-1E, the EA-1F carried an APS-31C radar under the starboard inner wing, and ALT-2 or ALT-7 jamming pods under each outer wing, with the electronics operated by two aviation electronics technicians (AT) from the rear cockpit. The "Electric Spad" was used for airborne electronic countermeasures, and was able to jam enemy radars as well as provide early warning capability with its APS-31C as the aircraft orbited off the enemy coast in support of strike missions.

One of the most important missions for the Skyraider in Vietnam was RESCAP, providing air cover and support to helicopters engaged in SAR operations to pick up downed aviators. The Navy helicopters involved in SAR missions inside North Vietnam were the Sikorsky SH-3 Sea King, which operated from the fleet carriers in four-helicopter detachments for antisubmarine defense, and the Kaman SH-2 Seasprite, which was operated from the destroyers and frigates operating off the North Vietnamese coast. The big twin-engine Sea King had long range and lifting capability, while the Seasprite was small and highly maneuverable. Until the summer of 1965, the Seasprite's only use for air rescue had been when the destroyer that carried it was operating as a plane guard with a carrier battle force. The fact that the Seasprite's base was a destroyer that might be operating as close as 12–20 miles offshore meant that it could provide a faster response than the carrier-based Sea Kings. The first rescue of an aviator in North Vietnam by a Seasprite happened in late August, 1965. The Skyraider had no trouble operating at a helicopter's speed, and its heavy payload and extended loiter time, coupled with excellent low-altitude performance, meant it could provide as much cover as needed if a search for the downed pilot in the thick jungles or a fight with enemy ground forces became necessary.

VA-25 "Fist of the Fleet" arrived in Southeast Asia on April 8, 1965, as part of Air Wing 2 (CVW-2) aboard USS *Midway*. The squadron was led by Commander Harry E. Ettinger, a Korean War Skyraider veteran who had flown from USS *Valley Forge* with VF-154. Shot down over North Korea in December 1951 and rescued from prison camp by anti-communist guerillas the next month, Ettinger's attempted rescue by Navy helicopter pilot Chief Naval Aviation Pilot Duane Thorin in February 1952 had provided novelist James A. Michener, who was aboard "Happy Valley" as a war correspondent, with the story that became his novel, *The Bridges at Toko-ri*. Unlike Michener's characters of Lieutenant Harry Brubaker and Chief Mike Thorney, Ettinger and Thorin had survived capture and imprisonment in North Korea, and both returned to service as naval aviators after their repatriation at the conclusion of the war.

Two days after their arrival on station in the Tonkin Gulf, the squadron launched its first missions, a RESCAP and SAR in the panhandle of southern North Vietnam. Their pace kept up with four Skyraiders launched on a SAR mission over Laos becoming the first *Midway* pilots to engage the enemy directly. VA-25's pilots engaged in almost daily RESCAP and road reconnaissance missions. April 15 saw the Skyraiders engage in a saturation bombing mission against an enemy stronghold in South Vietnam, which was followed the next day by the successful destruction of the Bai Duc Tho highway bridge in the panhandle.

The squadron's first major success came on April 18, the night of Easter Sunday, when Lieutenant Commander Harold E. Gray, Jr., and Lieutenant (jg) L.O. Woodbury spotted a long convoy of trucks southwest of Vinh. Reporting the contact to the ship, the two made several runs on the convoy, hitting vehicles at either end which blocked escape. At dawn, *Midway* launched a large strike of Skyraiders and Skyhawks that turned the convoy into junk. Gray and Woodbury again got lucky four nights later when they spotted another 15–20 truck convoy and hit it.

The squadron flew similar missions through May and June. The most memorable mission of their Southeast Asian tour happened on June 20, 1965. *Midway* was off the line that day, but when word was received that an Air Force F-105 pilot had bailed out near Dien Bien Phu, the duty RESCAP flight was launched to support the attempted rescue. The four Skyraiders were led by Lieutenant Commander Ed Greathouse and his wingman, Lieutenant (jg) Jim Lynne, in the first section, with Lieutenant Clint Johnson and wingman Lieutenant (jg) Charlie Hartman in the second. The Skyraiders had a typical RESCAP ordnance load underwing: four LAU-3/A 19-shot cylindrical pods of 2.75-inch FFARs and full loads of 20mm cannon rounds.

The four Skyraiders of Canasta Flight went "feet dry" north of Thanh Hoa, remaining 1,000 feet beneath a stratus cloud deck and maintaining an altitude of 10,000 feet, a height that was considered reasonably safe in 1965. Visibility below the cloud layer was excellent, and Greathouse ordered a "combat spread." The division's two sections took position about 1,000 feet apart, which enhanced their ability to maneuver while still maintaining an effective lookout. When they were approximately 90 miles south of Hanoi, the radar picket destroyer in the Gulf of Tonkin called "Canasta, bogies in the air." Minutes later came the chilling warning, "Canasta – they're on your six, four miles. Blips are merging."

Johnson's wingman Lieutenant (jg) Hartman recalled:

After that call, I looked behind us and saw them. As the number four, I was on Johnson's wing to the left, flying straight and level at about 10,500 feet. I don't mind telling you that my heart was really pumping. I was stunned. You don't see enemy fighters every day in your life. But there they were, a pair of silver MiG-17s heading roughly in the same direction we were.

Hartman called the bogies, but realized his section leader had lost his radios. Greathouse remembered:

The MiGs were in right echelon, offset about one mile to the right. I believe they passed without seeing us. Jim Lynne and I spotted them at about our seven or eight o'clock and watched them continue on. Initially, I thought they might be headed toward another flight of Spads from VA-196, which was operating in the area ahead of us, but when the MiGs were about one-and-a-half to two miles ahead, they executed a rapid reversal toward my section. My guess is they didn't spot us at first because we were just below the overcast. Their radar operator on the ground probably realized they had overshot and their reversal was very likely a response to a call from the controller. I transmitted "Heads Up" to the flight as they turned.

Hartman remembered, "The familiar story of the number four man being the first to be downed on an initial attack raced through my mind." However, after the MiGs turned, they and the A-1s confronted each other directly. The two formations were approaching each other at a closing speed of 600 knots. Seeing the MiGs turn toward the Skyraiders, Greathouse radioed a curse. All four A-1s executed split-S maneuvers as they dived for the trees below.

The MiGs and Skyraiders were now low in a valley between two ridgelines nearly 2,000 feet high, which left the ground hilly and interrupted by limestone karsts. The Skyraider pilots stayed below 500 feet, occasionally dipping to 50 feet just over the treetops, as they followed the river that ran through the valley. So long as they stayed low, they were in their element, low and slow, while the fast-moving jets consumed fuel at a high rate at low altitudes, which might distract the enemy pilots.

As one of the MiGs turned directly toward Hartman's plane, Greathouse ordered them to release their 300-gallon drop tanks. As Hartman punched off the tanks, his Skyraider seemed to leap straight up from the sudden loss of weight just at the tracer rounds from the attacking MiG passed through the sky exactly where he had been an instant before. Seeing Hartman's tanks drop and the tracer rounds, Johnson thought for a moment his wingman had been hit.

Amazingly, the MiG flashed past the two Skyraiders and made a sharp turn to the north. For a moment, the Navy flier thought they might be running out of fuel.

With Hartman and Johnson on the north side of the formation, Greathouse and Lynne jinked aggressively near a karst to the south side of the valley as the other MiG pursued them.

The next critical few seconds were confusing. Hartman described the fight as:

> like being in a mixmaster. There was a swirling fight involving four or five full-circle turns, with us trying to either stay out of the MiG's sights or get a shot at him. The MiG pulled up after the fifth circle. He then rolled sharply to the left in order to get into position for a head-on pass at Greathouse and Lynne. As he turned toward them, Johnson and I had a head-on shot at the MiG. We both opened fire. I saw the MiG's canopy shatter as the shells struck both it and the fuselage, but the jet kept coming toward us, trailing a thin plume of flame and smoke. The pilot was probably incapacitated, because it flew between us pretty much straight and level. I think when he turned to get a shot at Greathouse and Lynne he either lost sight of us or forget we were there.

A moment later, the enemy jet fell off on its wing and slammed into the ridge. A red-and-black fireball erupted. The second MiG was last seen disappearing into the distance. Hartman recalled, "The whole affair lasted about three minutes. We joined up, excited as hell, and headed back to the ship. It was dark when we landed." Once aboard *Midway*, a post-flight check found that Hartman had fired 90 rounds and Johnson 50.

Hartman and Johnson were each awarded the Silver Star for their achievement, while Greathouse and Lynne were awarded Distinguished Flying Crosses. VA-25 never let the pilots of VF-21, the air wing's Phantom squadron, forget which squadron had shot down a MiG.

Sixteen months later, Skyraiders again confronted MiG-17s. As the tempo of operations in Southeast Asia increased, the Navy sought to supplement the forces available by bringing antisubmarine warfare (ASW) carriers onto the line as "limited attack" carriers beginning in 1966; these air wings did not include dedicated fighter (VF) squadrons, being composed of A-4 Skyhawk and A-1 Skyraider squadrons, and would see most of their action in support of US troops in South Vietnam. The first ASW carrier to undertake the "limited attack" role was USS *Intrepid* (CVS-11), which made her first of three Southeast Asia deployments in this role when she departed Norfolk, Virginia for Southeast Asia on April 4, 1966, with CVW-10, the "Champagne

Air Wing," embarked. The air wing was composed of two Skyhawk squadrons, VA-15 – descended from VB-15, the top-scoring Helldiver unit of World War II – and VA-95; for the only time in the war, two A-1 squadrons, VA-165 "Boomers" and VA-176 "Thunderbolts," each equipped with 12 Skyraiders, were aboard the carrier.

Arriving in Southeast Asia in early May, *Intrepid* launched her first strikes from Dixie Station on May 15, 1966. The ship and her air wing operated primarily from Dixie Station for three Tonkin Gulf line periods between May and September 1966, with the Skyraiders suffering no losses until September, though they were hit by ground fire on 24 sorties; during the third line period in late August–September, VA-165 lost two A-1s while VA-176 lost one, all over North Vietnam. By 1966, the air over North Vietnam was extremely dangerous for the Spads, particularly in the areas around Hanoi and Haiphong, where SAM batteries were increasing weekly.

The Skyraiders primarily flew in the southern region of the panhandle, below the 20th parallel, where they could operate in a less demanding environment while their carrier remained on Dixie Station, off South Vietnam. VA-176's Lieutenant (jg) William T. "Tom" Patton remembered:

> There were so many A-1s on *Intrepid* that the planners weren't always sure what to do with us. Mostly, we were turned loose and told to be careful. In my own case, most of the targets I hit during 40 missions over the north were of my own choosing. We frequently roamed at will, exercising our own judgment, hitting bridges, trucks, barges and the like. We actually blew up two ammo depots and were involved in one small Alpha Strike.

Most operations were coastal and inland armed recon missions. The primary mission over the north was RESCAP/SAR, and the *Intrepid* Skyraiders flew 108 RESCAP missions, loitering off the coast for up to five hours, ready to head inland to assist a rescue. The A-1s engaged the enemy during 11 of these missions, resulting in the recovery of six fliers.

Intrepid left Subic Bay for her fourth line period on October 1, 1966; this would prove to be the most memorable period of the deployment. On October 9, Papoose Flight, a RESCAP flight led by Lieutenant Commander Leo Cook with wingman Lieutenant (jg) Jim Wiley, while

Patton was wingman to second section leader Lieutenant Pete Russell, was launched to provide cover if necessary for a major three-carrier Alpha strike on targets in the Hanoi area. Although the monsoon normally meant there was poor weather at this time of year, on this day the weather was clear with excellent visibility and calm seas. The four "Spads" hugged the coastline southeast of Hanoi, with Cook bringing them as close to "feet dry" as was safely possible in order to maximize their RESCAP capabilities.

Patton later recalled:

Looking at the no-man's land between us and the target, I wondered whether anyone in his right mind would even try to take four A-1s in there. If someone did go down, we'd have to take a direct route to save time, and the direct route would carry us over some deadly flak sites, not to mention SAM emplacements.

The pilots had been in "Indian Country," as the highly defended region of Hanoi was known to American pilots, before, but on those missions they had had the luxury of choosing where to enter and exit, avoiding enemy gun emplacements.

Soon the attackers winged past the Skyraiders, heading for the sanctuary of the Tonkin Gulf. It seemed to Patton that all the fighters and bombers had escaped successfully, but soon they learned that a VF-154 F-4B had been hit by a 100mm AAA shell as it rolled in to attack the railway bridge at Phu Ly; the crew had ejected 20 miles southwest of Hanoi. Patton checked his navigation charts, which had the known AAA and SAM locations noted in hand-drawn black circles. The F-4 crew had gone down in a heavily defended area. "I felt we could get in, but I was worried about the helo's chances. He'd be a sitting duck," Patton recalled. "I didn't envy Cook having to make the go-ahead decision. It was a long shot, but I admired his guts."

Cook and Wiley turned inland and headed for the location of the shoot-down, while Patton and Russell weaved around the slower UH-2 Seasprite with Patton in the rear, ready to attack any source of ground fire. The aircraft flew inland between 8,000 and 9,000 feet, hoping this was high enough to escape the AAA, though SAMs were another matter, since this was a perfect height for a missile attack. A-1s did not carry the SAM warning devices that other aircraft had; their only warning would be if they spotted the launch and were able to evade. The Seasprite had enough fuel for ten minutes over the downed aircrew.

As Patton, Russell, and the helicopter crossed the coastline, they were startled as the air around them lit up with flak when black and white clouds exploded in a barrage. Patton remembered that "When I saw that first curtain of AAA, I thought it would be impossible for the helo to get through. The pilot must have felt that way, too. Either that, or he became disoriented, for he quickly swung around to the east and began heading back out toward the water." Patton directed the helicopter back to the west and they continued on.

Once in the vicinity of the downed crew, Patton rolled in on one of the gun sites:

> I made several firing passes, scattering 20mm shells wildly. I thought the runs would keep a few North Vietnamese heads down, but there was no noticeable effect on the volumes of flak. I think the runs boosted the morale of the helo crew, though. Also, I was careful to use only two of my four cannons. I wanted plenty of 20 mike-mike on hand for possible use later on. All of a sudden the shooting stopped. It was as if we had passed through a waterfall into the clear. We had made it through unscathed, except for the helo, which took some hits, but none bad enough to cancel the mission.

Cook then radioed that he had sighted four MiG-17s in the area. Russell called the radar picket destroyer offshore, requesting immediate air cover. They then learned that the F-4s and F-8s on CAP had run low on fuel, and an in-flight tanker was unavailable. They were on their own.

Suddenly, Wiley called out, "I've got three MiGs taking turns on me! Please get some fighter cover in here!" Russell responded, "Right, Pud, we're on our way with two Spads and a helo!"

Thick cloud covered the mountainous area where the survivors were. Cook and Wiley became separated and one MiG went after Cook, who managed to evade by sticking close to the hillside. The other three MiGs formed a racetrack pattern and took turns rolling in on Wiley, who dived for the hillside. As he banked around a mountain to the left, one of the enemy jets broke to the right, then made a steep turn to the left, putting himself in front of Wiley, who fired a burst. The shells tore off the MiG's wingtip and a vapor trail spurted. While no one saw it crash, Wiley was later credited with a "probable."

Patton and Russell arrived right with the helo moments later. "We were strung out but we spotted two of the MiGs, and maneuvered for a head-on pass." Russell fired at the belly of the lead MiG as it hurtled directly toward him. The enemy fighter passed so close that his Skyraider shook in the wake from the jet's exhaust. The MiG wasn't seen again and Russell was also credited with a "probable."

Patton was still at 9,000 feet:

I shoved the throttle to full power, then pushed over. A MiG was darting along above the trees and heading in my direction, but its pilot didn't see me. I counted for four seconds until I figured he was in range, then rolled into a split-S. I dove straight down, gathering speed to 300-plus knots and pulled out at the MiG's four o'clock.

Vapor streamed from the Skyraider's wingtips as Patton pulled Gs to recover from the dive. Despite feeling the dive was too steep, he fired at the enemy fighter in front of him. The pilot realized Patton was on him and pulled up hard toward the Skyraider, executing a reverse turn:

This was a fatal mistake on his part. He was climbing, losing speed, while I still had plenty. Maybe his reversal would have worked against another MiG-17, but in this case it was premature on his part because I ended up at his six o'clock. I'd been tight as a clenched fist till this point, but now I felt myself relax, knowing the advantage I had.

I waited patiently until he filled my gunsight reticle. This was, of course, the most exciting moment in my life. I'll never forget it. The most obvious first impression I had when up close to the enemy fighter was the coke bottle shape of the fuselage. The only marking I remember was the red star midway along the fuselage. Both the MiG and I were climbing, me in close trail on him. I fired the cannons. My wings trembled, and the 20 mike-mike sounded a reassuring, deep staccato as they streamed into the tailpipe of the MiG. I was so close I could see metal fragments flying from the tail, which was literally disintegrating. I started firing at 500 feet and closed to 100 feet. Both the MiG and I were pointed up at a 75-degree angle when my guns quit. I later learned that two were empty and the other pair had jammed. The MiG still hadn't exploded, so I fired three Zunis one right after the other.

The Zunis flew straight and true trajectories but narrowly missed the jet:

> The MiG then flipped over and plummeted toward a mass of clouds below. I bent my aircraft around and followed him. Just before the MiG disappeared into the white mass, I fired the last rocket, which must have missed also. Enveloped by cloud, I switched my visual scan to the gauges in order to right myself. I wasn't keen to smash into one of the surrounding mountains. I popped clear at 500 feet and was bottoming out from the dive when, off to my left, I saw the pilot eject from the MiG.

Most of the action was witnessed by the helicopter crew from their position above the clouds, but not the ejection or the crash. Leo Cook and the others were several miles away, and didn't see what happened either. However, in short order they flew over the crash site. Patton was officially credited with the kill based on the helicopter crew's observations and Cook's authentication of the crash site. Later, it was learned four MiGs had launched but only three returned to base, one with a seriously damaged wingtip.

Patton later explained, "I think the 20 mike-mike disabled the engine. Maybe the MiG pilot made that last plunge through the clouds to reach a lower altitude at which to eject. Perhaps he felt that punching out earlier would have made him a helpless target floating down in his 'chute."

Sadly, the F-4 crew that Papoose Flight had tried to rescue had been captured shortly after they reached the ground. Patton was awarded the Silver Star, while Cook, Wiley, and Russell each received the DFC. Patton's victory marked the last aerial victory by an American pilot flying a piston-engined airplane.

While the two MiG-killing missions were the high-point of the war for Skyraider RESCAP and SAR operations, the missions were always difficult and often costly to the would-be rescuers.

On July 24, 1965, Lieutenant (jg) Nick Daramus, who joined VA-25 while they were deployed to Southeast Asia, found his first RESCAP/ SAR mission to be one of the most memorable missions of his career.

Daramus was assigned as wingman to Lieutenant "Abe" Abrahamson on a two-plane RESCAP flight. Not long after they took off, a USAF rescue coordination aircraft summoned them to provide cover for the rescue of an F-105 pilot who had ejected after being hit by AAA over Laos.

Though the area was blanketed with thunderstorms rising to 12,000 feet, Abrahamson led the two Skyraiders below the clouds which had created a ceiling 800 feet above the thickly forested expanse surrounded by hills below. As Daramus later remembered:

> We located the survivor, although it took quite a while, even though he helped by transmitting to us on his survival radio. There's nothing quite so small and undetectable as a human being in the jungle. Abe and I had difficulty keeping each other in sight because of extremely poor visibility and the need to keep a wary eye on the terrain. It wouldn't do to smash into one of those hills.

The jungle below was thick, but not very high, featuring tall grass and banana plants with sizable leaves. They soon located the pilot, who was hiding beneath a banana plant. With the survivor's location known, they flew to the west to join the inbound helicopter and led it to the location for pickup. Overall, the rescue was routine. The intermittent ground fire was quickly silenced with 2.75-inch FFARs in conjunction with their 20mm cannon:

> Abe and I were about to escort the chopper out of the danger zone when the rescue coordinator on-scene notified us an Intruder had just been bagged. Our helo pilot radioed his thanks and said he could find his way home okay. So we departed to find the A-6 crew. The pilot and bombardier-navigator [B/N] were down in an area which my charts verified was noted for heavy concentrations of AAA and small arms fire. It was a place to be avoided whenever possible. Today, that wouldn't be possible.

The two pilots encountered AAA as they picked their way through the clouds and hilly landscape, but were unscathed. They established radio communication with the A-6 crew and figured out that the two were nearly half a mile apart. They had landed in a clearing of rice paddies in neat square-shaped patterns approximately two miles on a side. The pilot had scrambled into a grove of small trees in the middle of the clearing, while the B/N was hiding among some large trees along the clearing's west side. The pilot reported he was in good conditions, but the B/N had a leg injury that hindered his ability to move. Minutes later, the two Skyraider pilots sighted enemy ground troops approaching.

Daramus later explained:

We were trying to pinpoint their locations by radio. If they had used signal flares, it would have been like bright arrows pointing at their precise positions. They called out movements of the troops while Abe was trying to transmit their location so that a helo could be sent. We didn't know it at the time, but two Marine Corps H-34 choppers that were based in South Vietnam, were on the way. Abe and I made coordinated rocket and strafing runs, covering each other from ground fire, trying to hold the oncoming enemy at bay. Finally, Abe determined that there was simply too much chatter on the airwaves. "You'll have to stay off the radio for awhile," he cautioned the survivors, "or we won't be able to get you out."

We swooped and circled for about an hour and got a stand-off with the enemy. As we circled, we'd see people heading for the clearing from a nearby village. As they approached, we would roll in and strafe them. Making a strafing run was a job in itself because of the low overcast, which made it very difficult to get a steep enough dive angle for accuracy. We'd have to pop up into the clouds in turns, then poke down through, which didn't leave much time to track, aim and fire a burst or two before pulling up.

Once there was radio silence, the two A-6 flyers were instrumental in securing their own rescue. When one of the Skyraiders flew over their position, they would report "On Top." "This enhanced our ability to know exactly where they were. But because they remained hidden in the foliage, we didn't see them until they finally fired tracers from their revolvers later."

The two Skyraiders had been on the scene for two hours when the first H-34 arrived. Daramus and Abrahamson were running low on ammunition and were making runs of the terrain without firing to discourage the enemy troops from moving toward the downed flyers.

Then the second H-34 showed up. "We kept the helicopters over the heavily forested hills, reducing their exposure to a minimum, until they made a final dash in." The Skyraider pilots then directed that the survivors reveal themselves by firing tracers so the helicopters could swoop down and collect them:

> The action now resembled that of a cage of excited monkeys. We had the two survivors, two helicopters and two Spad pilots all talking on the same frequency trying to achieve two separate pickups within the same area at the same time. The survivors left their sanctuaries at the right time, even though they were reluctant to enter the clearing, knowing the bad guys were nearby. The pilot got to his helicopter in short order and clambered aboard. The B-N took longer because of his injury, but he made it too.
>
> We then hustled out of there as fast as we could, but found it impossible to stay with the choppers because of the terrain and the poor weather. The helo pilots assured us that they could find their way home and flew off, unescorted, with two happy warriors on board. Abe and I joined up and headed home. We logged 7.8 hours in the saddle that day. What a great airplane to do it in. With the A-1, it was a piece of cake!

Pilots who were rescued by Skyraiders had good reason to be glad of the airplane's hours-long loiter time, since the actual SAR could take a while to get organized and arrive. On July 27, Ed Greathouse and Jim Lynne were on rescue patrol when a formation of F-105s attacked two North Vietnamese SAM sites 30 miles west of Hanoi. No fewer than six of the Thunderchiefs and their pilots were shot down during the attack or on the way back to their base in Thailand. Greathouse recalled:

> Jim and I arrived for RESCAP duty around 1300 hours, just as the last fighter was leaving. There was only one evader on the ground. Visibility was so good that I could easily see the city and its airport. There were several AAA batteries in the immediate vicinity, but our evader was on a good-sized ridge.
>
> We got in touch with him on the emergency radio and pinpointed his location. We told him to stay put while we left the area, since we didn't want to give away his location to the enemy. We flew 60 miles

to the south, close to the Laotian border, to await a helicopter. Every hour or so we would return and talk with the downed pilot for a few minutes. Finally, around about 1600 hours, we were advised a helicopter was on the way, but that it would be slow in coming since it had to refuel several times en route. It would arrive at dusk.

The Jolly Green Giant arrived at the border ready to go to work, despite the fact the pilot had no maps or knowledge of the area. Using our direction-finding gear, we talked him to our position near the Black River, then escorted him to the ridge.

The rescuers arrived as darkness was setting in.

Greathouse spotted several enemy trucks and ground troops in the area soon after they arrived. At the same moment, a flight of F-105s made their presence known. Despite runs that the Thunderchiefs made to dissuade them, the North Vietnamese spread out in the flat lands surrounding the high area where the survivor was hiding. The helicopter paid out 200 feet of its rescue cable down through the jungle canopy as the enemy continued to advance toward the survivor's location. The downed pilot managed to get into the sling and the rescue crew began reeling in the cable.

After they had reeled in about 50 feet, the cable became fouled and would not retract further. The rescued pilot was dangling 150 feet below the helicopter. With the enemy moving closer, the Jolly Green Giant pilot sighted what looked like an abandoned military camp nearby. The F-105 pilot hung on as the CH-3C pilot tried to land on the parade ground. Unfortunately, at the last moment a flagpole was spotted, in a position that prevented a safe touchdown. The F-105 pilot got out of the sling while the helicopter moved toward a rice paddy 300 feet distant. Greathouse orbited above. "Because of the mud and water in the paddy, the helicopter couldn't sit down, so the pilot moved away another 50 yards or so, looking for a better spot." As it did so, the survivor ran after it in a race over a course that would have challenged an Olympic runner. "That pilot was really high-stepping and splashing through there. The trucks were a mere quarter-mile away, rumbling toward the paddy." The two Skyraiders and the four F-105s kept them at bay with strafing runs.

The suppression attacks were successful and a joyful Captain Frank J. Tullo of the 12th Tactical Fighter Squadron, 18th Tactical Fighter

Wing, scrambled aboard the Jolly Green Giant, which promptly lifted off and flew off. Greathouse and Lynne escorted the helicopter to the Laotian border where the pilot radioed he could make it home on his own. The two Skyraiders swung east to return to *Midway*. Since they had been airborne over six hours, the carrier directed them to land at Da Nang and fly out to the carrier the next day.

The most successful Skyraider pilot in the dangerous business of RESCAP/SAR was Commander Gordon H. Smith of VA-152 "Wild Aces" during two Vietnam tours aboard USS *Oriskany*, the carrier that would serve more deployments to Southeast Asia during the war than any other. A naval aviator since receiving his Wings of Gold on October 20, 1948, Smith flew 38 missions in F4U-4 Corsairs with VF-33 aboard the carrier *Leyte* in Korea during the Chinese intervention in the winter of 1950. Interviewed after the Vietnam War, Smith recalled that:

> By the autumn of 1965, each pilot in the squadron was a seasoned veteran with more than 100 combat missions. We had been in the Tonkin Gulf for more than six months, and almost all of our flying had been into North Vietnam. We had spent a week or two in the south at the beginning of the tour, and when we moved to the north we soon learned that there was a world of difference between the two in terms of survival. We also learned that the north was no place for the Spad, especially in Route Packages IV, V and VI. By then we had gained a reputation for being a bunch of tigers in the SAR game, having led the effort in 12 successful rescues. Some of our reputation was well deserved, but much of it was derived from a combination of luck and hype.

Two years previously, during a "non-combat" tour to Southeast Asia during the Laotian Crisis aboard USS *Hancock*, Smith had participated in developing and planning SAR operations, which included soliciting the support of the hill tribesmen in Laos. "SAR tactics had been on my mind for some time, and before we made this deployment, the squadron expended considerable effort on training in this area. We certainly weren't the greatest experts, but we were more knowledgeable than the other units on Yankee Station during that first year of flying up north."

On November 6, 1965, Smith participated in the first attempt at a night rescue in enemy territory, to retrieve an F-105 pilot who had parachuted near Phu Ban, 25 miles south of Nam Dinh. During the course of the rescue attempt, two USAF A-1Es would be lost and their pilots captured, while a CH-3C Jolly Green Giant with a crew of four was also shot down, with one of its parajumpers retrieved by a Sikorsky SH-3A Sea King of HS-2, embarked in USS *Independence*.

Smith remembered:

I had just returned from a successful road recce mission. As I was finishing my debriefing, it was reported someone had picked up two beepers 15 miles south of Hanoi. After studying the maps, I requested that we immediately launch a SAR CAP, but the request was refused because it was within two hours of sunset, and by the time we got on scene it would be dark. I appealed, arguing that if we waited until dawn there could be no rescue in view of the presumed number of enemy personnel and defenses in the area. With reluctance, I was finally granted approval to go have a look-see and report back. I was advised that the E-1B radar picket would be up on "Middleman" so that we could talk directly with the ship and CTF-77.

Smith and his wingman, Lieutenant Gary Gottschalk, launched and headed to the scene, arriving just after sunset:

We made a number of passes over the area but could not raise hide nor hair of any beeper, although we did draw some 37mm fire from three locations. By now it was pretty dark, and from our relatively low altitude the muzzle flashes from the AAA batteries really stood out. In spite of our seeming lack of success, we weren't yet ready to give up.

The ground south and southwest of Hanoi is a low flat plain, which gives way to the west to some karst outcroppings which lead to sharp hills that rise as high as several thousand feet:

We had been searching at the edge of the flat plain, and decided to move our efforts into the base of the hills. I knew the area fairly well, but two of the 37mm sites were new to me, and weren't on my map plot. As we moved our search five to ten miles further west, we suddenly heard an intermittent beeper, but could not get a direction on it. We had now been airborne for about four hours, and I was beginning to be concerned about our fuel if we had to stay considerably longer, although we had enough for another hour or so on station.

As the Skyraiders flew back and forth, Smith found he could receive the beeper signal in a narrow cone to the northwest of the downed airman:

Apparently, he was in a niche in the karst, and the terrain blocked out the transmissions except in one direction. I wanted to get a helicopter in there, but we certainly needed a better location first. I tried to make voice contact on his survival radio but to no avail. We could hear him try to transmit, but all we were receiving was a "rasping" noise. Apparently, he could hear us but we couldn't hear him.

Smith asked if he had a flashlight, but got no response. "I asked him several other things and finally I mentioned a cigarette lighter. I told him that I was going to make a run on where I thought he was, and when I came close he was to light the lighter. I did, and he did, and there he was off to our left."

Smith called to get a helicopter in and was surprised that the response was immediately in the affirmative:

We then had to bide our time and worry about our fuel, which by then was running rather low. After waiting about 35 minutes, we got a call from the helicopter off the SAR destroyer reporting that he was on his way in. I was expecting that he would be escorted in, and was somewhat surprised to see that he was alone. The problem now was how to put the helicopter on the right spot, since it was difficult to pick out detailed ground features because of the darkness. Gary got the helicopter in position, and I told him I would come by, flash my lights, make a run and turn on my lights as soon as I was over the survivor. The helo driver was concerned about whether he'd be able to see the guy, so I told him he'd be the one with the cigarette lighter.

As Smith pulled up from his run, "I got a lot lower than I wanted, and I found myself face to face with the top of a tree. I clipped some branches, but except for scaring the hell out of me, it didn't do any damage, other than to my ego. I didn't say a word." He looked back and saw the helicopter heading in. To divert the enemy from the oncoming rescuer, Smith pulled up and turned on his lights, then made two runs on the AAA sites. "They started firing, and it apparently worked, for they didn't fire at the helicopter at all. I must have lucked out and got a bunch of amateurs, because they didn't come close to me either."

Several minutes later, the helicopter pilot radioed he had the survivor and was heading back out. Smith had intended to escort the helicopter to the beach, but just as he turned toward the ocean:

We heard another beeper. It turned out there were two beepers transmitting simultaneously, which probably explains why we weren't able to previously get a homing bearing. We now had our work cut out for us. There was at least one more downed airman here, and we needed to locate him soon while we still had some fuel left. This second guy was much easier to pinpoint than the first one, since we were able to home in on his beeper. Additionally, we were able to establish voice communications with him, and he gave us directions as we closed in on him. I finally located him in a crevice at the base of a large karst outcropping.

Smith radioed the ship and explained the situation, advising that he needed a relief, and recommended there be a visual hand off through the night so the evader could be picked up at first light:

We were first told that relief would be on scene in about an hour, which to us was totally unsatisfactory. We pleaded to get someone there *immediately*. In reply we got the standard "Wait, Out," but shortly were advised that relief was on the way. At that point I figured that if we left within the next few minutes, we had barely enough fuel to get back to the ship. I concluded that Gary had a bit more than I did because I'd wasted a lot tooling around making runs.

It was clear both pilots were in trouble. Smith advised that, if necessary, he would remain on the scene until he could give a visual hand off, and would ditch in Brandon Bay if he ran out of fuel. The response was immediate. "Admiral Ralph Cousins came on the horn, identified himself and directed that I head home NOW. I responded that he was cutting out, that I was transmitting blind, and that I intended to wait for relief."

Two F-4s suddenly appeared and Smith directed Gottschalk to head home, and tried to show the Phantoms where the pilot was:

> It was a bit frustrating because I couldn't get them to come down low enough to show them much. However, I finally got them to see me, and I made a run marking "on top" by turning my lights on. Of course this immediately drew some fire, which startled the F-4 drivers, but by now I was used to it. As before, the shooters were lousy shots, and I don't believe that they came very close.

Smith turned for home, convinced he was going to go in the water:

> I was preparing myself, both mentally and physically, for that event. I tightened my shoulder straps to the point that it hurt. Suddenly, I picked up the ship's TACAN [TACtical Air Navigation] and couldn't believe what I was seeing because the carrier was 20 degrees to the right and 40 miles closer than I thought it would be. This just couldn't be, but I wasn't going to argue about it, except for a while I was convinced that there was something wrong with my TACAN. Finally, the ship confirmed my position and I figured that I had a good chance of making it.

Thirty miles from the carrier, Smith ran into a small thunderstorm and thought his luck had turned bad. "However, once these cleared, there was the ship seven miles ahead of me. The LSO told me that we wouldn't change frequencies, and to call the ball. I came back with '507 Ball. State Zero,'" the call indicating that he saw the landing lights and that his fuel state was approaching empty, and he likely could not go around again. The LSO's calm response was "Roger Ball, Roger Zero." Smith proceeded to catch the three wire without any fuss.

Smith figured he was in trouble, which was confirmed by the debriefing. Commander Albert E. Knutson, VA-152's commander, was furious that Smith had once again risked another Skyraider. Smith was able to explain himself, but then learned that the admiral "wanted my head for disobedience of a direct order." Smith had a "private session" with the admiral, during which his best support came from *Oriskany*'s skipper, Captain Bart Connelly.

Smith wouldn't learn for another 30 years how it was that *Oriskany* turned up where she did:

> Captain Connelly had been following my situation closely, and decided to help out a bit. He cleared the bridge of all personnel except for himself and the officer of the deck, Lieutenant (jg) Bruce Bell, and headed west in violation of all the rules. He wanted no witnesses, and he swore Bell to secrecy. There is no question that without Connelly's aggressive action I would not have made it back that night.

Smith convinced Captain Connelly to allow a pre-dawn launch to go in and pick up the survivor he had left behind before it was too late. Such approval was difficult to get, since it disturbed the air department's operation cycle:

> *Oriskany*'s cycle ran from noon to midnight, and the fact that we returned after midnight screwed everything up by delaying the re-spot of the deck and preparations for the next day's cycle. Now I was asking that we conduct a launch out of sequence in the middle of our down period. On the other hand, I had first-hand knowledge of the on-scene situation, the location of the downed airman, the terrain and the location of the air defenses. I believed that if we could go in and do a quick snatch, we stood a better than even chance of being successful.

Smith launched with Lieutenant Gordon "Gordie" Wileen as his wingman an hour-and-a-half before sunrise on November 7. They picked up HS-2's SH-3A Sea King and proceeded to the target area:

> The trip in from the beach was uneventful. The weather was hazy, and we were over an undercast, which was typical around dawn in that part of the world. The clouds had settled in the valleys, with some of the hills protruding above the tops. It took me a while to get oriented, but once I did, I was able to visualize the terrain below the clouds in detail.

Breaks in the clouds began to appear as it started to get light. Smith told the helicopter pilot to hover over a ridgeline where he would be safe, while Wileen circled for protection:

> I then proceeded to find a hole in the clouds in order to get below and scout out the situation. As I approached the downed airman at low altitude, his beeper came on. I then felt confident that we could pick him up as soon as the clouds broke up a bit more. At the same time it occurred to me that it was possible that the guy had already been captured, and that the enemy were using his beeper to set up a trap. This had happened on two other occasions that I knew of. However, I quickly put that idea aside and focused on positive thoughts.

Smith began receiving AAA. "It appeared that the bad guys had brought in the first team, because they were far more accurate than the night before." Smith's plan was for him and Wileen to make runs on the AAA sites to draw their fire while the helicopter came in for the pickup:

> As I popped up through the clouds, I looked for the helicopter and he wasn't where he was supposed to be. I looked to my right and there he was, just where I didn't want him. I screamed on the radio for him to move to the southeast. As he started to turn, the bad guys opened up and everything started to fall apart quickly. The helicopter pilot announced that he'd been hit, and I immediately saw that he was streaming fuel – and a lot of it. He stated that he would continue to the southeast as the best and safest way to the water, and I concurred.

As Smith began reporting the situation to *Oriskany*, Wileen announced he was hit and on fire. "He was behind me, and when I turned I could see him trailing a lot of smoke, but no flames. Now we had a helluva situation on our hands. I told him to head straight out and not wait for us." Smith turned to escort the Seasprite back toward its home destroyer:

> The helicopter driver concluded that he was losing fuel at almost 200 pounds a minute. It didn't take a mathematical genius to figure that he probably didn't have enough to get beyond the beach. If he was to take the shortest route to the water we would have to cut across the

southern part of the Red River valley, and if we continued slightly to the right of our present heading it would take us right across Than Hoa. Either way, we would have been extremely vulnerable. So I told him to turn right to a heading of 240 degrees. Of course he thought I'd gone completely insane, but we finally talked it out. Besides, I told him to "Trust me" – and he did.

Thirty-five miles ahead was Hill 5500, the tallest point in North Vietnam. Smith knew that the top was barren, and extremely remote:

I'd often thought that if I ever found myself on the ground in that region, that's where I'd want to be. I figured that it would take days for the bad guy to get there. The helicopter was losing fuel at a faster rate than we previously thought, and it was going to be very tight. We finally made it and the SH-3A sat down on the very top of the hill, but with little fuel remaining. I congratulated the crew on getting down in one piece, and told them that we should have someone to pick them up within an hour.

The Sea King crew was duly rescued by a Navy UH-2 and an Air Force HH-3E Jolly Green Giant. By this time, the three CH-3C crewmen who had been shot down the previous day had been taken prisoner by the North Vietnamese.

Smith learned from Wileen that his hydraulic system had been shot up and he was going to divert to Da Nang where he could land wheels up. Since the rescue chopper for the downed Sea King was inbound with an escort, Smith turned to join Wileen:

I sorely wanted to see what we could do to go back and get that poor bastard we'd left in that karst 18 miles from Hanoi. It was clear though that we'd never get approval to mount another effort under the circumstances. Besides, I was getting tired, and it was showing. I hadn't had any sleep in the last 30 hours, and I'd been airborne more than 15 of the last 22 hours. The adrenalin rush was gone, and I was having a sinking spell.

Smith arrived at Da Nang, to find Wileen still orbiting, waiting for the field to be cleared for his wheels up landing. Smith went ahead and landed. "After giving Gordie a hug and downing four cups of coffee, I returned to the ship. Another day in the Tonkin Gulf."

Gordon H. Smith was awarded the Silver Star for his actions during this mission. Six months later, VA-152, with Commander Smith now the squadron commander, made their second deployment to Southeast Asia with CVW-16 aboard *Oriskany* on May 26, 1966. Commencing operations from Dixie Station on June 30, the "Wild Aces" flew 128 sorties against enemy positions in South Vietnam in just eight days, after which *Oriskany* transferred to Yankee Station, where the squadron again put their RESCAP and SAR expertise to use. On one of their first missions "up north" on July 12, Smith led the rescue of VF-162 F-8E pilot Lieutenant (jg) Richard F. Adams, who had successfully ejected and evaded over North Vietnam during the 1965 deployment and was down a second time northeast of the port of Haiphong. Smith's four "Wild Aces" Skyraiders penetrated deeper into North Vietnam than any preceding Navy rescue attempt. A month later, Smith and his squadron assisted in rescuing two USAF pilots shot down near Dong Hoi on July 27. On August 10, the squadron covered the rescue of two VF-111 F-8 pilots. Ten days later they covered the pickup of a USAF pilot shot down near Ha Cong. Over the course of two Vietnam tours, Commander Gordon H. Smith led 23 RESCAP/SAR missions, making successful rescues on 11 occasions. Smith was hit by AAA on August 28, 25 miles south of Thanh Hoa and his Skyraider was set afire. Staying with the plane long enough to get out over the Tonkin Gulf as the fuselage behind the cockpit burned fiercely, he finally kicked himself vertically out of the cockpit just as the flames reached it. Striking the tail as he fell away, his parachute deployed just before he hit the water. He was quickly picked up by a Seasprite launched from a nearby destroyer. Three days later, two "Wild Aces" Skyraiders covered the rescue of a VFP-63 RF-8A pilot from the middle of Haiphong Harbor.

Smith was awarded seven Silver Stars for his leadership in these missions. He was considered the Navy's leading expert on RESCAP, and was admired and respected by every pilot in the squadron. He rose to rear admiral before retiring in 1979 with 6,482 flying hours, of which 6,200 were in propeller attack aircraft.

By 1967, North Vietnam was considered "too hot" for the Navy's remaining Skyraider squadrons, the majority of which had transitioned over the previous four years to either the A-6 Intruder or the A-4

Skyhawk. Among the last squadrons to see action from a carrier deck was the veteran VA-52, flying as part of Air Wing 19 from *Ticonderoga*. Fourteen of the 21 pilots assigned were combat veterans. Over four line periods between November 1966 and April 1967, the "Knightriders" flew mostly RESCAP and coastal reconnaissance patrols.

The last combat tour of the A-1 was undertaken by the Skyraiders of VA-215 "Barn Owls," the squadron that had flown the first strikes over North Vietnam at the outset of *Rolling Thunder*. The squadron went aboard USS *Bon Homme Richard*, which left Alameda NAS for Southeast Asia on January 26, 1967. The "Barn Owls" were led on this, their third deployment, by Commander George Carlton.

Four months later, on May 22, 1967, Commander Carlton flew his most memorable RESCAP, a night mission to attempt a rescue of the two crewmen of a shot-down USAF F-4 Phantom, call sign "Starlight Four," that had gone down 30 miles north of Hon Gay. As Carlton recalled:

> Myself, CAG Commander Jack Monger, Bonnie Dick's captain Captain C.K. Ruiz and our division commander Rear Admiral Vincent P. de Poix, all studied the charts, complete with AAA and SAM plots, and I recommended a go. Admiral de Poix was concerned the location was too close to the MiG base at Kep, but Monger and I agreed that VPAF fighters were not known to fly at night.

The RESCAP was set with four A-1s for cover, four F-8s for escort, an A-3 tanker to support the Crusaders and the "Willie Fudd" (E-1B Tracer) to provide radar warning of any enemy aerial reaction. The launches began at 2100 hours and were separated by 15–20 minutes, with the E-1 going first, followed by the A-1s, A-3, and finally the F-8s, which allowed the force to arrive on station at 2215 hours with maximum fuel. "As we were leaving the flag briefing room, CAG asked me, 'Who's leading this one?' He knew the answer. Squadron COs fly more hours, and invariably lead first-of-a-kind missions. This would not be an exception."

The launch, join-up and flight north went well. As the Skyraiders approached the SAR destroyer that would send its SH-2 Seasprite in to make the pickup, Carlton sent the second section to escort the helo. "They would take it to a point ten miles southeast of Cam Pha to await my orders. With the E-1, F-8s and A-3 in position south and east of Cam Pha, we were all set to have a go."

Approaching the off-shore islands northeast of Cam Pha, Carlton determined that the path of least resistance would be along an easterly route ten miles north. He detached his wingman to provide high cover for the helo as it headed in for the pickup:

Thinking that a single Spad throttled back to 160 knots would cause less of a stir, I turned off the external lights and proceeded in at an altitude of about 2000 ft, throttling back and leaning the carburetor mixture to reduce the exhaust flames as much as possible. In rich mixture, the R-3350 engine put out huge, bright red exhaust trails along both sides of the fuselage. On the other hand, in lean mixture the exhaust was a soft, light blue color. It was about as stealthy as one could get in a Skyraider.

As Carlton flew on, he could see some lights from Hon Gay. "Estimating that I must be within five miles of our estimated datum, I tried the first contact. 'Starlight Four, this is Barn Owl One, over.'" The response was quick. "Barn Owl, you're loud and clear." Carlton set up an orbit and told Starlight Four to show a light. He looked down and saw a dim light. "'Kill it,' I radioed. The light went out. 'Barn Owl Three, bring 'em in. The datum's good.' 'Roger' was the response." Carlton climbed to the east, thinking that lady luck was with them. At 130 knots, it would take the helicopter 20 minutes to arrive.

The F-8s came "feet dry" as high cover while the A-3 tanker remained just offshore. Fifty miles south, the E-1 had a radar view of the whole scene. "During the helo's transit, I climbed up to 6,000 feet and eased into position to be ready with guns and rockets as needed." The helicopter, showing a vertical white light for identification and coordination purposes, moved in. "After an exchange with the downed airman, who was assured by the helo crew that he had a good shot at being rescued, the pilot started his approach to a hover. All was looking okay from my perch. Suddenly, the blackness erupted as I could see muzzle flashes from positions a half-mile or so west of the scene." Immediately after, the SH-2 pilot reported he'd been hit and that his co-pilot was wounded. Carlton radioed, "Abort! Abort! Barn Owls get out too," as he rolled in on the gun flashes:

After flipping on the master arming switch and turning the external lights to bright and flashing, I steadied in the run and fired bursts at the muzzle flashes that were now coming in my direction. The tracers were going right into the flashes as I pressed home the attack. The AAA diminished, and I became concerned about when to pull up, not knowing how high the terrain was. Thinking that I was well below normal weapons release altitude, I squeezed off one more burst and pulled the stick back as hard as I dared, at the same time pushing throttle, prop and mixture controls full forward. Thankfully, the A-1 climbed like the proverbial homesick angel.

Once clear, Carlton checked in with the helicopter and found the co-pilot was stable and they would be "feet wet" in 15 minutes:

I throttled back and headed downhill west of Cam Pha. Nearing the coast at 500 feet and 300 knots, AAA flashes began blinking brightly off my left wing. I realized my external lights were still on bright and flashing, I cut them and stood on the right wingtip, pulling the nose through 45 degrees to get away.

He leveled the wings and spotted the coastline ahead. "I continued downhill, crossing the beach no higher than 50 feet. The emotions one feels upon going feet wet after hanging it out a bit over a hostile beach are unparalleled."

Picking up the other three Skyraiders over the SAR destroyer just as the helicopter landed, the "Barn Owls" headed back to *Bonnie Dick* and landed. Once aboard, Carlton was put in radio contact with Commander Hank Bailey, CO of VA-115 aboard *Hancock*. "Hank and I discussed the SAR scene, and the best routes in and out. I wished him luck and headed for the showers. It was now well past midnight – all in a day's work." VA-115 covered the rescue of one of the F-4 crew the next day, but the second was captured.

VA-25 made the final Navy Skyraider deployment to Southeast Asia aboard *Coral Sea*, departing Alameda NAS for WestPac on July 26, 1967. Throughout the last of 1967, the Skyraiders were primarily employed on RESCAP/SAR operations, along with limited offensive operations including attacks on shore batteries firing at US destroyers. During the ship's in-port period at Subic Bay following its first assignment at

Yankee Station, the Skyraiders were finally fitted with APR-27 radar warning receivers that would indicate a SAM launch. During their next in-port period, the airplanes were fitted with the Yankee rocket seat extraction system.

The final major combat action for the Skyraider with the Navy came with the Tet Offensive, launched in January 1968. *Coral Sea* moved down to Dixie Station and VA-25 flew many close air support sorties in northern South Vietnam. When the Marines at Khe Sanh came under siege, the Skyraiders were part of the aerial onslaught that broke the siege. The unit's final mission was a strike against NVA artillery around Khe Sanh on February 20, 1968. Fittingly, the final trap of a combat mission was made by Lieutenant (jg) Theodore "Ted" Hill, Jr., the very last student pilot to graduate from "Skyraider school" who trapped in A-1H BuNo 135300 NE-405.

Coral Sea returned to Alameda on April 6, 1968. On April 10, VA-25 conducted a farewell ceremony for the Skyraider at NAS Lemoore. Lieutenant (jg) Hill, the last Navy Skyraider pilot, started up the engine of BuNo 135300, the last Skyraider to return from a combat mission, taxied between rows of saluting sideboys, and took off. He made a farewell pass before turning east to fly BuNo 135300 to NAS Pensacola, where it is still on display at the National Museum of Naval Aviation.

The EA-1F "Electric Spads" were finally retired by VAQ-33 after Detachment 11 flew from *Intrepid* during the carrier's third and final Southeast Asia deployment, from June to December 1968, with the last combat mission flown on December 27.

The Skyraider continued to fly combat with the VNAF, which would operate the aircraft until the end came on April 30, 1975. USAF air crews would continue to bless the Skyraider as they were pulled from the Southeast Asian jungles under the watchful eyes of fellow Air Force pilots flying A-1s known as "Sandy," the call sign for Skyraiders involved in RESCAP missions up to the end of US involvement in Vietnam in 1973.

IO

"THE FORREST FIRE"

The danger of fire aboard an aircraft carrier loaded with aircraft, aviation fuel, and explosive ordnance is the greatest threat to naval aviation. On October 26, 1966, at 0728 hours, the first of three aircraft carrier fires that would occur during the war happened aboard USS *Oriskany* when a flare in a locker that held 250 Mark 24 magnesium flares and 2.75-inch rocket warheads, located just off the forward hangar deck next to the Starboard sponson, inadvertently ignited. The sailor handling the flare threw it in the locker and dogged the door shut, failing to notice he had inadvertently lit the fuze. *Oriskany* was heading into the wind, preparing to launch aircraft, and the fire was not noticed until it emitted smoke through the open air vent.

General Quarters was sounded. Firefighting teams attempted to cool the area near the burning locker, but the high pressure inside made it impossible to open the door so directly fighting the fire was impossible. Ten minutes later, the pressure inside became so great the doors blew out. A helicopter on the forward port side of the hangar deck caught fire. Sailors in the area worked to move the bombed up and fully fueled aircraft to the flight deck to prevent them catching fire. The heat and smoke were drawn forward into the "officer's country" berthing quarters forward of the hangar which were occupied by pilots of the air wing. Soon the forward half of the ship was afire. Staterooms and passageways were filled with smoke as the flames burned through four levels, trapping many pilots in their bunks or in smoke-darkened passageways, killing some in their beds and others as they desperately tried to escape.

One pilot trapped in his stateroom found a wrench and opened the porthole. Continually soaking sheets and blankets in his wash basin and wrapping himself in them, he kept his head out the porthole, unable to escape with the fire in the passageway. Finally, a sailor discovered him and managed to get him a firehose, a battle lantern, and an Oxygen Breathing Apparatus, which he used to fight the fire and cool the stateroom. Nearby, Commander Richard M. "Dick" Bellinger, XO of VF-162 "Hunters," was in a similar situation. He stripped naked and forced his way through his porthole, despite weighing 207 pounds. Once on the flight deck, he managed to obtain protective clothing and organized firefighting parties.

At approximately 1030 hours, the ship's fire marshal informed Damage Control Central that the fire on the hangar deck and in officer's country was under control. Twenty-four pilots were dead, including newly installed CAG Commander Rodney B. Carter, who had led CVW-16 for only two weeks. In addition to the naval aviators, 19 other officers and men of the ship's company had been killed. One of the wounded died a day later, for a total 44 casualties. Knocked out of action, *Oriskany* sailed to Subic Bay, replaced on station by *Coral Sea*. Once at Subic Bay, the damage was found to be extensive enough to force the ship to return to the United States, where she entered the Hunter's Point Naval Shipyard in San Francisco for repairs that would take until June 1967 to complete. In the aftermath, several sailors, including the chief ordnance officer, were charged with 44 counts of manslaughter for actions immediately before the fire and court-martialed, though all were acquitted. The investigation determined that magnesium flares could ignite when jarred in certain cases, which was declared the reason that the first flare ignited.

The ongoing naval bombing campaign created a demand for general-purpose bombs ("iron bombs") that greatly exceeded domestic production rates. With the military concentrating in the early 1960s on nuclear weapons and more advanced ordnance such as the AGM-12 Bullpup, AGM-62 Walleye, and AGM-45 Shrike, production of conventional "iron bombs" nearly ceased. With the ever-increasing tempo of bombing operations in Southeast Asia after 1965, stockpiles of modern bombs nearly vanished until production was able to ramp up, which only ended the "bomb shortage" in the fall of 1967. Inadequate inventories of 13 different types of bomb were reported beginning in mid-1966. In April 1966, newspaper headlines across the

United States heralded the fact that the Department of Defense had repurchased 5,570 bombs from West Germany that had been sold for scrap at $1.70 apiece, for $21.00 each. Subsequently, the Pentagon was forced to admit that 18,000 bombs sold to various nations had been repurchased for prices considerably in excess of what they had been sold for. Throughout the controversy, Secretary McNamara denied there was a bomb shortage, stating at one time in response to media questions, "All this baloney about lack of bomb production is completely misleading." The "credibility gap" in Washington between official statements and reality began to take on canyon-like dimensions.

The inventory of bombs was critically low by 1967. The greatest shortage was for the new 1,000-pound Mark 83, which was favored by the Navy for its power-to-size ratio. A carrier-launched A-4E Skyhawk, which could carry a total load of 8,400 pounds, could carry up to 3,000 pounds of ordnance on its centerline rack with two drop tanks on the inner wing stations, or a single 400-gallon tank on the centerline and two Mark 83 thousand-pounders on each inner wing rack. The Skyhawks also carried unguided 5-inch Mark 32 "Zuni" rockets on the outer wing stations, which had a reputation for electrical difficulties and accidental firing. Flying an average of two missions a day, the carrier's magazine could be emptied in a matter of days with intensive operations. By the spring of 1967, the Navy was forced to take World War II and Korean-era "fat bombs" out of long-term storage and send them out to the carriers. Unlike the modern bombs, these bombs were highly vulnerable to fire, which could rapidly lead to an explosion. With the increased use of old bombs and Zuni rockets, in 1967 a carrier deck was potentially an even more explosive environment than normally.

The worst carrier fire of the Vietnam War, made worse by the presence of the old bombs and the unreliable rockets, broke out on USS *Forrestal* on July 29, 1967. The first "super carrier," named for James Forrestal, former Secretary of the Navy and first Secretary of Defense, who had led the fight in 1949 to save naval aviation – a fight that would lead to the creation of the *Forrestal* and the super carriers that followed – had operated with the Atlantic Fleet since her 1955 commissioning. She departed Norfolk Naval Base in May 1967, headed for her first wartime deployment in Southeast Asia. After stopping in Rio de Janeiro for a "show the flag" visit, she rounded the Cape of Good Hope and steamed across the Indian Ocean, arriving in Subic Bay in June. On board was Air Wing 17 – VF-11 "Red Rippers" and VF-74 "Be-Devilers" flying F-4B Phantom IIs; VA-46 "Clansmen" and VA-106 "Gladiators" flying A-4E Skyhawks; VA-65 "Tigers" in A-6A Intruders; detachments of RVAH-11 "Checkertails" with the RA-5C Vigilante; VAH-10 "Vikings" operating KA-3B Skywarriors; VAW-33 "Knighthawks" operating EA-1F Skyraiders; and VAW-123 "Screwtops" providing early warning with E-2A Hawkeyes.

The wing had flown 150 sorties since July 25. Bomb usage was such that *Forrestal* had rendezvoused for an underway replenishment with the ammunition ship USS *Diamond Head* (AE-19) on July 28. Among the ordnance transferred from *Diamond Head* were six Korean War-era AN-M65A1 GP 1,000-pound bombs. Several of the old bombs were more than ten years old and had spent some of that time stored improperly in open-air Quonset huts in an abandoned ammunition dump on the periphery of Subic Bay after having been exposed to the heat and humidity of Okinawa or Guam before ending there.

According to one *Diamond Head* crew member, when the ship arrived at Subic Bay to pick up ordnance for the Yankee Station carriers, base personnel who prepared the old bombs for transfer had assumed that *Diamond Head* had orders to dump them at sea. Informed that the bombs were destined for active use aboard the carriers, the commanding officer of the Subic Bay naval ordnance detachment was so shocked that he initially refused to approve the transfer in the belief a paperwork mistake had been made. With his refusal delaying *Diamond Head*'s departure, he only signed the transfer forms after receiving written orders from CinCPac that explicitly absolved his unit of responsibility for the bombs' terrible state.

Unlike the modern thick-cased Mark 83 bombs, which were filled with Composition H6, these AN/M65A1 bombs were thin-skinned and filled with Composition B, which was an older explosive that possessed greater shock and heat sensitivity. It could also become more powerful – up to 50 percent by weight – and much more sensitive if it was old or was improperly stored. *Forrestal*'s ordnance handlers, none of whom had ever even seen an AN/M65A1 before, found to their shock that the bombs taken aboard from *Diamond Head* were in terrible condition. They were coated with "decades of accumulated rust and grime" and their original packing crates, some of which were stamped with production dates as early as 1953, were moldy and rotten. The most alarming find, most dangerous of all, was when several of the bombs were discovered to be leaking liquid paraffin phlegmatizing agent from their rusty seams; this was unmistakable evidence that the bombs' explosive filler had degenerated due to excessive age and exposure to moisture and heat.

Lieutenant R.R. "Rocky" Pratt, a pilot in VA-106, later remembered the striking concern felt by the ordnance handlers, many of whom were afraid to even handle the bombs, while one ordnance officer wondered out loud if the old weapons would survive the shock of a catapult-assisted launch without a spontaneous detonation and suggested they be immediately jettisoned. The ordnance department reported the situation up the chain of command to *Forrestal's* Captain John Beling, stating that the bombs were, in their opinion, an imminent danger to the ship that should be immediately jettisoned overboard. Faced with the need for 1,000-pound bombs for the next day's missions, the captain demanded that *Diamond Head* take the old bombs back and exchange them with new Mark 83s; he was informed there were no new bombs available.

With orders to conduct strike missions over North Vietnam the next day and concluding he thus had no choice but to accept the bombs in their current condition, Captain Beling agreed to the ordnance handlers' demands that all the AN-M65A1 bombs be stored on deck in the "bomb farm" area between the starboard rail and the carrier's island until they were loaded for the next day's missions rather than in the magazine where an explosion could easily destroy the ship.

On July 29, plane handlers packed the aft area of the flight deck wing-to-wing with 12 VA-46 Skyhawks, seven VF-11 Phantom IIs, and two RA-5C Vigilantes, 21 aircraft loaded with bombs, rockets, ammunition, and fuel. Several of the AN-M65A1s hung from the racks of the waiting aircraft while the others were in the bomb farm near the island next to other bombs. The VF-11 Phantom flown by Lieutenant Commander James E. Bangert and Lieutenant (jg) Lawrence E. McKay was in position on the aft starboard corner of the flight deck, pointing about 45 degrees across the deck and armed with four LAU-10 underwing rocket pods, each of which contained four unguided 5-inch Mark 32 "Zuni" rockets. These were protected from an accidental launch by a safety pin which was only removed immediately prior to launch from the catapult.

At about 1045 hours, *Forrestal* turned into the wind and increased her speed to 32 knots in preparation for launching the strike. At 1051 hours, when Bangert switched from external to internal power, an electrical power surge happened; one of the rockets in the pod on external stores station 2, which was later found to be missing the safety pin, fired. The Zuni flew about 100 feet across the flight deck, severing a deck crewman's arm and rupturing the 300-gallon wing-mounted external fuel tank on the VA-46 Skyhawk in which Lieutenant Commander Robert "Bo" Browning sat awaiting launch. Fortunately, the Zuni's warhead safety mechanism prevented a detonation and the rocket broke apart on impact. Highly flammable JP-5 jet fuel spurted from the ruptured drop tank and spread on the deck under the A-4s of Lieutenant White and Lieutenant Commander John S. McCain III to the side of Browning. The fuel was ignited by fragments of burning rocket propellant, creating an instantaneous conflagration. McCain later remembered a "whooshing" sound, followed by a low-level explosion. An instant later, the two A-4s in front of him caught fire as the burning fuel raced beneath them. Another burning fragment punctured the external fuel tank of an A-4 just aft of the jet blast deflector for catapult number three.

The now-raging fire was fanned by the 32-knot wind that swept the deck and the exhaust of at least three jets. Fire Quarters was sounded at 1052 hours, followed by General Quarters a minute later. Condition ZEBRA, requiring all hands to secure ship for maximum survivability, including closing the fire-proof steel doors separating the ship's compartments, was declared at 1059 hours.

A moment later, one AN-M65A1 bomb fell from an A-4 to the deck, rolling six feet before coming to rest in a pool of burning fuel between White's and McCain's aircraft.

Damage Control Team 8, led by Chief Aviation Boatswain's Mate Gerald Farrier, specialized in flight deck firefighting. In their training, they had learned that a 1,000-pound bomb could still be extinguished and cooled without an explosive cook-off after direct exposure to a jet fuel fire for a full ten minutes. However, this information referred to the new Mark 83 1,000-pound bombs, which were filled with relatively stable Composition H6 explosive and had thicker, heat-resistant cases. Based on their training, the men operated in the belief that they had a ten-minute window to extinguish the fire before the casing would melt and give a low-order explosion.

Chief Farrier, who did not take the time to put on protective clothing, attempted immediately to smother the bomb with a PKP fire extinguisher in order to delay spread of the fuel fire and give the pilots an opportunity to escape. Despite his effort to cool the bomb, the casing suddenly split open and the explosive began burning brightly. Farrier recognized that a lethal cook-off was imminent and shouted orders for the team to withdraw; however, at one minute 26 seconds from the time the fire started, the bomb exploded, with the unstable Composition B enhancing the explosion's power. Farrier and all but three of his men were killed instantly, while another 27 were injured.

McCain, who had exited his A-4, saw another pilot on fire and turned to help him when the bomb detonated, knocking him backwards ten feet and wounding him with shrapnel. White had managed to climb out of his burning aircraft but was killed in the explosion. VA-46 pilot Lieutenant Ken McMillen successfully escaped while Lieutenant (jg)s Don Dameworth and David Dollarhide were injured by the explosion as they exited their aircraft. Lieutenant Commanders Gerry Stark and Dennis Barton were missing.

Oriskany helicopter pilot Lieutenant David Clement, who had been asked to fly plane guard for *Forrestal* after making a flight to the carrier, was off her stern and saw the event. He later remembered, "There was a horrendous explosion that shook my chopper, 'Angel Two-Zero.' It seemed as if the whole stern of the *Forrestal* had erupted. Suddenly there were rafts, fuel tanks, oxygen tanks, trop tanks and debris of every description floating in the water below." Clement and his crew, Ensign Leonard M. Eiland, Jr., Aviation Machinist's Mate (Jets) 3rd Class James D. James, Jr., and Airman Albert E. Barrows soon rescued five crewmen who jumped, fell, or were knocked from the carrier in the next 60 minutes. They would later bring medical supplies to the stricken ship. While they made the rescues, continuing explosions on the flight deck rocked their SH-3A. "Her stern was a mass of twisted steel, with holes in the flight deck, a vacant space where there had been many aircraft and a towering column of black and gray smoke and flames." Two flight deck crewmen who were tossed overboard by one of the explosions and fell 70 feet into the water, were picked up by Clement's helicopter and deposited back on the flight deck, where they resumed fire-fighting.

A crater was blown in the armored flight deck by the detonation, while men on deck were sprayed with bomb fragments and shrapnel from destroyed aircraft. The burning fuel poured through the crater into occupied berthing compartments below. Every airplane on the aft deck, all fully fueled and loaded with bombs, was damaged. The seven F-4s caught fire. Several men jumped or were blown into the ocean. Ten seconds after the first detonation, two more of the unstable bombs exploded, while a fourth blew up 44 seconds after that. By 1055 hours, seven or eight 1,000-pound bombs, one 750-pound bomb, one 500-pound bomb, and several missile and rocket warheads that were heated by the fire exploded. The explosions of several of the AN-M65A1 bombs, filled with the badly degraded Composition B, were estimated to be as much as 50 percent more powerful than a standard 1,000-pound bomb. A ninth explosion was attributed to sympathetic detonations of an AN-M65A1 and a newer 500-pound M117 H6 bomb positioned beside each other in the bomb farm.

Fortunately, the newer Composition H6 bombs either burned on the deck without detonating under the heat of the fires or were jettisoned overboard. Explosive ordnance demolition officer Lieutenant (jg) Robert Cates noticed there was a 500- and a 750-pound bomb lying in the middle of the flight deck. As he recalled, "They hadn't detonated; they were just setting there smoking. So I went up and defused them and had them jettisoned."

Fire suppression efforts during the first critical minutes were prevented by the ongoing detonations, which tore seven holes in the flight deck. Nearly 40,000 gallons of burning JP-5 from ruptured aircraft fuel tanks poured across the deck and into the holes in the deck and the fire reached into the aft hangar bay and berthing compartments. Fifty night crew personnel asleep in berthing compartments under the aft flight deck were killed by the fire while an additional 41 crewmen were killed in interior compartments in the ship's aft section. The below-deck fire was fed by clothing, bedding, and other items and burned with an awesome fury. Men who tried to locate shipmates trapped in the flame-filled compartments were driven out by fire and smoke. The hangar deck aft was so thick with smoke it was impossible to see even a few feet.

Crewmen from all over the ship rallied to fight the fires and control damage, pushing aircraft, missiles, rockets, bombs, and burning pieces over the side. Many 250- and 500-pound bombs were manually jettisoned by rolling them across the deck and over the side. Many men without firefighting or damage control training took over for the depleted teams. Unknowingly, some inexperienced firehose teams using seawater washed away the foam others were spreading in attempts to smother the fire. Twenty-four-year-old engineering officer Ensign Robert R. Schmidt and his damage control team continued to fight their way into compartment after burning compartment, some of which were virtually inaccessible. He recalled:

> I asked for volunteers, and I immediately had two or three who followed me back into the guts of the fire. Several times, people would come up to me and say, 'What can I do? How can I help?' At first, I couldn't find work for all the people who wanted to help. I can't give enough praise to the sailors I supervised. They fought the fire and did all the dirty jobs. These kids worked all night, 24–28 hours, containing the fire. I've nothing but praise for the American sailor.

At 1105 hours, escorting destroyer USS *George K. MacKenzie* (DD-836) came alongside the burning carrier and pulled men from the water while directing fire hoses onto the fires. USS *Rupertus* (DD-851) maneuvered as close as 20 feet to *Forrestal* for 90 minutes, while her firefighters directed fire hoses at the burning flight deck and into the hangar deck. By 1147 hours, the fires on the flight deck were brought under control and all flight deck fires were out by 1215 hours. At 1447 hours, *Forrestal* reported that the compartment fires still burned but progress was being made. The below deck fires continued for many more hours.

Cates and his crew of ordnancemen continued their struggle to defuse bombs before they could explode. One of his men volunteered to be lowered through a hole in the flight deck to defuse a live bomb that had fallen to the 03 level. The compartment was on fire and smoke-filled. After the bomb was defused, Cates was lowered into the compartment so he could attach a line to the bomb to pull it out and jettison it. He and one of his men moved toward the stern:

> We started picking up everything we could find that had explosives in it and threw them over the side. Some squadron pilots came up to me as we went aft I don't know who they were. They helped me take a Sidewinder missile off a burning F-4. We just continued working our way aft and taking what ordnance we found off aircraft and throwing it over the side.

CTF-77 had ordered *Forrestal* to steam toward a rendezvous with the hospital ship USS *Repose* (AH 16). Escorted by USS *Henry W. Tucker* (DD-875) the carrier made rendezvous with the hospital ship at 2054 hours that evening. The crew began transferring the dead and wounded at 2253 hours. Firefighter Milt Crutchley recalled that, "The worst was going back into the burned-out areas later and finding your dead and wounded shipmates. It was extremely difficult to remove charred, blackened bodies locked in rigor mortis while maintaining some sort of dignity for your fallen comrades."

Crewmen cut additional holes in the flight deck to let in air in order to fight fires in the compartments below the flight deck. By 1844 hours, the ship's carpenter shop was still on fire and fires were still burning in the aft compartments. At 2033 hours, Damage Control reported the fires in the 02 and 03 levels were contained; however, they were too hot to enter. Finally, at 0020 hours on July 30, 14 hours after the accident happened, all fires were controlled and were ultimately declared out throughout the ship at 0400 hours.

The number of casualties had quickly overwhelmed the ship's medical teams. Casualties in the fire were 134 men dead and 161 injured in the worst loss of life aboard a US Navy ship since World War II. Of the 73 aircraft aboard, 21 were destroyed and 40 were damaged.

Forrestal arrived at Naval Air Station Cubi Point on July 31, where repairs were made over the next three weeks sufficient to allow the carrier to return to the United States. She departed on August 11 and steamed back across the Indian Ocean and around Africa. She arrived at Naval Station Mayport, Florida on September 12, where the air group personnel were disembarked. She returned to Norfolk on September 14, where she underwent repairs in the Norfolk Naval Shipyard from September 19, 1967 to April 8, 1968. During the refit, 175 feet of the flight deck was replaced, as well as 200 compartments on the 03, 02, and 01 decks. Repairs cost $72 million, equal to more than $602 million in 2021 dollars.

An Aircraft Carrier Safety Review Panel was convened at Subic Bay on August 5. The board found that, "Poor and outdated doctrinal and technical documentation of ordnance and aircraft equipment and procedures, evident at all levels of command, was a contributing cause of the accidental rocket firing." The report pointed out that the doctrine and procedures employed were not unique to *Forrestal*. Further, the report stated that safety regulations should have prevented the Zuni rocket firing. A triple ejector rack electrical safety pin was designed to prevent any electrical signal from reaching the rockets before the aircraft was launched, but high winds could sometimes catch the tags and blow the pins free. In addition to the pin, a "pigtail" connected the electrical wiring of the missile to the rocket pod. Navy regulations required the pigtail be connected only when the aircraft was attached to the catapult and ready to launch, however, this was not followed since it slowed down the launch rate. The *Forrestal's* Weapons Coordination Board and Weapons Planning Board had agreed four weeks before the accident to "Allow ordnance personnel to connect pigtails 'in the pack', prior to taxi, leaving only safety pin removal at the cat." The memo, written on July 8, 1967, was circulated to the ship's operations officer. The investigation found that the pigtail was connected early, that the safety pin on the faulty Zuni missile was likely blown free, and that the missile fired when a power surge occurred as the pilot transferred his systems from external to internal power.

In the wake of the *Forrestal* disaster, the Navy revised its firefighting practices and modified weapon handling procedures to avoid a similar problem in the future. USS *Forrestal* never returned to Southeast Asia.

The third carrier fire was also caused by a misfired Zuni. Fortunately, on January 14, 1969, USS *Enterprise* was not in the Tonkin Gulf, and the Navy training in the aftermath of the "Forrest Fire" paid dividends. The world's first nuclear-powered aircraft carrier was off Hawaii in the midst of an Operational Readiness Inspection (ORI), a time most would agree was the second-worst for such an event to happen, *Forrestal's* timing being the worst.

The ship had turned into the wind at 0810 hours in anticipation of launching 16 armed aircraft at 0830 hours. According to the later investigation, at 0815 hours, "an MD-3A jet aircraft starter unit was positioned on the starboard side of an F-4J... such that its exhaust outlet was in line with and within twenty-four inches of a loaded LAU-10 ZUNI rocket launcher mounted on the starboard wing of the aircraft."

Several people on deck, including an ORI inspector, noticed the improperly parked starter unit, with its exhaust flowing over the rocket tube, but no one took action. When the overheated Zuni exploded, it created the exact same chain reaction that had happened back in 1967 aboard *Forrestal*. The explosion sent shrapnel flying, which punctured fuel tanks that sprayed JP-5 which ignited, and in turn detonated ordnance.

Again, holes that were blown in the flight deck allowed burning fuel to flow into the ship's interior. However, thanks to the training mandated since the *Forrestal* incident, all of the ship's company and the majority of the embarked air wing had been given firefighting training.

Another major difference was there was no ancient ordnance aboard; the modern bombs took enough time before they detonated to allow sailors near the fire to jettison other ordnance. The ship's captain ordered a change of course to blow the flames clear of undamaged aircraft, so that the fire didn't spread across the deck as had happened in 1967.

All fires were extinguished by 1138 hours. The cost was 27 dead and 371 injured. Estimates of damage were over $10 million for the ship and an additional $44 million for the 15 aircraft destroyed and 17 damaged.

The investigation concluded that "sound damage control organization, training and execution minimized casualties and prevented the initial fire from spreading beyond the Fly Three area of the flight deck to any significant degree." However, flight deck personnel were found to be still largely deficient in their knowledge of weapons specifics, specifically their cook-off times.

Given the facts of operating aircraft off a ship at sea, aircraft carriers continue to be the most dangerous surface warship on which to serve.

TOP GUN

In naval aviation history, the Vietnam War is divided into two periods: "Before Top Gun" and "After Top Gun." The changes effected in Navy pilot training during the three-and-a-half years between the end of *Rolling Thunder* and *Linebacker* revolutionized air combat.

Throughout *Rolling Thunder*, both the Navy and Air Force were frustrated at the results of air combat with the VPAF. Naval Aviation leadership looked at the fact that Navy aircrews were flying what were considered among the most modern fighters in the world – the F-4 Phantom II and F-8 Crusader – in combat with a relatively primitive foe, yet the kill ratio was only 2.5:1. In World War II, the Navy's kill ratio was 14:1. The official Air Force kill ratio for the Korean War, claimed at 12:1, made the Vietnam kill ratio appear unsuccessful. (In reality, the claimed kill ratio in Korea was the result of unexamined wartime propaganda, which was not realized in 1968.) To those leaders, something had to be done.

The most obvious problem was that the Sidewinder and Sparrow missiles used by the F-4 Phantom did not perform as had been expected before the war, with a result that many combats that should have resulted in a sure kill saw the enemy fly away to fight another day. Missiles regularly failed to launch or track; too often, when they did track, they still failed to explode or missed the target altogether. The Sparrow was particularly problematic, with a 63 percent failure rate, while 29 percent that did launch within the envelope missed the target. Firing a Sparrow took five seconds between lock-on and launch, an impossibly long and unsuitable time in a fast-moving dogfight environment. The missile was additionally optimized for a target flying straight and level, such as a nuclear bomber, rather than a swiftly maneuvering fighter. The missile's huge white smoke plume also identified it and warned the pilot of the aircraft it was fired against.

The Sidewinder was not as problematic as the Sparrow, but it still suffered from a 56 percent failure-to-launch rate. It also failed to acquire and missed the target 28 percent of the time due to being fired outside its envelope when crews took the "tone" as an indicator that it was ready to fire rather than just an indication that it had sensed a heat source. It was also distracted by clouds and ground-clutter when fired at a target above or below the aircraft launching it. Fortunately this miss rate dropped to 13 percent with the improved AIM-9D. One thing not considered at the time these missiles were first designed, which became important in the aerial environment of Southeast Asia, was that a fighter armed with these weapons could go from the -40 degrees Fahrenheit of high altitudes above 25,000 feet to the warm humid tropic air beneath 10,000 feet in a matter of minutes, going quickly back and forth between these extremes. Such temperature changes had a very negative impact on the electronics inside the missiles in the days before "solid state" electronics.

The aircraft itself presented technical problems, as related by Lieutenant John Nash. "The radar was unreliable. The F-4 cockpit was not configured or designed to function in the high-G air combat maneuvering (ACM) environment. We [VF-121/Top Gun] supplied ACM cockpit optimization recommendations in 1968–69 which helped considerably, but these 'too little-too late' modifications didn't make it to the squadrons until the war was over."

There was the additional problem that most Phantom aircrews had no previous training for air combat, since the prewar mission profile for the airplane had not foreseen the Phantom engaging in air-to-air combat, rather acting as a defense fighter tasked with shooting down nuclear-armed Soviet bombers at long range. Outside of the F-8 Crusader community, the Navy had ceased any air combat maneuvering training well before the war and "hassling" by pilots as a way of increasing their proficiency was officially frowned upon and could even lead to dismissal from the service. Some, like Lieutenant Denny Wisely, who scored two air-to-air victories during *Rolling Thunder* to become the leading "MiG-killer" in the Navy at the time, had been fortunate early in their careers to be assigned to squadrons where such activity was unofficially allowed, with the pilots engaging in such activity in the restricted airspace near San Clemente Island north of San Diego. As Wisely recalled, "A guy would spot another airplane, or even a pair, pull alongside and 'flip the bird' to make the challenge. If the other guy was up for it, he'd respond with the same, and we'd go at it till one or the other 'cried uncle' by waggling his wings."

Prior to their disestablishment in 1960, the Fleet Air Gunnery Units, with one such unit in the Atlantic Fleet and one in the Pacific Fleet, had trained naval aviators in air combat maneuvering. However, a doctrinal and strategic shift, resulting from perceived advances in missile, radar, and fire control technology, resulted in the widespread belief that the era of the classic dogfight was over. Only the F-8 Crusader community maintained any effort to continue this training, though what training was done did not involve the essential use of dissimilar aircraft in the process.

With the operational schedule becoming less frantic after the cessation of *Rolling Thunder*, and with chief of naval operations Admiral Thomas H. Moorer's approval from the top, "hassling" came back to the fighter squadrons in 1969 as ACM training returned. To Moorer's credit, when this resulted in an increase of the accident rate and there were calls in both the service and the halls of Congress to discontinue this activity, the Navy's leaders maintained that such training would pay dividends in increased skill and ability of pilots who would be better able to survive combat.

While Navy pilot training was designed to "stream" student pilots into fighter, light attack, medium or heavy attack after primary training, with first assignments out of flight school to squadrons in the respective "community," the Air Force did not differentiate between fighters and other aircraft types in pilot training once the Universal Pilot Training (UPT) program was put in place in 1960. It was not unusual for Air Force pilots whose logbooks were filled with time in bombers or transports to find their next assigned duty in the cockpit of an F-105 or F-4. Combat experience demonstrated this was a bad idea, since many who came to fighter squadrons in Southeast Asia from a non-fighter background were disproportionately represented in losses. However, top Air Force leadership – dominated as it was by officers whose experience in the Strategic Air Command meant they did not understand the needs of fighter pilots – refused all entreaties from those returned from combat to change the training syllabus to better train pilots for the war they faced.

For both the Air Force and Navy, *Rolling Thunder* became a Rorschach test, with each service drawing nearly opposite conclusions. The Air Force concluded that air losses were mostly due to unobserved attacks from the rear by North Vietnamese MiGs, and that the problem was therefore a technology problem. The response was the development of the F-4E Phantom, which carried an internal M61 Vulcan cannon that replaced the external SUU-23 Vulcan gun pods carried under the aircraft's belly by Air Force F-4Cs and F-4Ds; development of improved airborne radar systems; and efforts to solve the targeting problems and reliability of the AIM-9B and AIM-7 air-to-air missiles. Significantly, the Air Force never considered adoption of the Navy-developed AIM-9D Sidewinder with its improved infrared seeker, which had proven itself more effective in combat following its introduction in 1966 and opted to arm the F-4D with the AIM-4 Falcon, a missile that never performed to expectations in air-to-air combat, with the result the F-4D was rewired to use the Sidewinder.

The Navy, on the other hand, concluded that the problem was one of aircrew knowledge of how to handle their aircraft in combat with their North Vietnamese opponents.

In March 1968, Admiral Moorer assigned Captain Frank Ault to research the failings of the air-to-air missiles used by the Navy in combat over North Vietnam. Ault was a combat veteran of World War II, who had commanded USS *Coral Sea* in 1966–67, over a tour in Southeast Asia and participation in *Rolling Thunder*. His reputation as a leader was such that he could assemble a staff of his choosing to engage in such a comprehensive investigation, as well as giving him the backbone to publish the findings without pulling punches. Ault quickly picked a capable staff for the review, later recalling:

I was given carte blanche to pick anybody I wanted, and to conduct the study in any manner I saw fit. I looked for people who were recognized by their peers/contemporaries as the most knowledgeable in their respective area of expertise. This resulted in a team of two officers and three civilians – each a self-starter, deeply experienced in their field, capable of independent thought, and with the courage of their convictions. All shared the common characteristics of listeners, not talkers. Compartmentalizing the study effort permitted me to focus narrowly on each of the five subject areas, and identify the specific credentials required in each case. I wasn't looking for "men for all seasons," but rather "men looking for reasons."

Ault's team of five experts came up with five basic questions to be addressed by the study:

1. Is industry delivering to the Navy a high quality product, designed and built to specifications?
2. Are Fleet support organizations delivering a high quality product to the CVA's (aircraft carriers) and to forward sites ashore?
3. Do shipboard and squadron organizations (afloat and ashore) launch an optimally ready combat aircraft-missile system?
4. Does the combat aircrew fully understand and exploit the capabilities of the aircraft-missile system? (Corollary question: Is the aircraft-missile system properly designed and configured for the air-to-air mission?
5. Is the air-to-air missile system (aircraft/fire control system/missile) repair and rework program returning a quality product to the Fleet?

The team commenced work on May 1968 and spent four months gathering information. The report was written over the next three months and released on January 1, 1969. Known in the naval aviation community as the "Ault Report," more formally the "Air-to-Air Missile System Capability Review," the comprehensive and hard-hitting report offered 104 recommendations. Its primary conclusion was that the problem of lack of success in air combat stemmed from inadequate air-crew training in air combat maneuvering.

Regarding the problem of missile reliability, the report found that the probability of a missile destroying its target in combat as experienced over North Vietnam was approximately ten percent. The majority of these missile failures were the result of out-of-envelope firings, which were the result of aircrew unfamiliarity with the dynamically changing launch acceptability regions (LAR) in an air combat. To change this, the report proposed creation of an instrumented range where aircrews could become familiar with the complexities of firing the missiles. The result was the development of the Air Combat Maneuvering Range (ACMR) at MCAS Yuma.

Another cause of missile failure was the rules of engagement, which required the air crew to visually identify the target before firing. The Sparrow missile had been originally developed as a beyond-visual-range (BVR) weapon, where the combat scenario was a fleet defense fighter firing the missile against incoming Soviet bombers, in an environment where there were no other "friendlies" in the immediate vicinity. Requiring both a visual identification, along with the fact that often there were other aircraft in the engagement that the missile might engage, meant that either the missile was not used, for fear of it going after a "friendly," or it was fired in such a manner that it lost its lock-on with the intended target.

The most important recommendation to improve air combat performance was the establishment of an "Advanced Fighter Weapons School" at NAS Miramar to revive and disseminate fighter community ACM expertise throughout the fleet. With the concurrence of Admiral Moorer, planning for the creation of the United States Navy Fighter Weapons School had begun in September 1968, when Lieutenant Commander Dan Pedersen, an experienced naval aviator who had gained his wings in 1957 and had first served in All-Weather Fighter Squadron 3 (VF(AW)-3), whose XO was 23-victory World War II ace Commander Eugene Valencia, was given the assignment of implementing the program. As he later related, he was told he would have no funding, no location, that his instructors would come from what was available at Miramar, the airplanes they used would be loaners, and "Oh, yeah, you have 60 days to stand this up." The new school was under the control of VF-121 "Pacemakers," the Pacific Fleet F-4 Phantom replacement air group (RAG) unit. Publication of the Ault Report gave Pedersen the kind of backing he had lacked to push through bureaucratic impediments and get the school up and running.

Eight F-4 pilot and RIO instructors from VF-121 comprised the initial staff: Mel Holmes and Jim Ruliffson had both made combat deployments and were considered among the best F-4 pilots in the Navy, thus Holmes was put in charge of focusing on aerodynamic issues associated with aerial combat tactics, while Ruliffson developed the syllabus on optimum missile use; John Nash, who had participated in flight tests of captured MiG21 and MiG-17, brought air-to-ground F-4 pilot experience, while Jerry Sawatzky was also rated excellent as a pilot; Darrell Gary and Jim Liang were exceptional RIOs; as were J.C. Smith and Steve Smith, who was also an extraordinary "scrounger." Wayne Hildebrand was a naval intelligence officer who was extremely knowledgeable about the VPAF's operations. All are known in Top Gun history as "The Original Bros." They were hand-picked by Pedersen, and all had experience as students in the Fleet Air Gunnery Unit program. Pedersen picked the "Bros" for what he saw as each one's specialized knowledge and skill in a particular skill field: aerodynamics, tactics, situational awareness, radar, and weapons deployment. Together, they built the Naval Fighter Weapons School syllabus and created the school with no support. Steve Smith, whom Pedersen had chosen in part for his ability to get things done without reference to the bureaucracy when necessary, was in charge of finding office space on the base. He found a dilapidated 10-by-40-foot trailer that appeared abandoned, then cajoled a crane operator into moving it into place next to a hangar with an offer of a case of Scotch for his effort. Office furniture was scrounged up and the "Bros" spent a weekend putting in flooring and repainting the trailer with red trim. The sign out front read "Navy Fighter Weapons School," but from the outset it was known as "Top Gun," the name borrowed from an annual air weapons competition held in the 1950s. The uniform patch design was drawn on a cocktail napkin in the Miramar Officers' Club bar during a happy hour.

Two top secret projects were crucial to developing the tactics that would be taught at the school. Project Have Doughnut involved tests of a MiG-21F-13 obtained by the Israelis when Iraqi Air Force pilot Captain Monir Radfa defected with it to Israel on August 16, 1966. After the Israelis had flown the fighter for 100 hours of flight tests, it was loaned to the US Air Force in January 1968 for three months of tests as part of the agreement to sell F-4E Phantoms to Israel, during which US pilots flew it on 100 sorties. Later in 1968, the air force obtained two MiG-17Fs from Israel which had landed by mistake at Beset airfield in northern Israel on August 12, 1968, when the pilots had gotten lost during navigation training. Tests of the MiG-21 and the MiG-17s revealed the truth about them and de-mystified many beliefs held by US aircrews. John Nash was among the few Navy pilots who were allowed to fly these airplanes. He later recalled:

Flying the MiGs revealed several of their feature characteristics. Both the MiG-17 and MiG-21 were great fighter aircraft. They could out-turn any fighter or tactical jet that the Navy had during that period. The MiG-21 could go faster and pull more Gs than anything we owned. However, it had zip for radar, zip for missiles, zip for rear visibility (although the F-4 was worse), was a single-piloted aircraft and bled energy like a mother. It was hard to see, and if it had been flown by equals to the Navy pilot in Vietnam, it would have been responsible for dozens of kills. The way the US conducted – or ignored – the air war, the MiG-21, in company with the MiG-17, should have wreaked havoc on US air forces, rather than just posing a nuisance to our war. The MiG-17 could turn forever, but its speed and energy bleed rates were poor. It was a single-piloted aircraft, with no radar and poor weapons and weapons range.

There is no better way to learn to fight MiGs than to fight MiGs. The Drill and Doughnut projects were quick, and only allowed a limited number of pilots to see and fight the MiGs. The projects did allow us to find ways to beat a superior turning fighter. Tactics were written as gospel, and we all trained like we would fight – *finally*! The ringer was that the projects used the best pilots, and the MiGs were never flown as effectively in combat as they were in these tests.

In 1972, more than one successful crew would return to their carrier and report "It was just like the training, except the Gomers [a slang term for the enemy pilots] weren't as good."

Lieutenant Ronald "Mugs" McKeown, another naval aviator who flew the MiG-17 against the F-4 in earlier Have Drill tests, described a fight between the two as "a knife fight in a telephone booth." He reported that the secret of success for a Phantom crew was to stay out of the MiG-17's gun range and use the Phantom's superior speed and rate of roll, performing a series of barrel rolls during an engagement that would eventually allow the F-4 to turn back and attack its opponent, noting that the wing loading of a MiG-17 was half that of an F-4, while the MiG's weight was 75 percent less than that of the Phantom, which meant that an F-4 should never attempt to "dogfight" the enemy fighter.

During the 1968 tests, the MiG.21 was determined comparable to the F-8 Crusader in terms of performance at around 15,000 feet. It was more maneuverable than the F-8 at very low speeds, though heavy "stick" forces meant the pilot had to put its long control stick to strenuous use. When compared to the F-4, the MiG-21 was found to rapidly lose energy when making steep turns at speeds under

400 knots. The acceleration of the F-4 was superior to the MiG-21, which also suffered severe buffeting when flown at low altitudes and high speed.

The Navy was able to test the second MiG-17F, which the Air Force had used mainly as a spare, from March to June 1969, during which it was flown against F-4s and F-8s in more than 200 test flights. The airplane was found to have a strong tendency to enter an uncontrollable roll to the left at 570 knots, while the flight controls became virtually inoperable at around 520 knots at low altitude. John Nash noted that the MiG-17, flying at 300 knots, could perform a 6-G 360-degree turn and lose no more than 5 knots. Were a Phantom to attempt the same maneuver, it would come out of the turn just above landing speed.

As with the Akutan Zero discovered in the Aleutians in 1942 and extensively tested against contemporary US fighters by both Air Force and Navy pilots, which provided the knowledge of how to effectively fight an airplane that had been viewed by its opponents as nearly supernatural in its abilities, testing the two aerial opponents provided knowledge that would change the nature of future aerial engagements. This was particularly true for Navy aircrews, who would meet MiG-17s in over half their engagements in 1972. Coupled with their increased skill from the Top Gun ACM training that spread throughout fleet fighter squadrons, Navy fliers' air combat performance in 1972 would approach what had been seen during the Pacific War in 1944–45.

The experience of flying in the Have Doughnut and Have Drill flight tests allowed the Top Gun instructors to develop new tactics. When flying an F-4 against the MiG-21, the F-4 pilot should keep their speed above 450 knots and disengage if the fight slowed, only re-engaging when they could regain a speed advantage and the chance to use their missiles. Like fighting the Zero in World War II, vertical maneuvers were recommended, particularly against the tight-turning MiG-17. Using the "Loose Deuce" team approach, an F-4 pilot could easily outrun a MiG-17, which allowed his wingman to drop in behind the enemy and fire a missile. It was also essential to keep the fight at a long enough distance to stay out of range of the MiG's guns. The most important development that came from this was a vertical maneuver called "the Egg," first created by the legendary Air Force pilot and air combat guru, John Boyd. This used the superior power of the Phantom to describe a towering parabola, allowing the F-4 to outrun its opponent in a climb, then come over the top and zoom down for the attack, thus remaining in the vertical plane where the bigger and heavier Phantom was superior to either MiG opponent.

With the intelligence on enemy aircraft performance and studying engineering information, the "Bros" determined that the US aircraft with flight characteristics most like the MiG-17 and the MiG-21 were the A-4 Skyhawk and the T-38 Talon. The A-4s were cadged from Miramar-based VC-7, while they managed to convince the Air Force to make a temporary gift of a pair of T-38s. Studying combat reports, they learned Soviet air combat tactics and determined that air training missions would be flown using these tactics With these airplanes, and Phantoms cadged from VF-121, they flew dogfights on various service training ranges, challenging any Air Force, Navy, or Marine fighters who would play, as they perfected their training ideas.

As related in the Navy Fighter Weapons School command history written in 1973, the unit's purpose was to:

> train fighter air crews at the graduate level in all aspects of fighter weapons systems including tactics, techniques, procedures and doctrine. It serves to build a nucleus of eminently knowledgeable fighter crews to construct, guide, and enhance weapons training cycles and subsequent aircrew performance. This select group acts as the F-4 community's most operationally orientated weapons specialists. Topgun's efforts are dedicated to the Navy's professional fighter crews, past, present and future.

Teaching aerial dogfight tactics and techniques through dissimilar air combat training, or DACT, the school obtained use of T-38 Talon trainers borrowed from the US Air Force as MiG-21 stand-ins, and A-4 Skyhawks provided by VC-7 to simulate the MiG-17. Marine-operated A-6 Intruders and USAF F-106 interceptors were also in the mix when available.

Regarding who was sent to the school and what the program hoped to do, Jim Ruliffson recalled:

> Who got sent to Top Gun was the prerogative of the fleet squadron commander. Through message traffic, we and our chain-of-command superiors (VF-121 CO and ComFitWingPac [Commander Fighter Wing Pacific]) encouraged them to pick one-cruise "polished nuggets,

pilots and RIOs," and, ideally, assign them to be the squadron Training Officer upon their return so that the unit could benefit from his/their experience for the rest of that turnaround training, and the subsequent cruise.

From the beginning, the school required that each instructor become expert in at least one area, such as the technical intricacies of missiles or air combat maneuvering. They were expected to deliver two-hour lectures with no notes, with neat handwriting and diagrams on the blackboard. In addition to technical knowledge and lecture skill, all instructors were required to be "good sticks," to have a high level of stick-and-throttle skill to enable them to challenge students flying aircraft with superior performance.

In practice, given the natural competitiveness of naval aviators, the most important part of training stressed the post-flight debrief. When a Phantom crew was "shot down" by an instructor in a TA-4 Skyhawk, it was necessary that the debrief be conducted in a way that avoided alienating the students. Thus, instructors went over the physics involved in the maneuvers, tactics, and other factors that affected engagements, with emphasis on learning the points under discussion rather than keeping any sort of score. This system greatly reduced the "ego factor."

The goal of Top Gun was to create a cadre of expert squadron training officers. While any aircrew would improve after several weeks of intensive flying and training, the school also presented lectures on "teaching and learning" and "briefing and debriefing" so the students could return to their units with the tools needed to pass on what they had learned.

Darrell Gary recalled that when Top Gun opened its doors, there was no rush for the seats. "The squadron commanders would look at us and say, 'I'm the best of the best, my people are the best of the best, who are you guys in the funky trailer with red trim telling us what to do?'" Still, Pedersen managed to recruit the first class of eight – four pilots and four backseaters – and held the first class on schedule, 60 days after he was ordered to establish the school. The first group of graduates returned to their squadrons with new knowledge regarding weapons and tactics. As they imparted this knowledge to other pilots, enthusiasm for the training spread. During three-and-a-half years between the end of *Rolling Thunder* in November 1968 and the beginning of Operation

Linebacker in May 1972, Top Gun became established as the Navy's center of excellence in the development of fighter doctrine, tactics, and training. When Jerry Beaulier, one of the initial class, became the first Phantom pilot in two years to shoot down a MiG in a dogfight in March 1970, the course began to sell itself. Before too long, there was a waiting list to attend.

Lieutenant Curt Dosé, who had made a combat tour aboard USS *America* with VF-92 in 1969–70 recalled his experience as a Top Gun student, "Although perhaps not as glamorous as the later movie of the same name, the intensity, quality, and value of the real Top Gun school far exceeded that of the movie."

The five-week course was intense:

> Every day started very early with classroom study of a variety of lessons, from Soviet history to public speaking, in addition to cutting edge, "loose deuce" fighter tactics. Then at least one, if not two flights followed, flying against the best fighter pilots in the world at that time. Thoroughly tired and drained after the debriefs, more classroom work or study followed. Then it was home after dark for more study until late at night. Then the next morning, the same routine commenced once again.

During his time at the school, Dosé rented a home in La Jolla with an ocean view. "I had no time to enjoy it. Nor was there any time for the inviting social life that my roommates were enjoying. But I didn't mind. There was no other place I wanted to be, nor anything I wanted more to do than to be a student at the best school ever."

In operation, students brought their own airplane from their squadron and their own ground crew. The four weeks of training initially included one week of air-to-ground weapons use and three weeks of air-to-air work, but it was soon determined that three weeks was insufficient time to cover the air-to-air curriculum adequately and the air-to-ground sequence was dropped. The students did 75 hours of classroom instruction and each flew 25 training flights to put what was discussed in the classroom into practice. After the first year, the course was extended to five weeks. MiG-killer Commander Ronald "Mugs" Mckeown, who commanded Top Gun in the postwar years, explained, "We don't teach basics at all. We expect, and demand, that they have a working knowledge of fighter tactics when they arrive. They are the best people in their squadrons and, hopefully, we will make them better."

When the North Vietnamese opened the Easter Offensive in the spring of 1972, there was at least one Top Gun graduate in every Phantom unit. Air combat began with a vengeance in early May, and the results were dramatic. Over the course of *Linebacker*, the Navy's kill ratio rose from 2.7:1 to 13:1, while the Air Force, which had not implemented a similar training program, actually had its kill ratio worsen in comparison with what had been achieved during *Rolling Thunder* after the resumption of bombing.

With the demonstrated success of Navy fighter crews, Top Gun was vindicated. The Navy Fighter Weapons School became a separate, fully funded command with permanently assigned aircraft, staff, and infrastructure. The school received its greatest compliment after the end of the war, when the Air Force initiated its own DACT program through the USAF Fighter Weapons School at Nellis AFB, with dedicated "aggressor squadrons." The Air Force also initiated a program that became well known as "Red Flag," which gives training to fighter, fighter-bomber, and bomber crews to provide the experience of an aircrew's first ten combat missions, the period when they are most at risk of loss in combat.

12

INTERREGNUM, 1968–72

In the three-and-a-half years between the end of Operation *Rolling Thunder* on November 1, 1968, and the commencement of Operation *Linebacker* on May 10, 1972, the United States and North Vietnam engaged in a stand-off. The United States claimed the right to fly photo reconnaissance missions over the North and maintain patrols off the coast, but it was a right unrecognized or agreed to by North Vietnam. The two sides saw the continued missions as opportunities to test each other's resolve on occasion. For the US units, all offensive actions against North Vietnam were prohibited, and any engagement with enemy fighters was only authorized in self-defense. Throughout 1969, there were momentary contacts between Navy fighters and VPAF fighters that flew south of the 19th parallel into the panhandle of North Vietnam, though the VPAF fliers always retreated north whenever they were confronted.

Throughout these years, interdiction operations continued over "neutral" Laos by both Air Force and Navy fighter-bombers. Operation *Commando Hunt*, known to the aircrews as the "Laotian Highway Patrol," was flown from 1968 to the opening of the Easter Offensive against the Ho Chi Minh Trail where it came out of North Vietnam before turning back into northern South Vietnam. The operation was the longest sustained air interdiction campaign ever conducted by any air force. *Commando Nail* operations saw A-6A Intruders using their all-weather radar mapping and bombing capability to locate bombing targets and illuminate them for attacks by the accompanying F-4s and A-7s. Most of these missions were over the three mountain passes – Ban Karai, Mu Gia, and Ban Raving – that were natural choke points since they were the only access from North Vietnam into the Laotian "panhandle." The mountains to either side of these passes meant they were the most dangerous area for night flying as attacking aircraft attempted to identify and destroy the first and last vehicles in a convoy to trap the rest for further destruction. While more than 700,000 tons of bombs were dropped during these operations, no more than a small percentage of the enemy's supplies were ever destroyed. As a result, the Navy's effort was reduced to save operating costs in late 1969, with USS *Shangri-La* (CVS-38) joining *Bon Homme Richard* in place of the larger carriers to maintain sorties in early 1970. *Shangri-La* was in poor operating condition and the majority of her deployment was spent undergoing repairs, a sign of the age and deteriorating condition of the Essex-class carriers. For example, *Hancock*, which had been due for decommissioning in 1969, had been extended four years and would make a final Vietnam tour in 1972. Ironically, this replacement of the more capable air groups coincided with an increase in attacks on ARVN outposts in May, which resulted in *America* and *Oriskany* returning to Dixie Station.

During the years of the bombing halt, the VPAF was able to replenish and improve its force. The much-improved MiG-21bis and MiG-21MF, known in the West as the "Fishbed-H" and "J," were supplied by the Soviet Union, while China sent Shenyang J-5 fighters that were the license-built version of the MiG-17, and enough Shenyang J-6 fighters developed from the Soviet MiG-19, the first supersonic fighter in the USSR. The J-6 was much improved in performance and reliability over the Soviet airplane, which had essentially been abandoned early in its development cycle in favor of the MiG-21. Sufficient numbers of these aircraft were received that the VPAF established another fighter regiment, the 925th Fighter Regiment, to operate the J-6 fighters. The fighter's heavy armament of three 30mm cannon would come as a nasty surprise to the naval aviators who came up against the J-6 in 1972.

On January 28, 1970, breaking from prior practice, two MiG-21s led by VPAF ace Vu Ngoc Dinh of the 921st Fighter Regiment flew into Laos, where Dinh shot down an Air Force HH-53B helicopter from the 40th Aerospace Rescue and Recovery Squadron with an Atoll missile as it attempted to rescue the crew of a downed F-105G Wild Weasel in southern Laos. Major Holly Bell and his five crew members were killed when the Jolly Green Giant exploded. As a result, the Navy began an experiment, keeping BARCAP flights off the coast of the panhandle where air response was allowed beneath the Vietnamese radar while flying other aircraft in an attempt to entice the MiGs to fly into the area, where their interception was allowed. On March 28, the new tactic worked.

The only MiG kill claimed by either naval aviators or USAF crews in Southeast Asia between August 1968 and January 1972 was scored by Lieutenants Jerome E. "Jerry" Beaulier and RIO Steven J. Barkley from *Constellation*'s VF-142 that day. Beaulier and Barkley were older than the usual first-tour aircrew, both having served as enlisted men before becoming officers, Beaulier in the Air Force and Barkley in the Navy. Beaulier had been a member of the first class at Top Gun the year before. While the school's goal was that the graduates would return to their squadrons and become training officers, Beaulier was assigned as NATOPS (Naval Air Training and Operating Procedures Standardization Program) Officer when he returned to the squadron. As Barkley remembered, "He had frequent opportunities to hold forth in the ready room, so some of what was absorbed at Top Gun made its way to a mix of willing ears. So, in a way, it was working even then, but not as some would suggest."

Barkley had been responsible the night before for assigning the flight schedule for the day. He and Beaulier had drawn the "spare," which meant that when the BARCAP mission was launched, they would man their Phantom, and start up, ready to go if one of the assigned aircraft was forced to abort the mission. By the time they did so, there was word among the aircrew that MiGs were airborne and there was a possibility of an engagement. As the two cursed their luck, the squadron commander's airplane which was set to go experienced equipment failure and they were suddenly on the schedule for the mission.

Once airborne, Beaulier became wingman for CAG Commander Paul Speer with RIO Lieutenant (jg) John Carter when the CAG's original wingman found his radar wasn't working on preliminary post-launch check. Speer, a veteran F-8 pilot who had transferred to F-4s when he became *Constellation*'s CAG, had shot down one of four MiG-17's shot down in the biggest fight of *Rolling Thunder* on May 19, 1967. The Red Crown controller aboard USS *Horne* (DLG-30) vectored them, informing them that the enemy was 21 miles distant and had just dropped tanks, and that they were "cleared to fire."

RIO Barkley recalled:

I was desperately looking for a radar contact as we crossed the beach – then the radar died! I fought it for five miles and then gave up. This was no place for Built-In Tests! I was really disappointed – the perfect set-up for a head-on shot, and no radar! I went heads-up as we were about to go into a fight, and the radar problem could be sorted out later.

By this time our section was really "hauling the mail." We were in the region of about 550 knots, and had moved down to about 22,000 feet as Red Crown White had estimated the MiGs' altitude at about 20,000–22,000 feet. CAG was north of us about a mile, and we were stepped down 2,000–3,000 feet.

As the Phantoms closed, Beaulier was first to sight the MiGs, thus taking lead in the engagement, calling the sighting and a turn into the MiGs at two o'clock and 22,000 feet. He led the two F-4s in a climbing turn into the enemy, who had not yet spotted the approaching fighters. Barkley continued, "Someone in our aircraft commented, 'They don't see us!' Neither Beaulier nor myself will admit to making that call, but somebody did and, as you might expect, that's all it took for both MiGs to see us and begin aggressive maneuvering." The fight began as the MiGs crossed in front of the F-4s from left to right. Speer was two miles behind Beaulier as the enemy fighters turned into the Phantoms:

The MiGs turned right into us and began a vertical turn down into us as they split into singles from the fighting wing formation they were maintaining. We turned right into the nearest MiG and kept a visual on the second aircraft, beginning our turn at about 18,000 feet and pulling 5Gs as we chased the lead MiG through a 360-degree turn.

Beaulier and Barkley had discussed air combat many times, and had determined they would not drop their tanks until they were sucked into a slow fight, to maximize their time in the fight.

The F-4 rapidly lost energy, especially with the three tanks that we were still dragging. As we struggled through the 90 degrees of turn, our airspeed was 400 knots, so I called "Tanks" when the speed was right, and off went the wing tanks as planned. We kept the centerline tank. I've often wondered what the MiGs thought when they saw a jet calmly jettison tanks in the middle of a life or death fight. Did they think we were organized, or just nuts?

Beaulier pushed the throttles to keep up with the MiGs, which had joined again as a fighting wing:

Somehow, they were head-on with CAG Speer, who was out of phase with us and the MiGs, and coming from the opposite direction! The lead MiG launched an Atoll at CAG. Remember, this was not his first real fight, but it was certainly John Carter's baptism of fire, and John was focused. He saw the launch and called CAG's attention to it, probably in a near-falsetto voice. CAG saw the launch. His response to Carter's frantic call was, "No chance." He never varied his course one degree, and the missile passed harmlessly. That's experience!

The two enemy fighters then went left and right respectively. Beaulier followed the MiG that turned right. "Beaulier was onto him, and my responsibility was to track the remainder of the fight. I followed the second MiG through our six, and then it turned west and disappeared, with CAG in close pursuit." Speer followed the enemy fighter toward Hanoi, turning back only when the MiG-21 lit afterburner and dived toward Kep. Alone over an overcast he got several SAM warnings and turned back.

In the meantime, Beaulier and Barkley were chasing the lead MiG:

We were lagging our descending MiG about 40 degrees when he apparently lost sight of us and reversed his course. Jerry quickly corrected his turn and put our Phantom at the MiG's dead six o'clock, with Sidewinder selected. With the Sidewinder furiously buzzing, we fired the first missile at approximately half a mile. It hit the MiG's tailpipe and exploded. With the second Sidewinder now howling, I suggested maybe a second shot might be in order, so we shot it and there was another explosion on the MiG, which was now engulfed in a fireball from the leading edge of the wing backwards. The nose and canopy were visible in front of the fireball. We pulled up at the MiG's four o'clock and took a look as the doomed aircraft descended into the cloud below us. We never saw an ejection.

As word spread through the fighter community of Beaulier's victory, the doubts some squadron commanders had expressed before about the value of sending crews to Top Gun vanished. Within a matter of months, the school had a waiting list.

The cessation of bombing provided North Vietnam the opportunity to repair the damage inflicted by the dropping of more than 640,000 tons of bombs, close to the tonnage dropped by the US Army Air Force on Germany in World War II. Defenses were strengthened, with more airfields upgraded to allow operation of MiGs, while the fighter force was increased with replacement and supply of additional and more modern fighters from the Soviets and Chinese. By 1972, there would be 13 airfields capable of operating MiGs, with the airfields distributed throughout the country. North Vietnamese forces in Laos and Cambodia increased, despite continuing US bombing of the Ho Chi Minh Trail in Laos as well as an unannounced B-52 bombing campaign in Cambodia, which led to the US incursion into eastern Cambodia in May 1970 to interdict enemy bases there.

The 1968 Ault Report did more than just improve aircrew capability through the creation of Top Gun. The primary purpose of the report had been to deal with the problems of the weapons used. During the 1969–72 respite from direct combat, the AIM-9G Sidewinder was developed and brought into the Navy's inventory. This "dogfight" Sidewinder was superior to the AIM-9D that the Navy used in *Rolling Thunder* and was vastly superior to the AIM-9B that the Air Force stubbornly continued to utilize. Further development resulted in the AIM-9G getting the Sidewinder Extended Acquisition Mode (SEAM). This slaved the missile's seeker head to the aircraft's radar. During the MiG engagements on May 10, 1972, the war's hottest day, the AIM-9G achieved a 42 percent success rate. The AIM-9H became available in September 1972. The first "solid state" Sidewinder, the missile had increased reliability and robustness, with fins using more powerful actuators that allowed it to turn more tightly, improving tracking of a maneuvering target. Available only in limited numbers, the 9H had an even higher kill ratio than the 9G, and was more capable at altitudes lower than 7,000 feet, where more than half of all victories against MiGs were obtained. The Sparrow was similarly upgraded to the AIM-7E-2, though it still had the problem of not being able to be used in the optimal BVR mode due to the continuing requirement of a visual IS before firing a missile.

By May 1972, the naval air force aboard the carriers in the Tonkin Gulf was very different from what had existed in 1968. In the intervening years, many naval aviators who were either frustrated over the way the war was being fought and their role in it, or had come to believe that the war was not worth fighting, had left the Navy at the expiration of their terms of service. The number of combat veterans in the squadrons was not as high as it had been before. Additionally, the low retention rate of first-term enlisted men who took their valuable technical expertise with them when they returned to civilian life, left carrier crews short of mid-level NCOs, reducing efficiency in both the squadrons and the ships' companies.

13

A NEW WAR

Following the failed South Vietnamese Operation *Lam Son 719* invasion of Laos, the leaders of North Vietnam discussed a potential offensive during the 19th Plenum of the Central Committee of the Vietnam Workers' Party in 1971. By that December, the Politburo had determined to launch a major offensive early in the next year. 1972 was a US presidential election year, and with the increasing antiwar sentiment among the population as well as the government of the United States, there was a possibility of affecting the outcome. After his election as president in 1968, in response to growing antiwar sentiment in the country and larger demonstrations in opposition to the war in 1969, President Nixon had announced a "Vietnamization" policy in late 1969 that would begin replacing US units with ARVN units, thus allowing him to begin withdrawing US combat forces in 1970. By 1972, US combat units were at their lowest ebb in Southeast Asia since late 1964, while ARVN forces were stretched to the breaking point along a 600-mile border; the poor ARVN performance in *Lam Son 719* promised an easy victory. There was also the possibility of taking a South Vietnamese provincial capital and proclaiming it the capital of the Provisional Revolutionary Government.

This Politburo decision was the culmination of political infighting over the previous three years between those Politburo members grouped around Truong Chinh, who supported continued low-intensity guerilla warfare in the South while rebuilding the North, known as the "Chinese model" for the manner in which Mao Zedong had fought the Chinese Civil War in the aftermath of the end of World War II, and the "South firsters" grouped around Defense Minister Vo Nguyen Giap and supported by First Party Secretary Le Duan, who supported the Soviet model of big military offensives. Giap's influence had declined after the failure of the 1968 Tet Offensive, but his star was once again ascendant following the defeat of the ARVN invasion force in 1971. While Le Duan had responsibility for planning the operation, Giap was sidelined, being assigned responsibility for logistical matters and approving operational plans, while PAVN chief of staff General Van Tien Dung was in charge of conducting the offensive.

As a result of this decision, the Nguyen Hue Offensive, known in the West as "the Easter Offensive," and officially known in North Vietnam as "the 1972 Spring–Summer Offensive," and as "the Red Fiery Summer" in South Vietnamese history, was put into operation. It would be the largest military offensive in Asia since the Chinese People's Volunteer Army crossed the Yalu River into North Korea during the Korean War. It was a radical departure from previous offensives such as the 1968 Tet Offensive, since it was not intended to wage war outright but rather to gain as much territory and destroy as many ARVN units as possible, to improve the DRV's negotiating position with regard to the Paris peace negotiations that were moving toward a conclusion. For the North Vietnamese, the operation name given to the invasion was steeped in symbolic Vietnamese history: in 1773, the three Tay Son brothers, led by Nguyen Hue the eldest, united Vietnam at a time when the country was rent by civil war and social unrest.

Following the 1971 announcement that Richard Nixon would visit the People's Republic of China in 1972, the Chinese leadership assured the North Vietnamese that they would supply even more military and economic aid. The Soviets, who wished to widen any rift between China and Vietnam, also agreed to provide additional aid. The result of both agreements was a flood of supplies and equipment necessary to equip and support a modern conventional army arriving in Haiphong in the fall of 1971. Foremost were 400 T-34, T-54, and Type 59 (a Chinese version of the T-54) medium and 200 PT-76 light amphibious tanks, hundreds of SAMs, including the shoulder-fired, heat-seeking SA-7 Strela (NATO name "Grail"), AT-3 Sagger antitank missiles, and heavy-caliber, long-range artillery. During the same period, 25,000 PAVN troops were provided specialized training, primarily in the Soviet Union and Eastern Europe. High-level

Soviet military personnel also arrived, remaining in Vietnam until March 1972.

US military commanders in Southeast Asia began to believe "something was up" with regard to the enemy's future plans when MACV sent several reconnaissance teams into the Mu Gia and Ban Karai pass areas in the fall of 1971, where a buildup of PAVN forces and equipment was discovered. In light of this, MACV concluded that the enemy was preparing an offensive to take place in the Central Highlands and the northern provinces of South Vietnam. The timing made sense, since there were only 69,000 US personnel in South Vietnam, with most in support roles. By November 30, 1971, the number would be reduced to 27,000.

In late 1971, naval aviators striking the Ho Chi Minh Trail in Laos began to report that it appeared there was an increase in traffic southbound, which might indicate that a buildup was in process for a ground offensive in the spring. Both the Navy and the Air Force increased their reconnaissance missions over the southern third of North Vietnam. This led to an increase in combat action in what had been a "no bomb" zone since November 1968, other than "protective reaction strikes" against any enemy action against US reconnaissance sorties over North Vietnam. This increased activity on the Trail, combined with more aggressive flying by MiGs and siting of SA-2 missiles further south than before, reinforced the belief that another offensive was indeed in the making.

By December 1971, the incidents of the enemy opening fire on Blue Tree reconnaissance flights resulted in an increase in the allowable "protective reaction strikes." The rules of engagement stated that if a reconnaissance aircraft encountered enemy fire, the crews could not call their carrier for a strike to hit the AAA or SAM site. However, if the Blue Tree aircraft was flying with an escort group when it was fired on, the escort could strike the enemy position in "reaction." Until the increase in enemy traffic was spotted and it became clear there was a likelihood that the war was going to heat up, the "protective reaction strikes" had been defensive. Beginning in December, they became planned strike operations against specific targets such as fuel storage facilities and MiG bases, with the "escort" composed of strike, flak suppression, and MiGCAP sections.

Between December 26 and 30 the Air Force and Navy conducted Operation *Proud Deep*, the first major strikes against targets in the

North since 1968, with a goal of hitting the growing stocks of supplies apparently being built up. While the operation had a positive short-term impact, the domestic political environment in the United States did not allow the Nixon Administration to wage a sustained campaign. Further reconnaissance missions were flown over North Vietnam after *Proud Deep*. One naval aviator recalled:

> The Air Force would fly a single RF-4 with an escort Phantom on their recon missions over the North. When the Gomers shot at them they'd turn and get away with their pictures and put themselves in for Air Medals. We'd fly an RA-5C with what amounted to an Alpha strike in trail. If one guy opened up on the "Vigi" with a pistol, we'd initiate a "protective reaction strike" and roll in with the whole air wing.

At least in the panhandle, the war was back on by January 1972. On January 19, 1972, two VF-96 F-4Js from *Constellation* flying MiGCAP for a 19-plane Alpha strike flying escort on such a Blue Tree mission engaged enemy jets for the first time since Beaulier and Barkley's fight in March 1970. The crews were Lieutenant Randall H. "Duke" Cunningham with RIO Lieutenant (jg) William P. "Willie" Driscoll, and Lieutenants Brian "Bulldog" Grant and Jerry Sullivan. The "protective reaction strike" was being flown in retaliation for the shoot-down of a VA-165 A-6A Intruder participating in Operation *Proud Deep Alpha*, a second series of limited-reaction strikes.

Constellation's Alpha strike's target was caves suspected of housing MiGs, as well as three SAM sites in the Quan Lang area. They had been briefed to expect SAMs while inbound and had changed their flight profile to avoid the threat, flying inbound over northern South Vietnam then turning up into Laos, then back east toward the target. Cunningham later recalled, "We were told that we would encounter AAA, SAMs and MiGs in the target area. Two MiG-21s were known to be operating out of Quan Lang field and six were based at Bai Thuong, about 60 miles to the north."

Cunningham had joined the Navy in 1966, but had not flown in Vietnam before the end of *Rolling Thunder*. He had been known in his previous squadron for wanting to engage MiGs and had a reputation for flying as close to North Vietnam as was allowed in 1969. His first RIO later recalled that Cunningham had been one of the few in the previous squadron who had applied himself to reading all the secret information that was supplied to the fleet from the Have Drill and Have Doughnut programs regarding enemy fighters, a habit he maintained in VF-96, where he was assigned to fly with Driscoll.

The MiGCAP flew behind the F-4s escorting the RA-5C recon aircraft, flying above and behind the Alpha strike package. Once over Point Alpha, the Vigilante drew fire. The A-7 Iron Hand and F-4 flak suppression flights aircraft began their run into the target, while the rest of the force continued to Point Bravo, 30 nautical miles south-east of Quan Lang. As the strike divisions turned toward the target, the two MiGCAP Phantoms made a slow, descending turn to approach the target north of the strike track, passing just north of the airfield and establishing an orbit point between the target area and the MiG base at Bai Thuong, thus positioned to intercept any jets coming from Bai Thuong.

Fifteen miles west of Quan Lang, Cunningham started picking up AAA radar on his Radar Homing and Warning (RHAW) gear. They were right between two SAM sites. Cunningham was northwest of the Quan Lang airfield when he received a SAM-launch warning and spotted the missile when it was launched from the northern site. "The missile was coming right up under Grant's belly – he couldn't see it. I called, 'Break left,' but he didn't break hard enough, so I called for a harder break." The missile passed ten feet from Grant's canopy and detonated at 25,000 feet. Cunningham then got a warning that the southern SAM site had him locked-up and he soon saw another SAM launch. He and Grant broke right and down. "This one kept tracking – I wasn't defeating it. So, I rolled inverted, waited until it was within half a mile of us, then pulled hard into a split-S. I put the stick in my lap and pulled about 9G's."

The SAM flashed past and exploded 1,000 feet above the Phantom. Cunningham recovered and headed northwest, spotting another SAM launched at him from the northern site. "The F-4 can pull only about 3–4G at 300 knots, so I engaged burner. I still had the tank, so I unloaded. I was hanging in the straps. I rolled into the missile, and as it approached me, I buried the stick in my lap." The SAM detonated nearby, flipping the Phantom from a nose low left bank to a 45-degree right bank, nose high, but caused no damage.

Moments later, Cunningham spotted what he initially identified as two A-7s three miles away, heading north through a canyon at 500 feet.

"It dawned on me that those two birds were in afterburner, and the A-7 doesn't have a 'burner!'" The "A-7s" were two silver MiG-21s, with the leader on the left at about 500 feet, while the second was in a fighting wing 300–500 feet above his leader. Cunningham called "Blue Bandits! North of the field!" Diving to about 200 feet, he accelerated to 500 knots and closed on the lead MiG from behind.

"I thought about punching off my tank, but at that speed we were having problems with it hitting the stabilator." Driscoll hit the boresight switch, calling "Locked-on, 50 knots closing – shoot, shoot, shoot your Sparrow." Instead, Cunningham hit the "heat" switch. "From the tail aspect I was much more confident with the Sidewinder than I was with the Sparrow." The F-4 was 300 feet over the jungle making 500 knots when Cunningham launched an AIM-9G at the lead MiG two miles ahead. When the missile launched, the wingman called it and the lead MiG broke hard to the right. The enemy fighter turned in front of him, still in afterburner, as the Sidewinder hit the ground. "They must have been H or J-model MiGs (MiG-21bis or MiG-21MF), as the MiG-21 just can't turn that fast without hydraulically-boosted controls."

Cunningham pulled up into a high-speed yo-yo and barrel rolled left to maintain position. "I expected the big cross-turn – they were trying to bring me right down between them. Instead, his wingman just left him – he pushed over and ran." The lead MiG reversed its turn and continued toward Bai Thuong. The reversal repositioned the MiG directly in front of Cunningham less than a mile distant, and he fired a second AIM-9, which went directly up the tailpipe. "The aft section of the MiG appeared to come off, the nose tucked down violently, and the aircraft hit the ground, tumbling head-over-tail – no 'chute was seen."

Cunningham quickly turned right and spotted the second MiG dead ahead, fleeing the fight, headed northwest and pulling away. Cunningham was doing 450 knots, still in afterburner. He chased the second MiG for about 30 nautical miles:

I was going to chase him right to Bai Thuong but my RIO asked me for our fuel state. I said, "Willie, don't bother me now. I'm chasing a MiG," and he replied, "No shit. I want your state RIGHT NOW!" I glanced at it and was astounded to see that we were down to 6500 pounds. We now barely had enough to exit through the SAMs to a tanker.

The Phantom was now at tree-top height and taking ground fire from both sides, with tracers passing over the canopy. Driscoll had a full system lock-on, and Cunningham tried a desperation shot. They were at 200 feet with the MiG at 400 feet three miles away. The Sparrow failed to launch, due to what was later discovered to be a shorted cable which prevented the ejector cartridge firing. Cunningham made it to the tanker with less than five minutes' fuel remaining when he hooked on.

Cunningham and Driscoll received a warm welcome back aboard *Constellation*. "It was the first kill in almost two years, and we had quite a welcoming committee. In fact, one of the enlisted men knocked the Admiral over to jump up and grab my arm to say 'Mr Cunningham, we got our MiG today, didn't we?!'"

Despite the growing concern expressed in US and South Vietnamese intelligence estimates of enemy intentions and events such as Cunningham's fight, the upper levels of US leadership continued to deny things were changing. Defense Intelligence Agency officers who briefed Secretary of Defense Melvin Laird in mid-January stated that the North Vietnamese would attack after the Tet holidays, using armored forces in a conventional attack across the DMZ. However, Laird was not convinced. In testimony before Congress in late January, the secretary stated that a large communist offensive "was not a serious possibility." However, on February 4, President Nixon authorized the Air Force to strike at SAM sites discovered in Laos and southern North Vietnam. The next day, he ordered the draw-down of Air Force units in Southeast Asia halted, leaving B-52s at U-Tapao in Thailand. When the expected offensive did not take place in February, MACV commander General Creighton W. Abrams was publicly ridiculed in the American press. At the end of March 1972, Ambassador Ellsworth Bunker traveled to Nepal, while General Abrams prepared to spend the Easter holiday with his family in Thailand. On March 10, the 101st Airborne Division, the major American combat unit in South Vietnam, completed its withdrawal from the country.

Nixon's successful visit to China at the end of February contributed to a belief on the part of US officials in Washington that the situation in Southeast Asia would remain unchanged. Their argument was that China did not want to risk its newly established relationship with the United States and thus would use its influence with the North Vietnamese to prevent any actions that would compromise that, given that the Chinese needed the friendship with the United States in its confrontation with the Soviet Union, which would outweigh any solidarity with their "revolutionary comrades."

Air action had slowed through the rest of January and February, though Blue Tree protective reaction strikes continued, which allowed the Navy to stage the largest "unofficial" bombing campaign against North Vietnam since *Rolling Thunder* had ended in 1968. Cunningham and Driscoll's performance had demonstrated that Beaulier's victory two years earlier wasn't a fluke. The next Navy MiG kill happened the afternoon of March 6, and the two aircrews from *Coral Sea*'s VF-111 demonstrated the value of the Top Gun training in maneuvering and teamwork, as they successfully took out a MiG-17 by sticking to the F-4's strong points and putting the enemy fighter into a "sandwich" for the victory.

Section leader Lieutenant James "Yosemite" Stillinger, veteran of a prior combat tour in the F-8 and a recent Top Gun graduate, and RIO Lieutenant (jg) Rick Olin were accompanied by wingmen Lieutenant Garry L. Weigand and RIO Lieutenant (jg) William C. Freckleton, assigned as Force CAP (FORCAP) to support a photo-reconnaissance mission to Quan Lang airfield. Yankee Station had been moved from its previous point some 400 miles from North Vietnam to a point only 150 miles off the coast, which placed the task force close enough to be in potential danger of attack by the VPAF. The FORCAP was assigned to take a position north of the task force to intercept any attempted attack, while also being cleared to intercept any enemy jets that were spotted by the RA-5C when they turned north to return to "safe" airspace in central North Vietnam. Weigand and Freckleton were originally assigned to fly wing for Top Gun "Original Bro" Lieutenant Commander Jim "Cobra" Ruliffson and RIO Lieutenant (jg) Clark van Nostrand. However, as the Phantoms were holding on the catapults, Ruliffson's jet sprung a hydraulics leak. Stillinger and Olin, the stand-by, replaced Ruliffson and assumed section lead. Once airborne, both aircraft were discovered to have radar problems, with Olin's having pulse search problems while Freckleton's experienced complete failure. The section continued, although only able to employ the four Sidewinders each carried.

The RA-5C was escorted by two F-4s from *Coral Sea* sister squadron VF-51, led by squadron CO, Commander Foster S. "Tooter" Teague with RIO Lieutenant Ralph M. Howell, and squadron operations officer Lieutenant Commander Jerry B. "Devil" Houston with RIO Lieutenant Kevin T. Moore. Quan Lang airfield had been extensively developed during the bombing halt and now in 1972 was home to 260 VPAF fighters: 135 MiG-17s, 95 MiG-21s, and 30 F-6s, Chinese-built MiG-19s. Recently, the enemy fighter force had been regularly harassing Air Force B-52 missions in Laos, providing cover for the buildup of supplies being positioned in that country for the coming offensive against South Vietnam.

The Red Crown controller aboard USS *Chicago* was Senior Chief Radarman (RDCS) Larry Nowell, who by the end of the initial *Linebacker* air campaign in July would be the most successful Red Crown controller, guiding the Navy jets in 13 MiG-killing sorties. Fighter crews called him by name and considered themselves lucky when their missions coincided with his watches. For this accomplishment, Chief Nowell would be awarded the Distinguished Service Medal in August 1972, only the second Navy enlisted man to receive the award during the Vietnam War.

Guided by Nowell, the VF-111 Phantoms arrived on station above Brandon Bay and took up an orbit. Moments after their arrival, the RA-5C called "Bandits! Bandits! Two Blue Bandits!" then "More! Red bandits! Red bandits! Two, no I think I see three Red Bandits!" Adrenaline started pumping at the news there were at least two MiG-21s and three MiG-17s airborne. The VF-51 escorts that had remained over Laos accelerated to join the Vigilante photo plane. They arrived over Quan Lang and were quickly engaged by four MiG-17s. Teague and Howell were able to get in position to launch a Sidewinder against one of the MiGs, which exploded close enough to damage it, but as Teague became involved with the others, he lost track of the jet and the kill was not confirmed. After a real tussle, the two Phantoms managed to evade their more numerous opponents and get out of enemy airspace safely.

Moments after Stillinger and Weigand arrived on station, expecting from having heard Teague's and Houston's radio calls that they might intercept the MiGs returning to their base, Chief Nowell advised them they had "bogeys" in their immediate vicinity. Weigand took position on Stillinger's right wing as Red Crown then vectored them northwest at 15,000 feet. Nowell informed them that they had a "bogey" at 326 degrees and 14 nautical miles, 80 degrees to their right. The controller called the bogey at eight and then six miles, but neither crew spotted the enemy. Nowell then called "Merge plot." The two were almost on top of the target, but neither crew saw anything. Stillinger called "No Joy! No Joy!" Nowell replied "Look low, look low, three miles."

Wiegand remembered, "We rolled up into a left bank, looked down, and there was the MiG! It looked as though he had just pulled his nose up to come after us." The MiG-17 was at an altitude of approximately 500–1,000 feet. Stillinger called "Tally ho!" Moments later Weigand replied, "Roger, Tally ho on one MiG-17!" The two Phantoms were at 3,000 feet in a descending right turn. Freckleton later praised Nowell's direction. "If he hadn't told us to look down exactly when he said to, we would have continued our starboard turn and the MiG would have come around behind our section and bagged one or both of us." Freckleton explained later, "We knew it was going to be pretty much an energy fight since the MiG could easily out-turn the F-4. We had to use our speed and energy to climb, dive, extend and pitch back, as opposed to laying on a 6G turn that would not get us inside the MiG's turn radius."

Stillinger's spread of the tactical information he had learned at Top Gun in the squadron was paying off. He directed Weigand to go to trail. Pulling up in "the egg," Stillinger pitched over the top and positioned himself in trail on the MiG out of a barrel roll. As he descended in a right turn, the enemy fighter suddenly reversed left and pulled up hard into him. Stillinger recalled later, "I don't know if he saw us or if his GCI said there was somebody behind him, but he turned." Stillinger was able to follow the MiG through several reversals, but was unable to put his nose on the enemy to fire. The enemy fighter continued to maneuver in the horizontal, turning from 15–20 degrees nose high to 15–20 degrees nose low, as Stillinger remained in the vertical. Each time he came off a vertical roll and started down, the MiG reversed course, forcing Stillinger to barrel roll or yo-yo away from the enemy fighter to regain position.

"I finally decided, 'To hell with maintaining energy' and decided to pull around the corner and shoot him. I was outside his plane of turn, looking up at him, and I could see his tailpipe. I had a very good tone." Stillinger pulled the trigger at a range of 4,500–6,000 feet, but the MiG rolled into him, pulling very hard. "That was the first time he really turned to its maximum, much tighter than anything he showed me before." The Sidewinder tried to turn back, then went ballistic. "I don't think it ever had a good chance, once the MiG pilot rolled and pulled extremely hard. He blanked out my view of the tailpipe, and I didn't have a tone on my next missile."

Stillinger rolled away and came back down, but the MiG turned and put "quite a bit of angle-off in that one turn." There was no way to get a better shot than what he had taken. Stillinger called Weigand: "I can't stay behind him. I'm going to unload and run. Do you have me in sight?" Perched to take over the fight, Weigand replied, "I am rolling in on the MiG."

Stillinger then maneuvered into a pure-pursuit attack, putting his nose on the MiG and lighting the afterburners as he came down:

> As I went by him, I went ahead and relaxed the G and rolled away a little bit, almost wings-level, passed 500 feet behind him, then rolled back and pulled so I was sure I could see him. This was where his slow rate of roll was pretty obvious. I went by and he lazily rolled around toward me. It took him so long to roll into tracking position that I think he was outside gun range because I never saw him fire at me.

Stillinger called Weigand in from overhead as he kept the MiG at four o'clock low to drag him out. The enemy pilot lit his afterburner and tried to close Stillinger's rear but did not enter a lead-pursuit track. Weigand remembered:

> I rolled up over the top of the MiG, then continued around in a left-hand roll, coming out below and behind him. I figured that he was preoccupied with Jim, and hadn't seen me. He pulled hard into Jim, then, just as I put my nose on him, he straightened up and pulled hard into me! I figured he had now seen me, and was going to come around and start fighting with me. But I pushed down, trying to get into his blind six, and he reversed back onto the flight lead, who was now directly in front of him. He hadn't seen me after all!
>
> When I had first rolled in on him I had a lot of excess airspeed, and started to overshoot. To correct, I went to idle and put the speed brakes out. As he reversed onto the lead, he lit his 'burner and got his speed up pretty good. I got the speed brakes in. He was fairly close to Jim, but his reverse had cost him position. We were down to 500 ft and Jim was pushing 600 knots and opening on him pretty fast. He

must have thought he had a chance at a gunshot though, and that's why he lit his 'burner and continued to jockey for position.

Seconds later, Stillinger called, "Okay, the MiG is now back at my right four o'clock. Shoot him, shoot him. We're holding him off." Weigand was directly behind the MiG and fired an AIM-9D. It went directly up the enemy's tailpipe and exploded. Several large pieces of the tail came off as the MiG flew straight ahead for a moment, then pitched over to crash and erupt in a fireball.

Moments after scoring the kill, Red Crown alerted them to more MiGs. Weigand recalled, "By this time the North Vietnamese Air Defense Controller had vectored four MiG-21s onto us. They were only about 15 miles away, and closing fast. We were low on fuel and couldn't afford another engagement, so we lit the 'burners and exited North Vietnam, supersonic at 1,200 feet, outdistancing them." Once they were safe, the two Phantoms rendezvoused with a KA-3B to take on fuel before returning to *Coral Sea*.

Weigand and Freckleton's kill was *Coral Sea*'s first victory since VF-151 had claimed a MiG-17 on October 6, 1965. It was the second kill for F-4B BuNo 153019, which as NH-110, flown by VF-213's Lieutenant Dave McRae with RIO Ensign Dave Nichols, had shot down an AN-2 on December 20, 1966. The fight had been a perfect demonstration of the "Loose Deuce" teamwork devised at Top Gun to out-fly and out-fight the MiG-17 by never engaging the enemy on his terms.

A week before the North Vietnamese offensive was scheduled to begin, the United States walked out of the Paris peace negotiations, citing "intransigence" by North Vietnam as its reason. Despite the continuing intelligence reports, the Pentagon was unconcerned that the two top US officials in South Vietnam were out of the country at the end of March.

The offensive commenced at 1200 hours local on March 30, 1972, when an intense artillery barrage opened up on the northernmost ARVN outposts in Quang Tri Province. The 30,000 troops of the 304th and 308th PAVN divisions, supported by more than 100 tanks, crossed the DMZ to attack I Corps, which covered the five northernmost provinces of South Vietnam. The North Vietnamese assaulted what the South Vietnamese military called "the ring of steel," the ARVN firebases just south of the DMZ, which were manned by the ARVN 3rd Division, which had been created in October 1971 to replace departing American troops. The PAVN 312th Division, supported by an armored regiment, crossed into the Central Highlands from Laos and moved along Route 9, past Khe Sanh, into the Quang Tri River Valley.

The 1st Division, which was considered the ARVN's best unit, lost its 2nd Regiment, while the 11th Armored Cavalry was brought up from the I Corps reserve to form the heart of the new division. Both these units were experienced, well trained and equipped and well led. Unfortunately, the other two regiments, the 56th and 57th, were manned by recaptured deserters, former prisoners, and regional and provincial forces that had never performed well. The leadership was composed of cast-off officers and NCOs from other units. There were few American advisors, since by then most served only at regimental, brigade and divisional headquarters. The division commander was newly promoted Brigadier General Vu Van Giai, former deputy commander of 1st Division.

The I Corps commander in overall charge of the defense was Lieutenant General Hoang Xuan Lam, an officer who was the epitome of the indecision and ineffectiveness of Saigon's upper military leadership. General Lam concentrated on administrative and ceremonial matters, leaving tactical decisions to his subordinate commanders.

Intelligence had failed to predict either the scale of the offensive or the attack method. The result was that the PAVN troops overcame ARVN troops who had expected something very different, giving the attackers the benefit of shock effect and a crucial psychological edge over the defenders. In response to the offensive, General Giai ordered the 3rd Division to withdraw on April 1 south of the Cua Viet River to allow the troops to reorganize. ARVN armored units were able to hold off a PAVN offensive that was reinforced by the 320B and 325C divisions briefly the next day, when the crucial Highway 1 bridge over the river at Dong Ha was blown up. As this fighting happened, the 324B Division moved out of the A Shau Valley, advancing on Fire Bases Bastogne and Checkmate which protected the city of Hue.

The offensive had been timed to make use of the seasonal monsoon that began over South Vietnam. The cloudy weather left 500-foot ceilings which negated VNAF or US air strikes. The advance troops were backed by antiaircraft units equipped with the new ZSU-57-2 self-propelled antiaircraft vehicle armed with two deadly 57mm guns, as well as the SA-7 Grail shoulder-fired antiaircraft missile, both of which were deadly against low-level bombing attacks.

On April 2, Colonel Pham Van Dinh, commander of the 56th ARVN Regiment, surrendered Camp Carroll, the artillery firebase halfway between the Laotian border and Quang Tri City on the coast, which was the linchpin of the northern and western defense line and the strongest obstacle to the attacking North Vietnamese, with barely a shot fired. Mai Loc, the last western fire base, was abandoned by the ARVN troops manning it that afternoon. The PAVN forces were now able to cross the Cam Lau bridge west of Dong Ha, giving them unrestricted access to western Quang Tri Province.

The US response to this offensive was initially limited, since there were only 27,000 US troops in South Vietnam, of whom only 10,000 were combat troops. Combat aircraft strength in Southeast Asia was less than half its peak strength in 1968–69. There were only three Air Force squadrons of F-4s and a single squadron of A-37s stationed in South Vietnam, with another 114 F-4 fighter-bombers at bases in Thailand. There were 83 B-52 bombers stationed at U-Tapao RTAFB, Thailand and Andersen AFB, Guam. Task Force 77 had four aircraft carriers assigned, but only two could be called on at any one time to conduct operations.

Operation *Linebacker*, which began in May, 1972, was intended to halt or slow transportation of supplies and materials for the PAVN invasion of South Vietnam. *Linebacker* was the first bombing campaign against North Vietnam since Operation *Rolling Thunder* was ended on November 1, 1968. However, the initial American response to the invasion was almost lackadaisical, with the most warlike response being the April 2 authorization of Navy ships to conduct gunfire support missions to South Vietnamese forces ashore when Dong Ha was threatened.

For the next three weeks, the PAVN advance was slowed by ARVN delaying actions, while the South Vietnamese defenders were able to launch several counterattacks. At dawn on April 27, the PAVN invaders advanced toward Dong Ha, which fell the next day, with other forces advancing to within a mile of Quang Tri City. While General Giai had planned a staged withdrawal from the city, the ARVN forces received conflicting orders from him and General Lam; they splintered, then collapsed into a retreat that left most of the province north of the capital to the enemy.

On April 29, General Giai ordered a general retreat to the My Chanh River, eight miles further south. As the retreat became a rout, US military advisors in Quang Tri were forced to call for emergency helicopter evacuation, with 132 survivors, including 80 US soldiers, evacuated from Quang Tri on May 1. The ARVN exodus was joined by tens of thousands of South Vietnamese civilians fleeing the fighting. The mass of refugees pushed and shoved its way south on Highway 1 and became a target for North Vietnamese artillery. PAVN infantry attacked the column from its flank, while leaderless ARVN units lost all unit cohesion.

Fire Support Bases Bastogne and Checkmate fell after staunch ARVN defense and despite B-52 bomber strikes that inflicted heavy casualties on the attackers. Quang Tri City fell on May 2. General Lam was relieved of command by South Vietnamese President Nguyen Van Thieu and replaced by Lieutenant General Ngo Quang Trung, IV Corps commander, who was ordered to defend Hue and retake captured territory. General Giai, who had conducted a reasonably good defense, was made the scapegoat for the collapse, tried for "desertion in the face of the enemy," and sentenced to five years in prison.

On April 5, the South Vietnamese were rocked by the start of a second offensive in the III Corps region, north of Saigon, with the PAVN forces advancing out of Cambodia into Binh Long Province, northeast of Saigon, ordered to take the towns and airfields at Loc Ninh, Quan Li, and An Loc, which because of its close proximity to Saigon was to be proclaimed the capital of the Provisional Revolutionary Government. An Loc was surrounded and endured a combined artillery, armored, and infantry attack on April 13. Despite a defense organized by US advisors led by senior advisor Colonel William Miller, the attacks persisted and PAVN troops eventually entered the town, seizing the airfield and pushing the ARVN into a perimeter of about a third of a square mile. On April 21, PAVN tanks forced their way through the perimeter but were held off and destroyed by antitank weapons and helicopter gunships. PAVN infantry dug in. The ARVN troops soon realized that the PAVN infantry did not advance with the armor, making the tanks prey for their antitank weapons. PAVN infantry would move forward without armored support. The failure of PAVN tactical coordination was the result of this equipment and training being recent.

The lack of coordination made it difficult to defend against the rain of bombs and rockets from incessant ARVN and US air strikes, which killed many of the enemy and made resupply difficult. The battle became a siege, with An Loc completely surrounded. The defenders could only be resupplied by air, which was difficult due to the loss of the airfield. However, 448 missions delivered 2,693 tons of air-dropped food, medical supplies, and ammunition. *Paris Match* called the battle "a Verdun or a Stalingrad" in the III Corps region.

Following the attack in the south, the third phase of the Nguyen Hue Offensive in the Central Highlands area that was the responsibility of II Corps aimed to seize the cities of Kon Tum and Pleiku, which would open the possibility of advancing east to the coast and splitting South Vietnam in two. North Vietnamese forces, commanded by Lieutenant General Hoang Minh Thao, included 50,000 troops of the 320th and 2nd PAVN divisions in the Central Highlands and the 3rd PAVN Division in the coastal lowlands. The invaders were opposed by the ARVN 22nd and 23rd Divisions, two armored cavalry squadrons, and the 2nd Airborne Brigade, all commanded by II Corps commander Lieutenant General Ngo Du. The North Vietnamese presence had become known in January and several B-52 strikes had been flown in hopes of slowing the enemy. The ARVN units were deployed forward toward the border to slow the PAVN advance. An offensive by NLF forces in Binh Dinh panicked General Du and almost convinced him to fall for the enemy deception and divert his forces from the highlands.

Eventually, John Paul Vann, the civilian director of the US Second Regional Assistance Group, who had first arrived in Vietnam as an Army military advisor in 1963, reassured Du that the Binh Dinh attack was only a ruse and persuaded him to remain ready for the main blow, which Vann was convinced would come from western Laos. Though officially a civilian, Vann had been granted the unique authority to command all US military advisors within his region. Vann's leadership would save the day in the Central Highlands as he worked day and night, using his extensive civilian and military contacts, to channel US support – particularly air support – to the region.

On April 12, the 2nd PAVN Division, elements of the 203rd Tank Regiment, and several independent regiments attacked the outpost at Tan Canh and the nearby base at Dak To. The ARVN armor moved out toward Dak To but was ambushed and destroyed. The defense

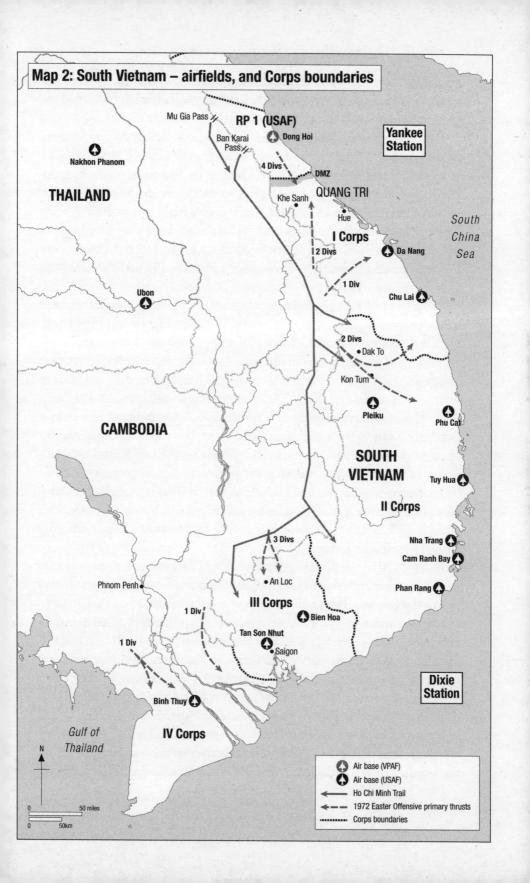

Map 2: South Vietnam – airfields, and Corps boundaries

Mu Gia Pass

RP 1 (USAF)

Nakhon Phanom

THAILAND

Ban Karai Pass

Dong Hoi

Yankee Station

4 Divs

DMZ

Khe Sanh

QUANG TRI

Hue

I Corps

South China Sea

2 Divs

Da Nang

1 Div

Chu Lai

Ubon

2 Divs

Dak To

Kon Tum

Phu Cat

Pleiku

CAMBODIA

SOUTH VIETNAM

Tuy Hua

II Corps

3 Divs

Nha Trang

Phnom Penh

An Loc

Cam Ranh Bay

1 Div

III Corps

Bien Hoa

Phan Rang

1 Div

Tan Son Nhut

Saigon

Binh Thuy

Gulf of Thailand

IV Corps

Dixie Station

N

0   50 miles

0   50km

Air base (VPAF)

Air base (USAF)

Ho Chi Minh Trail

1972 Easter Offensive primary thrusts

Corps boundaries

northwest of Kon Tum quickly disintegrated. While the rest of the 22nd Division covered the coast there were few forces left to defend the provincial capital of Kon Tum.

The North Vietnamese southern advance inexplicably halted for three crucial weeks, while the northern crisis waned as ARVN forces were reorganized and held in southern Quang Tri Province. With General Du increasingly unable to make decisions, Vann dropped all pretext of South Vietnamese command, took over and issued orders. Placing Colonel Ly Tong Ba, commander of the 23rd Division, in charge of the defense of Kon Tum, Vann used B-52 strikes to hold the North Vietnamese and reduce their numbers while finding additional troops to stabilize the situation.

President Nixon's first thought when informed of the offensive was to consider ordering a three-day attack by B-52s on Hanoi and Haiphong. National Security Advisor Henry Kissinger, who was alarmed that such an act would jeopardize formalization of the Strategic Arms Limitation Treaty (SALT I) when the president visited Moscow in May, convinced Nixon to reconsider. However, the president announced privately, "These bastards have never been bombed like they're going to be bombed this time." On April 4, he authorized B-52 bombing missions against the enemy in South Vietnam and bombing North Vietnam south of the 18th parallel. Considering the Joint Chiefs' initial response to be lacking proper strength, the president determined that only a massive escalation of force could prevent a total collapse in South Vietnam with a resulting loss of US prestige just before the coming summit meeting with Soviet leader Leonid Brezhnev.

Both USAF and VNAF units had flown support missions, weather permitting, since the offensive began, supported by the carriers *Coral Sea* and *Hancock*. However, the growing monsoonal weather pattern over the south limited such air support. *Kitty Hawk* had returned in February on her seventh Vietnam deployment with CVW-11 aboard. Having completed her first Dixie Station line duty in late March, she was recalled early from Subic Bay on April 3 in response to the North Vietnamese attack. On April 4, an RA-5C of RVAH-6 was launched on a Blue Tree mission to Quang Lang airfield in North Vietnam. The "Vigi" was covered by A-7E Corsair IIs of VA-192 and VA-195, and escorted by Phantoms of VF-114. Once the North Vietnamese opened up on the Vigilante with antiaircraft fire, the covering squadrons immediately responded with a "protective reaction strike" that hit several AAA sites, including what was officially described as the "incidental destruction" of two MiG-21s that were on the airfield at the time.

Following the president's decision to escalate the US response, forces were alerted on April 6 and units began moving toward Southeast Asia. *Constellation* was ordered to immediately join *Coral Sea*, *Hancock*, and *Kittyhawk* to put four carriers on station; *America* would soon arrive in Southeast Asia from the Atlantic Fleet and *Saratoga* was ordered to change her deployment from the Mediterranean to Southeast Asia. On the US west coast, *Midway* and *Oriskany* were ordered to speed their deployment preparations. By June, the Seventh Fleet would grow from 84 to 138 ships.

The Soviets and Chinese both publicly denounced the American response, but neither was willing to jeopardize the thawing relationship with the United States and the possibility of stepping back from the continuing Cold War nuclear confrontation. Thus, requests for additional support and aid from its socialist allies by North Vietnam met with cool responses. The leadership in Hanoi realized they were now on their own, facing the final act of direct American military involvement in the wars of Southeast Asia that would commence in May.

Following President Nixon's decision in favor of US intervention to militarily support South Vietnam against the Easter Offensive and his April 4 authorization for aerial attack against the North Vietnamese transportation system south of the 20th parallel, Task Force 77 launched 680 sorties in the ten days following, a tenfold increase over the previous three months. A persistent thick monsoonal overcast over northern South Vietnam during the first half of April severely limited aerial attacks on enemy troops. Operation *Freedom Train* began with a series of attacks on April 6 in which Navy pilots flew 106 sorties against targets in Quang Binh Province. On April 10, Air Force B-52s attacked Vinh, following up with a major bombing mission against Thanh Hoa on April 13. Surface units of Task Force 77 shelled Haiphong Harbor on April 16.

Navy ships operating off the coast of North Vietnam became actively engaged in the air war as combat operations heated up in the spring of 1972.

Just before 0400 hours on the morning of April 15, USS *Worden* (DLG-18) was operating as Red Crown and pulling North SAR duties about eight miles off the first sea buoy outside Haiphong. A nine-year-old frigate of the Leahy class, she was armed with RIM-2 Terrier SAMs fore and aft and two twin 3"/50 gun mounts as well as an eight-round anti-submarine rocket (ASROC) box forward of the bridge. At 0347 hours, Lieutenant (jg) Guy Thomas had just reported to the bridge as JOOD (Junior Officer of the Deck) of the 0400–0800-hours watch when the ship was hit by two missiles; one struck the AN/SPS-48 air search radar, the other hit above the bridge. Thomas later recalled, "There were four officers standing in the front of the bridge starting turnover of the watch. We heard it coming, and then BOOM! The first one hit the SPS-48, then a second hit – BOOM! – a flash and shrapnel ran through the bridge." Thomas was knocked down and hit by shrapnel in his thumb.

The bridge personnel assumed they had been hit by the North Vietnamese. The OOD (Officer of the Deck) called General Quarters and ordered the helmsman to turn out to sea at flank speed. The ship's CO, Captain George Shick, was in CIC at the time of the hit and immediately came onto the bridge and took control. In the initial confused moments as *Worden* ran to the southeast, the aft gun mount opened fire on what was believed to be a surface contact while warnings came from the CIC of signals by "Pot Head" surface search radars used on small missile boats and "Snoop Plate" submarine search radars. It quickly became obvious that *Worden* was seaworthy and her engineering plant were uncompromised, but all active sensors were dead, including the SPS-48 (3D air search), SPS-29 (2D air search), and SPS-10 (surface search) radars and three of the four SPG-55 guidance radars required to operate the SAMs. The ASROC box was also punctured by multiple fragments although the eight weapons themselves seemed undamaged. Boatswain's Mate 1st Class (BM1) Stirling, the Boatswain of the Watch, who had been standing on the bridge wing, was killed when shrapnel took off part of his head. Of the 14 men on the bridge at the time of impact; nine were wounded, including the helmsman, who lost part of his hand. Several were quickly transferred by helicopter to USS *Tripoli* (LPH-10) for medical attention.

Worden was able to steam to Subic Bay under her own power and was repaired over ten days, after which she returned to the Tonkin Gulf and resumed combat operations. At Subic, investigation of fragments from the missile warheads quickly revealed they came from two AGM-45

Shrike ARMs. It was quickly determined that no Navy aircraft had fired any missiles that night. It was eventually determined that the missiles had been fired by an Air Force F-105G Wild Weasel that had mistaken their SPS-48 for a North Vietnamese Fan Song SAM radar, despite their location off the coast in the Tonkin Gulf.

The possibility of an enemy aerial attack on Navy ships off the coast of North Vietnam became a reality four days after *Worden*'s "friendly fire" incident, on April 19, 1972. USS *Higbee* (DD-806) was five miles off the coast near Dong Hoi, with USS *Lloyd Thomas* (DD 764), USS *Sterett* (DLG-31), and the Commander of the Seventh Fleet (Com7thFlt) flagship USS *Oklahoma City* (CLG-5), participating in an Operation *Sea Dragon* fire mission against transportation targets on Highway One ashore, when radar picked up two bogeys coming out of the mountains and flying low over the gulf waters. *Higbee*'s crew didn't know it, but they were about to become the first US Navy ship bombed by an enemy air force since 1945 when she was attacked by a special force that the VPAF had organized the year before to engage in shipping strikes. When plans were initiated for the 1972 offensive, North Vietnamese leaders realized that the Seventh Fleet would likely re-activate *Sea Dragon*, in which surface ships had shelled the North Vietnamese coast throughout the years of *Rolling Thunder*, and the VPAF was directed to create a strike force that could oppose these operations.

Ten pilots of the MiG-17-equipped 923rd Fighter Regiment had been picked and trained in anti-shipping maneuvers by a military advisor known as "Ernesto" from the Cuban Air Force who was a specialist in anti-shipping attack, trained for such a role to oppose an invasion of the island nation by the United States after the failure of the Bay of Pigs invasion. The special force was led by MiG-17 pilot and ace Nguyen Van Bay. By March 1972, six pilots were considered capable of flying maritime attack missions. A special hidden airfield had been constructed by the 28th Technical Brigade at Gat, in Quang Binh Province, carefully camouflaged to escape detection by US photo recon flights. Several MiG-17s were modified to carry a 250-kilogram (550-pound) bomb under each wing on the mount for the underwing drop tanks the fighters normally carried. The 403rd Radar Unit moved into position near the Dinh River opposite the port of Nhat Le, where it kept track of US warships operating off the coast.

The day before the planned attack, VPAF pilots Le Hong Diep and Tu De took off from Kep airfield to deliver two of the special attack aircraft, flying to Gia Lam and then Vinh before delivering them to the secret airfield at Gat, to throw off US radar tracking them. Tu De later remembered, "We flew just above the ground after taking off from Vinh, to stay below the enemy radar." That night, the 403rd Radar Unit picked up four US ships off the coast of Quang Binh Province as they took up station five to seven miles to sea from the villages of Quang Xa and Ly Nhan Nam.

Nguyen Van Bay later recalled the attack:

Le Xuan Di, and I were preparing for the attack. At 0930 hours, the 403rd radar unit reported four ships 40 kilometers [25 miles] from Le Thuy and 120 kilometers [75 miles] from Dinh, and three ships 80 kilometers [50 miles] from the Sot river. However, due to the foggy weather, we could not take off. At noon the radar unit reported the ships had moved to the south and only two remained in position. By 1500 hours the first group of four ships was 15 kilometers [nine-and-a-half miles] from Ly Hoa and the second two-ship formation was seven kilometers [two-and-a-half miles] from Quang Trach, while three more warships were 18 kilometers [11 miles] from Ly Hoa. At 1600 hours, a new group of ships was spotted 16 kilometers [nearly four miles] from Nhat Le.

At 1605 hrs we received our orders to take off. When we were over Ly Hoa, we saw the ships and noted puffs of smoke, that they were firing on the shore. We received the order to attack.

Le Xuan Di turned left toward the fleet, overflying the other ships as he took aim at *Higbee* and increased his speed. The destroyer had just experienced a "hot round" in one of the two 5-inch guns in her aft mount, and the crew had evacuated onto the fantail when the MiG-17 flew low overhead and dropped two bombs on the ship, then broke to the left. Both his bombs hit the destroyer:

While Le Xuan Di was attacking his target I flew on, and upon reaching the Dinh river I spotted two ships to the northeast. I was too close, and did not have time for a proper attack, so I overshot them. I had to return for a second pass. Le Xuan Di asked me on the radio: "All right?" I answered "Not really," since I thought I had missed my target. After returning to base at 1622 hrs, I was told that a 30 meter [99-foot]-high column of smoke was seen out at sea, and later something burst into flames.

The attackers were over the task force only 17 minutes, with Le Xuan Di badly damaging *Higbee*'s superstructure and completely destroying the aft 5-inch mount, while wounding four crewmen with his two bombs. Nguyen Van Bay's critical view of his performance was borne out by the fact that *Oklahoma City* sustained only minor damage. *Sterett* claimed to have achieved a radar lock on Bay's MiG, shooting him down with two Terrier missiles, but Bay successfully returned to Gat airfield. The task force also reported exchanging fire with two North Vietnamese torpedo boats, but the North Vietnamese later stated that none of their ships had participated in the action.

Dong Hoi and Vinh airfield were attacked in retaliation the next day. Several days later, the secret airfield at Gat was discovered and attacked by a 30-aircraft Alpha strike. *Higbee* managed to steam under her own power to Da Nang despite having a damaged rudder, where she tied up alongside the repair ship USS *Hector* (AR-7). AP war correspondent Don Davis, who had just come off an assignment aboard USS *Buchanan* (DDG-14) which was also tied up to *Hector*, went aboard *Higbee* and later remembered that the ship's fantail "looked like a junkyard floating in a pool of dirty oil." The photo Davis took of the damage would play widely in US newspapers. He also recalled that the local naval authorities weren't happy there was a reporter present. Interestingly, the official history of USS *Higbee* in the Dictionary of American Naval Fighting Ships (DANFS) contained a short paragraph recounting the event as late as 2017, but as of 2019, all mention of the event has been removed from the DANFS record and the Naval History and Heritage Command record for the ship. When queried, NHHC stated there was no "official record" of such an event. The attack is recorded in detail in *Aerial Battles in the Skies of Vietnam*, the official history of the VPAF.

May 6 saw aerial activity heat up in a preview of what would come on May 10. VF-111's sister squadron, VF-51, finally got the opportunity to test their F-4s against MiGs. Lieutenant Commander Jerry "Devil" Houston recalled how enthusiastic the squadron had been when they were informed they would receive F-4s in place of their well-worn F-8s:

> What we didn't know was that our F-4s would be coming from Marine Corps rejects. The jets we were assigned had been preserved in whatever state they had been in a couple of years earlier when the Corps had declared them unairworthy. Maintenance Tiger Teams from all the F-4 squadrons at Miramar were assigned the job of going to MCAS El Toro and performing overdue scheduled maintenance, and getting those hulks capable of flying to Miramar. [Squadron Maintenance Officer] Chuck Schroeder succeeded in the Herculean undertaking of getting those over-the-hill rustbuckets ready for deployment, despite competing against my backbreaking training schedule.

Houston and RIO Lieutenant Kevin Moore, with maintenance officer Schroeder and RIO Lieutenant Rick Webb as their wing, were TARCAP for an Alpha strike that day against the VPAF's Bai Thuong airfield. Minutes after going "feet dry," Red Crown warned of MiGs in the air and the A-6 Intruder crews began calling MiG sightings. Houston soon spotted a camouflaged MiG-17 attacking three A-6s. As Houston came up behind the MiG, wingman Shroeder came under attack from a second MiG. RIO Moore attempted to warn Shroeder, but the old Phantoms had radio problems and Shroeder never heard Moore's repeated calls. Houston's MiG was in a high-speed chase of CAG Roger "Blinky" Sheets, who had interposed his A-6 between the MiG and the other two Intruders to drag it away.

Houston later recalled that the MiG was going so fast that the pilot couldn't have maneuvered out of the way since the control forces were so strong "He'd have bent the control stick first."

> We were behind the MiG for a long time with good tone and we couldn't, or wouldn't, shoot because he was directly behind the A-6. Although we had our pipper on the MiG and were getting good tone, we couldn't be sure that the tone wasn't being produced by the A-6 as well, and we couldn't get the bomber pilot to break. Here was the opportunity we had waited all our lives for and it was going to worms because the A-6 wouldn't break! The Marines had modified their radios to transmit the Sidewinder growl over the UHF radio

when the transmit button was pressed. That effectively put us without communications during the most important couple of minutes in my airborne career. I didn't know that Sheets couldn't hear my frantic calls to "Break and get the hell out of there." All he heard was the transmitted Sidewinder tone.

Finally, when the MiG was at minimum Sidewinder range, Houston fired:

The 'winder came off and went straight down, then straight up! And as we flew through the hump-backed smoke trail of the Sidewinder, it straightened out and headed for the MiG. Sheets saw the missile come off the rail and broke, having played the role of ultimate decoy to the end! The MiG couldn't break, and the Sidewinder flew up his tailpipe, blowing his tail off. We were so low that the explosion of the missile was followed immediately – just bam! bam! – by the explosion the MiG made as it impacted the karst ridge.

Coral Sea's strike against the Bai Thuong airfield was so successful that *Kitty Hawk* canceled cyclic operations and quickly organized an Alpha strike for a follow-up bombing. Recent Top Gun graduate Lieutenant Commander Pete "Viper" Pettigrew's VF-114 "Aardvarks" F-4 was prepared so quickly that the Phantom was launched with only two Sparrows and two Sidewinders, half the normal load.

Pettigrew and RIO Lieutenant (jg) Michael J. McCabe were assigned as one of two BARCAP Phantoms, while Lieutenant Robert G. Hughes and RIO Lieutenant (jg) Adolph J. Cruz were flying MiGCAP with squadron XO Commander John Pitson. At post-launch rendezvous, Pitson discovered his F-4 had radar failure, so Pettigrew and McCabe took lead of the MiGCAP section. Soon after crossing the beach, the strike received a warning from Red Crown of enemy air activity. They soon discovered they were being vectored onto their own strike formation. When GCI "ace" Chief Nowell came on the net, Pettigrew recalled breathing a sigh of relief. Nowell gave them a new vector to a bogey 30 miles distant. McCabe quickly obtained a lock on the target. He then lost the target, but Hughes acquired it at 15 miles. McCabe re-spotted the bogey when it was 12 miles distant and it was soon revealed as four MiG-21s in a finger-four "welded wing" formation. The Phantoms were at 7,000 feet and the enemy fighters at 4,000 feet; they gave no indication they had spotted the approaching American jets.

Pettigrew recalled:

We had visually acquired all four enemy jets, and from the time we first spotted them, we never lost sight of any of them throughout the engagement. It was now about 1830 hours, and we were low, looking into the sun to see them. When the sun goes down and you're looking into a haze, sometimes an airplane will show up very well at long range because it's much darker than any of the surrounding haze. This is how they appeared – very, very dark shapes, which stood out very well.

Pettigrew and Hughes then turned into the two second-section MiGs. Pettigrew described the initial attack:

They didn't have much airspeed, so we immediately had about 90 degrees off on them. You might almost call it a hat stern conversion – quite a bit hotter than you would want to run. However, they didn't seem to be turning very hard. In fact, the first section continued back to almost our "7–8 o'clock" before they really started turning, which gave them so much distance behind us that they never got back into the fight again.

Hughes was in the better position to take them and Pettigrew handed off to him. Hughes picked the number four MiG. Pulling in behind he fired a Sidewinder that ripped off part of the enemy jet's tail. "It didn't appear to me that he ever saw me, or knew that I was coming."

Only a few degrees out of position to attack the next MiG, Hughes closed rapidly to a range of 6,000 feet:

I was looking right up his tailpipe from a distance of about a mile. I got a tone and pulled the trigger. However, by the time the Sidewinder came off the rail after pulling the trigger I'd lost the tone. I tried it again, got another tone, pulled it again, and the same thing happened once more! I was really pissed by this time. I had wasted two good 'Winders, and I didn't know if it was my fault or if the guy was really warping my cone.

The first had missed to the right, while the second went ballistic. Obtaining another good tone, Hughes fired his last AIM-9 and watched as it exploded, shredding pieces off the MiG's tail. He saw another missile fly up the MiG-21's tailpipe, blowing the fighter to pieces.

When Pettigrew saw Hughes' two missiles fail:

I got back on the inside of the turn a little bit aft of Hughes at a height of 800 feet. We were both within ten degrees of the MiG's tail, and I looked up and pulled my nose up onto the MiG. By this time, he was at a height of about 4000 ft, and I got a tone and went to arm. I was pulling to the inside of the turn, and just as I was about to fire, I saw another missile come off Hughes's F-4. I think I fired about the same time that his missile came off the rail. We had about a one-second difference in the missiles.

Hughes's missile hit first, knocking pieces off the stabilator, and about a second later mine hit and the MiG disintegrated. There wasn't anything left of it. As I flew some 200 feet wide of the point of impact, the pilot's 'chute opened just off my left wing – we almost ran into him.

The entire engagement had lasted for little more than a minute. The lead section of MiGs turned around and was two miles behind but unable to close. Warned by Red Crown, Pettigrew and Hughes headed for the water, where they picked up a tanker then returned to the carrier.

In reviewing the incident, Pete Pettigrew later commented to the Project Red Baron interviewers:

We were talking the whole time. It's not very difficult after you've done it so many times before. I thought I'd seen this type of fight fought before against A-4s. A lot of things become instinctive. Hughes and I had never flown together before, yet we had no problem at all communicating. I think we knew exactly what each of us was thinking, or all four people knew exactly what the others were thinking the whole time. I think it was primarily because of the training.

Bob Hughes remembered:

> There was no question about the fact that Pettigrew was on my wing the whole time. He crossed a couple of times to keep inside of the turn or abeam of me, and called out his position, so I knew exactly where he was the whole time we were going in. That was really nice knowing you have the support to go ahead and attack with somebody there to watch out for you.

According to the Project Red Baron report, Pettigrew and Hughes "demonstrated a high degree of mutual support and co-ordination during this engagement. They were able to take advantage of the element of surprise, achieve two quick kills, and separate from the area without being seriously threatened by any of the MiGs. Good radio procedures enabled them to effectively press home their attack."

14

OPERATION *LINEBACKER*, 1972

Operation *Linebacker* began on May 10, which was later called "the war's longest day." Alternating attacks by Air Force units flying from Thailand and South Vietnam, and Navy units from the four aircraft carriers at Yankee Station resulted in the largest series of air battles of the entire war. An indication of the intensity comes from VPAF claims to have shot down seven F-4s with the Air Force and Navy admitting to the loss of five. In return, naval aviators claimed two MiG-21s and seven MiG-17s, including the only triple victory in one mission by Lieutenants Randy Cunningham and RIO Willie Driscoll of VF-96, as a result of which they became the only US Navy aces of the Vietnam War. *Constellation*'s VF-92 and VF-96 were responsible for seven of the nine MiG kills claimed by the Navy that day.

May 10 began for the Navy with a first Alpha strike that morning from *Constellation*, with Kien An airfield near Haiphong the target. TARCAP was flown by a VF-92 section composed of Top Gun graduate Lieutenant Curt "Dozo" Dosé and RIO Lieutenant Commander James "Routeslip" McDevitt, flying wing on Lieutenants Austin "Hawk" Hawkins and RIO Charles J. Tinker. Each was armed with four AIM-7E-2 "dogfight" Sparrows and four AIM-9G "dogfight" Sidewinders. Neither Dosé nor McDevitt knew that Hawkins planned to divert to nearby Kep airfield, where the VPAF based a large force of MiGs, following completion of the TARCAP support for Air Wing 9's strike. The air wing's tour had been extended to deal with the Easter Offensive, and Hawkins had yet to run across any MiGs. The plan to "troll" the enemy airfield in hopes of drawing up some opponents was unauthorized and such attempts to provoke enemy action were strictly forbidden. He had only informed his RIO, Tinker, of his intentions and had made Tinker promise not to tell anyone.

The Alpha strike included four other VF-92 Phantoms for flak suppression and two Iron Hand A-7Es from VA-146, with the strike force composed of nine VA-146 A-7Es and five VA-165 A-6As, followed by five EKA-3B Skywarriors providing ECM and tanker support.

The CAP crews heard many MiG calls on Guard as they flew toward the target, but neither crew could establish a radar contact or spot any enemy fighters. As the strike force departed, Red Crown advised, "Bandits, northeast at 35 nautical miles." The two F-4Js turned northeast and made a radar search; no contact was established with the reported bandits.

Hawkins and Dosé then headed toward Kep airfield, flying at 6,000 feet and 600 knots. Spotting the field eight miles distant, they turned north and Dosé took position in combat-spread on Hawkins' left. As they got closer, both pilots spotted two MiG-19s in revetments at the near end of the runway, with two MiG-21s holding short of the runway before takeoff at the other end. Suddenly, McDevitt called out, "MiGs rolling!" when he spotted the two other MiG-21s that were already on the runway as they accelerated for takeoff. Dosé later recalled:

> Sure enough, there were two MiG-21s on a section take-off, about a third of the way down the runway, accelerating towards us fast. I called for the tactical lead and said, "Come port and down." Hawkins called for afterburner, which I think I had already done, or did simultaneously, and we came slicing down in an in-place turn back along the runway at about 1,000 feet. We were straddling the runway, with me on the right and Hawkins on the left. By this time the MiGs were airborne. They were two miles off the end of the runway when we first started coming down, and I could see they were in afterburner and were climbing pretty much straight ahead.

As the two Phantoms closed, the MiG-21s jettisoned their centerline tanks and pulled left in a gentle climbing turn while both tanks hit the ground and exploded. Both enemy fighters were at about 100 feet when

Hawkins called, "You take the one on the right, and I'll take the one on the left."

Dosé closed on the right-hand fighter:

I had a tone before I even looked. I did check the null while I was still closing to make sure that I had the Sidewinder on him. There was no doubt about it. It was a beautiful tone, and we squeezed off the first Sidewinder and watched it. The missile guided very nicely, but it seemed like it took forever to come off, and it took forever to get there. It finally detonated immediately behind the MiG. I thought I had him, but he kept flying, so I immediately fired a second Sidewinder. The two were in a sort of "loose cruise" or "fighting-wing" formation, not more than 100 ft apart. I fired the second Sidewinder at exactly the same track-crossing angle as the first one. The second Sidewinder went down to their altitude, appeared to level off, and then disappeared up the MiG's tailpipe. Nothing happened for a couple of seconds and then the whole thing burst into a huge 100-foot wide ball of flame. The MiG came tumbling out of the forward edge of that ball of flame, nose over tail twice, then went into the ground with no ejection.

Dosé immediately pulled his nose into the lead MiG on the left and fired his third Sidewinder. It guided to the MiG and detonated about 10 feet to the rear. At almost exactly the same moment, Hawkins fired two AIM-9s at the same target, with both exploding just aft of and below the MiG. Hawkins fired a third Sidewinder just as the MiG broke into it in a 90-degree bank. The last Sidewinder passed about 15 feet behind the enemy fighter's tailpipe and exploded when it hit the ground.

Hawkins pulled as hard as he could to stay with the MiG but couldn't make the turn. He pulled back on the stick, shoved in the rudder, and made a high-G roll up and around his opponent, certain the MiG would either crash or level his wings, allowing Hawkins to fire his fourth Sidewinder. The MiG and the two pursuers circled Kep airfield during the entire engagement. Dosé saw the sky full of flak bursts behind them and a third MiG-21 diving at Hawkins' "five o'clock." He called "Bug out," but Hawkins didn't want to disengage, telling Dosé, "No, I can get this guy." The third MiG closed so fast, he passed right behind

Hawkins. Reaching the southern end of the airfield, he disengaged vertically, then rolled over just as the MiG he'd pursued launched an Atoll that went ballistic and missed.

Hawkins headed for the beach in full afterburner, 50 feet above the karst, followed by Dosé. They continued to jink as they looked for the third MiG to their rear. During these evasive maneuvers, they became separated and each exited North Vietnam alone, with Hawkins going south of Haiphong, while Dosé flew out to sea north of the port. Rejoining when they hit the tanker, they returned to *Constellation*. Dosé later recalled, "If not a noble departure, it was at least a successful one at near Mach below 50 feet, with MiG-21s behind us firing Atoll missiles."

Back on the carrier, Hawkins was in trouble for his unauthorized trip over Kep, despite Dosé's victory. Tinker recalled:

Once we got back to the boat, everyone was excited about Curt's MiG kill, but Hawk was in deep shit for leaving the strike to go trolling. The elephants were still deciding our fate when we manned up for the strike on Hai Duong. We were punished by tying us to an Iron Hand A-7 as escort. Hawk was told, "If you don't come back with him, don't come back at all!"

Speaking to the Red Baron interviewers afterwards, Hawkins noted:

The thing that I think could be learned from the engagement itself is that with the missile, lookdown is the same as angle-off as far as tracking is concerned. It's something that's got to be remembered. I think something that's not stressed enough is the fact that a simple six o'clock shot is not good enough – you've got to know all the parameters. If you've got 200–300 knots overtake, pressing to three-quarters of a mile or one mile, you're pushing it. The missile was guiding on the plume itself, plus the fact that it was a look-down shot as it went past the tailpipe, and the missile detonated directly below the aircraft. I saw both of mine blow up the same way. If I had it to do over again, knowing what happened to my Sidewinders, I'd make sure that I was at the same altitude as the MiGs before I'd shoot. I wouldn't shoot with any look-down. In this particular engagement a gun would have made all the difference due to the close range. It would have been no trouble at all to have achieved a smooth gun-tracking position, as he was in a position where there was nothing he could do but turn. It seems that there have been so few times that I've launched on a hop where I ended up with eight missiles that I could use. You're always wondering, "When is that damned missile going to detune on me?"

Dosé commented:

The one big mistake I made was, as soon as we got out of there, and we knew that there were MiGs behind us, we should have jettisoned our tanks, and we never did. I never thought about it. I have no doubt in the world, especially with the unimaginative defensive tactics that the MiG was using, that if I'd had an M-61 cannon, I could have hosed him right out of the sky.

Dosé's most interesting comments related to his Top Gun experience, and its influence on his combat. "During the whole engagement I felt that I had been there before. We've done so much training in this environment that you look at an airplane with a certain closure, and a certain airspeed, and say 'Let's come this way,' because that's the way you have done it before, and you know that it works."

While Hawkins was explaining himself to his squadron commander, *Constellation* launched her second Alpha strike of the day, which would end up part of the biggest air battle to happen in the Vietnam War as more MiGs rose to oppose the attackers than any mission before or after. The 70-plane strike included groups from three carriers, with their targets being the railways siding of the Haiphong–Hanoi railroad, and the Hai Duong and Cam Pha rail bridges.

The two TARCAP sections launched by VF-92's sister squadron VF-96 "Fighting Falcons" included Lieutenants Michael J. "Matt" Connelly and RIO Thomas J. J. Blonski. The TARCAP F-4Js were each armed with four AIM-7E-2 Sparrows and four AIM-9G Sidewinders. Lieutenants Randy Cunningham and Willie Driscoll, victors against MiGs in January's "protective reaction strike" and an escort mission two days before this, were escort for an Iron Hand A-7E flown by VA-147's Lieutenant Norman Birzer, with Lieutenants Brian "Bulldog" Grant and RIO Jerry Sullivan on their wing, while a second escort section was led by former Blue Angel Lieutenant Steven Shoemaker and RIO Lieutenant (jg) Keith V. Crenshaw. MiGCAP was flown by VF-92 XO Commander Harry L. Blackburn with RIO Lieutenant Stephen Rudloff and VF-96 XO Commander Dwight Timm with RIO Lieutenant Jim Fox.

The TARCAP went "feet dry" south of Haiphong and turned north up the Red River to the targets. Connelly and Blonski's section was to the left of the strike force with the other TARCAP section to the right. As the strike group turned to the target, Air Group 9 CAG Commander Lowell "Gus" Eggert called "Play ball! Play ball!," the radio code to prepare for battle. Each TARCAP section passed the other in combat spread as they made a level cross-turn. Connelly and his wingman headed south to set up a barrier against MiGs coming from Bai Thuong.

Connelly heard an A-7 pilot scream that there were MiGs on his tail, so excited he failed to provide his position. Connelly replied, "Where are you?" When he looked down, he saw the A-7 flown by Birzer at his three o'clock low, three miles distant with two MiG-17s right behind. Connelly called "Tally-ho" and made a 6G turn to engage. When he did, Blonski yelled "We just lost the damned radar! We've got a black scope!" As Connelly desperately tried to keep visual contact with the enemy fighters, he lost his wingman, remaining alone for the rest of the engagement. The MiG wingman spotted Connelly when he rolled in and broke right.

Connelly slid into position 8,000 feet behind the lead MiG and 30 degrees angle-off just as Birzer started to roll wings-level with the "Red Bandit" close behind. Connelly, worried a Sidewinder might track on the A-7, fired nevertheless to get the MiG off Birzer's tail. The missile had a good tone, but didn't guide. Spotting it, the enemy pilot used the MiG-17's turning ability to break hard enough to nearly meet Connelly head-on. Breaking back into the MiG, Connelly found himself at the bottom of a big dogfight with enemy jets "all over the place."

He later explained the fight to the Red Baron interviewers:

To come back and try to reconstruct what followed after that on a blackboard is impossible. I don't even know if the first MiG I shot down was the same guy that I initially shot at. I don't think it was, but everything was so confusing, and there were so damned many of them! They were all over the place! If you were chasing one, and looked over and saw another one that was less angle-off, and you had less degrees to pull to get at his six, you just went after him. The whole thing transpired at about 7,000 feet. I had enough energy to maintain the bottom of the fight, and control it pretty well. I didn't want to go up with the other F-4s because I could pick the MiGs up easily. They were always about 1,000 ft above me when I picked them up, and I had plenty of altitude over the ground, so I wasn't worrying about it that much.

Turning back into the lead MiG and finding a sky full of 20-plus MiGs, Connelly spotted a third MiG-17 that was turning right at about 300 knots, which had apparently not seen him. Realizing he was closing too fast, Connelly pulled power to idle and popped his speed brakes. As the enemy fighter ahead started to roll wings-level, he brought the speed brakes back in. A moment later he had a good tone and fired an AIM-9 that went straight up the MiG's tailpipe, and it exploded in a fireball. Back on *Constellation*, he found the Sidewinder's exhaust had burned a hole in his left speed brake.

Quickly spotting a fourth MiG-17 in a right turn, Connelly executed an attack similar to his first, but as he drifted toward its six o'clock, the MiG reversed left, which put Connelly on the inside of its turn. Apparently not having seen the approaching F-4, it rolled out wings-level. "I had a really good tone and I took my time because I only had three Sidewinders. I'd wasted the first, the second one worked, and I really wanted to make the third one work, too." When he was 4,000–5,000 feet behind the enemy fighter, Connelly fired his last Sidewinder, but just as he did, the tone dropped off. The missile made a corkscrew and detonated beside the MiG's rear fuselage. Momentarily, Connelly thought he'd missed, but Blonski called, "Wait a minute, his tail's gone!" Smoke then started streaming and as the MiG rolled left, the pilot ejected.

While he watched the MiG go down, an F-4 passed less than 1,000 feet above him. An instant later, a MiG-17 was 30 feet out, off his left, almost flying wing at the same speed. "I thought, 'You almost had your ass shot off!' I don't know what the hell I was doing or how we got that way. If you lined up ten Gomers tomorrow, I could recognize him, since he wasn't flying with an oxygen mask. I was looking at him and he was looking at me."

Connelly slow rolled over this fifth MiG, putting it off his right wing. He then performed a rolling scissors. The MiG followed him, then the enemy pilot dumped his nose and disengaged. "He wouldn't have had to do too much of anything if he had continued his slow fight until he got behind and started to pepper us. For the life of me I can't figure out why he broke off." Despite being left with four Sparrows he couldn't use due to the radar failure, Connelly set off after two more MiG-17s:

> I used the old philosophy "It's easier for me to chase them than to have one of them behind me." I chased one of them around for a while, and he was pulling pretty hard. He finally dropped his nose and started diving for the deck. I thought he was going to go home, so we started to make a turn towards the beach. Then another one flew right in front of me. He was turning to the left and I just followed him. He did the same thing as the other one, and I don't think he ever saw me. I was right behind him, and just chasing him around. I could have been in an excellent gun position – all I would have had to do was add a little more power and catch them.

As he made another full-circle sweep before heading out, Connelly saw Cunningham's F-4 with a MiG-17 pulling up below him. He called, "F-4 heading 180 degrees. You've got a MiG-17 coming up behind you. Unload, full 'burner – you can outrun him." There was no response. Connelly pulled his nose toward the MiG and selected radar as he called a second warning. Cunningham finally heard his warnings and unloaded in full afterburner.

Two miles from the enemy and at a 20-degree aspect angle, Connelly put his pipper on the MiG. His radar was still black, but the missile select lights were on. He squeezed the trigger, hoping to force the MiG to break off. "Normally a Sparrow comes out and starts doing ballistic trajectories. This one came off and started going right at him. The trouble is, before the Sparrow got to the guy, I pulled my nose away from him and headed for feet-wet." The Sparrow passed right over the MiG as it turned to disengage and missed. "The second that it came off the rail and flew a hundred yards, the MiG just snapped right off Cunningham's F-4. All of a sudden the guy was nose down, diving away, and we resumed our heading out."

Connelly later told the Red Baron interviewers, "Neither of the MiGs maneuvered while the missiles were in flight. Neither had a wingman. They were out there by themselves. Every guy we engaged was single, aside from the first two." In contrast, the Americans were much better trained and disciplined:

The most significant thing was the section integrity. Sections were made and dissolved in seconds. We maintained mutual support. The whole fight was contained within about a four-mile area, and you could see the other black-nose airplanes. You'd see a guy with a MiG behind him, and you would come on the radio and say, "Keep pulling to port." I heard a lot of that on the radio. Sections were made and dissolved in just seconds with that kind of quick mutual support.

As to the F-4's lack of a gun, Connelly also said, "There's no doubt in my mind that if we'd had gas and guns, we probably would have bagged five that day. It would have been easy." Blonski said of the engagement, "If all the MiG drivers that day had the benefit of the training that we've had, and if they'd had a chance to fly against an airplane comparable to the F-4, it might have been disastrous, because we made mistakes. We've never experienced that many MiGs in a confined area at one time."

In addition to Connelly's two MiG-17s, Shoemaker and Crenshaw scored a MiG-17, while Cunningham and Driscoll put in the best one-fight performance by a Navy aircrew in the war, shooting down three MiG-17s to become the Navy's only aces of the war before they were forced to eject from their badly damaged Phantom after barely making it "feet wet" to be picked up by a helicopter and returned to the carrier.

After fighting MiG-17s and MiG-21s through most of the war, Navy fliers finally shot down two MiG-19s on May 18. These were actually Chinese-supplied Shenyang J-6s developed from the Soviet MiG-19S, flown by the 925th Fighter Regiment, which had only engaged in combat with Air Force fighters before this engagement. Designated "Farmer-C" by the NATO identification system for Soviet fighters, the MiG-19 was known to US aircrews in the Vietnam War as the "White Bandit," in line with the MiG-17 "Red Bandit" and MiG-21 "Blue Bandit." Like the MiG-17, the "White Bandits" did not carry missiles at this time. The two victories were scored by two F-4Bs from *Midway*'s VF-161 flown by Lieutenants Henry A. "Bart" Bartholomay and RIO Oran R. Brown as lead with Lieutenants Patrick E. "Pat" Arwood and James M. "Taco" Bell flying wing. Their opponents were Pham Ngoc Tam and Nguyen Thang Long, who had been involved that morning in a fight with Air Force F-4Ds from the 421st Tactical Fighter Squadron of the 366th Tactical Fighter Wing, in which Tam had shot down the F-4D flown by First Lieutenants W.D. Ratzel and weapon systems officer (WSO) J.B. Bednarek, neither of whom had survived, despite the VPAF pilots reporting they had seen their parachutes open. The four MiG-19s then diverted to Kep airfield to refuel.

Midway's Alpha strike was briefed to strike the Haiphong–Hanoi highway and rail bridge. The strike force consisted of 11 A-7Bs of VA-93 and three A-6As from VA-115, with MiGCAP support from two VF-161 F-4Bs and flak suppression from a division of four VF-161 F-4Bs.

Following launch from *Midway*, Bartholomay and Arwood took on fuel from VA-115's KA-6Ds then coasted in north of Hon Gai. The original plan was that they would then follow a ridge of hills to Kep, where they would take up CAP station five miles south of the airfield. The route provided radar cover from the ridge and allowed them to evade the defending SAM sites.

North Vietnamese GCI ordered the four 925th Regiment MiG-19s flown by Pham Ngoc Tam, Nguyen Thang Long, Nguyen Hong Son and Vu Viet Tan at Kep to take off and intercept the Navy formation. Pham Ngoc Tam and Nguyen Thang Long became separated from the others and remained at low altitude. As they had not finished refueling, they turned back to Kep to land and finish refueling after several minutes of unsuccessful search.

Bartholomay had experienced a problem when he tanked and the two Phantoms were delayed. Thus, they were forced to fly straight up the Red River, over Haiphong, then on to Kep in order to arrive on station on schedule. They arrived on station in combat-spread, with Arwood on Bartholomay's right. Minutes later they received a warning call from Red Crown that bandits were airborne. When Bartholomay checked his wingman, he saw two sun-flashes down low against a ridge line approximately seven to eight miles distant. Calling for a right turn, he lit afterburner. Arwood crossed to Bartholomay's left while also lighting afterburner. Both now spotted the bogeys and closed up as they accelerated to 650–675 knots and closed the distance.

Bartholomay soon identified the two contacts as "White Bandits," then told Arwood he would go shooter with Arwood as protective cover. Pham Ngoc Tam and Nguyen Thang Long had just entered the break for landing on their approach to Kep airfield. The two Phantoms arrowed directly over the VPAF base toward them. Bartholomay later told the Red Baron interviewers:

> They appeared to see us about a mile west of Kep, as they started a left turn, still in trail. I was at 300 to 500 feet, crossing the northern edge of the runway and the MiGs were level with me. I told Arwood that I was going to push them around to port. Moments later I saw both their tanks come off simultaneously.

Tam and Long stayed in a level 3–4G turn for 360 degrees as Bartholomay pursued them, about a mile-and-a-half to their rear:

> To let Arwood and Bell get out of phase with me and come in for a shot, I started a lag-pursuit at about 550 knots, pushing them around. Two or three times in the first 180 degrees of turn I tried to pull my nose up to them for a shot, but they recognized it and added another G or two and spoiled my solution.

As Bartholomay and Arwood completed the first 360, the two MiGs were in close formation in front of them. Arwood was about 3,000 feet high on the inside of the turn, and had Tam's MiG in his sight. "I had my pipper on him and was at a range of about 4,500 feet, but I couldn't get a tone, so I kept trying. He was almost wings-level, with maybe a little right turn. I felt like I was almost dead six. I was closing on him, so I fired the missile anyway."

When Arwood fired, Tam broke hard left as wingman Long continued right. Bartholomay recalled, "I felt that guy really laid on the G when Arwood shot his missile. He almost pulled the wings off." The Sidewinder went ballistic and passed about 190 feet behind Tam's MiG. Bartholomay followed Long as he turned right while Arwood pitched up into a nose high left turn to follow Tam's MiG. He remembered, "The lead MiG was heading in a south-easterly direction, and I was high

above him, coming down. As he continued his extension maneuver, he
was rolling his aircraft from a 90-degree left to a 90-degree right bank.
He was not really changing his flightpath any, but was rolling in an
attempt to regain me visually."

Tam suddenly executed a hard left turn, causing Arwood to
momentarily lose sight of him. Continuing his left turn, he regained
visual contact in a lag-pursuit position behind Tam's MiG. Tam briefly
continued his left turn, then pulled his nose up slightly and started
to reverse right. Arwood was now behind Tam's MiG, and could see
Bartholomay closing on Long's MiG ahead.

Bartholomay was behind and below Long's MiG. "He gave a flip-
flop of his wings about three times and padlocked me at his five-thirty
as I was pulling my nose up to him. As soon as he saw me, he pulled
6–7G and gave me a beautiful plan view, then extended." Bartholomay
tried again to pull his nose up and put the pipper on the MiG, but
Long again made a 7G turn and pulled away. Bartholomay unloaded
and extended about two miles west, then accelerated to 550 knots as
he picked up his nose and pulled hard left into the MiG while Long
continued his left turn. "I lost sight of him for about five to ten seconds,
but my RIO still had him. He said, 'Okay, he's at your nine o'clock
going to your eight-thirty. I said, 'We're going to cause an overshoot
here – call my turn.'" RIO Brown watched Long go back to about their
seven o'clock, then told Bartholomay, "Pull up now." "I pulled up high
into him and rolled to his outside and there he was, overshooting. It
worked."

Bartholomay continued his roll, but Long pulled up in front of
him and rolled to the outside. "As we both completed our rolls, I was
looking at him at about ten o'clock some 1,000 feet above me, both of
us getting slow. I'd say he was at about 250 knots and I was doing about
220 knots, because he was still giving me nose-to-tail separation."

Tam, who was being chased by Arwood, pulled his nose to the right
and was in position on Bartholomay's tail, about a mile behind the
Phantom. Bartholomay unloaded since he didn't want to slow down
while Tam was closing on him. He later recalled:

As it turned out, the wingman MiG had some hairy idea of dragging
me out or trying to get away, because we simultaneously lowered
our noses and started to extend. We went from about 220 knots to

400 knots, maintaining the same position and accelerating together. He was 1–2,000 feet in front of me. My nose was behind him and I couldn't really pull it up.

As they accelerated to about 400 knots, Bartholomay was gaining on Long's MiG. "I know he didn't see me back there because he started pulling up, and my RIO was calling the other MiG back about a mile-and-a-half, and closing."

Just as Tam pulled his nose onto Bartholomay, Arwood fired his second Sidewinder, which tracked and exploded about five feet behind and to the right of the MiG. An instant later, Arwood saw parts come off the MiG, followed by a bright flash in the tailpipe. As the MiG went out of control, Tam ejected successfully.

Bartholomay remembered, "Arwood shot his second missile and my RIO told me, 'He got it – he got it.'" A few seconds later, Bartholomay pulled up and fired a Sidewinder at Long's MiG. "It looked like the guy had gone into afterburner, and it apparently hit him in the tail because he spewed fuel or something. Then he pitched nose-up and went into a flat spiral." Just before the MiG went into a flat spin, Long was able to eject nearly over Kep airfield.

The fight had taken place within a few miles of the runway at Kep airfield at altitudes between 150 and 6,000 feet. Both crews were surprised at the lack of AAA or SAMs, or any other MiGs. Feeling lucky, they joined up and headed back over the gulf where they found a tanker, then flew back to *Midway*.

The Red Baron evaluation of the engagement was critical; both Bartholomay and Arwood "Violated basic combat-spread principles when they separated for one-on-one attacks. The absence of other threats in the area allowed their split section to operate successfully." Like the other successful MiG-killers in 1972, Bartholomay credited his success to the training he received at Top Gun, and the influence the school had on overall fleet tactics. "Our ACM training was a direct result of Top Gun's influence on re-defining fighter tactics, and our squadron's insistence on spending more hours training its aircrews in these tactics than other squadrons did."

Five days later, former Top Gun instructor Lieutenant Commander Ronald "Mugs" Mckeown and RIO Lieutenant Jack Ensch scored two MiG-17s destroyed. By the end of *Linebacker* in December, two more

MiG-17s and five MiG-21s had been shot down by Navy aircrews, for a total of 26 MiG-17s, MiG-19s and MiG-21s shot down by Top Gun graduates or aircrews who had been trained by graduates in their squadrons. In Red Baron interviews, all these successful crews attributed their success to the realistic training they had undergone before entering combat. The Navy's decision to concentrate on how their aircrews fought, as opposed to the Air Force's concentration on the equipment they fought with, was demonstrated by a victory ratio that was close to the scores of Hellcat pilots over the Pacific a generation earlier. The Air Force paid the ultimate compliment of instituting realistic ACM training and adopting the Navy's "Loose Deuce" in the years after the end of the war. Both "TOPGUN" – as the program became known – and the Air Force "Red Flag" have continued in the years since, the result of the hard-won lessons over Vietnam.

15

THREE DFCs IN SEVEN DAYS

While Navy fighter pilots set new scores in air combat, the pilots of the attack squadrons went after the enemy's supplies. Operations were maintained at a high level throughout Operation *Linebacker* as the A-4s, A-6s and A-7s supplied the "Sunday Punch" to bring the Easter Offensive to a halt.

While *Constellation*, *Kitty Hawk*, *Coral Sea*, and *Hancock* were immediately available to meet the Easter Offensive, the Navy quickly sent two carriers from the Atlantic Fleet: USS *Saratoga* was preparing to deploy with the Sixth Fleet in the Mediterranean with CVW-3 aboard; instead, she sailed from Mayport, Florida, on April 11 for her only service in Vietnam, arriving at Subic Bay on May 8. USS *America* with CVW-6 was alerted on June 2 that she would not deploy to the Mediterranean as scheduled and departed Norfolk on June 5 for a third Vietnam tour, arriving in late June after rounding the Cape of Good Hope and crossing the Indian Ocean. USS *Midway*, with CVW-5 embarked, expedited her return to the Tonkin Gulf from Alameda, California, arriving in mid-May; her 327-day 1972–73 cruise would go into the record books as the second-longest carrier deployment in the Vietnam War, only two days short of *Coral Sea*'s 329-day deployment in 1964–65. *Constellation* was actually on her way back to the United States, having offloaded ordnance at Subic Bay, and stopped at Yokosuka before crossing the Pacific back to San Diego. Commander J.M. Seely, XO of Intruder-equipped VA-165, recalled, "Our cruise on 'Connie' started in August 1971, and we were on our way home via Yokosuka, loading motorcycles in the hangar bay on April 1, 1972, when the word came down that we were extended indefinitely. We unloaded the motorcycles and headed back to Yankee Station." On June 5, *Oriskany* departed early for her seventh deployment, arriving at Subic Bay on June 21; this final tour would make her the longest-serving carrier of the war. At times over the next six months, there would be six and even seven carriers on the line at Yankee Station.

Commander Charles "Chuck" Sweeney reported aboard USS *Hancock* in July 1972, as replacement XO for VA-212 "Rampant Raiders." Joining the navy with a Bachelor of Science degree in Engineering, he was commissioned in April 1958 and received an immediate assignment to the Naval Flight Test Center at NAS Patuxent River, where he flew as crew in test programs he was working in. "Jim Lovell, later commander of Apollo-13, took me flying one day, and convinced me I should volunteer for Navy carrier aviation." After pinning on his Wings of Gold in 1961, Sweeney flew Grumman S-2 Trackers for the next three years, when he received orders to the Naval Post Graduate School at Monterey. Graduation in 1966 saw the war in Southeast Asia now in full swing. "Prior to graduation, I volunteered for A-4 Skyhawks and went through the jet transition course at NAS Kingsville and the A-4 RAG at NAS Lemoore."

Sweeney's squadron, VA-22 "Fighting Redcocks," went aboard USS *Bon Homme Richard* in March 1969 as part of CVW-5 for their fourth deployment to Southeast Asia. With *Rolling Thunder* having ended the previous November, the air wing flew air support missions from Dixie Station off South Vietnam. One of Sweeney's most satisfying missions came during this tour:

We were tasked as RESCAP support for a mission against a SAM site north of the DMZ. We were carrying gun pods instead of bombs, and were just approaching the DMZ when we got a call from a group of Marines that they needed support from anyone in the vicinity since they were being overrun just south of the DMZ. We replied we were on the way.

When we got there, we had an overcast ceiling at 2,000 feet, and the Rules of Engagement (ROE) required a pullout by 3,500 feet. We decided to hell with the ROE and went in at 1,800 feet. The Marines popped green smoke to mark their position and we were strafing NVA troops! It was the closest I ever got to a target. We came out of that run at about 300–400 feet AGL [Above Ground Level] and saw figures falling and others were running. We made multiple runs till we were out of ammo and the NVAs were retreating. That was the closest and most meaningful air support I ever gave anybody.

Returning to the United States in October 1969, CVW-5 deployed again to Southeast Asia in April 1970. Sweeney recalled, "All our missions were against South Vietnamese or Laotian targets due to the bombing halt." When they returned in November, VA-22 learned they would be giving up their Skyhawks to re-equip with the A-7E "Corsair II." Sweeney left the "Fighting Redcocks" soon after, assigned as operations officer for the A-4 Replacement Air Group (RAG) at Lemoore.

Nineteen months later, Sweeney's return to combat flying was abrupt:

LCDR Frank Green, the Executive Officer of VA-212, was killed on July 10, 1972, when he was hit by North Vietnamese triple-A and flew into the ground at night. I was ordered to replace him. I went aboard Enterprise for two days over July 19–21 to re-qualify for night traps with VA-127. I left for WestPac on July 28 and joined VA-212 aboard *Hancock* on July 30. I flew my first mission on August 1.

Over the next two months, Sweeney would see more dangerous combat than he had in his previous two tours, as VA-212's A-4Fs flew mission after mission over North Vietnam.

September 6, 1972 saw Sweeney's first memorable mission:

Our strike was the last launch of the day. I was leading a division, looking for targets of opportunity. With the crappy weather, we split up and the second section leader spotted a group of trucks in a camouflaged park near the Thanh Hoa Bridge. It was the only target of any consequence we spotted, so we made a bombing run on them and got several direct hits.

On the third run, defensive fire got heavy and Sweeney's wingman, Lieutenant (jg) Will Pear, was hit in his engine. He pulled off the target trailing smoke and fire. Sweeney quickly spotted the flaming A-4. "He was climbing, with what looked like a huge fire coming from the rear fuselage, but the engine was still running. I told him to turn toward the water."

Fortunately the Skyhawk's engine was still providing sufficient power to allow Pear to climb and head toward the coast. Sweeney closed on the damaged Skyhawk. "He managed to climb to 6,500 feet before the engine quit and the airplane caught fire like a Roman Candle. We were about fifteen miles from the Thanh Hoa Bridge and around a mile offshore at that point. There was a high sea state and the overcast above us, with a very bright sunset under the clouds." Pear managed to eject safely and got into his raft once he was in the water.

Sweeney's role changed from strike leader to on-scene commander of a SAR mission:

It was approaching sunset when this happened and I knew we would lose the light pretty quickly. I received offers of help from the Air Force and other Navy units but opted to use assets from my air wing. The nearest rescue helo was aboard the USS *Gridley* [DLG-21]. It was shut down and tied down for the night, but they told us they could be ready to go quickly and be on-scene in fifteen minutes. While they were getting things together, I ordered the other section to head for the *Gridley* and escort the helo to the scene as soon as they were ready to go.

In the meantime, two other sections from the air wing arrived, and I assigned them to suppress any flak that opened up. I got a little too close to shore while orbiting and they began shooting at me. I decided I was going to hit that target later. I was orbiting over Pear at about 2,000 feet and trying to keep him in sight as we were losing the light. The big problem was that those ten foot waves down there were pushing him toward the beach. Fortunately, the waves were strong enough to prevent the North Vietnamese on the beach launching their boats. I ordered two A-4s to make a strafing run on them which put a stop to any more attempts on their part.

As the two attacking A-4s pulled up from their strafing run, the flight took fire from an antiaircraft site on a nearby island. "I told them to remember the target and to hit it after the rescue when the helo was safely out of the way. They made a very successful attack later."

"After what seemed like forever but was probably something around ten minutes, I got a call from the helo that they were five minutes out and asking if I had the survivor in sight. I advised that I did and that he was drifting toward shore." The HH-3A Sea King of Detachment 110, HC-7 "Sea Devils," finally arrived, flying low over the now-dark ocean:

They passed over Pear's position and dropped a swimmer who made contact with him. The helo then went some distance before dropping a smoke light about 1,000 yards from the raft. I thought they had missed him, but I later learned they did that to confuse the enemy as to what they were really doing. I also found out that while they were maneuvering around to confuse the enemy, they lost sight of the two men in the water for a little while. When the swimmer said they were ready for pickup, I sent the flak suppressors after two triple-A sites and dispatched my second section to be ready for the coastal defense gun that I knew would open up. When the Sea King came to a hover to pick up the two men in the water, the shore gun opened up and bracketed the smoke light which was 1,000 yards from the helo. The helo crew members also heard some small arms fire during the pickup but were not hit. The section took out the coastal defense gun and the helo with the swimmer and Pear aboard headed back to the *Gridley*.

After the successful rescue, Sweeney and his second section were headed after the third AAA site that had shot at them earlier when he received a radio call from the task group commander asking him to report when all aircraft were "feet wet" and ordering them to return to the carrier.

I still had my six 500 pound bombs and knew we only had a couple more minutes to go for a successful hit. He couldn't see me, so I just replied "roger." We rolled in on the site and it was satisfying as I had secondary explosions and I saw the gun fly up in the air. As soon as I got back out over the water, I immediately radioed the task group commander that we were feet wet and heading for the *Hancock*. It was the very last flight of day and really dark on the water by this point. It was night when we got back to the ship, and everyone landed safely.

This action would lead to the award of the first of three DFCs Sweeney would receive for missions flown over the next ten days.

Linebacker continued through the summer and fall in a hard-fought attempt to cut off supplies to North Vietnamese forces in South Vietnam as operations picked up tempo. The carriers of Task Force 77, now commanded by Vice Admiral Damon W. "Hutch" Cooper, commander of the carrier *Ticonderoga* during the original Tonkin Gulf Incident that had put the United States directly into the Vietnam War, struck targets previously on the forbidden list throughout North Vietnam.

Operations were affected by the fact that the monsoon was in full swing. Strikes launched with forecasts of good weather often found themselves dealing with heavy rain and low clouds over treacherous mountains in poor visibility. Sweeney remembered:

On September 12, we were assigned to hit an antiaircraft artillery repair facility thirty miles from the Chinese border. That was the furthest north anyone from our air wing had gone up to that point, because they had been worried about upsetting the Chinese as had happened back in Korea. I was assigned to lead the Alpha strike with thirty-five aircraft.

The weather was "iffy," but the Skyhawks continued on even as they were informed that North Vietnamese MiGs had taken off from Kep and were headed toward their position. "Fortunately for us, the weather was bad enough that the MiGs turned around, which frustrated our fighter pilots, but the F-8s were probably the reason the MiGs turned tail." The target was hit solidly, though there were no secondary explosions; all aircraft recovered safely despite encountering moderate to heavy defensive fire.

The next day, Sweeney flew in a two-squadron Alpha strike against a rail yard on the southern outskirts of Hanoi:

The mission was set up to look like we were headed for a strike on the Thanh Hoa Bridge, so that if the North Vietnamese sent any MiGs up, they might not be prepared when we went after the real target. The plan was that we would divert from our course toward the bridge at the last minute and turn to hit the rail yard which was ten minutes' flying time northwest. My division was on the left side of the formation. Just before the formation was supposed to turn right and head for the target, we spotted the smoke from a SAM launch. It took a minute or so before I realized it was headed toward my division. When a SAM was launched against you, you waited till it looked like a flying telephone pole, then you flew barrel roll around it, which would exceed the G limits of the SAM and hopefully it would go ballistic – out of control. My problem at this moment was that we were going to have to execute a barrel roll to the left just as the rest of the strike force turned right.

Sweeney's division made a successful defensive roll but were thrown out of formation. "We went left while everyone else went right, and were so far back when we recovered that we had to cut the corner to catch up." Once over the target, Sweeney realized things were not as he had been briefed to expect:

My target was actually underwater due to the floods from the monsoon. There was triple-A flying everywhere. I saw a train about 500 yards away and made a run on it. We hit the train, which had sustained fires and secondary explosions, and came out of our pass into the middle of a lot more triple-A. Then we had another SAM fired at us, which we managed to evade. This was definitely the hottest mission I had ever flown.

By mid-September it was becoming clear the North Vietnamese offensive in South Vietnam had been blunted, though fighting would continue into the middle of October. Shortly after this hot mission to Hanoi, the pilots of CVW-21 were glad to hear that *Hancock* had finally received orders to return to the United States at the end of the month:

Ordinarily, when a carrier was leaving the line to go home, you got sent down to Dixie Station off South Vietnam to fly your final missions. However, with operations like they were, we learned we'd be staying on Yankee Station till we were relieved. Not only that, but we soon found that our last mission – which was going to be my 200th – would be against the Thanh Hoa Bridge, the toughest target in North Vietnam.

Originally built by the French, the Thanh Hoa Bridge had been sabotaged by the Viet Minh during the First Indochina War in 1946, and rebuilt in 1957:

When they rebuilt that bridge, they basically over-built it. It became one of the strongest bridges in the world. There must have been a few hundred strikes flown against it, from the very beginning of the war, with no real success and lots of airplanes shot down. We were one of the first air wings to have Laser-Guided Bombs (LGB), which is probably why they gave us the assignment. Everyone was a little spooked about this being our final mission. In the end, they knew we were coming and got their smoke generators working in time so the target was partially obscured. While we scored a few more hits, we didn't take her down. The Air Force had hit it good back in May, but it wasn't finally considered destroyed until VA-82 hit it with Walleyes a couple weeks after our attack. The good thing was that we didn't lose anyone. After losing the CO in May and the XO in July, and two other air wing pilots who became POWs in August and September, the squadron felt we had put in our service.

Sweeney learned he was to receive a second and third award of the DFC for the missions of September 12 and 13, in addition to the award for the September 6 mission – three in one week!

It may sound strange that these missions merited the Distinguished Flying Cross, the fourth-highest combat award, but that shows just how rough those missions over North Vietnam were in 1972. I saw more direct combat in the two months of August and September 1972 than I did in both of my previous tours combined. Admiral Stan Arthur, who at that time was CO of VA-164 on the *Hancock*, received 11 DFCs for missions he'd flown during the Easter Offensive, and my CO, Commander "Duke" Peacher, was awarded 13 DFCs during the same time frame.

Coral Sea arrived in December, 1971, with the first and only Marine squadron to fly from a carrier deck during the Vietnam War aboard. Marine All-Weather Attack Squadron 224 (VMA(AW)-224) "Bengals," a former Skyhawk squadron that had converted to the Intruder in 1968, was normally stationed at MCAS Cherry Point, North Carolina. The "Bengals" came aboard with nine A-6A bombers and three KA-6D tankers. Initially the squadron had a leadership problem due to the Marines' lack of carrier experience at senior levels. Initial operations aboard the carrier did not go well and things didn't improve when they entered combat with the *Proud Deep* and later *Freedom Train* strikes, the initial response to the North Vietnamese offensive. Fortunately, changes in air group leadership allowed the squadron to improve their record in April.

On April 6, CVW-15's CAG, Commander Tom Dunlop, was shot down in a VA-22 A-7E by a SAM. His replacement was Commander Roger "Blinky" Sheets, a fighter pilot who was remembered by VF-51 MiG-killer Lieutenant Commander Jerry "Devil" Houston as "a Don Knotts look-a-like, with more guts than a slaughterhouse." Sheets believed in leading from the front. He quickly saw the problem with the "Bengals" lack of carrier experience and took the squadron over, after which the unit rapidly became a highly effective fighting organization. Among the junior and mid-level officers was Captain Charlie "Vulture" Carr, a former enlisted man and warrant officer, who was experienced beyond his years, and regarded as one of the better NFOs in Marine aviation. Sheets picked him for his B/N, and the squadron never looked back.

On April 9, the "Bengals" led the wing in a strike on Bai Thuong airfield, with Sheets and Carr in front. The target was hit hard and all returned without loss. That night the squadron suffered its first loss when NL-505, crewed by Major Clyde D. Smith and First Lieutenant Scott Ketchie, was hit by AAA over the Ho Chi Minh Trail in Laos. The Intruder was loaded with 12 Mark 82 500-pounders and a dozen Rockeyes and was hit in the left wing while dive-bombing a truck convoy. Both crew ejected.

Smith came down next to the burning wreckage. The remaining bombs were cooking off from the intense flames and shrapnel was flying everywhere. When he heard Ketchie pass overhead through the top of the jungle canopy, he triggered his emergency beeper and made a voice Mayday call; Ketchie made no response. The crew of another A-6 accompanying Smith's plane reported hearing two beeper signals clearly, coming from the dense jungle below. Using direction finding equipment aboard the Intruder, they were able to pinpoint both men's positions.

Smith recalled later:

The sun had just set and it was very dark. There was a lot of noise close by. I assumed it was Scott and almost called out. Somebody or something was moving through the woods in a hurry. About an hour later, I heard shouting and several shots. At that moment, I felt certain that he had been captured.

Smith continued to seek a hiding place in the jungle:

> About 2200 hours, I heard another aircraft overhead nearby and turned on my beeper. A voice speaking perfect English came up on the rescue frequency. He came in clearly, sounded very close, and asked me where I was. I replied, "I'm in the vicinity of the wreckage," to which the voice said, "We'll be there in a few minutes." It was totally dark by then, and we had been briefed that no rescues were ever attempted at night. I asked him his call sign, but there was no answer. Nothing like that happened again.

Smith's Intruder continued to burn throughout the night. He heard North Vietnamese trucks in the darkness as they negotiated what sounded to him like a very rough road. When dawn came, the truck traffic ceased and he heard movement all around in the bush. He could now see he was in an open area on the side of a small ridge, next to a gully filled with elephant grass four or five feet high. When the sounds of movement went away and he felt he was safe, Smith moved into the dense foliage at the bottom of the gully and remained hidden there for the next four days.

At around 0900 hours, Smith heard an OV-10 Bronco overhead and was able to establish radio contact. The "Nail" (call sign for USAF air controllers over the Ho Chi Minh Trail) forward air controller (FAC) pilot was searching for Ketchie and him. Thirty minutes later, an Air Force helicopter with A-1 "Sandy" Skyraiders flying support arrived overhead. There were a large number of enemy AAA sites in the immediate area and all aircraft took a tremendous amount of fire. Smith remembered, "Listening to these professionals calmly going about their job under fire was something that would stay with me for the rest of my life." The enemy were too numerous and too close for a successful pickup. The pilot flying "Sandy 01" radioed "We'll be back" as the force flew off.

The weather closed in for the next three days, making a successful rescue attempt impossible. Early in the morning of April 13, Smith learned from the radio that there was a massive rescue mission going on

35 miles east of him to pick up Lieutenant Colonel Iceal Hambleton, navigator of an EB-66, call sign "Bat 21," who had been shot down on April 2 during the early stages of the Easter Offensive. Nail 45 told him "It looks good, I think we can do a good tune on you today." That afternoon, Air Force F-4s arrived overhead and began bombing the enemy AAA sites as the FAC circled. Over the next hour there was non-stop bombing as Navy, Air Force, and Marine aircraft attacked the NVA positions surrounding Smith, who later recalled, "To the credit of everyone involved, not one life or aircraft was lost and no one hit the survivor on the ground!"

At about 1700 hours, Major Jim Harding, "Sandy 01," the SAR commander, told Smith to get ready and stay up on the radio, that the rescue helicopter was coming in. At that point, "Sandy 01" had seven A-1s and four FACs who were controlling 10–15 fighters suppressing the AAA sites, while two Jolly Green Giant helicopters were in a holding pattern ten miles away.

Harding ordered "Sandy 02" to "Go get Jolly 32 and bring him in." As Sandy 02 led Jolly 32 forward, he fired smoke rockets to mark Smith's hiding place.

Jolly 32 pilot Captain Ben Orrell and co-pilot First Lieutenant Jim Casey brought the big helicopter in low over the jungle. As they began their run-in, enemy ground gunners opened up with everything they had. Crew Chief Technical Sergeant Bill Brinson manned the 7.62mm Vulcan mini-gun at the back ramp while door gunner/winch operator Airman First Class Bill Liles and door gunner Airman First Class Kenneth Cakebread manned the mini-guns to either side and returned fire.

Jolly 32 maneuvered over Smith's position. Sandy 01 called "Pull up Jolly, pull up, you're right over the survivor." No one in the helicopter could spot Smith. When he popped a flare, the helicopter's downwash pushed the red smoke down the gully. He flipped it over and ignited the night end, which hit him with sparks. Jolly Green 32's crew still couldn't see him. Smith moved upslope into the open. He could see the helicopter at the top of the ridge, with its rotor blades cutting off tree tops and slinging them in every direction.

In the midst of the chaos, Liles spotted Smith and Orrell told him to lower the hoist. As the penetrator neared the ground, Smith grabbed it and snapped the climber's snaplink on his torso harness to the cable. Immediately, Liles took up the slack. When Smith reached the door,

Liles rolled him in and said, "Get the hell out of the way" then yelled to Orrell, "He's in the door, let's get the hell out of here!" as he swung the mini-gun into the open door and opened fire in the direction Smith had come from. As Jolly 32 pulled away, four A-1s rolled in to strafe and rocket the enemy troops on the ground. Ninety minutes later, Jolly Green 32 landed at Nakhon Phanom Airbase in Thailand.

Unfortunately, during the first day of the SAR operation, Ketchie's emergency radio stopped transmitting. In 1992, an NSA correlation study of all communist radio intercepts pertaining to missing Americans was finally declassified and made public; it contained five North Vietnamese radio messages correlated to this incident. The fifth message reported the capture of one pilot on April 10. Lieutenant Ketchie was not among those POWs returned in 1973, nor were his remains ever returned.

Following the commencement of the North Vietnamese Spring Offensive, *Constellation* and *Kitty Hawk* launched eight A-6s on April 16 to hit SAM sites in Route Package 6 preceding USAF strikes. Commander Seely recalled, "These were single airplane, night, low-level missions, and there was a lot of opposition, especially SAMs. One of our BARCAP F-4s counted 51 missiles and I heard a later count of more than 100, all against our A-6s." Seely and his B/N, Air Force exchange officer Major Sid Dodd, had four SAMs explode near them just before and after bomb release, but fortunately their Intruder was undamaged. The Intruders successfully cleared the way for the Air Force bombers.

On May 6, CVW-15 flew a daylight Alpha strike against Bai Thuong airfield after intelligence reported the presence of more than 25 MiGs. The Intruders were led by Sheets and Carr, each carrying 16 Rockeyes. The big bombers swept over the field at 100 feet, while the A-7Es and F-4Bs feinted attacks from medium altitudes. On the way in, Carr spotted bandits airborne about ten miles from the target. CAG Sheets popped up and rolled onto the airfield, flying under several surprised MiGs orbiting over the base; the enemy fighters immediately punched off their external fuel tanks which fell among the attacking A-6s, fortunately without any contact.

With "bombs away," the Intruders turned and headed for the coast, 50 miles distant, flying as fast and low as possible. Sheets saw a MiG-17 lining up on his section leader and turned his aircraft to offer it as bait. The MiG dropped behind and opened fire, while Sheets was doing more than 450 knots, 100 feet above the ground! He kept the MiG at bay until VF-51's "Devil" Houston and RIO Lieutenant Kevin Moore shot the MiG down with a Sidewinder. All the A-6s returned to *Coral Sea* safely, where Sheets and Carr flew alongside the carrier and performed a victory roll along with the victorious Houston.

May 9 saw the Intruder's most important mission of the war: Operation *Pocket Money* – the mining of Haiphong Harbor.

Mining the most important North Vietnamese harbor had been high on the military's lists of requests from the early planning days of *Rolling Thunder*. While some limited attacks had been finally allowed by the Johnson Administration, attempting to mine Haiphong was only allowed once in 1967, and the event was unsuccessful. The reason given for allowing Haiphong to become a sanctuary was its use by merchant ships from many "friendly" countries, as well as ships from the Soviet Union and China. The possibility of military intervention by the Soviets or the Chinese if one of their ships was lost, or harm to NATO if a "friendly" was sunk, was considered too high a price to pay. Over the past seven years, nearly 85 percent of the war materials used by the North Vietnamese had entered the country through Haiphong.

Despite the fact that President Nixon was scheduled to meet with Soviet Premier Alexei Kosygin in Moscow in June for an important summit, the administration quickly gave permission for mining the harbor once it was decided to re-enter the war with a significant force following the opening of the Easter Offensive. On May 5, JCS chairman Admiral Thomas H. Moorer ordered CNO Admiral Elmo Zumwalt to plan a mining mission under the code name *Pocket Money*.

The first mission of the operation was assigned to *Coral Sea*. CAG Sheets worked out the mission requirements with air wing mine warfare officer Lieutenant Commander Harvey Ickle, VA-22 operations officer, and Captain Charlie Carr, who as B/N in the lead plane would establish the critical attack azimuth and timing of the mine releases. Three "Bengals" Intruders would each carry four 1,000-pound Mark 52 magnetic mines to be dropped in the harbor's inner channel, and six A-7s from VA-22 and VA-94 would each carry four 500-pound Mark 36 Destructors (Mark 82 bombs with acoustic mine fuzes) which they would drop in the outer portion of the channel. Reconnaissance had identified 36 foreign-flag ships in port: 16 Soviet, five Chinese, five Somalian, four British, three Polish, two Cuban, and one East

German. As soon as word was received that the mines were in the harbor, President Nixon was scheduled to announce their work in a Washington, DC press conference.

The strike plan included movement of the guided missile cruisers USS *Long Beach* (CGN-9) and USS *Chicago* (CG-11) north from the Positive Identification Radar Advisory Zone (PIRAZ) station off Hon Mat to a point in the Tonkin Gulf 40 miles off Haiphong to provide antiaircraft defense to the mining strike. A free-fire zone above 1,000 feet over the harbor was proposed for the cruisers to use their RIM-8 Talos missiles to engage MiGs flying from Phuc Yen and Kep airfields near Hanoi. Sheets lowered that to 500 feet, since the minelayers would stay under that and he had never seen MiGs above a few thousand feet.

Following the meeting on May 8 at which these decisions were taken, Rear Admiral Rembrandt C. Robinson, Commander of the Seventh Fleet Cruisers and Destroyers (ComCruDes7thFlt), and his staff returned to his flagship USS *Providence* (CLG-6) aboard a SH-3 Sea King. While approaching the ship, the helicopter lost power. It managed to touch down on the edge of the helo deck, then rolled overboard, hit the water upside-down, and quickly sank. Only the crew and the staff aviation officer survived, when they realized they were hunting for the door on the wrong side because they were upside-down. Admiral Robinson and two other staff officers drowned.

At dawn on May 9, an Air Force EC-121 Warning Star arrived off Haiphong from Da Nang to provide airborne early warning for the strike. Minutes later, destroyers USS *Richard S. Edwards* (DD-950), *Berkeley* (DDG-15), *Buchanan* (DDG-14), and *Myles C. Fox* (DD-829), commanded by Captain Robert Pace, who had succeeded Admiral Robinson, moved inshore and opened fire on the antiaircraft batteries defending the harbor. *Kitty Hawk* launched 17 aircraft that were to make a diversionary air strike against the Nam Dinh railroad siding. The strike force found bad weather over the primary target, so struck the secondary targets at Thanh at 0840 hours and Phu Qui at 0845 hours.

The main force of VMA(AW)-224 Intruders led by Sheets and Carr and the A-7Es of VA-22 and VA-94 led by VA-22 XO Commander Leonard E. Giuliani, with a VAQ-135 EKA-3B for ECM support, launched from *Coral Sea* at 0840 hours. At the same time, *Long Beach* and *Chicago* went to General Quarters. At 0842 hours, two MiGs were picked up by *Chicago*'s radar in a holding pattern just north of

Haiphong awaiting the incoming strike force. *Chicago* fired two Talos missiles, destroying one MiG. Minutes later, North Vietnamese coastal artillery batteries opened fire on the cruiser, which moved out of gun range before suffering any damage, while able to maintain missile coverage for the mission.

The *Coral Sea* bombers flew on into the harbor, taking up position in formation so that the mines would be properly laid. With Carr in the lead, they began releasing the mines at 0859 hours and at 0901 hours Sheets radioed the ship to verify the mines were in the water. *Coral Sea* then forwarded the message to the White House where President Nixon had been speaking slowly in order to avoid jeopardizing the mission. Upon receiving the message he looked up at the cameras and stated:

> I have ordered the following measures, which are being implemented as I am speaking to you. All entrances to North Vietnamese ports will be mined to prevent access to these ports and North Vietnamese naval operations from these ports. United States forces have been directed to take appropriate measures within the international and claimed territorial waters of North Vietnam to interdict the delivery of supplies. Rail and all communications will be cut off to the maximum extent possible. Air and naval strikes against North Vietnam will continue.

The 72-hour delayed arming time on the mines at Haiphong announced by the president expired at 0900 hours Vietnam time on May 12. Nine ships at Haiphong, including one British and four Soviet, had taken advantage of the delay to depart the port, while 27 ships would remain there until July 1973. Soviet and Soviet-bloc ships which were en route to Haiphong at the time were diverted to different destinations, thus avoiding a direct confrontation with the mine fields. Non-Soviet ships refused to enter the harbor when they were informed by their insurance companies that the mining was not an event the companies would cover.

On May 11, *Coral Sea*, *Kitty Hawk*, and *Constellation* flew additional mining missions against the ports of Thanh Hoa, Phuc Loi, Quang Khe, and Dong Khoi. This was followed on May 12–13 with missions to seed mines at Cua Sot, Cap Mui Ron, and the river mouths Cua Day and Cua Lac Giang, south of Don Son, as the beginning of a mining campaign that eventually planted over 11,000 Mark 36 Destructor and 108 special Mark 52-2 mines – 8,000 in coastal waters and 3,000 in inland waterways – by December 1972. During this operation, an unforeseen event happened when there was a spontaneous detonation of dozens of the mines throughout North Vietnam on August 4, 1972. The Navy later determined that the event had been caused by increased magnetic radiation from a geomagnetic storm that had been triggered by a coronal mass ejection on the Sun; scientific study confirmed this explanation in 2018.

While the overall campaign of mining throughout the waterways of North Vietnam is considered one of the most significant naval air operations of the war, the mining of Haiphong alone is generally considered the most significant operation in the campaign, since it prevented the arrival of further supplies, such that the second North Vietnamese offensive that fall was cut short without achieving any of its goals. As a result of the mining, during the last eight months of the war, North Vietnam's supplies were limited to those that could be brought by rail from China, with the supply trains also open to air attack, reducing overall supplies received by 75–85 percent. By October, North Vietnamese ground operations had come to a halt, and the Paris peace negotiations were within sight of a final agreement. US negotiators in Paris offered to remove the mines in order to encourage North Vietnam to release the US prisoners of war.

By the time *Coral Sea* departed for return to the United States, she had spent 148 days on the line at Yankee Station since arriving the previous December. Both ship and air wing should have been awarded a Presidential Unit Citation for the mining missions; instead they were awarded the Navy Unit Commendation. In addition to the mining, CVW-15's fighters had shot down five MiGs, while 16 aircraft had been lost, 12 falling victim to enemy action. VMA(AW)-224 had flown 2,800 sorties during their tour, which re-established a tradition of Marine air units serving aboard carriers which continues to this day.

Operation *Linebacker* saw the A-7E Corsair II become the primary light attack aircraft aboard the carriers at Yankee Station. The Air Force had been interested in the A-7 from the time the Navy had chosen it as the new light-attack aircraft, due to its heavy bombload and range/loiter capability and speed, which made it altogether a much more "survivable" airplane than the A-1 Skyraider that had been adopted from the Navy. Seeing the problems created by the early versions powered by the disappointing Pratt & Whitney TF30, the Air Force had chosen to proceed with their version, the A-7D, which would be powered by the Allison TF41 turbofan, a license-built British Spey, which provided nearly 3,000 pounds more thrust than the TF30 that powered the A-7B. The A-7D also replaced the original pair of troublesome Colt Mark 12 20mm cannon with a single General Electric M61A1 Vulcan with 1,000 rounds.

Seeing the overall performance increases of the A-7D, the Navy ordered its own version of the sub-type, designated A-7E, which flew for the first time on March 9, 1969. It differed from the Air Force version in retaining the probe-and-drogue aerial refueling system. The heart of the A-7C was the inertial navigation platform and sophisticated computer, which provided accurate navigation and precise weapon delivery. The new Head-up Display (HUD) allowed the pilot to see flight and weapons system data on a "combiner glass" that provided the traditional gunsight display, as well as computer-generated visual bombing data, while the projected map-display system showed the track over the ground. This digital bombing and navigation system was highly accurate. Endurance, accuracy, and a wide selection of underwing ordnance made the A-7E a real improvement over the previous Corsair IIs. The A-7E first entered service with VA-146 and VA-147 the following July; these were among the first 60, which were designated A-7C to distinguish that they were still powered by the TF30 due to delays in delivery of the TF-41. The two squadrons re-equipped with the definitive A-7E in October 1969 and went aboard USS *America* at Norfolk, Virginia, as part of CVW-9 in January 1970.

The A-7E flew its first combat mission on May 26, 1970, when *America* and her air wing arrived on Dixie Station after rounding the Cape of Good Hope and crossing the Indian Ocean. Among the pilots in the squadron was Air Force exchange officer Captain Ralph F. Wetterhahn, who had shot down a MiG while flying F-4s with the 8th Tactical Fighter Wing in Operation *Bolo* back in 1967. While most Navy pilots didn't use the A-7's new gun, Wetterhahn loved firing the cannon. At one point he told other squadron pilots that he fired the weapon as he pulled out of a bombing pass to keep the AA gunners down. When one replied that doing so would reveal his position to the gunners from the flash of fire, he replied, "Hell, they see the whole airplane the whole time during the day and miss, so because they see a two-second burst at night, they'll suddenly get more accurate?"

Wetterhahn recalled his experience with the A-7E during his tour, comparing it with his experience in the F-4:

I felt more comfortable in the A-7E over North Vietnam than I did in the F-4. The cockpit rearward visibility was dramatically improved, and even though we didn't have afterburner, the plane could turn! You could look out at either wing and see what bombs or missiles you had left. The armament switches were laid just under the instrument panel glare shield for easy access. And the Projected Map Display controlled by the Inertial Navigation System was fantastic. Since the doppler radar was integrated with the INS to control drift, the map positioning, both day and especially at night, was fantastic. I led all of our squadron Blue Tree recce escort missions over North Vietnam on my cruise in VA-146. We flew as two ship escorts for the RA-5C Vigilante recce birds. The load was Shrikes for the SAMS, AIM-9s for the MiGs, Mark 82 bombs for the gun pits, and 1,000 rounds of 20mm for all of the above. Unfortunately, the Air Force D model was thrown together before the Navy E model. Much of the above cockpit improvements were missing.

Two years later, the A-7E got the chance to prove itself in the high-threat environment of North Vietnam, where the Corsair II truly came into its own.

During *Linebacker*, the A-7s were seldom threatened by the VPAF, but during the initial *Linebacker* strikes on May 10, 1972, two A-7s did duel with an enemy fighter. Two A-7s, one from VA-147 and one from VA-146, encountered VPAF ace Duong Trung Tam, a MiG-17 pilot of the 931st Fighter Regiment, during a midday strike against the marshalling yards of the Hai Duong railway that connected Haiphong and Hanoi. Lieutenant George T. Goryanec was first to become involved with Duong just after dropping his bombs on the target. When the MiG-17 attempted to close on him, Goryanec turned into the attacker and cut loose a burst of fire. The MiG turned away and Goryanec headed for the coast.

Lieutenant Allan E. Junker of VA-146 wondered why he had seen no SAMs during the squadron's approach to the target, taking this as a sign of potential enemy fighter activity. He dropped his eight Mark 82 bombs and turned for the coast. Separated from his division, Junker was alone when he spotted what he first identified as an A-6 coming toward him. Moments later he realized his mistake as the MiG-17 turned to get on his tail. Junker was in a pickle, since VA-146 had turned their AIM-9Ds over to the air wing's F-4 squadrons due to a shortage. He also had no gun due to a run of malfunctions in the squadron's Corsair IIs. His only hope was to outfly the enemy pilot.

Radioing that he was being tracked by a MiG-17, Junker dived for the deck. He knew a MiG-17 could definitely out-turn an A-7 and was faster. His one advantage was that the A-7E was clearly the MiG's superior in roll-rate; it was what he had to work with. Jinking up and down and side to side as he flashed over the North Vietnamese countryside at 500 knots and around 100 feet, he could see the MiG in his rearview mirrors. The MiG pilot used his superior speed to close the distance and opened fire – red golf-ball-sized shells whizzed past him with the MiG so close he could hear the sound of the gunfire. He pulled hard into a roll and managed to put a little distance between himself and the relentless enemy. Tip vortices spun as he desperately threw the A-7 left then right, pulling more than 6Gs. Ahead, he could see the coastline come into view.

The MiG was now above him at his "two o'clock," turning left for a firing pass when he heard the squadron XO, Commander Fred Baldwin, on the radio. "I'm above you, roll right and throw him off!" Junker rolled right as told and the MiG passed behind him. Baldwin too was unarmed and could only call turns. For what seemed like an eternity to Junker, he rolled left, right and reversed course in his effort to stay out of the enemy's gunsight. Suddenly, a Corsair II flashed into view. George Goryanec had heard Baldwin on the radio. Fortunately, VA-147 had working guns. Goryanec engaged the MiG with several bursts of fire and saw hits on the right wing.

Junker was now able to outrun the MiG, but realized he was heading toward Hanoi! Quickly reversing course, he dived till he was just above the ground and ran for the coast. The MiG fell behind, then turned away as Junker crossed the coast and headed on out over the Tonkin Gulf. When he finally trapped aboard "*Connie*," he received a huge welcome as he managed to pull himself out of the cockpit, his flight suit soaked with sweat. "People shook my hand and hugged me," he recalled.

Several weeks later at the Cubi Point officers' club after *Constellation* came off the line, one of Junker's fellow VA-147 pilots had a chance meeting with Lieutenants Ken Cannon and Roy Morris from *Coral Sea*'s VF-51, where he learned the rest of the story. Cannon and Morris were returning from their strike with flight leader Lieutenant Commander Chuck Shroeder and RIO Lieutenant (jg) Dale Arends when they heard Junker's frantic call for help. Racing toward Junker's position, they came across a MiG-17 headed for Kep still ready for a fight. There was later evidence indicating that this was Duong Trung Tan. He engaged Shroeder and quickly obtained an advantageous position behind Shroeder's Phantom, but didn't open fire – having likely used up his ammunition on Junker. Cannon and Morris rolled in behind him and shot him down with a Sidewinder.

Throughout the 1972 air battles, the VPAF only claimed one A-7 shot down. The event happened on May 23 and the victor making the claim was a MiG-21 pilot. Navy records list VA-93's Commander Charles Barnett shot down in A-7B BuNo 154405 by a SAM on that date.

Commencing on May 24, carriers at Yankee Station began regular night operations. During June and July, 30 percent of the total Navy attack effort in North Vietnam was night sorties, including 45 percent of the armed recce effort. These missions were primarily flown by A-7 Corsair IIs and A-6 Intruders, with the A-7s flying as many night sorties as they did day sorties, while the Intruder squadrons flew more night than day armed reconnaissance sorties. Of the eventual seven carriers serving in the theater by the end of June, three or four were constantly in operation from Yankee Station through the end of September.

Shortly after nightfall on August 6, Lieutenant James R. Lloyd of *Saratoga*'s VA-105 "Gunslingers" was one of two A-7Es flying an armed reconnaissance mission near Vinh. The pilots picked up a warning signal that a Fan Song SAM radar was tracking them. Moments later they spotted the flame of a SAM launch. The two pilots started jinking but moments later when he was at 3,500 feet flying at 300 knots, Lloyd's airplane was hit and caught fire. The hydraulics failed and the controls stiffened as the left wing started to disintegrate. Lloyd ejected and landed safely near My Ngoc, 20 miles northwest of Vinh.

USS *England* (DLG-22) was at the northern SAR station, ten miles off the coast, with HH-3A Sea King "Big Mother 60" of Detachment 110 of HC-7 aboard. The helicopter was tied down for the night and pilot

Lieutenant Harry J. Zinser, co-pilot Lieutenant William D. Young, and crewmen AE3 Douglas G. Ankeny and AMHAN Matthew Szymanski were asleep in preparation for a midnight alert when word of Lloyd's shoot-down was received at 2210 hours. The crew was awakened as *England* sounded emergency flight quarters and "Big Mother 60" lifted off the destroyer's helo deck at 2220 hours for the 113-mile flight to the rescue location.

The HH-3A arrived two miles east of Hon Matt Island at 2320 hours, with Lloyd's wingman providing cover; the crew finally located him at 0222 hours on August 7 with radio vectors from Lloyd despite enemy fire, false pencil flares, and strobes meant to throw them off while the enemy searched for him. At 0223 hours, Zinser landed the big helicopter in a rice paddy. Lloyd came out of hiding and ran across the paddy, jumping through the open door a minute later. With the lights of enemy troops searching nearby, "Big Mother 60" lifted off and headed back out to sea. Lloyd was disembarked on USS *Cleveland* (LPD-7) at 0300 hours.

North Vietnam's air defense effort during *Linebacker* changed dramatically as compared to the summers of 1967 and '68, which had seen fairly intensive air-to-air combat and a large number of SAM launches. In 1972, while there was an increase in Navy attack sorties, there was a decrease in the number of air-to-air combat incidents and SAM firings in June and July after the significant battles in May. In June 1972, the VPAF took the MiG-17 out of first-line combat, so that afterwards almost all VPAF aircraft sighted or engaged were MiG-21s.

September saw a decrease of 800 in tactical air attack sorties flown as compared to the sortie rate in August, with 3,934 sorties flown into North Vietnam. Night sorties declined from 45 percent of total armed reconnaissance sorties over the summer to 31 percent in September. Nearly 50 percent of Navy tactical air sorties that month were close and direct air support missions in South Vietnam flown from Dixie Station.

Operation *Linebacker*, which would later be called *Linebacker I* following the *Linebacker II* campaign in December, came to an end on October 23, 1972, when the United States ended all sorties into North Vietnam above the 20th parallel as a goodwill gesture to promote the Paris peace negotiations. Air combat in South Vietnam escalated that month as North Vietnam increased small-scale attacks throughout the country in an effort to increase the territory it held before the potential cease-fire. The enemy's lack of supplies due to the mining of Haiphong brought the offensive to an early end without achieving its objectives. With this, the naval air war in Vietnam was considered over. When the Paris Peace Accords were signed in January 1973 and fellow naval aviators returned from imprisonment in North Vietnam, and the ships departed the waters of the Tonkin Gulf, there was a collective sigh of relief from those who had sacrificed so much.

16

END GAME, APRIL 1975

April 1975 saw the wars in Southeast Asia come to an end. The only unexpected aspect of this event was its date. That it happened as quickly as it did when it did, surprised all parties involved.

The Paris Peace Accords that were signed in January 1973 and touted in the United States as ending formal US involvement, did not end the fighting in South Vietnam. In truth, the "Peace Accords" were little more than a face-saving gesture for the Nixon Administration. When talks between the United States and North Vietnam broke down at the end of October 1972, Nixon's response had been what came to be known as "the Christmas Bombing" of Hanoi, after which the North Vietnamese returned to the talks, which quickly resulted in the Peace Accords. In truth, that final spasm was better described by an unnamed aide to Secretary of State Kissinger: "We bombed them into accepting our concessions." With the Accords, President Nixon was able to claim he had achieved his oft-mentioned "Peace with honor." But, in the end, there would be neither peace nor honor.

Most of those in Washington who understood the real situation in Southeast Asia believed it was very likely that South Vietnam would fall; as Frank Snepp, chief CIA strategy analyst in Vietnam, famously described the policy, what was wanted was a "decent interval." The Nixon Administration collectively hoped that others would be blamed for the inevitable tragedy that would be hung around America's neck.

Almost immediately following the final US troop withdrawals from South Vietnam, both the North Vietnamese and their southern allies, and the South Vietnamese government, began violating the cease-fire as each side moved to gain control of as much territory as possible, since such occupation would provide the occupier with control of the regional population should there be further negotiations or a renewed war.

The fighting was not small-scale. Four divisions of the PAVN were involved in what was called the "Land-grabbing-and population nibbling" campaign designed to take strategic positions in the Central Highlands and along the South Vietnam/Cambodia border. A new International Commission of Control and Supervision (ICCS) to monitor the cease-fire's implementation had been established, but it soon fell into squabbling over details between the communist and non-communist delegates: since any decisions made had to be unanimous, this doomed any attempt to stop the numerous cease-fire violations. Within a matter of months, the ICCS ceased to function meaningfully and slipped quickly into irrelevance.

As a result of the Enhance and Enhance-Plus programs that had supplied $753 million dollars' worth of new aircraft for the VNAF, and more armored vehicles, artillery, helicopters, and other equipment to the ARVN, the Saigon government had what was – at least on paper – the fourth-largest military force in the world. However, due to lack of training for the personnel who were to operate and maintain all this gear, and the complete dependence on the United States for spare parts, fuel, and ammunition, maintenance and logistics problems that could not be resolved became widespread. The major cutbacks in US aid meant artillery batteries that had previously fired 100 rounds per day were reduced to firing only four rounds daily, while infantrymen found themselves reduced to 85 bullets per month, which was insufficient for one minor firefight. Over the two years following the US withdrawal, the armed forces "voted with their feet." In 1974, records showed that at any given time no more than 65 percent of authorized manpower was present for duty. Promotion in the upper reaches of the officer corps was controlled by political loyalty rather than professional ability. Politically, the endemic corruption and incompetence eventually forced President Thieu to sack Generals Nguyen Van Toan and Nguyen Vinh Nghi, respectively the commanders of II Corps (the Central Highlands) and IV Corps (the Mekong Delta), for their notorious corruption despite the fact they were perhaps his two best commanders, proven leaders who were popular with their troops and successful in battle.

North Vietnam's losses in the 1972 battles were being made good by increased Soviet and Chinese aid. In 1973, the communist-bloc countries increased their support by 50 percent over that provided in 1972, a total 2.8 million metric tonnes (3 million US tons) of goods with a value of $330 million, which – according to CIA estimates – increased in 1974 to 3.5 million metric tonnes (3.9 million US tons) valued at $400 million. During the same period, aid to Saigon dropped from $2.2 billion in 1972 to $965 million in 1974.

By the end of 1973, a serious political debate over future military policy was underway among the North Vietnamese leaders. In December 1973, the Central Committee of the Communist Party of Vietnam was convened to review the progress of military actions undertaken in the south. Defense Minister Vo Nguyen Giap and PAVN Chief of Staff General Van Tien Dung urged an increase in military operations, arguing that passivity would affect army morale. They were countered by Premier Pham Van Dong, who believed such action would reduce reconstruction activity in the north.

In the end, Resolution 21 was approved, charting something of a middle course; the plan called for "strategic raids" to regain territory taken by the ARVN following the signing of the Peace Accords. The action would test the reactions of both the ARVN and the US government. Between March and November 1974, ARVN forces in Quang Duc Province and at Bien Hoa were attacked in operations that saw the PAVN take the military initiative while troops gained experience in combined arms operations that were a step up from the infantry fighting in the war. The "strategic raids" resulted in the ARVN expending ammunition that could not be replaced, while the PAVN gained control of jump-off points should any new offensive result. Most importantly, the Northern leadership saw that the B-52s did not return.

As a result, the North Vietnamese Politburo agreed in October 1974 that the war had reached its "final stage" and voted on the Resolution of 1975 that outlined the strategy to be followed in 1975 and 1976: in 1975, the army would consolidate gains, eliminate South Vietnamese border outposts, and continue the buildup in the south in preparation for the final general offensive in 1976.

The PAVN leaders decided an attack in the Central Highlands would have the greatest chance of success. This plan was challenged by the military commander in the south, Lieutenant General Tran Van Tra, whose staff presented a plan for a direct attack against Saigon. In the face of northern opposition, Tra proposed a "test" attack in Phuoc Long Province, which would demonstrate the ARVN's fighting ability and answer the question of what a US response would be. Tra's plan had potential for great gain at low risk. In the end, the argument was resolved by First Party Secretary Le Duan's conditional approval; he finished the meeting by warning General Tra: "Go ahead and attack... [But] you must be sure of victory."

During the same period that these decisions were made in Hanoi, President Thieu's belief that President Nixon's promise to return American air power to the war should any serious violations of the agreement occur was badly shaken by domestic political events in the United States. While "peace candidate" George McGovern had lost the 1972 presidential election, the antiwar faction of the Democratic Party had successfully increased their ranks in both the House and Senate. On July 1, 1973, Congress passed the Case–Church Amendment to the Fiscal Year 1974 Pentagon Budget, which stopped short of complete prohibition of any direct or indirect US combat activities over or in Laos, Cambodia, and both North and South Vietnam. Nixon's veto of the War Powers Act Congress had passed in October 1973 to try to reassert the traditional congressional role in declaring and financing wars as defined in the Constitution was overridden on November 7, 1973; with that now law, there would be little or no opportunity for the president to make good the promise he made to the Saigon government. Additionally, Nixon's attention was increasingly drawn to the growing Watergate scandal.

Even with the increasing antagonism between the president and Congress, Thieu remained confident the United States would not allow his government to fall. However, many other South Vietnamese leaders took a more realistic view. VNAF commander General Dong Van Khuyen later recalled: "Our leaders continued to believe in US air intervention even after the US Congress had expressly forbidden it... They deluded themselves." The Arab Oil Embargo, with the resulting "oil shock" in 1974, saw the South Vietnamese economy largely destroyed by the resulting inflation; a government spokesman was forced to admit that spring that the Saigon government was "being overwhelmed" by inflation. By the time Nixon was forced to resign the presidency on August 9, 1974, the Saigon government was unable to pay the troops; this led to even greater absenteeism and loss of morale.

The 1975 Spring Offensive, officially known as "the General Offensive and Uprising of Spring 1975," developed rapidly into a war-ending campaign following initial success in Phuoc Long Province. Phuoc Long, the northernmost provincial capital in III Corps, 75 miles northeast of Saigon, came under attack on December 13, 1974, when the PAVN force, composed of the CT-7 and 3rd divisions, an independent infantry regiment, and armored, antiaircraft, and heavy artillery support, moved out of Cambodia. The South Vietnamese defenders included five Regional Force battalions, 48 Popular Force platoons and four territorial artillery units. They were reinforced by the 2nd Battalion, 7th Infantry Regiment of the ARVN 5th Division, two artillery sections, and three reconnaissance companies. The battle started with the elimination of static outposts to isolate the city. A heavy artillery bombardment on December 27 covered the attack by infantry supported with armor. The hope of a counterattack or relief effort by the ARVN was doomed by thousands of refugees who took to the roads, while desertion in the ARVN grew as soldiers left in search of family members. This would become common in the later attacks, spreading rapidly among the regular forces.

An emergency meeting at the Independence Palace in Saigon on January 2 saw III Corps commander General Dung present a plan to relieve Phuoc Long using the Airborne Division which was turned down due to there being no reserve forces available; with all overland routes in enemy hands, such an attempt would depend completely on airlift, and the VNAF no longer had such capability. Finally, the defenders of Phuoc Long could not hold off the two PAVN divisions long enough for relief to arrive. The meeting ended with the decision to surrender Phuoc Long City and Province, since the region was strategically less important than Tay Ninh, Pleiku, or Hue. Fighting continued until January 6, 1975, after which Phuoc Long became the first provincial capital permanently taken by the PAVN. Out of 5,400 ARVN troops originally committed, only 850 managed to escape. More important, there was no reaction by the United States. According to General Cao Van Vien, Chief of the ARVN General Staff, "Almost gone was the hope that the United States would forcibly punish the North Vietnamese for their brazen violations of the cease-fire agreement... What more encouragement could the communists have asked for?"

The North Vietnamese Politburo received news of the victory during their Twenty-third Plenum; the General Staff was immediately ordered to develop a follow-up plan in light of the proof that the United States would not re-intervene despite the weakness of the ARVN having been exposed. Le Duan declared: "Never have we had military and political conditions so perfect or a strategic advantage so great as we have now."

On March 10, preceded by an intense artillery bombardment, the PAVN 10th Division assaulted Buon Mai Thuot, pushing into the city and seizing the ammunition depot – the ARVN supplies became the solution to the North's own ammunition shortage. Three days later, the ARVN 44th Regiment, 23rd Division and a battalion of the 21st Ranger Group were brought by helicopters to Phuoc An, 20 miles east. Advancing into the thousands of refugees fleeing the highlands, the ARVN attack disintegrated when they came into contact with the 10th Division and the troops joined the civilian exodus. Phuoc An fell on March 18.

There is an apocryphal story that, following the ARVN defeat in the Central Highlands, some of President Ford's aides pleaded with him to act to repel the North Vietnamese invasion. Ford, who had succeeded to the presidency following Nixon's resignation in the face of impeachment over Watergate, and was well aware of the attitude of antipathy by Congress toward any further American involvement in Southeast Asia, responded: "If I do that, those guys over there (i.e., the House of Representatives) will impeach me." The remark has never been found in any official record, but in fact the story reveals the ground truth regarding domestic US politics at this point: most of the American people, and certainly their representatives, wanted no more to do with any wars in Southeast Asia.

The retreat from the Central Highlands became a rout in which the 23rd Infantry Division, as well as Ranger, armor, artillery, engineer, and signal units were lost in ten days. Buoyed by the easy success, the PAVN 10th, 316th, and 320th divisions moved toward the coast. A similar collapse occurred in the northern provinces of I Corps, with Da Nang taken by the end of the month.

The day after Buon Mai Thuot was attacked, Thieu was finally forced to realize there was no longer any hope of the United States providing the $300 million supplemental aid package he had asked for. In a meeting with generals Quang and Vien, he discussed redeployment of the armed forces to "hold and defend only those populous and flourishing areas which were most important." Those were the III and IV Corps zones, which he called "Our untouchable heartland, the irreducible national stronghold."

The rapidity of the ARVN collapse surprised the North. By March 25, the Politburo decided it was no longer necessary to wait another year to begin the final offensive. Le Duan pressured the General Staff to take advantage of their gains in the highlands since there were only two months before the monsoon began. General Dung was ordered to move the northern forces 370 miles south in order to capture Saigon by May 19, the late President Ho Chi Minh's birthday. In what was perhaps the most complex logistical feat of the war, the army managed to move into position by early April. On April 7, Le Duc Tho – who had shared the 1973 Nobel Peace Prize with Henry Kissinger for the Paris Peace Accords – arrived at General Dung's headquarters near Loc Ninh as the Politburo representative responsible for overseeing the final offensive.

Those at the top of the US intelligence community had little doubt the South Vietnamese government would fail to meet the challenge, regardless of any actions the United States might take to provide support. However, neither the CIA nor any other intelligence agency realized how fast this would happen. Evacuation of Southeast Asia was not discussed at the White House until April 6, when Secretary of State Kissinger informed President Ford that evacuation plans must be set up to deal with the emergency they now faced.

South Vietnamese forces regrouped and defended Phan Rang and Xuan Loc in early April, but the loss of political and military will to continue was ever more obvious as the TV sets of the world were treated to footage of ARVN soldiers being forced off airliners at gunpoint or falling to their deaths as they hung onto Huey skids for dear life. President Thieu resigned on April 21 in hopes that a new leader could reopen negotiations with the North Vietnamese. It was too late.

US Army, Navy, Air Force, and Marine personnel in the Defense Attachés Office (DAO) had commenced planning for a helicopter evacuation on April 1. Beginning in late March, the embassy had encouraged all dependents and non-essential staff to fly out to the Philippines and await further developments. On April 7, Nikki A. Fillipi, an Air America pilot, and Marine Lieutenant Robert Twigger of the DAO, set out to identify possible landing zones in Saigon for the coming evacuation. Over the next few days, they surveyed 37 buildings and selected 13 as Landing Zones. Workers from Pacific Architects and Engineers then removed obstructions from the sites and painted an "H" that was the exact "footprint" for the skids of a Huey helicopter on each. All the work had to be accomplished in accordance with Ambassador Martin's order that he would not tolerate any outward sign that the Americans intended to abandon South Vietnam.

Beginning on April 12, Task Force 76 gathered off the coast. Brigadier General Richard E. Carey, commander of the 9th Marine Amphibious Brigade tasked with organizing support of the evacuation, flew to Saigon to meet Ambassador Martin; he later remembered, "The visit was cold, non-productive and appeared to be an irritant to the Ambassador." Planning by the Marines was made more difficult by Ambassador Martin's strict adherence to the terms of the Paris Peace Accords, which limited total American military personnel in the country to no more than 50; for each specialist brought in, someone else had to first leave.

In the United States, Erik Shilling, the former American Volunteer Group pilot who had flown the first US offensive mission of the Pacific War back in 1941 remaining involved in the subsequent wars – including the aerial re-supply of the French position at Dien Bien Phu in the First Indochina War – until he left Laos in 1970 to join his old wartime comrades at Flying Tiger Airlines, convinced the airline management at the end of March to expand the number of flights in South Vietnam to facilitate the evacuation he saw coming. He later recalled, "I had so many Vietnamese friends I had flown with and fought with, who I knew would face a very dark future; I wanted to do everything I could to help them." Since he also knew how the children of Americans by Vietnamese women were viewed in the larger Vietnamese society, "I especially wanted to organize evacuation for as many of those kids as we could get out of there. After the C-5 crash [April 4, carrying 250 Vietnamese children, with 153 children and adults killed in the crash] our effort became even more important." Air Force C-141 and C-130 cargo planes were joined by planes from Flying Tiger Airline, World Airways and Air America in the evacuation. Within a week, the restriction that each evacuee had to be in a seat with a seatbelt, which reduced the passenger load on a C-141 to 94 and 75 in a C-130, was scrapped. C-141s were taking off with as many as 314 passengers aboard while C-130s were departing with up to 240 people crowded in their cargo holds.

Following the evacuation of Phnom Penh, *Okinawa*, *Hancock*, and the two landing ships *Vancouver* and *Thomaston* left the Gulf of Thailand on April 14, bound for the South China Sea and rendezvous with the rest of Task Force 76, now operating off the port of Vung Tau.

USS *Coral Sea* departed Subic Bay on April 10, headed for Perth, Australia, to take part in the annual Battle of the Coral Sea celebration. Men who had heard tales of the reception that the ship named for the battle that saved Australia had received when she first visited Sydney for the observance in 1964 looked forward to a week-long party with great anticipation as they headed south across the South China Sea; the "shellbacks" aboard made preparation for crossing the equator and initiating the "pollywogs" into Neptune's Realm. Hours after the ship left harbor, newly minted RIO Ensign Richard Heinrich, orders in hand assigning him to VF-51 aboard *Coral Sea*, arrived at NAS Cubi Point after hitching a ride from Clark Air Force Base where he had arrived in the Philippines. Informed that his ship was gone, Ensign Heinrich was advised to sit back and enjoy a few days in the Bachelor Officer Quarters while a flight to Australia was arranged so he could meet the carrier on arrival.

While *Coral Sea* steamed across the South China Sea, USS *Enterprise* was conducting flight operations north of the Philippines. Lieutenant Commander Kenneth "Dutch" Rausch of VA-27 was paying attention to the news from Vietnam and wondering if he'd be flying combat operations over the country anytime soon, this time in an A-7E rather than the A-4 Skyhawks he had flown during the war. The night of April 17, the carrier and her escorts received orders to proceed to the old Dixie Station off the central coast of South Vietnam to provide cover for the gathering fleet of rescue ships, should the North Vietnamese object to this American involvement in the end of the Southeast Asian wars. At the same time, *Coral Sea* received orders canceling the trip to Australia and ordering the ship to rendezvous with the newly formed task force off South Vietnam.

In Subic Bay on April 16, the veteran carrier *Midway* was ordered to put her air group ashore and depart to join Task Force 76. The carrier had several Air Force helicopters aboard, but her primary role would be as an empty deck to serve as an emergency landing field for evacuees. Off Vietnam, *Midway* was joined by *Hancock*, still carrying HMM-453's helicopters. Also aboard was HC-1's Detachment 2, whose Sikorsky UH-3 Sea King helicopters were rumored through scuttlebutt to be tasked with in-country SAR for US aircraft that might be shot down. In light of this, Lieutenant Bill Crumpler, who had last flown Huey gunships in Vietnam with the legendary HAL-3 "Seawolves," the most-decorated Navy squadron in the war, was asked by the other pilots and crews – none of whom were veterans – what they might expect. "I told them if we got that nasty job," Crumpler recalled, "that the first thing we should do is midnight requisition some green paint so those white upper fuselages wouldn't be so damned obvious." The pilots and crewmen were privately anxious that their rumored involvement could lead to the United States once again rejoining the war. "Fortunately, cooler heads prevailed, and it was announced there would be no in-country SAR mission for us."

In Hanoi, a group of pilots who had flown MiG-17s until the fighter was removed from front-line service in 1972 was organized to move south and operate captured VNAF aircraft in order to provide battlefield air support for the army. Among the pilots was now-Senior Lieutenant Tu De, whose first experience of combat had been the "Higbee Incident" three years earlier. Others involved were Nguyen Van Loc, Han Van Quang, Hoang Mai Vung, and Tran Cao Thang; all came from the 923rd Fighter Regiment. VPAF commander Tran Hanh, the first VPAF pilot to shoot down an American plane in the air battle on April 4, 1975, at the Dragon's Jaw, ordered the operation into action and accompanied the pilots and supporting ground crews when they flew to the captured airfield at Da Nang in an Ilyushin Il-14 transport. Tu De later recalled that there were "many" Cessna A-37B light attack aircraft and Northrop F-5As that had been abandoned on the airfield by the retreating VNAF, all left because of varying degrees of damage there was no time to repair. "With the assistance of several technicians of the other air force, we identified several A-37s that could be repaired the easiest, and took the necessary parts from the others." Two surrendered VNAF A-37 pilots explained the flight manuals to the North Vietnamese pilots while the aircraft were made operational.

The first repaired A-37 was declared airworthy on April 25. Flying with an ex-VNAF pilot in the right seat to provide guidance, Tu De quickly got the feel of the aircraft and after a 15-minute flight he landed, dropped off the "instructor" and made a solo 15-minute flight. After his success, the other pilots spent the rest of the day getting checked out. The other four A-37s were declared operational over the next two days. By the end of the day on April 27, each of the former MiG-17 pilots had made three solo flights in the A-37s and Colonel Tran Hanh gave the unit the name "Victory-minded Squadron" and declared them ready to undertake operations. That night, the five aircraft were fully fueled with an extra drop tank under each wing, and each was armed with four Mark 82 500-pound bombs.

The same day that the "Victory-minded Squadron" arrived at Da Nang, 40 Marines in civilian clothes from the 9th Marine Amphibious Brigade on *Hancock* were flown to the embassy in Saigon by Air America helicopters to reinforce the 18 Marine Security Guards assigned to defend the embassy; six Marines were assigned to protect Ambassador Martin.

April 27 saw Saigon come under fire from PAVN 122mm rockets for the first time since 1973. The evacuation coordinators from 7th Air Force limited incoming flights at Tan Son Nhut to C-130s because of their greater maneuverability during landing and takeoff, which would make them less vulnerable to the shoulder-fired SA-7 Strella SAMs used by the advancing PAVN forces. Over the preceding eight days, nearly 40,000 American and South Vietnamese refugees had been evacuated from Tan Son Nhut.

The morning of April 28, the persistent Ensign Heinrich stepped out of a helicopter onto *Coral Sea*'s flight deck. He later described his complicated journey from Subic Bay to the fleet off Vietnam: "I went down to the Subic Bay harbor master and did my best to see how I could get out to the ship. I was told unless I was a bomb, crude oil or Marine, I could forget about it until she came into port." Not to be deterred, he discovered USS *Denver* (LPD-9) was soon departing for the coming operation:

I managed to catch a ride out to her and get on board just as she was preparing to get underway. After several days at sea, I talked my way onto a helo that was jumping around several of the ships. I did a quick cross deck to the *Enterprise* and finally touched down on the *Coral Sea*. I remember walking into the VF-51 ready room with all my stuff and the squadron officers were pretty surprised, to say the least, to see this FNG walk in. I was so new I wasn't even carrier qualified yet, so I ended up with a front row seat to see it all. The main thing was everyone was wondering if the next flight would see them fighting the other side in our own planes they had captured. No one knew what to expect.

Little did the pilots on *Coral Sea* know, but just such an operation had gotten underway at about the same time Heinrich walked into VF-51's ready room. At Da Nang, the five A-37s took off and flew at low level to Thanh Son airfield, where they refueled. They departed Thanh Son at 1700 hours after the heat of the day so that they could take off with full loads, headed for Tan Son Nhut airfield – again at low level to avoid radar detection by the ships offshore.

At 1805 hours, the controllers in the tower at Tan Son Nhut reported what was thought to be five VNAF A-37s inbound. Moments later, those on the field realized the A-37s were not landing when they strafed aircraft on the ground. The Mark 82s tumbled from their wings and exploded on the field. Six exploded close enough to severely damage several C-130s and two were set on fire. At the time, it was thought the pilots of the A-37s were VNAF pilots who had defected, since no one thought North Vietnamese pilots could have made the transition to the American aircraft in the short time since airfields in South Vietnam had been abandoned. This mistaken view of the VNAF has been part of the "official history" ever since.

Once he had dropped his bombs, Lieutenant Tu De pulled out of his strafing run and spotted a C-130 ahead that had just taken off and was turning toward the gulf. He flew past the big transport and from a distance of 75–100 feet waggled his wings at the pilots in the cockpit and later recalled thinking to himself, "I wish you a safe flight to America." He then banked away and made a pass over Saigon at an altitude of 300 feet, drawing fire from the Presidential Palace.

The other four pilots each took a separate course as they turned away from their attack, in order to break up any pursuers. In fact, three VNAF F-5s that were airborne in the vicinity did attempt to give chase but lost the A-37s in the smoke and haze surrounding Saigon. The five VPAF pilots returned safely to Da Nang by 1950 hours.

Following the VPAF attack, PAVN forces that had moved near Tan Son Nhut fired rockets and artillery at the airfield after dark. At 0330 hours on April 29, a 122mm rocket hit Guardpost One at the DAO Compound. Two members of the Embassy Marine Security Guard Battalion, Corporal Charles McMahon and Lance Corporal

Darwin Lee Judge, were killed instantly in the explosion. McMahon, who was 11 days short of his 22nd birthday, had arrived in South Vietnam ten days earlier while Judge, who was two-and-a-half months past his 19th birthday, had been in-country since early March. They were the last two American combat deaths in the Vietnam War.

Twenty minutes later, a C-130E from the 776th Tactical Airlift Squadron was hit by another 122mm rocket as it taxied toward the terminal to pick up refugees after dropping off a BLU-82 "Daisy Cutter" on the far side of the field for the VNAF. The crew were able to get out of the aircraft when it caught fire. Between 0430 and 0800 hours, over 40 rockets and artillery shells struck the DAO compound.

At dawn on April 29, a VNAF AC-119G gunship that had spent the night dropping flares and strafing the approaching PAVN forces was joined by two A-1 Skyraiders that began patrolling the perimeter of the airfield until one was hit by an SA-7 at 0645 hours and went down. At 0700 hours, the AC-119 began an attack run to the east of the airfield when it was hit by an SA-7 and set afire, crashing in flames. Shortly after that, VNAF aircraft began taking off in disorganized formations. A-37s, F-5s, C-7s, C-119s, and C-130s headed for Thailand while pilots and crews of UH-1s loaded family members aboard their helicopters and took off, flying out to sea in search of the ships of Task Force 76. At 0800 hours Lieutenant General Tran Van Minh, the VNAF commandeer, accompanied by 30 staff members, arrived at the DAO compound and demanded evacuation. The VNAF was no longer an organized force.

At 0700 hours, General Smith advised Ambassador Martin that further fixed-wing evacuation from Tan Son Nhut was impossible as the enemy had the field surrounded, and that Operation *Frequent Wind* – the evacuation of Saigon – should commence. Martin refused to accept General Smith's word and insisted on visiting Tan Son Nhut to see things for himself. He arrived at 0930 hours to find the field afire and abandoned.

In Washington, President Ford learned of the loss of the C-130 and the deaths of the two Marines in the midst of a meeting with his energy and economic advisors. He scribbled a note to NSC Deputy Director Lieutenant General Brent Scowcroft that it was time to decide how to end things in Vietnam. In the subsequent meeting, it was determined that evacuation by commercial flights, by military airplanes, or by sea was no longer feasible; no final decision was reached. Two hours later, Ambassador Martin – who had returned to the embassy from Tan Son Nhut – called to inform the president that two C-130s attempting to land at Tan Son Nhut had been forced to abort due to rocket fire in the airfield, which was no longer operational. With that, everyone, including Ambassador Martin, agreed they had to go with the helicopter evacuation. At 1108 South Vietnam time April 29, Commander Task Force 76 received the CinCPac order to execute Operation *Frequent Wind*.

At 1406 hours, two Hueys carrying General Carey and Colonel Alfred M. Gray, Jr., the commander of Regimental Landing Team 4, landed at the DAO Compound. As the helicopter made its approach to the compound, they had a front row view of the PAVN's firepower while Tan Son Nhut was shelled with ground, rocket, and artillery fire. The two officers quickly established a command post in preparation for the arrival of the Marine CH-53s and the ground security force.

Lieutenant Colonel Herbert Fix, CO of HMM-463, had received orders to commence the evacuation at 1400 hours. The Marine air crews and Marine infantrymen rapidly manned their CH-53D Sea Stallion helicopters. "Gentlemen, start your engines." The laconic command, copied from the Indianapolis 500 auto races, echoed from *Hancock*'s 1MC. Moments later, the CH-53s lifted off the deck and took up a tight formation as they flew through the dark, ominous rain clouds that hovered over the South China Sea, bouncing in the blustery wind. Forty minutes later, they flew over the city and saw Tan Son Nhut in the distance. Soon Fix spotted the landing zone (LZ) in the tennis court near the DAO compound. Landing two at a time, the helicopters unloaded Battalion Landing Team (BLT) 2/4's command groups Alpha and Bravo, Fox Company and reinforced Hotel Company at 1506 hours; the Marines quickly moved to reinforce the 125 Marines of the Embassy Security Battalion who were already present. The second wave of 12 CH-53s landed at 1515 hours, bringing in the rest of the BLT. A third wave of two CH-53s from Marine Heavy Helicopter Squadron 463 (HMH-463) and eight CH-53Cs and two HH-53s of the Air Force's 40th Aerospace Rescue and Recovery Squadron operating from *Midway* arrived shortly afterwards. The helicopters quickly picked up waiting evacuees as more Air America Hueys fluttered in with others.

Air America had committed 24 of 28 available helicopters, and 31 pilots had agreed to remain in Saigon for the evacuation. When the shelling subsided at Tan Son Nhut at 0830 hours the Air America helicopters started flying to the designated rooftop landing zones in Saigon to pick up evacuees and fly them either to Tan Son Nhut for evacuation or out to the ships offshore. The pilots found the traffic around *Midway* and *Hancock* impossible, with desperate VNAF helicopters flying out to the fleet, and were only able to make more than one trip by touching down on the amphibious ships to discharge their passengers. *Time* magazine correspondent William Stewart recalled his flight:

> I sat in cold panic as the chopper took off. For the next three minutes as we gained altitude, we held our breaths. We knew the communists had been using heat-seeking missiles, and we were prepared to be shot out of the sky. As I turned around to see who was aboard, Buu Vien, the South Vietnamese Interior Minister, smiled and gave a thumbs-up signal. Forty minutes later we were aboard the USS *Denver*, safe.

Ensign Heinrich recalled what it was like on *Coral Sea* when the Vietnamese helicopters began arriving:

> There were so many that when they landed, we'd get the people out and have to push the helo overboard to make room for another to land and keep the deck open for our own ops. Some of the pilots who went into the water had their valuables – gold and jewelry and such – around their necks and had to decide whether they wanted to sink or swim because the weight of the stuff was dragging them down.

Coral Sea and *Enterprise* launched fighters to provide possible air cover over the city. RIO Lieutenant (jg) Teddy Prendergast flew with Lieutenant Commander Kenneth "Frog" Burgess and later recalled: "We flew over Saigon at about ten thousand feet. Looking down, it was just insane, all the crowds in the street, helicopters taking off from building roofs and flying every which way. I was amazed there weren't any midairs." Burgess remembered the Saigon flight as the most memorable of those he had flown since the carrier took position south of Cap St Jacques. "I must have logged a hundred hours. We were flying two and three missions a day."

Another drama unfolded that day on Con Son Island, site of the largest South Vietnamese prison. There, VNAF Major Buang-Ly was determined he would find a way to get his wife and five children out of the country. Communist forces had arrived on the island intent on freeing their fellow fighters. Finding a Cessna O-1 "Bird Dog," a light observation plane, abandoned on the island's airfield, the major and his wife stuffed their children, who ranged in age from 14 months to six years, into the airplane and he managed to take off as communist forces arrived on the field and opened fire at the airplane. He had no idea where to go, and headed out to sea. Unknown to him, the carriers *Midway* and *Hancock* were operating some 50 miles out, in the general direction he was heading. An hour later, he spotted ship's wakes in the sea, then found the carriers and their escorts. Vietnamese helicopters surrounded the two carriers, circling in hopes of landing, while crews tried to spot the recently landed Hueys to the side to provide open space on their flight decks.

Commander Vern Jumper, air boss of *Midway*, later remembered what happened:

> Suddenly, out of nowhere, this little Bird Dog appeared overhead and circled the ship. He made three passes right over the flight deck at about 100 feet, trying each time to drop a note. The first two blew over the side, but the third one stayed on deck. It said "I can land on your runway, would you please move the helicopters to the other side of your runway. I have one more hour of fuel. Would you please rescue me?" It was signed Major Buang, wife and five children.

Jumper went to the bridge to confer with Captain Chambers. "At first I suggested we have him ditch alongside the ship, put swimmers in the water, and save him. But Captain Chambers said, 'We're not going to do that. If he ditches in the water, he'll lose those five kids.' That was very true because it would have nosed over and we would have never gotten the kids out of there."

Chambers ordered Jumper to clear the angle deck by pushing the helicopters over the side. He later recalled "There were about ten million dollars worth of helicopters there and I thought to myself I was probably ending my career, but I did it anyway." As the deck crew pushed the helicopters overboard, two others landed in the midst of the activity. Their crews and passengers were pulled out and they were put over the side with the rest. Finally, the deck was clear.

Jumper remembered:

We turned into the wind. This guy made a couple passes at the ship just to look. I had no radio communications with him. I couldn't talk to him. He could see that we were ready for him. We had 30–40 knots right down the angle deck, and he started his final approach. He made a beautiful carrier landing without a tail hook. He touched down right in the wire area – we'd stripped the wires off the deck because that would have fouled him up. He touched down right where he should have, bounced once, rolled up the deck and was stopped before he got to the end of the angle deck. My flight deck crew ran out to grab him before he went over the side. The major and his wife jumped out of the cockpit, pulled the seat forward, and out tumbled the kids. She was holding a baby in her arms. My flight deck crew and all the other guys that were working on the flight deck in the squadrons and the ship's company were whooping and hollering and making so much noise. They were so proud, so glad that they saved this guy.

While some of Captain Chambers' superiors might have initially been upset about the loss of the helicopters, film of the landing was broadcast across the United States the next day. Major Buang-Ly's stunning escape made headlines from coast to coast with the photo of the O-1 on *Midway*'s deck on every front page. Captain Chambers and his crew were heroes. (The airplane can be seen today aboard *Midway*, now a museum in San Diego.)

VA-27's Lieutenant Rausch flew three patrols over the South Vietnamese coast that day with Lieutenant Tom Gravely. They saw refugees on shore getting in boats and heading out to sea. "It was the saddest sight I ever saw," he recalled. Having completed their third patrol, they headed back to *Enterprise* and came under fire from the ground:

We were just going feet wet near Vung Tau when we started taking tracers. Tom spotted the source and decided to get in a duel with a

ZSU-23 quad AAA. He made a strafing run and dropped ordnance. The AAA stopped, but as he rejoined, I saw a spray of something coming from the airplane's underside. I pulled in close and made a visual inspection. He had a small hole just ahead of the main gear. He'd taken a hit in the bleed air system which caused hot air to burn through some of the hydraulic systems.

The two A-7s coasted out over the Tonkin Gulf. It was soon apparent that Gravely's airplane was not going to make it to the carrier. Twelve miles from the ship, he reported a loss of longitudinal control and ejected. "I stayed with him till the SAR bird got there and pulled him out of the water. I landed last bird on the last recovery." No one wanted to list the event as a combat loss. "The skipper had a word with me about what had happened and we determined it could have been a mechanical failure, which made it an operational loss. I wrote up the report saying exactly that. Nobody was interested in a reason to re-fight the war." Lieutenant Tom Gravely was the last naval aviator to punch out over the Tonkin Gulf.

The most memorable moments of the evacuation occurred at the American Embassy in Saigon. By the time Prendergast and Burgess and the others from VF-51 flew over the city that morning, some 10,000 people were gathering around the embassy in hopes of finding a way out of the country, while around 2,500 evacuees were in the embassy and consular compounds awaiting transport to the DAO compound for evacuation. The crowds outside the embassy blocked traffic and the gates had been closed to prevent them from surging onto the embassy grounds. This prevented use of the buses that had been organized to transport evacuees to the DAO compound. Those who were eligible for evacuation who had not gotten to the embassy in time had to find their way through the crowd and make themselves known to the embassy staff or Marine guards manning the walls. They then had to be lifted over the walls while those below tried to use them as a way to get into the compound. One who managed to get out later recalled that "You could smell the desperation and fear in the air."

Inside the embassy, the crisis was worse. Some staff and evacuees had taken alcohol from the embassy's stores and were now wandering around in varying states of inebriation. Others were busy removing intelligence documents and US currency from safes and taking it to the incinerator. No one knew how much of the money actually made it from the safes to the incinerator in the confusion, but one staffer later estimated that more than five million dollars were burned.

Ambassador Martin created difficulties throughout the event. Despite all evidence to the contrary, he had remained optimistic that a negotiated settlement could be reached and that the United States would not be forced to pull out of South Vietnam. During the final days, in a doomed effort to avert the spread of defeatism and panic, he refused to allow Major James Kean, who commanded the Marine Security Guard Battalion, to have his men cut down the large tamarind tree and the other trees and shrubbery that blocked use of the embassy parking lot as a helicopter landing zone.

Finally, following his return from Tan Son Nhut, where the enormity of the catastrophe had finally broken through his defenses, Martin gave the order to clear the parking lot. Kean's Marines went to work at 1000 hours and by noon they had cleared the LZ. With the LZ on the embassy roof for the lighter Hueys and CH-46s, the parking lot LZ allowed the heavier CH-53s to come in. The Air America helicopters picking up people from the rooftop LZs throughout the city now began bringing them to the embassy. When Kean saw the first CH-53s heading toward Tan Son Nhut around 1500 hours, he contacted Task Force 76 to inform them of his airlift requirements. This created additional problems, since those offshore had assumed all evacuees had been taken to the DAO compound; only two helicopters were scheduled to evacuate Ambassador Martin and the Marines from the embassy.

Finally, a CH-46 arrived at 1700 hours, bringing the first of 130 Marines from 2/4 BLT from the DAO compound to reinforce perimeter security. The helicopter departed filled with evacuees. The last evacuees departed the DAO compound at 1900 hours and Kean was told operations at the embassy would cease at sunset. He responded that the LZ would be well lit and requested operations continue. He positioned vehicles around the parking lot to light it with their headlights. Informed by a CH-53 pilot who landed at 2130 hours that Task Force 76 commander Admiral Whitmire had ordered operations to cease at 2300, Kean went to Ambassador Martin and asked him to contact the White House and ensure the airlift continue. Martin did so, and Task Force 76 received orders that flights were to continue. Despite pilot fatigue and the poor visibility due to bad weather, darkness and smoke, General Carey managed to convince the admiral they should maintain the effort.

With helicopters landing at the embassy every ten minutes, Kean informed General Carey at 0215 hours that there were 225 Americans and 850 non-Americans left and that another 19 lifts would complete the evacuation. At 0300 hours, Ambassador Martin ordered Kean to move the remaining evacuees to the parking lot, which became the final perimeter. Word was received at 0327 hours that President Gerald Ford had ordered the evacuation ended when the 19 additional flights had been made. With that number already exceeded, Kean went to the rooftop LZ at 0430 hours and used a helicopter radio to contact Carey, who told him the president had ordered the airlift limited to Americans only. At 0458 hours, Ambassador Martin finally boarded an HMM-165 CH-46, call-sign "Lady Ace Nine," for evacuation to the task force command ship, USS *Blue Ridge*.

In the meantime, Kean had returned to the ground floor and ordered his men to withdraw into the chancery. The last were stepping inside as the crowd surrounding the embassy broke open the gates and surged into the compound. They bolted the chancery door while Seabees on the sixth floor locked the elevators; the Marines withdrew up the stairs, locking the grill gates behind them.

The men gathered on the roof, searching the night sky for the helicopters coming for them. Below on the ground floor, someone drove a water tanker through the chancery door and the crowd surged into the building, battering their way through the grill gates in a desperate final attempt to get to the roof. Kean managed to establish radio contact with the fleet, to learn that when Lady Ace Nine's pilot transmitted "Tiger is out," the inbound helicopter crews thought the mission was complete and turned back.

The Marines managed to seal the doors to the rooftop and used Mace to force back the crowd inside. Sporadic gunfire passed overhead. Twenty minutes later, CH-46s arrived and evacuated most of the Marines and the Seabees. Kean and ten Marines were left on the roof. After an anxious wait, CH-46 "Swift 22" of HMM-164 arrived overhead at 0700 hours. With the last Americans aboard, Swift 22 lifted off the embassy rooftop at 0753 hours and landed on USS *Hancock* at 0830 hours.

By the time aircraft ceased operation from Tan Son Nhut on April 28, 50,493 people – including 2,678 Vietnamese orphans – had been evacuated. Following the activation of Operation *Frequent Wind*, 122 Marine pilots logged 1,054 flying hours in 682 sorties, airlifting 395 Americans and 4,475 Vietnamese and third-country nationals from the DAO compound and 978 American and 1,120 Vietnamese and third-country nationals from the embassy.

While these dramatic events were underway in Saigon, Marine CH-46 YT-14 of HMM-164 spent the day as *Hancock's* SAR helicopter, first launching at 0600 hours. Crew chief/right gunner Corporal Stephen R. Wills and first mechanic/left gunner Corporal Richard L. Scott spent the day aboard as the helicopter operated for 17 hours. A CH-46D carried 1,200 pounds of jet fuel in each stub wing, giving it a flight endurance of two hours; YT-14 made several "hot refueling" landings during the day without shutting down. At 1300 hours, Captain William C. Nystul and First Lieutenant Michael J. Shea relieved the originally assigned pilot and co-pilot.

By 2200 hours, the fatigued pilots had been flying continuously for almost ten hours and the two crewmen had worked continuously for 17 hours. Twice in their final flight hour they were on final approach when they were sent back out to their orbit point for another possible SAR mission. Wills remembered:

We were at our orbit point when Captain Nystul radioed for clearance for a landing approach back to the *Hancock*. We were down to about 30 minutes of fuel. We were given the OK to return, refuel and then go back out. On our inbound approach, I looked out the rear of the ship and saw a light at our six o'clock position coming in on us. I made it out to be another aircraft. I told Captain Nystul and then I cleared him for a hard right turn. That other aircraft missed hitting us by less than 100 ft. For the next 15 minutes there was no conversation in our aircraft, except for a comment made by Captain Nystul that "Some one is going to die up here tonight." As we approached the ship, he asked me if we were clear for a left turn. I gave the OK and no sooner than that, I heard "Pick it up, Pick it up, Pick it up." I braced myself, thinking that we were about to be in a mid-air with another aircraft.

Sergeant Chris Woods, crew chief of "Swift 22" aboard ship saw what happened next:

> The traffic pattern around the *Hancock* was very congested with aircraft landing, dropping off passengers, refueling, etc. I can't remember if I was doing a turnaround inspection or trying to get some rest. I heard the air boss yell "PULL UP! PULL UP! PULL UP!" over the 5MC speakers. He kept yelling "PULL UP!" until the aircraft impacted the water. I ran out in front of my aircraft to see a left running light angling towards the water that continued down until there was a flash caused by the aircraft impacting the water. I remember hearing several hovering helicopters trying to pick up survivors. Pandemonium was everywhere.

Two Navy SH-3s, one Marine CH-53 and finally another CH-46 tried to rescue YT-14's crew. Corporal Wills later related:

> I came to under water. I was only able to inflate one side of my LPA. The right side was torn. When I hit the surface I found that my radio was gone, along with my pistol. I found my pen flares and fired two of them. I started yelling to see if anyone else got out. Corporal Scott yelled back. He was about 50 yards from me.

The SH-3s tried to get the two Marines with their hoist but the men couldn't hook up. The rotor wash from the CH-53 kept pushing them under. "Swift 07," another HMM-164 CH-46D, piloted by Captain Steve Haley and First Lieutenant Dean Koontz, launched immediately, and picked up Scott by hoist, then made a water-landing in pitch-black conditions, and water-taxied to the struggling and seriously injured Wills, who was unable to get into the rescue harness due to his injuries. The cabin was filling with seawater as crew chief Sergeant Lon Chaney pulled Wills through the cabin door by hand.

The rescue was completed at 2330 hours. The bodies of Captain Nystul and Lieutenant Shea were never recovered. A burial at sea ceremony was held aboard *Hancock* at twilight on April 30 for the last two naval aviators to die in Vietnam.

Following the fall of South Vietnam, the United States was faced with the question of how to help the thousands of refugees created by the event. The front lines of this operation became the Subic Bay naval base, commanded by Rear Admiral Doniphan B. "Don" Shelton, the former night fighter pilot in Korea who had been the last man to fly over the North Korean port of Hamhung during the evacuation of North Korea following the intervention in the war by the Chinese People's Volunteer Army. Admiral Shelton later recalled what was done:

> By early April, we had a pretty good idea that things were going bad over in southeast Asia. I received advance direction from CinCPacFlt that the South Vietnamese who were expected to leave that country were officially designated as refugees, which gave me the money and ability in advance to turn our recreation site, Grande Island, into a tent city. The effort received the designation Operation *New Life*. We would ultimately process 43,000 Vietnamese refugees through Grande Island between mid-April and mid-August.
>
> The SeaBees built the refugee camp in about 10 days and we were ready to start receiving them by April 15. The tent floors were made with double layers of wood pallets in the event of rain, and there was running water, private showers, and laundry facilities. Once things got going, we operated the camp like a city with a mayor, city officials, a daily newspaper, doctors, dentists, etc. My wife worked every day with a Vietnamese interpreter to create the Bull Horn bulletin board to keep everyone informed of how things were going.
>
> When the evacuation began, they were arriving at first at Clark AFB aboard C-5s, C-141s and C-130s. Later they came by boats and were picked up by our ships in the Tonkin Gulf. The government of the Philippines requested we limit their stays in the country to 14 days, so we had to make the operation as efficient as possible. When the refugees arrived, they were immediately interviewed by American Embassy and Subic Bay officials to determine their status. They were then processed through a shower facility minus their clothes, given haircuts and deloused. They were then issued five sets of clothes and their valuables were inventoried with a receipt and stored in a Marine M-48 Tank with two Marine guards right there and another in a banyan tree on site with a rifle. Only one woman ever claimed her valuables weren't returned when she left, and we paid her $2,500 on the spot. Food was prepared at Cubi Point and brought to the

camp by helo. The most popular meal was cheese burgers with lots of catsup.

We had 500 Cambodians who we housed at first on the beach beyond the Cubi Point runway for about a week, before their head man asked to see me and requested they be housed with the Vietnamese; we did that and there were no problems. We also included them in running the city functions.

Vice President Nguyen Cao Ky came into Subic on the *Denver*. The Philippines government had told me that he could not set foot on Philippine soil. I agreed and we transported him from *Denver's* flight deck to Cubi in a helo, where he then walked on double planks into the C-130 that flew him on to Guam and then the States.

I rank our treatment of these people by the fact that, when it came their turn to move on to the United States, they wanted to stay where they were. Overall, I consider Operation *New Life* the best job I had in a 40-year navy career.

As the ships of Task Force 76 departed for the Philippines, Ensign Heinrich and the rest of those aboard *Coral Sea* now looked forward to their delayed participation in the Battle of the Coral Sea celebration in Perth. But first, the ship paid a visit to Singapore, arriving on May 6 and remaining until the morning of May 9. Once again at sea, the ship's shellbacks resumed their plans for the initiation of the pollywogs, which took place aboard the carrier and her escorts on May 10 as the task force neared the Lombok Strait, entrance to the Indian Ocean.

There was still one act left in the Southeast Asian epic.

17

SOUTHEAST ASIAN FINALE

While the end game played out in South Vietnam, the war in Cambodia that had begun in May 1970 with the US invasion of the then-neutral country came to an abrupt end. On February 17, 1975, the US-allied Khmer Republic armed forces were forced to retreat from the villages and strongpoints they held along the Mekong River that provided the only connection to outside support from South Vietnam. The capital of Phnom Penh was quickly surrounded by the Khmer Rouge, leaving the city completely dependent on aerial resupply through Pochentong Airport. The United States mobilized an airlift of food, fuel, and ammunition, but military support was limited by the Case–Church Amendment, which restricted spending appropriated funds for military operations in Southeast Asia. BirdAir operated the airlift under contract to the United States, flying C-130 and DC-8 cargo into Pochentong from U-Tapao air base in Thailand. On March 22, two aircraft were hit by Khmer Rouge rockets that forced a suspension of the airlift the next day, but it was resumed on March 24, in the desperate hope the Khmer Rouge could be held off until the monsoon began in May. Khmer Republic president Lon Nol resigned on April 1 and left for exile in Thailand in hopes his departure could lead to peace negotiations. That day the final Khmer Republic position at Neak Luong fell and its captured artillery soon made its presence felt as Phnom Penh came under bombardment.

The United States executed Operation *Eagle Pull* on April 12. Marine CH-53s from HMH-462 aboard USS *Okinawa* (LPH-3) landed 360 Marines of the 2nd Battalion, 4th Marines Battalion Landing Team carried by USS *Vancouver* (LPD-2) and *Thomaston* (LSD-28) of Amphibious Ready Group Alpha (Task Group 76.4) at Phnom Penh Airport. The older Essex-class carrier USS *Hancock* had recently joined the fleet with HMH-463's helicopters providing reinforcement. The Marines secured LZ Hotel at the airfield at 0720 hours and HMH-462 helicopters evacuated 84 Americans and 205 Cambodians and third country nationals to the fleet, with three CH-53s at a time landing for pickups. By 1040 hours, the last were aboard the helicopters and headed out to sea. HMH-463's CH-53s then extracted the Marines, with the last departing at 1059 hours to the accompaniment of rocket fire from the Khmer Rouge as USAF OV-10s flew air cover overhead. The evacuation caught the Cambodian government by surprise; Phnom Penh and the provincial capitals still held by the government were filled with millions of refugees. By the end of the day, Khmer Rouge forces were closing in on the airport.

Over the course of April 15, attempts to negotiate peace through China were rebuffed by the Khmer Rouge. On April 16, shelling set the Shell Oil depot on fire. That afternoon the Khmer Republic Air Force flew its last mission, bombing the field as the enemy entered it, using T-28Ds that had remained behind to cover the departure of 97 other aircraft loaded with civilian dependents, who then escaped to Thailand.

On April 17, the Khmer Rouge occupied Phnom Penh. Captured members of the Khmer Republic forces were taken to the Olympic Stadium and executed, with senior leaders forced to write confessions before their executions. The Khmer Rouge ordered the evacuation of Phnom Penh, emptying the city. With that, Cambodia descended into a dark age of mass genocide by the victorious Khmer Rouge that would only end in 1979 after the deaths of some two million Cambodians when forces supported by Vietnam took control.

Following the April 30 fall of Saigon, the Khmer Rouge demanded the departure of all Vietnamese forces from their long-occupied base areas in Cambodia. This demand was met by a North Vietnamese refusal to leave areas they claimed were Vietnamese territory. On May 1, Khmer Rouge forces landed on Phu Quoc, an island claimed by Cambodia but previously controlled by South Vietnam, then captured the Tho Chu Islands the next day. Five hundred Vietnamese residents were evacuated to the mainland and later executed. Fearing the CIA would use merchant ships to supply their opponents, and to stop further Vietnamese incursions, the Khmer Rouge began patrolling coastal waters on May 1. The next day, seven Thai fishing boats and their crews were captured. On May 4, their gunboats pursued a South Korean freighter in an action that prompted the South Korean Transportation Ministry to warn shipping in the area. On May 7 they detained a Panamanian ship near Poulo Wai for 36 hours before releasing the ship following interrogation of the crew, and fired on a Swedish vessel in the same area.

The afternoon of May 12, the US container ship SS *Mayaguez*, loaded with 107 containers of routine cargo, and 77 containers of US government and military cargo taken on in Saigon on April 21, passed Poulo Wai Island en route to Sattahip, Thailand.

At 1418 hours, a Khmer Navy Swift Boat approached *Mayaguez* and fired across her bow. When Captain Charles T. Miller ordered the engines slowed to maneuvering speed, a rocket-propelled grenade (RPG) was fired over the ship. Ordering the radio room to transmit an SOS, Miller brought the ship to a halt. Seven Khmer Rouge soldiers led by battalion commander Sa Mean boarded the ship and he ordered Miller to proceed to the east of Poulo Wai. As this happened, a crewman broadcast a "Mayday" that was heard by an Australian vessel. At 1600 hours, when *Mayaguez* arrived off Poulo Wai, 20 more Khmer Rouge soldiers came aboard. Sa Mean, who did not speak English, pointed at a chart and signed that Miller should proceed to Ream on the Cambodian mainland, but the captain mimed the ship hitting rocks and sinking because the radar wasn't operating. Radioing his superiors, Sa Mean was ordered to keep the ship at Poulo Wai and *Mayaguez* dropped anchor at 1655 hours.

The US embassy in Jakarta, Indonesia, learned of *Mayaguez*'s SOS and Mayday signals and passed on the information. The news reached the National Military Command Center in Washington at 0512 hours Eastern Daylight Time (EDT). President Ford was briefed by Brent Scowcroft and the National Security Council (NSC) was convened at 1221 hours. CinCPac Admiral Noel Gayler had previously ordered reconnaissance aircraft to locate *Mayaguez*.

In the belief that the forced withdrawal from Cambodia and South Vietnam had severely damaged the reputation of the United States, and to avoid a comparison with the "Pueblo Incident" in 1968, where failure to use military force to halt capture of an intelligence ship by North Korea had led to an 11-month hostage situation, a decision was made to keep *Mayaguez* away from the Cambodian mainland. The White House issued a statement that President Ford considered this an act of piracy, though the claim had no foundation in maritime law. Secretary of Defense Schlesinger ordered *Mayaguez* located to prevent her movement to the Cambodian mainland. At 0200 hours on the morning of May 12, *Coral Sea* had just passed through Lombok Strait when the crew awakened to the captain's announcement over the 1MC public address system that the ship was turning around to "take care of one last problem," as Ensign Heinrich later remembered.

With no diplomatic communication with Phnom Penh, a message was sent by Secretary of State Kissinger to the Chinese Liaison Office in Washington demanding that *Mayaguez* and her crew be immediately released, but the note was not accepted. George H.W. Bush, head of the US Liaison Office in Beijing, was ordered to deliver the note to the Chinese Foreign Ministry as well as pass on an oral message that "The Government of the United States demands the immediate release of the vessel and of the full crew. If that release does not immediately take place, the authorities in Phnom Penh will be responsible for the consequences."

P-3 Orions picked up *Mayaguez* on radar and she was visually identified at 0814 hours on May 13. After drawing fire, the VP-17 patrol plane pulled off and another took up a radar surveillance from further out. Shortly after this, Captain Miller was ordered to get *Mayaguez* underway and she departed at 0845 hours, following a Swift Boat. The P-3 continued tracking her on radar.

Admiral Gayler ordered Seventh Air Force commander Lieutenant General John J. Burns to send combat aircraft to the area and at 1300 hours two unarmed F-111s that had been diverted from a training mission made low-level high-speed passes over the ship, When they departed, Sa Mean ordered Captain Miller to drop anchor approximately a mile north of Koh Tang Island. Shortly thereafter two F-4Es arrived and fired their cannon in the water ahead of the ship. They were followed by A-7D Corsairs and F-111s that fired into the sea ahead and astern of the ship to indicate she should not be moved further. At 1615 hours, the crewmen were put in two fishing boats that took them closer to the island.

Coral Sea and her escorts would arrive the next day, but they had no troops aboard. *Hancock* and *Okinawa* both had Marines aboard, but neither could arrive before May 16 and 18 respectively. The only unit available was 2nd Battalion, 9th Marines, then training on Okinawa. The unit was ordered to return to camp the night of May 13. At dawn on May 14, the unit boarded C-141s at Kadena AFB to fly to Thailand. While the regiment had been the first US ground combat force to land in Vietnam in April 1965, by May 1975 only a few officers and NCOs were combat veterans.

Planning for the rescue involved the assignment of nine Air Force HH-53C "Jolly Green Giants" from the 40th Aerospace Rescue and Recovery Squadron and ten CH-53 "Knives" of the 21st Special Operations Squadron at Nakhon Phanom RTNB to stage the assault. The differences between the two would become important: the HH-53 was able to refuel by air; it carried 450 gallons of fuel in self-sealing tanks, was armor plated, and carried three 7.62 miniguns. The CH-53 could not be refueled by air, carried 650 gallons of fuel in non-self-sealing tip tanks; it lacked armor and was only armed with two miniguns. The HH-53 was less vulnerable to ground fire and could remain in the area indefinitely as long as it had access to a tanker.

The Air Force had a plan to retake *Mayaguez* using an assault force of 75 troops from the 56th Security Police Squadron to be dropped onto the containers on *Mayaguez*'s deck the morning of May 14. Five HH-53s and seven CH-53s were ordered to proceed to U-Tapao for staging, but CH-53 "Knife 13," crashed en route killing its crew and 18 security policemen. With this loss and the discovery that the containers would collapse under the weight of the helicopters, while the men would be exposed if they rappelled down to the deck, the plan was canceled. The NSC decided to wait for *Coral Sea* to arrive off Koh Tang and the Marines to arrive in Thailand before making a rescue attempt.

At dawn on May 14, the *Mayaguez* crew was loaded onto a fishing boat that left Koh Tang in company with two Swift Boats, headed for Kampong Som on the mainland. Two F-111s, followed by a pair of F-4Es and a pair of A-7Ds, made firing passes, firing first in front of the Swift Boats and then directly at them, causing one to turn back. An AC-130H Spectre gunship engaged the second Swift Boat before an A-7D strafed it and sank it. The pilots reported seeing 30–40

Caucasians on board the fishing boat. A communications link had been established between the White House and the orbiting fighters, whose pilots reported they could try to shoot the rudder off the fishing boat, but this was turned down because there was too much chance of harming the crew. At 1010 hours, the fishing boat arrived at Kampong Som, where the local Khmer Rouge commander, apparently fearing an American attack, refused to accept responsibility for the crew. With that, the boat moved further down the coast and anchored off Koh Rong Sanloem Island. Unfortunately, the orbiting fighters lost track of the boat after it entered Kampong Som, which was the crew location transmitted up the chain of command.

Uncertainty regarding the location of the crew dominated the rescue plan. Planners believed some were still on the ship, some on Koh Tang, and others on the fishing boat at Kampong Som. The NSC opted to proceed with a simultaneous attack by Marines to retake the ship and attack Koh Tang, with diversionary attacks on Cambodian shipping and bombing of mainland targets by *Coral Sea*'s air wing. The rescue plan was finalized: 600 Marines of Echo and Golf companies from 2nd Battalion, 9th Marines in five CH-53 Knives and three HH-53 Jolly Greens would seize and hold Koh Tang. Two of the helicopters would make a diversionary assault on the West Beach to cover the six that put the main assault on the wider East Beach. The Marines would then take the nearby compound where it was believed the crew was held. This initial assault wave would be backed up by two more waves of helicopters in order to land all of 2nd Battalion, 9th Marines on Koh Tang. It was estimated that only 20–30 Khmer Rouge were present; the planners in Thailand had not received the reports of heavy antiaircraft fire coming from the island and the number of gunboats sighted had not been passed on. Due to fear of harming the nearby crew, there would be no preparatory air strike.

Mayaguez would be seized by 57 Marines from Delta Company, 1st Battalion, 4th Marines. Volunteers from Military Sealift Command would be brought to *Mayaguez* by the destroyer *Holt*, for a ship-to-ship boarding an hour after the assault on Koh Tang. With *Mayaguez* retaken, *Holt* would take up a blocking position with USS *Wilson* to intercept any Khmer forces reacting to the operation. A strike force from *Coral Sea* would hit targets on the mainland. The Air Force plan for B-52s to bomb the port facilities at Kampong Som and Ream Naval Base was dropped, with President Ford allowing only attacks by carrier-based aircraft. The assault would take place on May 15.

Unfortunately, none of *Mayaguez's* crew were on Koh Tang Island. Rather than 20–30 defenders, the Khmer Rouge commander of Kampong Som District had sent a force of 100 troops to the island on May 1 to defend against a possible Vietnamese attack. The defenses were centered on the two beaches to either side of a narrow peninsula. On East Beach, two heavy machine guns were dug in at each end of the beach, with fortified fighting positions equipped with two M60 7.62mm machine guns, several RPGs, and two DK-82 recoilless rifles set up behind a sand berm, all connected by a shallow zig-zag trench. On West Beach, a heavy machine gun, an M60, RPGs, and a 75mm recoilless rifle were in connected firing positions. Both strong points were supported by a 60mm mortar position behind them, with an 81mm mortar positioned in the middle of the island that could fire on either beach.

At 0613 hours on May 15, three HH-53s transferred Marines to *Holt*. As the destroyer slowly came alongside *Mayaguez*, A-7Ds overhead saturated the ship with tear gas and at 0725 hours the Marines executed one of the first hostile ship-to-ship boardings since the Civil War. An hour-long search revealed the ship was empty.

The Koh Tang assault was a disaster. Expecting only light opposition, the helicopters instead faced heavy fire from a large force. At 0630 hours, the two CH-53s approaching East Beach were met by intense fire. Their lack of armor, self-sealing fuel tanks, and defensive weapons proved fatal. Two RPG grenades hit Knife-31, igniting the left fuel tank and ripping open the nose of the helicopter; it crashed in a fireball 150 feet offshore that killed the co-pilot, five Marines, and two Navy corpsmen while another Marine drowned when he swam from the wreck; three Marines were cut down trying to reach the beach and a tenth died clinging to the burning wreckage. The ten surviving Marines and three helicopter crewmen swam for two hours before they were picked up by *Wilson's* whaleboat. One of the survivors was the Marine forward air controller, who used an Air Force survival radio to direct air strikes from the water until the battery failed.

Knife 23 crash-landed when its tail section was blown off by an RPG grenade, but the 20 Marines and five-man crew were able to get out successfully and set up a defensive perimeter. They would be cut off for 12 hours and saved by the co-pilot, who used his survival radio to call in air strikes.

The remaining four helicopters were diverted from East Beach to West Beach and managed to land their Marines between 0630 hours and 0700 hours. Jolly Green 41 only managed to get in on its fifth attempt with support from an AC-130 gunship. Knife 32 and Jolly Green 41 and 42 managed to land 81 Marines of Golf Company on West Beach while Jolly Green-43 landed the 29 Marines of the battalion command and mortar platoon, led by company XO Major Randall Austin, half a mile distant to the southwest. By 0700 hours, 109 Marines and five Air Force crewmen were on Koh Tang in three isolated positions and under close fire by Khmer Rouge troops.

With Knife 21, 23, and 31 destroyed by enemy fire and Knife 22 and 32 and Jolly Green 41 and 42 too badly damaged to continue operations, only Jolly Green 11, 12, and 43 were left to bring in the follow-up force. Knife 51 and 52, which had been assigned for SAR, were reassigned to carry troops.

Covered by suppressive fire from an AC-130, Jolly Green 13 landed on East Beach in a hail of enemy fire at 0815 hours, 300 feet from the surrounded Marines. When they were reluctant to break cover and run through the heavy fire to the helicopter, Jolly Green 13 managed to lift off with its fuel line ruptured by enemy fire and stayed airborne long enough to make an emergency landing in Rayong, Thailand.

The three HH-53s and two CH-53s picked up 127 Marines of the second wave at U-Tapao between 0900 hours and 1000 hours. At 1150 hours, Knife 51 and 52 and Jolly Green 43 arrived over Koh Tang and prepared to land on East Beach. During the approach, Knife 52's fuel tanks were punctured by enemy fire; the pilot aborted the landing and managed to make it back to U-Tapao with fuel streaming. Knife 51 and Jolly Green 43 abandoned their attempts and took up a holding pattern.

In the meantime, shortly before the ship was retaken, the Khmer Rouge information and propaganda minister announced from Phnom Penh that there was no plan to hold the ship and crew, and they had only been detained to find out what they were doing in Cambodian waters. The broadcast was picked up by the CIA and translated for the NSC by 0715 hours Cambodian time. Skeptical of the Khmer

Rouge, the White House stated at 0815 hours that the operation would continue until the ship and crew were safe.

The Khmer Rouge followed the statement by informing the crew at 0630 hours that they would be allowed to go back aboard the ship, but only after they agreed to a statement that they had not been mistreated. At 0715 hours they were loaded aboard the Thai fishing boat, which was escorted by their original captor Sa Mean and his men in a Swift Boat. Once away from the island, Sa Mean took the guards off first and instructed the crew to return to their ship and call off the Americans. At 0935 hours, the fishing boat was spotted by an orbiting P-3 that mistakenly identified it as a gunboat. Moments later the crew was spotted aboard and at 0949 hours *Wilson* came alongside and brought the crew on board. The White House received news of the crew's release, and at 1127 hours Cambodian time President Ford announced the recovery of *Mayaguez* and rescue of the crew, failing to mention that the crew had been released by the Khmer Rouge.

The president refused to cancel the *Coral Sea* air strikes with the Marines still on Koh Tang. VF-51's Ken Burgess later recalled, "No one in VF-51 was looking forward to the possibility of being the last guy to die in a war we'd already lost. That opinion wasn't limited to our ready room." A strike force of VA-95 A-6As and A-7Es from VA-22 and VA-95, escorted by VF-51 and VF-111 F-4Ns, bombed barges and oil storage facilities at Kompong Som, cargo planes and T-28s at Ream airfield, and other boats at Ream naval base starting at 0905 hours.

Lieutenant Commander James A. Lair, strike leader for a flight of two VA-22 and one VA-94 A-7E, recalled this final strike of the war:

> Our CAG, who was in an A-6, found a Khmer Rouge Swift Boat that was headed toward *Mayaguez* at high speed and notified the Airborne Command Center. They immediately contacted me and asked if we had ordnance. Each of my A-7s had four Mark-20 Rockeyes. We were cleared to destroy the Swift Boat. We expended all the Rockeyes with no damage to the Swift boat, because the boat's high speed and the time of fall for the Rockeye let it outrun the bomb's lethality pattern. I then made a low angle strafing run and sank the gunboat with my M61 Vulcan. As a result of our experience with high speed targets, the A-7 was subsequently outfitted with a computerized Constant

Computer Impact Point (CCIP) targeting device on the HUD that could account for a target's speed.

Other than Lair's battle with the Swift Boat, nothing else of note happened and all aircraft were safely recovered. Ken Burgess recalled, "We were all happy that the defenses weren't that well-organized and everybody came home safe."

With the ship and crew recovered, the task force received orders to "immediately cease all offensive operations against the Khmer Republic [and to] disengage and withdraw all forces from operating areas as soon as possible" from the Joint Chiefs at 1155 hours. On receiving the order, the orbiting EC-130 airborne command center sent a recall to the second assault wave which turned back. Major Austin managed to convince General Burns that he needed reinforcement to keep his separated units from being overrun and the helicopters turned around and headed for Koh Tang.

At 1210 hours, Knife 51, followed by Jolly Green 43, 11, and 12 managed to land 100 Marines on West Beach. There were now 205 Marines on West Beach and 20 Marines and five airmen on East Beach. Under cover of mortar fire and A-7 air strikes, Major Austin and his Marines managed to reach Golf Company at the northern end of West Beach at 1245 hours.

The Khmer Rouge had moved back from the beach positions, and gunfire at West Beach had been reduced by 1400 hours. Major Austin asked the airborne command center if he should attempt to push across the 1,100 feet separating his men from the isolated unit on East Beach, but was informed that another pickup would be attempted. Jolly Greens 11 and 43 approached East Beach at 1415 hours but had to pull off due to heavy fire that damaged a fuel line on Jolly Green 43, forcing it to make an emergency landing aboard *Coral Sea* at 1436 hours; it was repaired and returned to operations by 1700 hours. The crew reported that they had been hit by fire coming from the semi-submerged Swift Boat shot up by an AC-130 the day before. With this information A-7s strafed the boat. Nail 68, an Air Force OV-10 FAC, took over control of air support at 1623 hours and called on *Wilson* to destroy the boat with her 5-inch guns. This new FAC brought an improvement in the air support, but the battle regained intensity at 1700 hours when the Khmer Rouge found an ammo dump and were able to resupply themselves.

A third rescue attempt at East Beach was made at 1800 hours when the sun set. Jolly Green 11 – with gunfire support from Jolly Green 12, Knife 51 and *Wilson's* whaleboat which was armed with four M60s – made its run in to the beach after Nail 68 brought in an AC-130 followed by *Coral Sea* F-4s and A-7s to hit the edge of East Beach. Jolly Green 11 was over East Beach at 1815 hours. With the wreckage of Knife 23 blocking the original LZ, pilot First Lieutenant Donald Backlund hovered just to the north, see-sawing up and down to make the helicopter a difficult target for the enemy. Because of this, only a few Marines could get aboard the rear ramp at a time, timing their jumps with the downward moves. Despite the helicopter being hit repeatedly, all 20 Marines and the five Air Force crewmen got aboard and Backlund delivered them to *Coral Sea*.

Ken Burgess was flying one of the F-4Ns providing cover. He later remembered, "Just after the helicopter made the pickup, the FAC ordered us to get out to sea so these five C-130s that had shown up with 'Daisy Cutters' could make their drop. There was a huge explosion." The 15,000-pound BLU-82 "daisy cutter" was the largest conventional bomb in existence at the time. The FAC had directed that one be dropped well south of the remaining Marines on West Beach, but the enormous blast sent a shockwave across the Marine position so strong that Major Austin radioed the airborne command center that no more should be dropped and the other four C-130s left with their weapons still aboard.

Shortly after the bomb was dropped, word was received from Jolly Green 11 that one Marine might still be in the wreckage of Knife 31. Jolly Green 12 went in to make a search, hovering above the wreck and lowering a crewman to check the wreck. There was no one there, but Jolly Green 12 took several hits and was damaged so badly it was forced to fly to *Coral Sea*.

The moonless night now provided sufficient cover to try to extract the remaining men on West Beach. Knife 51 and the quickly repaired and returned Jolly Green 43, joined by recently arrived Jolly Green 44, began the withdrawal at 1840 hours, protected by gunfire from the AC-130 and *Wilson*, which was standing by offshore. Knife 51 lifted out 41 Marines, followed by Jolly Green 43, which picked up 54; they were taken to *Coral Sea*. As Jolly Green 44 loaded 44 Marines, the shrinking perimeter came under intense attack and the remaining Marines were in danger of being overrun. Because a round trip to *Coral Sea* took 30 minutes, pilot First Lieutenant Bob Blough took the Marines to the nearby *Holt*, hovering over the destroyer in complete darkness with only the front wheels touching down as the Marines dropped onto the ship. Five minutes later, Blough returned to West Beach and picked up 34 more Marines. This time, due to engine trouble, he had to fly out to *Coral Sea*. Thirty-two Marines were still on the island.

At 2000 hours, Knife 51 landed under fire and began loading in the dark. Company commander Captain Davis and Gunnery Sergeant McNemar searched for stragglers. When two more Marines stumbled out of the darkness, parajumper Technical Sergeant Wayne Fisk left the helicopter and made one last search for stragglers. Finding none, he leaped into the hovering Knife 51 and the CH-53 left Koh Tang 2010 hours, headed for the *Coral Sea*.

Total American losses included 18 dead and 50 wounded. Thirteen dead were left on the beach. Unfortunately, there were still Americans on the island.

Shortly after Knife 51 departed, pilot First Lieutenant Brims informed the FAC that some Marines aboard claimed there were still Marines on the ground; this was contradicted by Captain Davis who stated all Marines were off Koh Tang. Just after 2020 hours, radioman Staff Sergeant Robert Velie in the C-130 airborne command center heard an American ask over the radio when the next helicopter would extract them. The caller gave Velie the authentication code that he was not the Khmer Rouge. The aircraft commander then advised *Holt* that Marines were still on the island. *Holt* replied that they should swim out to sea for rescue, but when this was passed to the caller, he said it was not possible because only one could swim. Velie then advised the caller to take cover since air strikes were inbound; the caller confirmed message received, but there was no further radio contact.

Two hours later, with the Marines now aboard three different ships, Echo Company commander Captain Stahl found three of his Marines were missing. After checking all ships, Lance Corporal Joseph N. Hargrove, Private First Class Gary L. Hall, and Private Danny G. Marshall, all members of a machine gun team that had been protecting the constantly shrinking perimeter's right flank, were missing.

The Marines volunteered to go back and get their fellows. Task Force 73 commander Rear Admiral Robert P. Coogan met with the

Marine leaders and Lieutenant (jg) R.T. Coulter, who had just arrived with a SEAL team, to consider the options. The admiral asked Coulter to go ashore with *Wilson*'s boat under a white flag with leaflets dropped and *Wilson* broadcasting the intentions to recover the American bodies and find the missing men; Coulter responded with a proposal to take his team ashore for a night reconnaissance, but Coogan had orders from Seventh Fleet to cease hostile action and decided there would be no rescue mission unless there was confirmation the Marines were alive.

The morning of May 16, *Wilson* cruised between the beaches broadcasting in English, French, and Khmer that they had no hostile intent and only wished to retrieve any Americans dead or alive and would send an unarmed boat ashore if the Khmer Rouge would allow them. No answer was received and no one spotted the missing Marines. With no indication that they were alive after three hours, *Wilson* departed the area. Hargrove, Hall, and Marshall were declared Missing in Action; their status was changed to Killed in Action (Body Not Recovered) on July 21, 1976.

In 1985, the Khmer Rouge commander at the Koh Tang battle informed the US Joint Task Force-Full Accounting (JTF-FA) that on the morning of May 16 he ordered a search for any remaining Americans. One of the searchers was hit by M16 fire, and one American with a leg wound was captured. The description matched Joseph Hargrove. The Khmer Rouge continued to search and located an abandoned M60, various equipment, and the covered body of a black American (presumably Ashton Loney, the first man killed in the assault). He was buried and the prisoner taken to headquarters. When he learned his soldier had died, the commander ordered the American shot. A week later, his men noticed that their leftover food was being disturbed and found bootprints in the mud. They captured two Americans whose descriptions matched Gary Hall and Danny Marshall. The commander was ordered to deliver them to the mainland, where they were taken to the Ti Nean Pagoda above Sihanoukville and shackled after being stripped to their underwear. A week later, on orders from Phnom Penh, each was beaten to death with an RPG launcher. Hall was buried in a shallow grave near the beach while Marshall was dumped on the beach.

In 1999, a JTF-FA team found bone fragments that might have belonged to Hall and Marshall, but DNA tests were inconclusive. Hargrove, Hall, and Marshall received Purple Hearts, but Hargrove was not given the medal until 1999, when Vietnam veteran pilot and author Ralph Wetterhahn published articles about the case. In 2016 the Defense POW/MIA Accounting Agency (DPAA) announced the recovery of Hall's ID card from an empty grave on Koh Tang and the recovery of a radio and flak jacket from near where Knife 51 had taken off.

Coral Sea received the Meritorious Unit Commendation on July 6, 1976 for her role in the Mayaguez incident. Ken Burgess remembered, "The whole thing was as messed-up as everything else in that messed-up war." It was an appropriate epitaph for a war that began in confusion and misinformation, which never changed throughout the decade it was fought.

BIBLIOGRAPHY

Anthony, Victor B. and Richard R. Sexton, *The War in Northern Laos 1954–1973* (Washington, DC, Air Force History Office, 1993)

Attinello, John S. et al, "Air To Air Encounters in Southeast Asia" (The Red Baron Report), Vols 1–3, Institute for Defense Analysis, 2001

Ault et al, "Report of the Air-to-Air Missile Systems Capability Review" (The Ault Report), Naval Air Systems Command, January 1, 1969

Baranek, David, "Top Gun: The Navy's First Center of Excellence," US Naval Institute Proceedings, Vol. 145, No. 9, September 2019

BDM Corporation, "A Study of the Strategic Lessons Learned in Vietnam, Vol. 1: The Enemy," US Army War College, 1981

Berman, Larry, *Planning a Tragedy: The Americanization of the War in Vietnam* (New York, W.W. Norton, 1982)

Birzer, Norman and Peter B. Mersky, *US Navy A-7 Corsair Units of the Vietnam War* (Oxford, Osprey Publishing, 2004)

Boniface, Roger, *Fighter Pilots of North Vietnam: An Account of their Combats 1965 to 1975* (Authors On Line, 2005)

Burgess, Richard R. and Rosario M. Rausa, *US Navy A-1 Skyraider Units of the Vietnam War* (Oxford, Osprey Publishing, 2006)

Davies, Peter E., *US Navy F-4 Phantom II Units of the Vietnam War 1964–68* (Oxford, Osprey Publishing, 2016)

Davies, Peter E., *US Navy F-4 Phantom II Units of the Vietnam War 1969–73* (Oxford, Osprey Publishing, 2018)

Davies, Steve, *Red Eagles: America's Secret MiGs* (Oxford, Osprey Publishing, 2012)

Dean, Ashley E., "Counterproductive Counterinsurgency: Lessons from the Misuse of Airpower in the American Vietnam Conflict and the United States' Fight against ISIS," unpublished Master's thesis, Louisiana State University, 2017

Directorate of Intelligence, "Intelligence Memorandum: The Effectiveness of the Rolling Thunder Program"; Washington, DC, Central Intelligence Agency, May 23, 1967

Elward, Brad and Peter E. Davies, *USN F-4 Phantom MiG Killers: 1965–70* (Oxford, Osprey Publishing, 2012)

Elward, Brad and Peter E. Davies, *USN F-4 Phantom MiG Killers: 1972–73* (Oxford, Osprey Publishing, 2014)

Fall, Bernard B., *Last Reflections on a War* (New York, Doubleday, 1967)

Fey, Peter, "The Effects of Leadership on Carrier Air Wing Sixteen's Loss Rates During Operation Rolling Thunder, 1965–1968," unpublished Master's thesis, US Army Command and General Staff School, 2006

Fey, Peter, *Bloody Sixteen: The USS Oriskany and Air Wing 16 during the Vietnam War* (New York, Potomac Books, 2020)

Grant, Zalin, *Over the Beach: The Air War in Vietnam* (New York, W.W. Norton and Company, 1986)

Halberstam, David, *The Best And The Brightest* (New York, Random House, 1972)

Hallion, Richard P., *Rolling Thunder 1965–68* (Oxford, Osprey Publishing, 2018)

Hankins, Michael M., "The Phantom Menace: The F-4 in Air Combat in Vietnam," unpublished Master's thesis, University of North Texas, 2013

Harris, Warren L., "The Linebacker Campaigns: An Analysis," unpublished Master's thesis, US Air Force Air War College, 1987

Hung, Nguyen Sy, *Air Engagements in the Skies over Vietnam (1965–1975) as Viewed from Both Sides* (Hanoi, People's Army Publishing House, 2013)

Karnow, Stanley, *Vietnam, a History* (New York, Viking Books, 1983)

Lin, Mao, "China and the Escalation of the Vietnam War: January to July 1965," unpublished Master's thesis, University of Georgia, 2004

McMaster, H.R., *Dereliction of Duty* (New York, Harper, 1997)

McNamara, Robert S., *In Retrospect: The Tragedy and Lessons of Vietnam* (New York, Times Books, 1995)

Mersky, Peter B., *US Navy and Marine Corps A-4 Skyhawk Units of the Vietnam War* (Oxford, Osprey Publishing, 2010)

Mersky, Peter B., *F-8 Crusader Units of the Vietnam War* (Oxford, Osprey Publishing, 2012)

Michel III, Marshall L., *Clashes; Air Combat over North Vietnam 1965–1972* (Annapolis, MD, US Naval Institute Press, 2007)

Morgan, Rick, *A-3 Skywarrior Units of the Vietnam War* (Oxford, Osprey Publishing, 2002)

Morgan, Rick, *A-6 Intruder Units of the Vietnam War* (Oxford, Osprey Publishing, 2012)

Nichols, John B. and Barrett Tillman, *On Yankee Station* (Annapolis, MD, US Naval Institute Press, 1987)

Office of the Historian, "Foreign Relations, 1964–1968, Vol. V, Vietnam 1967; Documents 135-152," Washington, DC, Department of State, 2001

Osborne, Arthur M., "Air Defense for the Mining of Haiphong," *Proceedings of the US Naval Institute*, Annapolis, MD, Vol. 100, No. 4, September 1974, pp. 113–115

Pedersen, Dan, *Top Gun: An American Story* (New York: Hachette, 2019)

Polmar, Norman and Edward J. Marolda, *Naval Air War: The Rolling Thunder Campaign* (Naval History and Heritage Command, Department of the Navy, 2015)

Pribbenow, Merle, "North Korean Pilots in the Skies of North Vietnam," Princeton: Woodrow Wilson Institute, November 2011

Sherwood, John, *Fast Movers: Jet Pilots and the Vietnam Experience* (Simon & Schuster, 2001)

Smith, John T., *Rolling Thunder: The Strategic Bombing Campaign Against North Vietnam, 1965–1968* (Walton-on-Thames, Air Research Publications, 1994)

Snepp, Frank, *Decent Interval: An Insider's Account of Saigon's Indecent End Told by the CIA's Chief Strategy Analyst in Vietnam* (University Press of Kansas, 25th anniversary edition, 2002)

Thomson, James C., "How Could Vietnam Happen? An Autopsy," *The Atlantic*; April 1968, https://www.theatlantic.com/magazine/archive/1968/04/how-could-vietnam-happen-an-autopsy/306462/

Tillman, Barrett, *MiG Master: The Story of the F-8 Crusader* (Annapolis, MD, US Naval Institute Press, 1990)

Toperczer, Istvan, *MiG 17 and MiG-19 Units of the Vietnam War* (Oxford, Osprey Publishing, 2001)

Toperczer, Istvan, *MiG-21 Units of the Vietnam War* (Oxford, Osprey Publishing, 2001)

Toperczer, Istvan, *MiG-17 and MiG-19 Aces of the Vietnam War* (Oxford, Osprey Publishing, 2016)

Toperczer, Istvan, *MiG-21 Aces of the Vietnam War* (Oxford, Osprey Publishing, 2017)

Van Staaveren, Jacob, *Gradual Failure: The Air War over North Vietnam, 1965–1966* (Washington, DC, United States Air Force, 2002)

Vietnam Task Force, "United States – Vietnam Relations, 1945–1967; Vol. IV: Direct Action: The Johnson Commitments, 1964–1968" (The Pentagon Papers), Office of the Secretary of Defense, 1969

Vietnam Task Force, "United States – Vietnam Relations, 1945–1967; Vol. IV: Section 7: Air War in the North: 1965–1968" (The Pentagon Papers), Office of the Secretary of Defense, 1969

Wilkens, John, "Top Gun at Fifty," *San Diego Union-Tribune*, June 16, 2019

Wisely, H. Denny, *Green Ink: Memoirs of a Fighter Pilot*, private publication, 2018

Zumwalt, Elmo R., Jr., *On Watch* (New York, Quadrangle Books, 1976)

SOURCES FOR DIRECT QUOTES

Arnold, Bob: Fey, Peter, *Bloody Sixteen: The USS Oriskany and Air Wing 16 during the Vietnam War* (New York, Potomac Books, 2020)

Barkley, Steven: Davies, Peter E., *US Navy F-4 Phantom II Units of the Vietnam War 1964–68* (Oxford, Osprey Publishing, 2016)

Batson, Jack: Davies, Peter E., *US Navy F-4 Phantom II Units of the Vietnam War 1964–68* (Oxford, Osprey Publishing, 2016)

Carlton, George: Burgess, Richard R. and Rosario M. Rausa, *US Navy A-1 Skyraider Units of the Vietnam War* (Oxford, Osprey Publishing, 2009)

Cunningham, Randall H. "Duke": Drendel, Lou, … *And Kill MiGs, Air to Air Combat From Vietnam to the Gulf War* (Carrollton TX, Squadron/Signal Publications, 1975)

Daramus, Nick: Burgess, Richard R. and Rosario M. Rausa, *US Navy A-1 Skyraider Units of the Vietnam War* (Oxford, Osprey Publishing, 2009)

Elkins, Frank: Fey, Peter, *Bloody Sixteen: The USS Oriskany and Air Wing 16 during the Vietnam War* (New York, Potomac Books, 2020)

Fraser, William: Davies, Peter E., *US Navy F-4 Phantom II Units of the Vietnam War 1964–68*, (Oxford, Osprey Publishing, 2016)

Greathouse, Ed: Burgess, Richard R. and Rosario M. Rausa, *US Navy A-1 Skyraider Units of the Vietnam War* (Oxford, Osprey Publishing, 2009)

Hartman, Charlie: Burgess, Richard R. and Rosario M. Rausa, *US Navy A-1 Skyraider Units of the Vietnam War* (Oxford, Osprey Publishing, 2009)

Hawkins, Austin "Hawk": Davies, Peter E., *US Navy F-4 Phantom II Units of the Vietnam War 1969–73* (Oxford, Osprey Publishing, 2018)

Houston, Jerry "Devil": Davies, Peter E., *US Navy F-4 Phantom II Units of the Vietnam War 1969–73* (Oxford, Osprey Publishing, 2018)

Jenkins, Harry: Levinson, Jeffrey L., *Alpha Strike Vietnam: The Navy's Air War 1964 to 1973* (New York, Pocket Books, 1989)

Junker, Allan: Levinson, Jeffrey L., *Alpha Strike Vietnam: The Navy's Air War 1964 to 1973* (New York, Pocket Books, 1989)

Leue, Dave: Levinson, Jeffrey L., *Alpha Strike Vietnam: The Navy's Air War 1964 to 1973* (New York, Pocket Books, 1989)

Li Dayun: Davies, Peter E., *US Navy F-4 Phantom II Units of the Vietnam War 1964–68* (Oxford, Osprey Publishing, 2016)

McCabe, Michael: Davies, Peter E., *US Navy F-4 Phantom II Units of the Vietnam War 1964–68* (Oxford, Osprey Publishing, 2016)

Miles, John: Fey, Peter, *Bloody Sixteen: The USS Oriskany and Air Wing 16 during the Vietnam War* (New York, Potomac Books, 2020)

Nash, John: Wisely, H. Denny, *Green Ink: Memoirs of a Fighter Pilot*, private publication, 2018

Nguyen Van Bay: Hung, Nguyen Sy, *Air Engagements In the Skies Over Vietnam (1965–1975) as Viewed From Both Sides* (Hanoi, People's Army Publishing House, 2013)

Patton, William T. "Tom": Burgess, Richard R. and Rosario M. Rausa, *US Navy A-1 Skyraider Units of the Vietnam War* (Oxford, Osprey Publishing, 2009)

Peck, Paul: Burgess, Richard R. and Rosario M. Rausa, *US Navy A-1 Skyraider Units of the Vietnam War* (Oxford, Osprey Publishing, 2009)

Pettigrew, Pete "Viper": Davies, Peter E., *US Navy F-4 Phantom II Units of the Vietnam War 1969–73* (Oxford, Osprey Publishing, 2018)

Ruliffson, Jim: Elward, Brad, and Peter E. Davies, *USN F-4 Phantom II MiG Killers, 1965–70* (Oxford, Osprey Publishing, 2016)

Seeley, J.M.: Morgan, Rick, *A-6 Intruder Units of the Vietnam War* (Oxford, Osprey Publishing, 2012)

Smith, Clyde: Morgan, Rick, *A-6 Intruder Units of the Vietnam War* (Oxford, Osprey Publishing, 2012)

Smith, Donald D. "D-D": Levinson, Jeffrey L., *Alpha Strike Vietnam: The Navy's Air War 1964 to 1973* (New York, Pocket Books, 1989)

Smith, Gordon: Davies, Peter E., *US Navy F-4 Phantom II Units of the Vietnam War 1964–68* (Oxford, Osprey Publishing, 2016)

Stockdale, James: Pentagon papers (Public Domain)

Swartz, Ted: Levinson, Jeffrey L., *Alpha Strike Vietnam: The Navy's Air War 1964 to 1973* (New York, Pocket Books, 1989)

Watkins, Don: Davies, Peter E., *US Navy F-4 Phantom II Units of the Vietnam War 1964–68* (Oxford, Osprey Publishing, 2016)

Weigand, Garry: Davies, Peter E., *US Navy F-4 Phantom II Units of the Vietnam War 1969–73* (Oxford, Osprey Publishing, 2018)

Wetterhahn, Ralph: Birzer, Norman and Peter Mersky, *US Navy A-7 Corsair II Units of the Vietnam War* (Oxford, Osprey Publishing, 2004)

Wills, Stephen: Barbour, Alan, Marine Helos in Operation Frequent Wind (popasmoke.com)

Woods, Chris: Barbour, Alan, Marine Helos in Operation Frequent Wind (popasmoke.com)

FROM INTERVIEWS WITH THE AUTHOR

Alberg, Lt CDR Don: VAH-2, 1968
Alderink, RADM James: Cubi Point, 1975
Blonski, RIO Thomas: VF-96, 1975
Burgess, LCDR Kenneth: VF-51, 1975
Cash, CAPT Roy Jr.: VF-33, 1968
Connelly, LCDR Matthew: VF-96, 1972
Crumpler, LCDR W. Hughes: HC-1 Det 2 , 1975
Davis, Don: Associated Press, 1972
Dosé, CDR Curt: VF-92, 1972
Heinrich, CAPT Richard: VF-51, 1975
Jumper, CDR Vern: USS Midway, 1976
Lair, RADM James: VA-22, 1975
Pham Phu Thai, Lt Gen: VPAF, 1968–1975
Prendergast, CAPT Tim: VF-51, 1975
Rausch, LCDR Kenneth: VA-27, 1975
Shelton, RADM Doniphan: CO Subic Bay, 1975
Shilling, Erik: Flying Tiger Airlines, 2003
Sweeney, CDR Charles "Chuck": VA-212, 1975
Tu De, Lt Col: VPAF, 1972–75
Williams, CDR Royce: VF-33, 1960–61; CAG 11, 1965–67
Wisely, RADM H. Denny: VF-114, 1965–68

GLOSSARY

AA	antiaircraft
AAA	antiaircraft artillery
ACM	air combat maneuvering
AFB	air force base
Alpha strike	Navy term for a large air attack by multiple squadrons of a carrier air wing
ARM	anti-radiation missile
ARVN	Army of the Republic of Viet Nam
ASA	Army Security Agency (US)
ASE	Allowable Steering Error
ASW	antisubmarine warfare carrier
BARCAP	Barrier Combat Air Patrol
BASE	basic automated checkout equipment
BLT	battalion landing team
BVR	beyond visual range
CAG	Commander Air Group
CAP	Combat Air Patrol
CIA	Central Intelligence Agency
CIC	Combat Information Center
CinCPac	Commander in Chief Pacific
CO	Commanding Officer
Com7thFlt	Commander Seventh Fleet

COMINT	communications intelligence
ComPatFor7thFlt	Commander Patrol Force 7th Fleet
CRITIC	critically important message
CVW	Carrier Air Wing
DACT	dissimilar air combat training
DAO	Defense Attachés Office
DFC	Distinguished Flying Cross
DIANE	digitally integrated attack and navigation equipment
DMZ	Demilitarized Zone (the border zone between North and South Vietnam between 1954 and 1976)
DRV	Democratic Republic of Vietnam (= North Vietnam)
DSU	direct support unit
ECM	electronic countermeasures
ELINT	electronic intelligence
EST	Eastern Standard Time
FAC	forward air controller
FFAR	folding fin air rocket
FORCAP	Force Combat Air Patrol
GCI	ground-controlled interception
helo	helicopter
HUD	Head-up Display
IFF	identify friend or foe
Iron Hand	term used for a mission aimed at suppressing SAM missile sites
JCS	Joint Chiefs of Staff
LSO	landing signal officer
LZ	landing zone
MACV	Military Assistance Command – Vietnam
MAP	Multiple Aim Point
MCAS	Marine Corps Air Station
MER	multiple ejector rack
MIA	missing in action

MiGCAP	MiG Combat Air Patrol
NAO	naval aviation observer
NAS	naval air station
NFO	naval flight officer
NKPAF	North Korean People's Air Force
NLF	National Liberation Front (also known as the "Viet Cong")
NOTS	naval ordnance test station
NSA	National Security Agency (US)
NSG	Naval Security Group
NVA	North Vietnamese Army
OPLAN	Operations Plan
ORI	Operational Readiness Inspection
PAVN	People's Army of Vietnam
PIRAZ	Positive Identification Radar Advisory Zone
PLAAF	People's Liberation Army Air Force (= Chinese Air Force)
POL	petroleum–oil–lubricant
POW	prisoner of war
RAG	replacement air group
RESCAP	Rescue Combat Air Patrol
RIO	radar intercept officer
RPG	rocket propelled grenade
RTAF	Royal Thai Air Force
RVAH	Reconnaissance Attack (Heavy) Squadron
RVN	Republic of Vietnam (= South Vietnam)
SAM	surface-to-air missile
SAR	search and rescue
SIF	Selective Identification Facility
SIGINT	signals intelligence
SOG	Special Operations Group
TARCAP	Target Combat Air Patrol
UN	United Nations

USAF	United States Air Force
VA	Attack Squadron
VAH	Heavy Attack Squadron
VAL	Heavier-than-air, Attack, Light
VAW	Carrier Airborne Early Warning Squadron
VC	Viet Cong (officially known as the National Liberation Front, or NLF)
VF	Fighter Squadron
VMA	Marine Attack Squadron
VMA(AW)	Marine All-Weather Attack Squadron
VNAF	Republic of Vietnam Air Force
VP	Patrol Squadron
VPA	Vietnam People's Army
VPAF	Vietnam People's Air Force
XO	executive officer

INDEX

References to maps are in **bold**.

Democratic Republic of Vietnam (DRV) *see*
North Vietnam
Dempewolf, Lt (jg) Philip W.   190
Dennison, Lt Terry   148
Denton, Cdr Jeremiah   195
Denver, USS   351–52, 364
Desoto patrols   16, 23–25, 27, 34
Di, Le Xuan   298–99
Diamond Head, USS   246, 247
DIANE system   196, 197–98
Dickson, Lt Edward A.   113
Diebert, Lt Cdr Bernie   199
Diem, Ngo Dinh   17, 25
Diep, Le Hong   298
Dinh, Dao   92
Dinh, Nguyen Dang   87
Dinh, Col Pham Van   290
Dinh, Vu Ngoc   87, 146, 270
Do, Nguyen Ngoc   87, 143
Dodd, Maj Sid   330
Dollarhide, Lt (jg) David   249
Dong, Ha   91
Dong, Pham Van   343
Dong, Tran   91
Dong Phong Thong Bridge   133
Doremus, Lt Cdr Robert   139, 140
Dosé, Lt Curt "Dozo"   266, 305, 306–8,
309
Douglas Aircraft   69
Driscoll, Lt (jg) William P. "Willie"   280,
282, 283, 305, 309, 313
Du, Lt Gen Ngo   292, 294
Duan, Le   278, 344, 346, 347
Dung, Pham   92
Dung, Gen Van Tien   278, 343, 345, 347
Dunlop, Cdr Tom   327

Easter Offensive (1972)   278, 288–92,
294–304
Eastman, Lt L.C.   145
Eaton, Lt Don   195
Eggert, Cdr Lowell "Gus"   310
Eiland, ENS Leonard M., Jr.   249
electronic intelligence (ELINT)   25, 27, 76
Elie, Lt Cdr Gayle O.   167
Elkins, Lt Frank   110, 181–82
Elliot, Lt (jg) Robert   167
Ellsberg, Daniel   44

engines   61
J57   55–56, 58
J65   69
J79   59–60, 63–64
JT3   52–53
VK-1F   82
England, USS   338–39
Ensch, Lt Jack   317
Enterprise, USS   78, 128, 172, 199–200,
253–54
and evacuation   349, 355, 357–58
Estes, Lt (jg) W.O.   170
Estocin, Lt Cdr Mike   192–93
Ettinger, Cdr Harry E.   217

Farrier, BM Gerald   248–49
Fegan, RIO Ronald J.   136, 138
Fellows, Lt Cdr Jack   199
Felsman, Cdr J.J.   62
fighter pilots   51
Fillipi, Nikki A.   347–48
Fix, Lt Col Herbert   354
Flagg, Lt (jg) Bud   147–48
Fleet Air Gunnery Units   257, 261
fleet defense fighters   51
Flint, Cdr Lawrence E., Jr.   62
Flynn, Lt Bob   200–1
Ford, Gerald   346, 347, 353–54, 360
and Cambodia   367–68, 371, 373
Formosa   16, 23
Forrestal, USS   57, 63, 77, 153, 245–53
Foster, Cdr Wynn F.   186–87
Fox, Lt Jim   310
Franke, Cdr W.A.   104
Fraser, Cdr William F.   136–37, 139
Freckleton, Lt (jg) William C.   284, 286, 288
Freeborn, Lt Guy   167–68
French Indochina   17
and First War (1946–54)   91, 92

Gary, Darrell   260, 265
Gayler, Adm   368
Geneva Agreement (1954)   91–92
George K. MacKenzie, USS   251
Germany   53, 83–84, 105
Giai, Brig Gen Vu Van   289, 290–91
Giap, Gen Vo Nguyen   91, 278, 343
Gilbert, Sir Martin   101

Tay Son brothers 278
Taylor, Gen Maxwell D. 32, 112
Teague, Cdr Foster S "Tooter" 284, 285
Teague, Lt (jg) J.E. 170
Terry, Lt Ross R. 146
Tet Offensive (1968) 127–28
Thai, Lt Gen Hoang Van 93
Thai, Lt Pham Phu 178
Thailand 111, 119, 120
Thang, Tran Cao 350
Thanh Hoa Bridge 133, 139–41, 325–26
Thao, Gen Hoang Minh 292
Thieu, Nguyen Van 291, 342, 344, 346–47
Tho, Le Duc 347
Thomas, Lt (jg) Guy 296
Thomas, Cdr Harry 122
Thomas, Lt Cdr Spence 134, 135
Thomaston, USS 349, 366
Thomson, James 97–98, 100
Ticonderoga, USS 25, 30–31, 33, 46, 111,
 128
 and second Tonkin Gulf attack 36, 37,
 40–41
 and VA-192 Sqn 190–91, 192
Timm, Cdr Dwight 310
Tinh, Col Gen Dang 92
Tinker, RIO Charles J. 305–6, 308
Toai, Mai Duc 159
Toan, Gen Nguyen Van 342
Tonkin Gulf Incident (1964) 15, 16,
 26–32, 35–42, 43–46, 48
Top Gun 141, 260–67, 274
tour of duty policies 108–9, 153
Tra, Lt Gen Tran Van 343–44
Trach, Lt Col Nguyen Phuc 93
Trembley, Lt (jg) J. Forrest 200
Truman, Harry S. 98
Trung, Lt Gen Ngo Quang 291
Tschudy, Lt (jg) Bill 195
Tuc, Lt Phan Van 134
Tullo, Capt Frank J. 229–30
Turner Joy, USS 12, 31, 33–34, 35–42, 46
Twigger, Lt Robert 347–48

United States Navy Fighter Weapons School
 see Top Gun
United States of America (USA) 17, 18–19,
 20–21, 32–33, 99, 110–11; *see also* Ford,

Gerald; Johnson, Lyndon B.; Nixon,
 Richard
Universal Pilot Training (UPT)
 program 257
Unruh, Lt Jerry 134
Urban, Cdr Hank 155, 156
US Air Force (USAF) 21–22, 33, 51, 127,
 153–54
 and Cambodia 369–72
 and Easter Offensive 290, 294–95
 and evacuation 347–49
 and Korean War 98
 and pilots 181–82
 and Rolling Thunder 107–8, 116,
 124–25
 and rules of engagement 97
 and training 257–58
 see also aircraft, US; Top Gun
US Army 101, 347–49
US Marine Corps 71, 101, 115–16, 126
 and Cambodia 365–66, 369–78
 and evacuation 347–49, 351, 359–62
 VMA-224 ("Bengals") 326–31
US Navy 21–22, 26, 51, 258–59
 and air combat 171–72
 and aircraft 55, 56, 62, 71
 and Easter Offensive 295–99
 and evacuation 347–49
 and jammers 163–64
 and Korean War 98, 100
 and loss rate 105–6, 121–22
 and *Rolling Thunder* 107–8, 119,
 124–25, 126
 and rules of engagement 97
 and training 256–58
 see also air combat; Top Gun
US Navy (units):
 VA-22 ("Fighting Redcocks") 320–21
 VA-25 ("Fist of the Fleet") 217–20
 VA-35 ("Panthers") 199–200
 VA-65 ("Tigers") 198–99
 VA-75 ("Sunday Punchers") 202–3
 VA-85 ("Black Falcons") 195–97
 VA-147 ("Argonauts") 208–10
 VA-192 ("World Famous Golden
 Dragons") 190–93
 VA-196 ("Main Battery") 200–2
 VA-215 ("Barn Owls") 239–41